THE SPORTING SPIRIT
Athletes in Literature and Life

THE SPORTING SPIRIT
Athletes in Literature and Life

Edited by ROBERT J. HIGGS *East Tennessee State University*
and NEIL D. ISAACS *University of Maryland*

With a Foreword by HEYWOOD HALE BROUN

Harcourt Brace Jovanovich, Inc.
New York • Chicago • San Francisco • Atlanta

ISBN: 0-15-583351-0

Library of Congress Catalog Card Number: 76-16435

Printed in the United States of America

Calligraphy on the cover created by Vladimir Yevtikhiev.

For permission to use the selections reprinted in this book, the authors are grateful to the following publishers and copyright holders:

BEACON PRESS For "The Play-Element in Contemporary Civilization" from *Homo Ludens* by Johan Huizinga, translated by R. F. C. Hull. Copyright 1950 by Roy Publishers. Reprinted by permission of Beacon Press.

THE BLACK SCHOLAR For "The Myth of the Racially Superior Athlete" by Harry Edwards. Reprinted from *The Black Scholar* (November 1971) by permission of the publisher.

LAWRENCE E. BRINN AND LOUISE CRANE For "Some Questions on Sports" from "Ten Answers: Letters from an October Afternoon, Part II" by Marianne Moore.

CURTIS BROWN, LTD. For "Runner" by W. H. Auden, Reprinted by permission of Curtis Brown, Ltd. Copyright © 1962 by The National Film Board of Canada.

ALAN DUGAN "On Hurricane Jackson" from *Poems* by Alan Dugan, published by Yale University Press. Copyright © 1961 by Alan Dugan.

ESQUIRE MAGAZINE For "Mind over Water" by Diana Nyad from *Esquire* (October 1975). © 1975 by Esquire, Inc. Reprinted by permission of Esquire Magazine.

FARRAR, STRAUS & GIROUX, INC. For "Say Good-bye to Big Daddy" from *The Complete Poems* by Randall Jarrell. Copyright © 1966, 1969 by Mrs. Randall Jarrell. Reprinted with the permission of Farrar, Straus & Giroux, Inc.

Pages 301–304 represent a continuation of the copyright page.

DEDICATION

To John Tinkler, Drake Bush, Charlie Hurt, John Gilbert, Bill Lawkins, David Duke, Mike Kelly, Wayne Lazar, Hammerin' Harvey Hecht, and Mallory Chamberlin and

Ralph Bean, Cary Anderson, Ed Trainer, Paul Dowell, Rabbit Adams, Bob Plemmons, Phil Schaefer, Sammy Burris, Bill Brown, and

Bobby Jack Fry, Charles Boynton, John Perry, Jim Kirkland, Hugh Welch, Bob Welch, Bernie Leggett, Jack Reese, Ken Bohringer, Ken Tolo, Bland Crowder, Harry Row, and Bernie Sisman, and

All the unsung heroes and anonymous ringers (and faithful fans) of the legendary mighty Knicks of Knoxville.

From their Hall-of-Fame old-timers' battery.

Preface

The literature of sport is a vast uncharted territory, yet it is one in which we all live; it is part of a society pervaded by the awareness, the values, and the spirit of sports. That our literature accurately reflects such involvement is a matter largely ignored by literary critics but largely taken for granted by writers and readers. For example, the most powerful passages in Hemingway are concerned with blood sports, and Fitzgerald describes an entire atmosphere and the perception of an American in Paris in the two-word sentence: "Football weather." There is really no exit from our ubiquitous stadiums.

For this reason we should learn as much as possible about the meaning of sports in our culture, and *The Sporting Spirit: Athletes in Literature and Life* is our contribution to that goal. It is a work that has grown out of a number of years of research as well as out of our classroom experience, which proved to us the popularity among students of the pervasive themes of sports in modern literature. "Sports Culture, USA," a course at the University of Maryland, has been offered twice, and over three hundred students have taken it. One of its attractions was the participation of scholars, athletes, sportswriters, and other guests, who stimulated the students, provided an enlightening diversity of views, and discouraged simplistic conclusions about sports, which in the past have come as frequently from the halls of academe as from the department of athletics.

A similar multifaceted approach is employed in *The Sporting Spirit.* The book is organized in four parts representing a general view of sport as seen by the literary artist, the athlete, the social critic, and the philosopher and historian, each section exhibiting a wide diversity of opinion. Each part is preceded by an introduction that provides a framework within which to see the various aspects of the subject. At the end of the book we have presented the students with questions that we hope will help them arrive at their own understanding of the issues involved.

For their visits to "Sports Culture, USA," where they helped examine the implications of sport for our sensibilities, literature, media, heroes, rituals, institutions, priorities, and values, we wish to thank Andrew Beyer, Richard Darcey, Donald Dell, David DuPree, Tom Fields, Steve Hershey, Kim Hoover, John Howard, Roy Jefferson, James Kehoe, Wally Keiderling, Howard LaBow, Stanford Lavine, John Lucas, Dorothy McKnight, Peter O'Malley, Abe Pollin, Shirley Povich, Don Ruck, Jack Russell, Jerry Sachs, George Solomon, Eric Stevens, Gerald Strine, Bill Tanton, Shelby Whitfield, and Jack Zane. We also wish to thank the students whose encouragement perpetuated the course and inspired the book and whose journals testified to the success of the experiment.

For their kind assistance with *The Sporting Spirit*, we are grateful to Berney Burleson, Reny, Julia, and Laura Higgs, Don Johnson, Edith Keys, Anne LeCroy, David McClellan, John B. Tallent, Jean Thomas, Peggy Vick, Joy Witty, Drake Bush, Liz Hock, Eben Ludlow, Judith Rundel, Abigail Winograd, and Sid Zimmerman.

Our dedication suggests how closely we have been involved in the spirit of the enterprise.

Robert J. Higgs
Neil D. Isaacs

Foreword

When small children gather around that powerful magnet, a sizable puddle, the result is often the invention of some game, possibly involving a stick, a milk carton, and a couple of stones. As the game progresses, if one player makes an unusual move the others will cry out in horror, "You can't do that! It's the rule!" It seems to me that this positive-negative statement, immediately obeyed by all but the most defiant, is at the heart of our love of sports and games. With their relatively simple codes and short time spans, they are the only parts of our lives which seem to have a recognizable shape.

Jean-Paul Sartre, an unlikely sports writer, once said that "Play is an activity of which man is the first origin, for which man himself sets the rules, and which has no consequences except according to the rules posited." Sartre went on to argue that play is therefore the only area in which humankind is free and that through it one can escape his or her own "natural nature."

Judge Learned Hand once remarked that a society which esteemed law above justice was a truly civilized society. It is a remark which at first makes the neck hairs bristle, but on second look it simply means that justice is, on the whole, a subjective idea, judged differently according to personal points of view and passions, while law is the set of rules written on the top of the box the game came in, those rules without which the game is as shapeless and unfair as life itself.

One of the things which seems now to be robbing sport of some of that freedom which arises, ironically, from the acceptance of rules is the notion that sport is not separate from life itself, but an integral part of it. Thus the Olympic games are increasingly an expression of national purpose, and the pressures on athletes toward political conformity make them a part of a uniformed army marching at the will of old men whose purposes are far from the autokinetic joys of young competitors.

So also in our professional sports, where the dictum has been proclaimed that "Winning is the only thing," it is taken for granted that competitors will make every effort to circumvent the rules through such things as unobserved dirty play, arguing with officials in order to intimidate them for the future, or simply to delay a game in which the opponent seems to have found, momentarily, a successful rhythm. Indeed, in recent seasons some of our athletes have begun to glory in observed dirty play under the wonderfully revealing title "Enforcement." Colleges argue not over the hypocrisy and corruption of their sports programs, but over the allowable degree of hypocrisy and corruption. Children are dragooned into acrimonious mini-versions of parental wars, and the elderly brood over the fact that despite having bought a book by Jack Nicklaus, they are unable to match his scores.

There are moments when sport seems to have performed the remarkable feat of making Sartre sound like an optimist and making Samuel Johnson's first dictionary definition of sport, "Tumultuous Fun," seem like a bitter joke. Still, as much of the material in this book reminds us, the pure in heart are sometimes discouraged, but haven't been defeated; while sport goes on flourishing like grass seed in the cracked cement of our stadia, and somewhere a group of children is gathering around a puddle ready to devise the game and accept the magic Rule, the thing which draws them together is the joyous mystery of games.

Heywood Hale Broun

Contents

THE SPORTING SPIRIT
Athletes in Literature and Life

Introduction

According to some scholars, Homer was the first to use the word "athlete" meaning one who contends for a prize in public games. With this in mind, it is not difficult to see why sports have served, since the greatest antiquity, as a metaphor of life. All of us are thus seen as sports people, players on the field striving for prizes and awards held in esteem by ourselves and others.

As Paul Weiss has pointed out in *Sport: A Philosophic Inquiry,* the athlete becomes a representative of humanity, making us aware of the possibilities of the body just as the scholar makes us aware of the possibilities of the mind. But athletes, in their struggles for recognition and achievement on and off the playing arena, also become fitting subjects for dramatic allegory when they play the roles of hero and villain, scapegoat and clown. It is no accident that poets from Homer to Auden have focused upon the person of action, who invariably is athletic, if not an athlete. And it is no accident that an athlete or ex-athlete is an important character in many of the most highly applauded American dramas: *Strange Interlude, The Petrified Forest, Death of a Salesman, Golden Boy, Cat on a Hot Tin Roof, Who's Afraid of Virginia Woolf?,* and *The Great White Hope.*

Fiction writers have manifested an equal fascination with the athlete. In Victorian England the virtues of a sound mind in a sound body were proclaimed to such an extent that writers concerned with athletics came to be regarded as a cult of sports enthusiasts. *Tom Brown's School Days* is perhaps the most famous work of its kind and certainly the most influential. Indeed, it was largely responsible for the establishment and perpetuation of the myth of the character-building qualities of the British public schools. While a similar cult has never evolved in America, and while sports fiction has never developed into a genre in the way that detective fiction or the western story has, sports in much American fiction have served as a focal point for the examination of social or personal values. Two among the multitude of works can serve as examples of the way in which sports have been used in serious American literature. William Faulkner's "The Bear" is a short story about the growing maturity and increasing awareness of a young boy during the several years he hunts for a huge, elusive, and mysterious bear. The hunting context serves to illuminate the boy's relation to the land and to history. Equally mythic, Bernard Malamud's *The Natural* deals with a baseball hero's journey from innocence to cynicism. Here the sports world serves as a microcosm of our society in which financial and psychological pressures debase the highest ideals and destroy personal worth. On a more popular level, the public-school values exemplified by *Tom Brown's School Days* were carried forward in the United States by juvenile literature, especially the "Frank Merriwell" series of dime novels. Centering on Frank Merriwell, an athletic young man from Yale, this series ran to over 200 titles and sold, according to some estimates, as many as 500 million copies. It seems obvious that sport plays a significant role on all levels of literature. The presence of sports in literature demands study, and of course this study requires a parallel examination of the meaning of sports in life.

So thoroughly and subtly have athletics filtered into every aspect of our consciousness that they have saturated our culture with the sports ethos. From the lowest grades of school through college, athletics, especially team sports, are an important part of the curriculum. Television and newspapers devote considerable time and space to reporting sports events. The events themselves are listened to on radio, watched on television, or attended by huge numbers of spectators. Since 1972 each Super Bowl has had an estimated television audience of over 70 million people. But perhaps most telling of all is the widespread use of sports language and values in nonathletic situations. A recent major work in ethics, for example, uses the concept of fair play in discussing various notions of justice; it proposes as the fundamental moral concept of rational systems of ethics a "doctrine of justice as fairness."

Sports are interwoven into the very fabric of our way of life. Not only have they provided us with such ethical terms as "fair play," they have also furnished us with the complex set of social ideas summed up in the words "team spirit," with metaphors of individual responsibility, as in the phrase "she carried the ball at the conference," and with such synonyms for cooperation revealed in sentences like "they will play ball with us in getting the contract." Perhaps most of all, sports have provided us with contemporary instances of excellence and heroism. To some modern critics the athlete is the only genuine hero remaining to a skeptical age. In this view, the athlete ranks with the medieval knight on his quest and the classical hero in his prowess. Behind Muhammad Ali stand Sir Gawain and Achilles.

Who is the athlete? What are his or her values? What does the athlete, as a universal hero, represent? What do athletes reveal about our hopes or about our view of the world? These are questions that a concerned society should ask. An approach to these questions perhaps lies in an examination of the relationship between mind and body. What is the best synthesis of the two? What happens to an individual or a society when either mind or body is emphasized at the expense of the other? The ancients, regardless of what they may have practiced, advocated a balance, as seen in such idealistic expressions as "strength and wisdom," "music and gymnastic," and "a sound mind in a sound body." Socrates felt that the very survival of the state depended upon the harmony of mind, body, and soul, and he used the athlete to illustrate his point.

The athlete was also used to illustrate a point by the modern historian Arnold Toynbee. He argued that there were two flaws in the Hellenic culture: specialization and egocentricity. By specializing, individuals concentrate their energies upon single activities, while through egocentricity talented individuals fail to use their gifts to benefit the common weal. Toynbee sees this nexus of failures as disruptive of society in the modern as well as in the classical world.

Toynbee's view is generally shared by Johan Huizinga and Lewis Mumford, while a dissenting view has been registered by Paul Weiss who presents a sort of "athletics for athletics' sake" argument, that is, an argument for looking at sport as an end in itself, without trying to find any social justification in it. In Weiss's view, the athlete as athlete is solely concerned with his or her athletic role. He discusses athletes in terms of what they can realistically accomplish rather than with reference to some exalted and abstract standard. The athlete's motivation, he contends, can be explained only through a desire for excellence and self-realization. Of all the intellectuals who have considered sports to any extent, none has had so generous an opinion of the athlete as Weiss.

As compelling as Weiss's arguments are, the fact remains that sport has never been regarded by most people as a thing in itself but invariably has been construed in a religious, political, or cultural context. This social view is evidenced by the ongoing debates over women and racism in sports, subsidization of athletes, and sport as an aspect of nationalism. The poet Robert Frost believed, like the Greeks, that athletics "are close to the soul of culture." For this reason he was concerned that college athletics, especially, should be kept from corruption. Justice, Frost believed, is necessary to physical prowess. This is a crucial point, for it hardly behooves us to train Olympic athletes who break previous records if we cannot also build a world devoid of such atrocities as the Munich massacre of 1972 and the "soccer war" of 1969.

Although there are many artists and writers who have praised sport and found significance in it as a symbol of culture, there has been a minority, from the ancient world to the modern, that has lamented society's preoccupation with sports and games and its apathy toward the life of the mind. Among those who have complained about excessive interest in sport have been Euripides, Galen, Castiglione, Matthew Arnold, and Thorstein Veblen. According to Veblen, sport was a form of conspicuous consumption, for "success as an athlete presumes not only a waste of time, but also a waste of money." He further argued that "the relation of football to physical culture is much the same as that of the bullfight to agriculture." Though few intellectuals have looked at sport in depth as Veblen has, a number have made casual remarks representative of the attitudes of many members of the academic community. Among these was the critic Joseph Wood Krutch, who wrote, "Just as those who have played football are supposed to be educated so those who learn square dances or play bingo at the parish house are supposed to be religious." The debate over the role and relevance of the athlete constitutes in itself an *agon* of sports.

Finally, literature of sport differs in theme from other literature but not in substance. Like all literature it raises questions about the nature of humankind: Who are we? What is good? What meaning can we give our lives? Simply because the literature of sport focuses on the athlete does not make it less aesthetic than any other type of literature. But, paradoxically, neither can it be judged by artistic considerations alone. The athlete in literature reflects the fact that sports permeate modern society on many levels of consciousness. One critic has claimed that sport has replaced religion as the opiate of the masses. Many contemporary authors, such as Philip Roth, have used sports to spin a mythological web around our culture. Ultimately sports literature is worthy of our attention because it reminds us of one inescapable fact: We have bodies as well as minds or souls. Sports literature does not and cannot define the best way for an individual to unite body and soul, but it does tell us that a conjunction of some sort is necessary. In 1816, in a letter to John Adams, Thomas Jefferson wrote that "of all human contemplations the most abhorrent is body without mind"; but in his novel *Joiner,* James Whitehead points to a condition of equal horror, the mind with no body, as the protagonist looks at the soldier in Grünewald's *Isenheim Altarpiece* struggling to stand on legs that will not support him. Fortunately we do not have to choose between such extreme conditions, but can choose instead from many combinations, depending to some extent on circumstances, but also on talents and tastes. There are many alternatives, or, as Pindar says in "Olympia 8,"

> Various goods have come
> to one man and another; there are many roads
> to happiness, if the gods assent.

from Olympia 8

Pindar

Mother of games, gold-wreathed, Olympia,
mistress of truth where men of prophecy
by burning victims probe the pleasure of Zeus of the shining
thunderbolt,
what story he has for folk
who strain in spirit to capture
magnificence of strength
and space to breathe after work's weariness:

his will is steered by men's prayers to favor of piety.
Then, O grove of Pisa beside Alpheos, shadowed with trees,
accept this our festival song with its burden of garlands.
Great is his fame forever
whom your bright victory befalls.
Various goods have come
to one man and another; there are many roads
to happiness, if the gods assent.

Translated by RICHMOND LATTIMORE

Autolycus

Euripides

Of the myriad afflictions that beset Hellas
none is worse than the breed of athletes.
Never, first of all, do they understand the good life,
nor could they. How can a man enslaved to his jaws,
subject to his belly, increase his patrimony?
Nor to abide poverty, to row in fortune's stream
are they able; they have not learned the fair art
of confronting the insoluble. Shining in youth
they stride about like statues in the square.
But comes astringent age, they shrink in rags.
Blameworthy is the custom of the Hellenes
who for such men make great concourses
to honor idle sports—for feasting's sake.
What nimble wrestler, fleet runner, sinewy
discus thrower, agile boxer, has benefited his city
by his firsts? Fight our enemy discus in hand?
In mellay of shields box the foe from the fatherland?
Confronted with steel, such silliness none remembers.
'Tis the wise and the good we should crown with bay,
who best guide the state, the prudent and the just,
whoso by discourse averts evil actions, banishes
strife and contention. Prowess of such sort
is to all the city a boon, to all Hellenes.

Translated by Moses Hadas

part 1

Contending Myths: The Athlete in Literature

In his book *The Hero,* Lord Raglan states that a ritual is an enactment of a myth, and since sport is so highly ritualistic, it lends itself readily to mythical interpretation. Athletes customarily engage in a wide variety of ceremonies, especially before and after the game. The introduction of teams to spectators, the clasping of hands, the meeting in the center of the ring, the jumping of the net, the cutting of the basket, and the awarding of "the game ball" are only a few familiar practices. Other customary practices are playing the anthems of nation and alma mater, holding pre- and post-game prayers, having half-time festivities, and indulging in locker room celebrations or post mortems. If these traditional forms of behavior constitute ritual, what is the myth being enacted? It may be the monomyth, a word coined by James Joyce and discussed by Joseph Campbell in *The Hero with a Thousand Faces.*

The monomyth is, in essence, the hero myth, the belief that meaning in life is achieved through valiant struggle. It is this monomyth, or hero myth, that explains the kinship between sports and literature. Statistics and records have an important function in our knowledge of sport. But if we seek to understand the human drama in sport, the heroic aspirations, successes, and failures, we must turn to the metaphorical account—that is, to literature—rather than to records of how the game was played.

Heroes in stories may play different roles depending on their values and achievements, and the attitudes and points of view of the witnesses to their deeds. Thus, within the monomyth we have various faces of the hero; we have contending myths. With athletes, the three types of heroes are the Apollonian, Dionysian, and Adonic figures. The first is a model of form, beauty, order, and control; the second is a model of abandonment, energy, and immersion in nature; and the third is a model of failure, despair, and rejection. The third, or Adonic, figure is usually represented by the scapegoat, the tortured cripple, or the sacrificial hero, all of whom are, to use a term from myth criticism, the *pharmakos*. In *The Birth of Tragedy*, Nietzsche describes the opposition of Apollo and Dionysius; and the contrast of Apollo and Christ (or the Adonic element) has been remarked on in several myth studies. American literature of sports tends to conform to both theories since the action invariably centers on the Apollonian element. Hence the typical figure is Apollo *agonistes*, the hero struggling against nature and other heroes to impose a structure on the world that would maintain his beauty and celebrate his self-worth.

A story may combine all three archetypal figures into one character, as in Bernard Malamud's *The Natural*, but the plot will always center on the battle between order and chaos—which raises a number of questions. What do these figures tell us about the quality of heroism? Is persecution or sacrifice required of them? Must they suppress or control their natural energies to achieve order? What motivates them to achieve perfection or success? The stories themselves also raise several questions. For example: Are other characters in the stories allowed to compete with the hero on the same terms? Is the hero's quest treated ironically or straightforwardly? What meaning does the heroic struggle yield?

The answers offered by the following selections are many and varied. J. F. Powers's "Jamesie" portrays the disillusioning effect a dishonest athlete has on an admiring young boy. Jamesie, obviously, is a hero-worshiper, but Lefty proves unworthy of his expectations by betraying the heroic ideal. In this story the conflict is within Jamesie, rather than Lefty, the athlete-hero. But in John Updike's "Ace in the Hole" and Irwin Shaw's "The Eighty-Yard Run," the *agon* is centered entirely in athletes or ex-athletes who are arrested in their development and seek meaning in reliving the past. Both characters are self-deceived, or in the terminology of criticism, are *alazon* figures. In contrast, James Thurber's Bolenciecwcz, is not self-deceived because he does not have a mind capable of deception; in this manner, Thurber effectively satirizes one of the most popular models in our society, the all-around student athlete. In a more serious tone, Budd Schulberg's "Crowd Pleaser" presents a boxing match in which the spectators' racist feelings make a scapegoat of the more skillful fighter. Other selections, less conveniently categorized, portray the would-be hero, the ex-hero, and witnesses to the heroic struggle. For those who have played or followed sport, the mythic drama depicted in verse and story will provide the shock of recognition.

A Baseball Experiment

Mark Twain

This experiment was baseball. In order to give the thing vogue from the start, and place it out of the reach of criticism, I chose my nines by rank, not capacity. There wasn't a knight in either team who wasn't a sceptered sovereign. As for material of this sort, there was a glut of it always around Arthur. You couldn't throw a brick in any direction and not cripple a king. Of course, I couldn't get these people to leave off their armor; they wouldn't do that when they bathed. They consented to differentiate the armor so that a body could tell one team from the other, but that was the most they would do. So, one of the teams wore chain-mail ulsters, and the other wore plate armor made of my new Bessemer steel. Their practice in the field was the most fantastic thing I ever saw. Being ball-proof, they never skipped out of the way, but stood still and took the result; when a Bessemer was at the bat and a ball hit him, it would bound a hundred and fifty yards sometimes. And when a man was running, and threw himself on his stomach to slide to his base, it was like an ironclad coming into port. At first I appointed men of no rank to act as umpires, but I had to discontinue that. These people were no easier to please than other nines. The umpire's first decision was usually his last; they broke him in two with a bat, and his friends toted him home on a shutter. When it was noticed that no umpire ever survived a game, umpiring got to be unpopular. So I was obliged to appoint somebody whose rank and lofty position under the government would protect him.

Here are the names of the nines:

BESSEMERS	ULSTERS
King Arthur.	Emperor Lucius.
King Lot of Lothian.	King Logris.
King of Northgalis.	King Marhalt of Ireland.
King Marsil.	King Morganore.
King of Little Britain.	King Mark of Cornwall.

The title has been supplied by the editors for this excerpt from *A Connecticut Yankee in King Arthur's Court.*

KING LABOR.	KING NENTRES OF GARLOT.
KING PELLAM OF LISTENGESE.	KING MELIODAS OF LIONES.
KING BAGDEMAGUS.	KING OF THE LAKE.
KING TOLLEME LA FEINTES.	THE SOWDAN OF SYRIA.

Umpire—CLARENCE

The first public game would certainly draw fifty thousand people; and for solid fun would be worth going around the world to see. Everything would be favorable; it was balmy and beautiful spring weather now, and Nature was all tailored out in her new clothes.

Dream of a Baseball Star

Gregory Corso

I dreamed Ted Williams
leaning at night
against the Eiffel Tower, weeping.

He was in uniform
and his bat lay at his feet
—knotted and twiggy.

'Randall Jarrell says you're a poet!' I cried.
'So do I! I say you're a poet!'

He picked up his bat with blown hands;
stood there astraddle as he would in the batter's box,
and laughed! flinging his schoolboy wrath
toward some invisible pitcher's mound
—waiting the pitch all the way from heaven.

It came; hundreds came! all afire!
He swung and swung and swung and connected not one
sinker curve hook or right-down-the-middle.
A hundred strikes!

The umpire dressed in strange attire
thundered his judgment: YOU'RE OUT!
And the phantom crowd's horrific boo
dispersed the gargoyles from Notre Dame.

And I screamed in my dream:
God! throw thy merciful pitch!
Herald the crack of bats!
Hooray the sharp liner to left!
Yea the double, the triple!
Hosannah the home run!

Jamesie

J. F. Powers

There it was, all about Lefty, in Ding Bell's Dope Box.

"We don't want to add coals to the fire, but it's common knowledge that the Local Pitcher Most Likely To Succeed is fed up with the home town. Well, well, the boy's good, which nobody can deny, and the scouts are on his trail, but it doesn't say a lot for his team spirit, not to mention his civic spirit, this high-hat attitude of his. And that fine record of his—has it been all a case of him and him alone? How about the team? The boys have backed him up, they've given him the runs, and that's what wins ball games. They don't pay off on strike-outs. There's one kind of player every scribe knows—and wishes he didn't—the lad who gets four for four with the willow, and yet, somehow, his team goes down to defeat—but does that worry this gent? Not a bit of it. He's too busy celebrating his own personal success, figuring his batting average, or, if he's a pitcher, his earned run average and strike-outs. The percentage player. We hope we aren't talking about Lefty. If we are, it's too bad, it is, and no matter where he goes from here, especially if it's up to the majors, it won't remain a secret very long, nor will he . . . See you at the game Sunday. Ding Bell."

"Here's a new one, Jamesie," his father said across the porch, holding up the rotogravure section.

With his father on Sunday it could be one of three things—a visit to the office, fixing up his mother's grave in Calvary, or just sitting on the porch with all the Chicago papers, as today.

Jamesie put down the *Courier* and went over to his father without curiosity. It was always Lindy or the *Spirit of St. Louis,* and now without understanding how this could so suddenly be, he was tired of them. His father, who seemed to feel that a growing boy could take an endless interest in these things, appeared to know the truth at last. He gave a page to the floor—that way he knew what he'd read and how far he had to go—and pulled the newspaper around his ears again. Before he went to dinner he would put the paper in order and wish out loud that other people would have the decency to do the same.

Jamesie, back in his chair, granted himself one more chapter of *Baseball Bill in the World Series.* The chapters were running out again, as they had so many times before, and he knew, with the despair of a narcotic, that his need had no end.

Baseball Bill, at fifty cents a volume and unavailable at the library, kept him nearly broke, and Francis Murgatroyd, his best friend . . . too stingy to go halves, confident he'd get to read them all as Jamesie bought them, and each time offering to exchange the old Tom Swifts and Don Sturdys he had got for Christmas—as though that were the same thing!

Jamesie owned all the Baseball Bills to be had for love or money in the world, and there was nothing in the back of this one about new titles being in preparation. Had the author died, as some of them did, and left his readers in the lurch? Or had the series been discontinued—for where, after *Fighting for the Pennant* and *In the World Series,* could Baseball Bill go? *Baseball Bill, Manager,* perhaps. But then what?

"A plot to *fix* the World Series! So that was it! Bill began to see it all. . . . The mysterious call in the night! The diamond necklace in the dressing room! The scribbled note under the door! With slow fury Bill realized that the peculiar odor on the note paper was the odor in his room now! It was the odor of strong drink and cigar smoke! And it came from his midnight visitor! The same! Did he represent the powerful gambling syndicate? Was *he* Blackie Humphrey himself? Bill held his towering rage in check and smiled at his visitor in his friendly, boyish fashion. His visitor must get no inkling of his true thoughts. Bill must play the game—play the very fool they took him for! Soon enough they would discover for themselves, but to their everlasting sorrow, the courage and daring of Baseball Bill . . ."

Jamesie put the book aside, consulted the batting averages in the *Courier,* and reread Ding Bell. Then, not waiting for dinner and certain to hear about it at supper, he ate a peanut butter sandwich with catsup on it, and left by the back door. He went down the alley calling for Francis Murgatroyd. He got up on the Murgatroyd gate and swung—the death-defying trapeze act at the circus—until Francis came down the walk.

"Hello, Blackie Humphrey," Jamesie said tantalizingly.

"Who's Blackie Humphrey?"

"You know who Blackie Humphrey is all right."

"Aw, Jamesie, cut it out."

"And you want me to throw the World Series!"

"Baseball Bill!"

"In the World Series. It came yesterday."

"Can I read it?"

Jamesie spoke in a hushed voice. "So you're Blackie Humphrey?"

"All right. But I get to read it next."

"So you want me to throw the World Series, Blackie. Is that it? Say you do."

"Yes, I do."

"Ask me again, Call me Bill."

"Bill, I want you to throw the World Series. Will you, Bill?"

"I might." But that was just to fool Blackie. Bill tried to keep his towering rage in check while feigning an interest in the nefarious plot. "Why do you want me to throw it, Blackie?"

"I don't know."

"Sure you know. You're a dirty crook and you've got a lot of dough bet on the other team."

"Uh, huh."

"Go ahead. Tell me that."

While Blackie unfolded the criminal plan Bill smiled at him in his friendly, boyish fashion.

"And who's behind this, Blackie?"

"I don't know."

"Say it's the powerful gambling syndicate."

"It's them."

"Ah, ha! Knock the ash off your cigar."

"Have I got one?"

"Yes, and you've got strong drink on your breath, too."

"Whew!"

Blackie should have fixed him with his small, piglike eyes.

"Fix me with your small, piglike eyes."

"Wait a minute, Jamesie!"

"Bill. Go ahead. Fix me."

"O.K. But you don't get to be Bill all the time."

"Now blow your foul breath in my face."

"There!"

"Now ask me to have a cigar. Go ahead."

Blackie was offering Bill a cigar, but Bill knew it was to get him to break training and refused it.

"I see through you, Blackie." No, that was wrong. He had to conceal his true thoughts and let Blackie play him for a fool. Soon enough his time would come and . . . "Thanks for the cigar, Blackie," he said. "I thought it was a cheap one. Thanks, I'll smoke it later."

"I paid a quarter for it."

"Hey, that's too much, Francis!"

"Well, if I'm the head of the powerful——"

Mr. Murgatroyd came to the back door and told Francis to get ready.

"I can't go to the game, Jamesie," Francis said. "I have to caddy for him."

Jamesie got a ride with the calliope when it had to stop at the corner for the light. The calliope was not playing now, but yesterday it had roamed the streets, all red and gold and glittering like a hussy among the pious, black Fords parked on the Square, blaring and showing off, with a sign, Jayville vs. Beardstown.

The ball park fence was painted a swampy green except for an occasional new board. Over the single ticket window cut in the fence hung a sign done in the severe black and white railroad manner, "Home of the Jayville Independents," but everybody called them the "Indees."

Jamesie bought a bottle of Green River out of his savings and made the most of it, swallowing it in sips, calling upon his will power under the sun. He returned the bottle and stood for a while by the ticket window making designs in the dust with the corrugated soles of his new tennis shoes. Ding Bell, with a pretty lady on his arm and carrying the black official scorebook, passed inside without paying, and joked about it.

The Beardstown players arrived from sixty miles away with threatening cheers. Their chartered bus stood steaming and dusty from the trip. The players wore gray suits with "Barons" written across their chests and had the names of sponsors on their backs—Palms Café, Rusty's Wrecking, Coca-Cola.

Jamesie recognized some of the Barons but put down a desire to speak to them.

The last man to leave the bus, Jamesie thought, must be Guez, the new pitcher imported from East St. Louis for the game. Ding Bell had it in the Dope Box that "Saliva Joe" was one of the few spitters left in the business, had been up in the Three Eye a few years, was a full-blooded Cuban, and ate a bottle of aspirins a game, just like candy.

The dark pitcher's fame was too much for Jamesie. He walked alongside Guez. He smelled the salt and pepper of the gray uniform, saw the scarred plate on the right toe, saw the tears in the striped stockings—the marks of bravery or moths—heard the distant chomp of tobacco being chewed, felt—almost—the iron drape of the flannel, and was reduced to friendliness with the pitcher, the enemy.

"Are you a real Cuban?"

Guez looked down, rebuking Jamesie with a brief stare, and growled, "Go away."

Jamesie gazed after the pitcher. He told himself that he hated Guez—that's what he did, hated him! But it didn't do much good. He looked around to see if anybody had been watching, but nobody had, and he wanted somebody his size to vanquish—somebody who might think Guez was as good as Lefty. He wanted to bet a million dollars on Lefty against Guez, but there was nobody to take him up on it.

The Indees began to arrive in ones and twos, already in uniform but carrying their spikes in their hands. Jamesie spoke to all of them except J. G. Nickerson, the manager. J. G. always glared at kids. He thought they were stealing his baseballs and laughing about it behind his back. He was a great one for signaling with a score card from the bench, like Connie Mack, and Ding Bell had ventured to say that managers didn't come any brainier than Jayville's own J. G. Nickerson, even in the big time. But if there should be a foul ball, no matter how tight the game or crucial the situation, J. G. would leap up, straining like a bird dog, and try to place it, waving the bat boy on without taking his eyes off the spot where it disappeared over the fence or in the weeds. That was why they called him the Foul Ball.

The Petersons—the old man at the wheel, a red handkerchief tied tight enough around his neck to keep his head on, and the sons, all players, Big Pete, Little Pete, Middle Pete, and Extra Pete—roared up with their legs hanging out of the doorless Model T and the brass radiator boiling over.

The old man ran the Model T around in circles, damning it for a runaway horse, and finally got it parked by the gate.

"Hold 'er, Knute!" he cackled.

The boys dug him in the ribs, tickling him, and were like puppies that had been born bigger than their father, jollying him through the gate, calling him Barney Oldfield.

Lefty came.

"Hi, Lefty," Jamesie said.

"Hi, kid," Lefty said. He put his arm around Jamesie and took him past the ticket taker.

"It's all right, Mac," he said.

"Today's the day, Lefty," Mac said. "You can do it, Lefty."

Jamesie and Lefty passed behind the grandstand. Jamesie saw Lefty's father, a skinny, brown-faced man in a yellow straw katy.

"There's your dad, Lefty."

Lefty said, "Where?" but looked the wrong way and walked a little faster.

At the end of the grandstand Lefty stopped Jamesie. "My old man is out of town, kid. Got that?"

Jamesie did not see how this could be. He knew Lefty's father. Lefty's father had a brown face and orange gums. But Lefty ought to know his own father. "I guess it just looked like him, Lefty," Jamesie said.

Lefty took his hand off Jamesie's arm and smiled. "Yeah, that's right, kid. It just looked like him on account of he's out of town—in Peoria."

Jamesie could still feel the pressure of Lefty's fingers on his arm. They came out on the diamond at the Indees bench near first base. The talk quieted down when Lefty appeared. Everybody thought he had a big head, but nobody could say a thing against his pitching record, it was that good. The scout for the New York Yankees had invited him only last Sunday to train with them next spring. The idea haunted the others. J. G. had shut up about the beauties of teamwork.

J. G. was counting the balls when Jamesie went to the suitcase to get one for Lefty. J. G. snapped the lid down.

"It's for Lefty!"

"Huh!"

"He wants it for warm up."

"Did you tell this kid to get you a ball, Left?"

"Should I bring my own?" Lefty said.

J. G. dug into the suitcase for a ball, grunting, "I only asked him." He looked to Jamesie for sympathy. He considered the collection of balls and finally picked out a fairly new one.

"Lefty, he likes 'em brand new," Jamesie said. "Who's running this club?" J. G. bawled. But he threw the ball back and broke a brand new one out of its box and tissue paper. He ignored Jamesie's ready hand and yelled to Lefty going out to the bull pen, "Coming at you, Left," and threw it wild.

Lefty let the ball bounce through his legs, not trying for it. "Nice throw," he said.

Jamesie retrieved the ball for Lefty. They tossed it back and forth, limbering up, and Jamesie aped Lefty's professional indolence.

When Bugs Bidwell, Lefty's battery mate, appeared with his big mitt, Jamesie stood aside and buttoned his glove back on his belt. Lefty shed his red blanket coat with the leather sleeves and gave it to Jamesie for safekeeping. Jamesie folded it gently over his arm, with the white chenille "J" showing out. He took his stand behind Bugs to get a good look at Lefty's stuff.

Lefty had all his usual stuff—the fast one with the two little hops in it, no bigger than a pea; his slow knuckler that looked like a basketball, all the stitches standing still and staring you in the face; his sinker that started out high like a wild pitch, then dipped a good eight inches and straightened out for a called strike. But something was wrong—Lefty with nothing to say, no jokes, no sudden whoops, was not himself. Only once did he smile at a girl in the bleachers and say she was plenty . . . and sent a fast one smacking into Bug's mitt for what he meant.

That, for a moment, was the Lefty that Jamesie's older cousins knew about. They said a nice kid like Jamesie ought to be kept away from him, even at the ball park. Jamesie was always afraid it would get back to Lefty that the cousins thought he was poor white trash, or that he would know it in some other way, as when the cousins passed him on the street and looked the other way. He was worried, too, about what Lefty might think of his Sunday clothes, the snow-white blouse, the floppy sailor tie, the soft linen pants, the sissy clothes. His tennis shoes—sneakers, he ought to say—were all right, but not the golf stockings that left his knees bare, like a rich kid's. The tough guys, because they were tough or poor—he didn't know which—wore socks, not stockings, and they wore them rolled down slick to their ankles.

Bugs stuck his mitt with the ball in it under his arm and got out his Beechnut. He winked at Jamesie and said, "Chew?"

Jamesie giggled. He liked Bugs. Bugs, on loan from the crack State Hospital team, was all right—nothing crazy about him; he just liked it at the asylum, he said, the big grounds and lots of cool shade, and he was not required to work or take walks like the regular patients. He was the only Indee on speaking terms with Lefty.

Turning to Lefty, Bugs said, "Ever seen this Cuban work?"

"Naw."

"I guess he's got it when he's right."

"That so?" Lefty caught the ball with his bare hand and spun it back to Bugs. "Well, all I can promise you is a no-hit game. It's up to you clowns to get the runs."

"And me hitting a lousy .211."

"All you got to do is hold me. Anyhow what's the Foul Ball want for his five bucks—Mickey Cochrane?"

"Yea, Left."

"I ought to quit him."

"Ain't you getting your regular fifteen?"

"Yeah, but I ought to quit. The Yankees want me. Is my curve breaking too soon?"

"It's right in there, Left."

It was a pitcher's battle until the seventh inning. Then the Indees pushed a run across.

The Barons got to Lefty for their first hit in the seventh, and when the next man bunted, Lefty tried to field it instead of letting Middle Pete at third have it, which put two on with none out. Little Pete threw the next man out at first, the only play possible, and the runners advanced to second and third. The next hitter hammered a line drive to Big Pete at first, and Big Pete tried to make it two by throwing to second, where the runner was off, but it was too late and the runner on third scored on the play. J. G. from the bench condemned Big Pete for a dumb Swede. The next man popped to short center.

Jamesie ran out with Lefty's jacket. "Don't let your arm get cold, Lefty."

"Some support I got," Lefty said.

"Whyn't you leave me have that bunt, Lefty?" Middle Pete said, and everybody knew he was right.

"Two of them pitches was hit solid," Big Pete said. "Good anywhere."

"Now, boys," J. G. said.

"Aw dry up," Lefty said, grabbing a blade of grass to chew. "I ought to quit you bums."

Pid Kirby struck out for the Indees, but Little Pete walked, and Middle Pete advanced him to second on a long fly to left. Then Big Pete tripled to the weed patch in center, clear up against the Chevrolet sign, driving in Little Pete. Guez whiffed Kelly Larkin, retiring the side, and the Indees were leading the Barons 2 to 1.

The first Baron to bat in the eighth had J. G. frantic with fouls. The umpire was down to his last ball and calling for more. With trembling fingers J. G. unwrapped new balls. He had the bat boy and the bat boy's assistant hunting for them behind the grandstand. When one fell among the automobiles parked near first, he started to go and look for himself, but thought of Jamesie and sent him instead. "If anybody tries to hold out on you, come and tell me."

After Jamesie found the ball he crept up behind a familiar blue Hupmobile, dropping to his knees when he was right under Uncle Pat's elbow, and then popping up to scare him.

"Look who's here," his cousin said. It had not been Uncle Pat's elbow at all, but Gabriel's. Uncle Pat, who had never learned to drive, sat on the other side to be two feet closer to the game.

Jamesie stepped up on the running board, and Gabriel offered him some popcorn.

"So you're at the game, Jamesie," Uncle Pat said, grinning as though it were funny. "Gabriel said he thought that was you out there."

"Where'd you get the cap, Jamesie?" Gabriel said.

"Lefty. The whole team got new ones. And if they win today J. G. says they're getting whole new uniforms."

"Not from me," Uncle Pat said, looking out on the field. "Who the thunder's wearing my suit today?"

"Lee Coles, see?" Gabriel said, pointing to the player. Lee's back—Mallon's Grocery—was to them.

Uncle Pat, satisfied, slipped a bottle of near beer up from the floor to his lips and tipped it up straight, which explained to Jamesie the foam on his mustache.

"You went and missed me again this week," Uncle Pat said broodingly. "You know what I'm going to do, Jamesie?"

"What?"

"I'm going to stop taking your old *Liberty* magazine if you don't bring me one first thing tomorrow morning."

"I will." He would have to bring Uncle Pat his own free copy and erase the crossword puzzle. He never should have sold out on the street. That was how you lost your regular customers.

Uncle Pat said, "This makes the second time I started in to read a serial and had this happen to me."

"Is it all right if the one I bring you tomorrow has got 'Sample Copy' stamped on it?"

"That's all right with me, Jamesie, but I ought to get it for nothing." Uncle Pat swirled the last inch of beer in the bottle until it was all suds.

"I like the *Post*," Gabriel said. "Why don't you handle the *Post?*"

"They don't need anybody now."

"What he ought to handle," Uncle Pat said, "is the *Country Gentleman.*"

"How's the Rosebud coming, Jamesie?" Gabriel asked. "But I don't want to buy any."

Uncle Pat and Gabriel laughed at him.

Why was that funny? He'd had to return eighteen boxes and tell them he guessed he was all through being the local representative. But why was that so funny?

"Did you sell enough to get the bicycle, Jamesie?"

"No." He had sold all the Rosebud salve he could, but not nearly enough to get the Ranger bicycle. He had to be satisfied with the Eveready flashlight.

"Well, I got enough of that Rosebud salve now to grease the Hup," Gabriel said. "Or to smear all over me the next time I swim the English Channel—with Gertrude Ederle. It ought to keep the fishes away."

"It smells nice," Uncle Pat said. "But I got plenty."

Jamesie felt that they were protecting themselves against him.

"I sent it all back anyway," he said, but that was not true; there were six boxes at home in his room that he had to keep in order to get the flashlight. Why was that the way it always worked out? Same way with the flower seeds. Why was it that whenever he got a new suit at Meyer Brothers they weren't giving out ball bats or compasses? Why was it he only won a half pound of bacon at the carnival, never a Kewpie doll or an electric fan? Why did he always get tin whistles and crickets in the Crackerjack, never a puzzle, a ring, or a badge? And one time he had got nothing! Why was it that the five-dollar bill he found on South Diamond Street belonged to Mrs. Hutchinson? But he *had* found a quarter in the dust at the circus that nobody claimed.

"Get your aunt Kate to take that cap up in the back," Uncle Pat said, smiling.

Vaguely embarrassed, Jamesie said, "Well, I got to get back."

"If that's Lefty's cap," Gabriel called after him, "you'd better send it to the cleaners."

When he got back to the bench and handed the ball over, J. G. seemed to forget all about the bases being crowded.

"Thank God," he said. "I thought you went home with it."

The Barons were all on Lefty now. Shorty Parker, their manager, coaching at third, chanted, "Take him out . . . Take him out . . . Take him out."

The Barons had started off the ninth with two clean blows. Then Bugs took a foul ball off the chicken wire in front of the grandstand for one out, and Big Pete speared a drive on the rise for another. Two down and runners on first and third. Lefty wound up—bad baseball—and the man on first started for second, the batter stepping into the pitch, not to hit it but to spoil the peg to second. The runner was safe; the man on third, threatening to come home after a false start, slid yelling back into the sack. It was close and J. G. flew off the bench to protest a little.

After getting two strikes on the next batter, Lefty threw four balls, so wide it looked like a deliberate pitchout, and that loaded the bases.

J. G. called time. He went out to the mound to talk it over with Lefty, but Lefty waved him away. So J. G. consulted Bugs behind the plate. Jamesie, lying on the grass a few feet away, could hear them.

"That's the first windup I ever seen a pitcher take with a runner on first."

"It was pretty bad," Bugs said.

"And then walking that last one. He don't look wild to me, neither."

"He ain't wild, J. G.; I'll tell you that."

"I want your honest opinion, Bugs."

"I don't know what to say, J. G."

"Think I better jerk him?"

Bugs was silent, chewing it over.

"Guess I better leave him in, huh?"

"You're the boss, J. G. I don't know nothing for sure."

"I only got Extra Pete to put in. They'd murder him. I guess I got to leave Lefty in and take a chance."

"I guess so."

When J. G. had gone Bugs walked halfway out to the mound and spoke to Lefty. "You all right?"

"I had a little twinge before."

"A little what?"

Lefty touched his left shoulder.

"You mean your arm's gone sore?"

"Naw. I guess it's nothing."

Bugs took his place behind the plate again. He crouched, and Jamesie, from where he was lying, saw two fingers appear below the mitt—the signal. Lefty nodded, wound up, and tried to slip a medium-fast one down the middle. Guez, the batter, poled a long ball into left—foul by a few feet. Bugs shook his head in the mask, took a new ball from the umpire, and slammed it hard at Lefty.

Jamesie saw two fingers below the mitt again. What was Bugs doing? It wasn't smart baseball to give Guez another like the last one!

Guez swung and the ball fell against the left field fence—fair. Lee Coles, the left fielder, was having trouble locating it in the weeds. Kelly Larkin came over from center to help him hunt. When they found the ball, Guez had completed the circuit and the score was 5 to 2 in favor of the Barons.

Big Pete came running over to Lefty from first base, Little Pete from second, Pid Kirby from short, Middle Pete from third. J. G., calling time again, walked out to them.

"C'mere, Bugs," he said.

Bugs came slowly.

"What'd you call for on that last pitch?"

"Curve ball."

"And the one before that?"

"Same."

"And what'd Lefty give you?"

"It wasn't no curve. It wasn't much of anything."

"No," J. G. said. "It sure wasn't no curve ball. It was right in there, not too fast, not too slow, just right—for batting practice."

"It slipped," Lefty said. "Slipped, huh!" Big Pete said. "How about the other one?"

"They both slipped. Ain't that never happened before?"

"Well, it ain't never going to happen again—not to me, it ain't," J. G. said. "I'm taking you out!"

He shouted to Extra Pete on the bench, "Warm up! You're going in!" He turned to Lefty.

"And I'm firing you. I just found out your old man was making bets under the grandstand—and they wasn't on us! I can put you in jail for this!"

"Try it," Lefty said, starting to walk away.

"If you knew it, J. G.," Big Pete said, "whyn't you let us know?" "I just now found it out, is why."

"Then I'm going to make up for lost time," Big Pete said, following Lefty, "and punch this guy's nose."

Old man Peterson appeared among them—somebody must have told him what it was all about. "Give it to him, son!" he cackled.

Jamesie missed the fight. He was not tall enough to see over all the heads, and Gabriel, sent by Uncle Pat, was dragging him away from it all.

"I always knew that Lefty was a bad one," Gabriel said on the way home. "I knew it from the time he used to hunch in marbles."

"It reminds me of the Black Sox scandal of 1919," Uncle Pat said. "I wonder if they'll hold the old man, too."

Jamesie, in tears, said, "Lefty hurt his arm and you don't like him just because he don't work, and his father owes you at the store! Let me out! I'd rather walk by myself than ride in the Hupmobile—with you!"

He stayed up in his room, feigning a combination stomach-ache and headache, and would not come down for supper. Uncle Pat and Gabriel were down there eating. His room was over the dining room, and the windows were open upstairs and down, but he could not quite hear what they said. Uncle Pat was laughing a lot—that was all for sure—but then he always did that. Pretty soon he heard no more from the dining room and he knew they had gone to sit on the front porch.

Somebody was coming up the stairs. Aunt Kate. He knew the wavering step at the top of the stairs to be hers, and the long pause she used to catch her breath—something wrong with her lungs? Now, as she began to move, he heard ice tinkling in a glass. Lemonade. She was bringing him some supper. She knocked. He lay heavier on the bed and with his head at a painful angle to make her think he was suffering. She knocked again. If he pinched his forehead it would look red and feverish. He did. Now.

"Come in," he said weakly.

She came in, gliding across the room in the twilight, tall and white as a sail in her organdy, serene before her patient. Not quite opening his eyes, he saw her through the lashes. She thought he was sick all right, but even if she didn't, she would never take advantage of him to make a joke, like Uncle Pat, prescribing, "A good dose of salts! That's the ticket!" Or Gabriel, who was even meaner, "An enema!"

He had Aunt Kate fooled completely. He could fool her every time. On Halloween she was the kind of person who went to the door every time the bell rang. She was the only grownup he knew with whom it was not always the teeter-totter game. She did not raise herself by lowering him. She did not say back to him the things he said, slightly changed, accented with a grin, so that they were funny. Uncle Pat did. Gabriel did. Sometimes, if there was company, his father did.

"Don't you want the shades up, Jamesie?"

She raised the shades, catching the last of that day's sun, bringing the ballplayers on the wall out of the shadows and into action. She put the tray on the table by his bed.

Jamesie sat up and began to eat. Aunt Kate was the best one. Even if she noticed it, she would say nothing about his sudden turn for the better.

She sat across from him in the rocker, the little red one he had been given three years ago, when he was just a kid in the first grade, but she did not look too big for it. She ran her hand over the front of his books, frowning at Baseball Bill, Don Sturdy, Tom Swift, Horatio Alger, Jr., and the *Sporting News.* They had come between him and her.

"Where are the books we used to read, Jamesie?"

"On the bottom shelf."

She bent to see them. There they were, his old friends and hers—hers still. Perseus. Theseus. All those old Greeks. Sir Lancelot. Merlin. Sir Tristram. King Arthur. Oliver Twist. Pinocchio. Gulliver. He wondered how he ever could have liked them, and why Aunt Kate still did. Perhaps he still did, a little. But they turned out wrong, most of them, with all the good guys dying or turning into fairies and the bad guys becoming dwarfs.

The books he read now turned out right, if not until the very last page, and the bad guys died or got what was coming to them.

"Were they talking about the game, Aunt Kate?"

"Your uncle was, and Gabriel."

Jamesie waited a moment. "Did they say anything about Lefty?"

"I don't know. Is he the one who lost the game on purpose?"

"That's a lie, Aunt Kate! That's just what Uncle Pat and Gabriel say!"

"Well, I'm sure I don't know——"

"You *are* on their side!"

Aunt Kate reached for his hand, but he drew it back. "Jamesie, I'm sure I'm not on anyone's side. How can I be? I don't know about baseball—and I don't care about it!"

"Well, I *do!* And I'm not one bit sick—and you thought I was!"

Jamesie rolled out of bed, ran to the door, turned, and said, "Why don't you get out of my room and go and be with them! You're on their side! And Uncle Pat drinks *near beer!*"

He could not be sure, but he thought he had her crying, and if he did it served her right. He went softly down the stairs, past the living room, out the back door, and crept along the house until he reached the front porch. He huddled under the spiraea bushes and listened to them talk. But it was not about the game. It was about President Coolidge. His father was for him. Uncle Pat was against him.

Jamesie crept back along the house until it was safe to stand up and walk. He went down the alley. He called for Francis.

But Francis was not home—still with his father, Mrs. Murgatroyd said.

Jamesie went downtown, taking his own special way, through alleys, across lots, so that he arrived on the Square without using a single street or walking on a single sidewalk. He weighed himself on the scales in front of Kresge's. He weighed eighty-three pounds, and the little card said, "You are the strong, silent type, and silence is golden." He weighed himself in front of Grant's. He weighed eighty-four pounds, and the card said, "Cultivate your good tastes and make the most of your business connections."

He bought a ball of gum from the machine in front of the Owl Drugstore. It looked like it was time for a black one to come out, and black was his favorite flavor, but it was a green one. Anyway he was glad it had not been white.

He coveted the Louisville Sluggers in the window of the D. & M. Hardware. He knew how much they cost. They were autographed by Paul Waner, Ty Cobb, Rogers Hornsby, all the big league stars, and if Lefty ever cracked his, a Paul Waner, he was going to give it to Jamesie, he said.

When Lefty was up with the Yankees—though they had not talked about it yet—he would send for Jamesie. He would make Jamesie the bat boy for the Yankees. He would say to Jake Ruppert, the owner of the Yankees, "Either you hire my friend, Jamesie, as bat boy or I quit." Jake Ruppert would want his own nephew or somebody to have the job, but what could he do? Jamesie would have a uniform like the regular players, and get to travel around the country with them, living in hotels, eating in restaurants, taking taxicabs, and would be known to everybody as Lefty's best friend, and they would both be Babe Ruth's best friends, the three of them going everywhere together. He would get all the Yankees to write their names on an Official American League ball and then send it home to Francis Murgatroyd, who would still be going to school back in Jay-ville—poor old Francis; and he would write to him on hotel stationery with his own fourteen-dollar fountain pen.

And then he was standing across the street from the jail. He wondered if they had Lefty locked up over there, if Uncle Pat and Gabriel had been right—not about Lefty throwing a game—that was a lie!—but about him being locked up. A policeman came out of the jail. Jamesie waited for him to cross the street. He was Officer Burkey. He was Phil Burkey's father, and Phil had shown Jamesie his father's gun and holster one time when he was sleeping. Around the house Mr. Burkey looked like everybody else, not a policeman.

"Mr. Burkey, is Lefty in there?"

Mr. Burkey, through for the day, did not stop to talk, only saying, "Ah, that he is, boy, and there's where he deserves to be."

Jamesie said "Oh yeah!" to himself and went around to the back side of the jail. It was a brick building, painted gray, and the windows were open, but not so you could see inside, and they had bars over them.

Jamesie decided he could do nothing if Mr. Burkey was off duty. The street lights came on; it was night. He began to wonder, too, if his father would miss him. Aunt Kate would not tell. But he would have to come in the back way and sneak up to his room. If it rained tomorrow he would stay in and make up with Aunt Kate. He hurried home, and did not remember that he had meant to stay out all night, maybe even run away forever.

The next morning Jamesie came to the jail early. Mr. Burkey, on duty, said he might see Lefty for three minutes, but it was a mystery to him why anyone, especially a nice boy like Jamesie, should want to see the bum. "And don't tell your father you was here."

Jamesie found Lefty lying on a narrow iron bed that was all springs and no covers or pillow.

"Lefty," he said, "I came to see you."

Lefty sat up. He blinked at Jamesie and had trouble getting his eyes to see.

Jamesie went closer. Lefty stood up. They faced each other. Jamesie could have put his hand through the bars and touched Lefty.

"Glad to see you, kid."

"Lefty," Jamesie said, "I brought you some reading." He handed Lefty Uncle Pat's copy of *Liberty* magazine.

"Thanks, kid."

He got the box of Rosebud salve out of his pocket for Lefty.

"Well, thanks, kid. But what do I do with it?"

"For your arm, Lefty. It says 'recommended for aches and pains.'"

"I'll try it."

"Do you like oranges, Lefty?"

"I can eat 'em."

He gave Lefty his breakfast orange.

A funny, sweet smell came off Lefty's breath, like perfume, only sour. Burnt matches and cigar butts lay on the cell floor. Did Lefty smoke? Did he? Didn't he realize what it would do to him?

"Lefty, how do you throw your sinker?"

Lefty held the orange and showed Jamesie how he gripped the ball along the seams, how he snapped his wrist before he let it fly.

"But be sure you don't telegraph it, kid. Throw 'em all the same—your fast one, your floater, your curve. Then they don't know where they're at."

Lefty tossed the orange through the bars to Jamesie.

"Try it."

Jamesie tried it, but he had it wrong at first, and Lefty had to reach through the bars and show him again. After that they were silent, and Jamesie thought Lefty did not seem very glad to see him after all, and remembered the last gift.

"And I brought you this, Lefty."

It was *Baseball Bill in the World Series.*

"Yeah?" Lefty said, momentarily angry, as though he thought Jamesie was trying to kid him. He accepted the book reluctantly.

"He's a pitcher, Lefty," Jamesie said, "Like you, only he's a right-hander."

The sour perfume on Lefty's breath came through the bars again, a little stronger on a sigh.

Wasn't that the odor of strong drink and cigar smoke—the odor of Blackie Humphrey? Jamesie talked fast to keep himself from thinking. "This book's all about Baseball Bill and the World Series," he gulped, "and Blackie Humphrey and some dirty crooks that try to get Bill to throw it, but . . ." He gave up; he knew now. And Lefty had turned his back.

After a moment, during which nothing happened inside him to explain what he knew now, Jamesie got his legs to take him away, out of the jail, around the corner, down the street—away. He did not go through alleys, across lots, between buildings, over fences. No. He used the streets and sidewalks, like anyone else, to get where he was going—away—and was not quite himself.

At the Ball Game

William Carlos Williams

The crowd at the ball game
is moved uniformly

by a spirit of uselessness
which delights them—

all the exciting detail
of the chase

and the escape, the error
the flash of genius—

all to no end save—

So in detail they, the crowd,
are beautiful

for this
to be warned against

saluted and defied—
It is alive, venomous

It smiles grimly
its words cut—

The flashy female with her
"mother" gets it—

The Jew gets it straight—it
is deadly, terrifying—

It is the Inquisition, the
Revolution

It
lives

day by day in them
idly—

This is
the power of their faces—

It is summer, it is the solstice
the crowd is

cheering, the crowd is laughing
in detail

permanently, seriously
without thought

The Eighty-Yard Run

Irwin Shaw

The pass was high and wide and he jumped for it, feeling it slap flatly against his hands, as he shook his hips to throw off the halfback who was diving at him. The center floated by, his hands desperately brushing Darling's knee as Darling picked his feet up high and delicately ran over a blocker and an opposing linesman in a jumble on the ground near the scrimmage line. He had ten yards in the clear and picked up speed, breathing easily, feeling his thigh pads rising and falling against his legs, listening to the sound of cleats behind him, pulling away from them, watching the other backs heading him off toward the sideline, the whole picture, the men closing in on him, the blockers fighting for position, the ground he had to cross, all suddenly clear in his head, for the first time in his life not a meaningless confusion of men, sounds, speed. He smiled a little to himself as he ran, holding the ball lightly in front of him with his two hands, his knees pumping high, his hips twisting in the almost girlish run of a back in a broken field. The first halfback came at him and he fed him his leg, then swung at the last moment, took the shock of the man's shoulder without breaking stride, ran right through him, his cleats biting securely into the turf. There was only the safety man now, coming warily at him, his arms crooked, hands spread. Darling tucked the ball in, spurted at him, driving hard, hurling himself along, his legs pounding, knees high, all two hundred pounds bunched into controlled attack. He was sure he was going to get past the safety man. Without thought, his arms and legs working beautifully together, he headed right for the safety man, stiff-armed him, feeling blood spurt instantaneously from the man's nose onto his hand, seeing his face go awry, head turned, mouth pulled to one side. He pivoted away, keeping the arm locked, dropping the safety man as he ran easily toward the goal line, with the drumming of cleats diminishing behind him.

How long ago? It was autumn then, and the ground was getting hard because the nights were cold and leaves from the maples around the stadium blew across the practice fields in gusts of wind, and the girls were beginning to put polo coats over their sweaters when they came to watch practice in the afternoons. . . . Fifteen years. Darling walked slowly over the same ground in the spring twilight, in his neat shoes a man of thirty-five dressed in a double-breasted suit, ten pounds heavier in the fifteen years, but not fat, with the years between 1925 and 1940 showing in his face.

The coach was smiling quietly to himself and the assistant coaches were looking at each other with pleasure the way they always did when one of the second stringers suddenly did something fine, bringing credit to them, making their $2,000 a year a tiny bit more secure.

Darling trotted back, smiling, breathing deeply but easily, feeling wonderful, not tired, though this was the tail end of practice and he'd run eighty yards. The sweat poured off his face and soaked his jersey and he liked the feeling, the warm moistness lubricating his skin like oil. Off in a corner of the field some players were punting and the smack of leather against the ball came pleasantly through the afternoon air. The freshmen were running signals on the next field and the quarterback's sharp voice, the pound of the eleven pairs of cleats, the "Dig, now *dig!*" of the coaches, the laughter of the players all somehow made him feel happy as he trotted back to midfield, listening to the applause and shouts of the students along the sidelines, knowing that after that run the coach would have to start him Saturday against Illinois.

Fifteen years, Darling thought, remembering the shower after the workout, the hot water steaming off his skin and the deep soapsuds and all the young voices singing with the water streaming down and towels going and managers running in and out and the sharp sweet smell of oil of wintergreen and everybody clapping him on the back as he dressed and Packard, the captain, who took being captain very seriously, coming over to him and shaking his hand and saying, "Darling, you're going to go places in the next two years."

The assistant manager fussed over him, wiping a cut on his leg with alcohol and iodine, the little sting making him realize suddenly how fresh and whole and solid his body felt. The manager slapped a piece of adhesive tape over the cut, and Darling noticed the sharp clean white of the tape against the ruddiness of the skin, fresh from the shower.

He dressed slowly, the softness of his shirt and the soft warmth of his wool socks and his flannel trousers a reward against his skin after the harsh pressure of the shoulder harness and thigh and hip pads. He drank three glasses of cold water, the liquid reaching down coldly inside of him, soothing the harsh dry places in his throat and belly left by the sweat and running and shouting of practice.

Fifteen years.

The sun had gone down and the sky was green behind the stadium and he laughed quietly to himself as he looked at the stadium, rearing above the trees, and knew that on Saturday when the 70,000 voices roared as the team came running out onto the field, part of that enormous salute would be for him. He walked slowly, listening to the gravel crunch satisfactorily under his shoes in the still twilight, feeling his clothes swing lightly against his skin, breathing the thin evening air, feeling the wind move softly in his damp hair, wonderfully cool behind his ears and at the nape of his neck.

Louise was waiting for him at the road, in her car. The top was down and he noticed all over again, as he always did when he saw her, how pretty she was, the rough blond hair and the large, inquiring eyes and the bright mouth, smiling now.

She threw the door open. "Were you good today?" she asked.

"Pretty good," he said. He climbed in, sank luxuriously into the soft leather, stretched his legs far out. He smiled, thinking of the eighty yards. "Pretty damn good."

She looked at him seriously for a moment, then scrambled around, like a little girl, kneeling on the seat next to him, her hands along his ears, and kissed him as he sprawled, head back, on the seat cushion. She let go of him, but kept her head close to his, over his. Darling reached up slowly and rubbed the back of his hand against her cheek, lit softly by a street lamp a hundred feet away. They looked at each other, smiling.

Louise drove down to the lake and they sat there silently, watching the moon rise behind the hills on the other side. Finally he reached over, pulled her gently to him, kissed her. Her lips grew soft, her body sank into his, tears formed slowly in her eyes. He knew, for the first time, that he could do whatever he wanted with her.

"Tonight," he said. "I'll call for you at seven-thirty. Can you get out?"

She looked at him. She was smiling, but the tears were still full in her eyes. "All right," she said. "I'll get out. How about you? Won't the coach raise hell?"

Darling grinned. "I got the coach in the palm of my hand," he said. "Can you wait till seven-thirty?"

She grinned back at him. "No," she said.

They kissed and she started the car and they went back to town for dinner. He sang on the way home.

Christian Darling, thirty-five years old, sat on the frail spring grass, greener now than it ever would be again on the practice field, looked thoughtfully up at the stadium, a deserted ruin in the twilight. He had started on the first team that Saturday and every Saturday after that for the next two years, but it had never been as satisfactory as it should have been. He never had broken away, the longest run he'd ever made was thirty-five yards, and that in a game that was already won, and then that kid had come up from the third team, Diederich, a blank-faced German kid from Wisconsin, who ran like a bull, ripping lines to pieces Saturday after Saturday, plowing through, never getting hurt, never changing his expression, scoring more points, gaining more ground than all the rest of the team put together, making everybody's All-American, carrying the ball three times out of four, keeping everybody else out of the headlines. Darling was a good blocker and he spent his Saturday afternoons working on the big Swedes and Polacks who played tackle and end for Michigan, Illinois, Purdue, hurling into huge pile-ups, bobbing his head wildly to elude the great raw hands swinging like meat-cleavers at him as he went charging in to open up holes for Diederich coming through like a locomotive behind him. Still, it wasn't so bad. Everybody liked him and he did his job and he was pointed out on the campus and boys always felt important when they introduced their girls to him at their proms, and Louise loved him and watched him faithfully in the games, even in the mud, when your own mother wouldn't know you, and drove him around in her car keeping the top down because she was proud of him and wanted to show everybody that she was Christian Darling's girl. She bought him crazy presents because her father was rich, watches, pipes, humidors, an icebox for beer for his room, curtains, wallets, a fifty-dollar dictionary.

"You'll spend every cent your old man owns," Darling protested once when she showed up at his rooms with seven different packages in her arms and tossed them onto the couch.

"Kiss me," Louise said, "and shut up."

"Do you want to break your poor old man?"

"I don't mind. I want to buy you presents."

"Why?"

"It makes me feel good. Kiss me. I don't know why. Did you know that you're an important figure?"

"Yes," Darling said gravely.

"When I was waiting for you at the library yesterday two girls saw you coming and one of them said to the other, 'That's Christian Darling. He's an important figure.' "

"You're a liar."

"I'm in love with an important figure."

"Still, why the hell did you have to give me a forty-pound dictionary?"

"I wanted to make sure," Louise said, "that you had a token of my esteem. I want to smother you in tokens of my esteem."

Fifteen years ago.

They'd married when they got out of college. There'd been other women for him, but all casual and secret, more for curiosity's sake, and vanity, women who'd thrown themselves at him and flattered him, a pretty mother at a summer camp for boys, an old girl from his home town who'd suddenly blossomed into a coquette, a friend of Louise's who had dogged him grimly for six months and had taken advantage of the two weeks that Louise went home when her mother died. Perhaps Louise had known, but she'd kept quiet, loving him completely, filling his rooms with presents, religiously watching him battling with the big Swedes and Polacks on the line of scrimmage on Saturday afternoons, making plans for marrying him and living with him in New York and going with him there to the night clubs, the theaters, the good restaurants, being proud of him in advance, tall, white-teethed, smiling, large, yet moving lightly, with an athlete's grace, dressed in evening clothes, approvingly eyed by magnificently dressed and famous women in theater lobbies, with Louise adoringly at his side.

Her father, who manufactured inks, set up a New York office for Darling to manage and presented him with three hundred accounts, and they lived on Beekman Place with a view of the river with fifteen thousand dollars a year between them, because everybody was buying everything in those days, including ink. They saw all the shows and went to all the speak-easies and spent their fifteen thousand dollars a year and in the afternoons Louise went to the art galleries and the matinees of the more serious plays that Darling didn't like to sit through and Darling slept with a girl who danced in the chorus of *Rosalie* and with the wife of a man who owned three copper mines. Darling played squash three times a week and remained as solid as a stone barn and Louise never took her eyes off him when they were in the same room together, watching him with a secret, miser's smile, with a trick of coming over to him in the middle of a crowded room and saying gravely, in a low voice, "You're the handsomest man I've ever seen in my whole life. Want a drink?"

Nineteen twenty-nine came to Darling and to his wife and father-in-law, the maker of inks, just as it came to everyone else. The father-in-law waited until 1933 and then blew his brains out and when Darling went to Chicago to see what the books of the firm looked like he found out all that was left were debts and three or four gallons of unbought ink.

"Please Christian," Louise said, sitting in their neat Beekman Place apartment, with a view of the river and prints of paintings by Dufy and Braque and Picasso on the wall, "please, why do you want to start drinking at two o'clock in the afternoon?"

"I have nothing else to do," Darling said, putting down his glass, emptied of its fourth drink. "Please pass the whisky."

Louise filled his glass. "Come take a walk with me," she said "We'll walk along the river."

"I don't want to walk along the river," Darling said, squinting intensely at the prints of paintings by Dufy, Braque and Picasso.

"We'll walk along Fifth Avenue."

"I don't want to walk along Fifth Avenue."

"Maybe," Louise said gently, "you'd like to come with me to some art galleries. There's an exhibition by a man named Klee. . . ."

"I don't want to go to any art galleries. I want to sit here and drink Scotch whisky," Darling said. "Who the hell hung those goddam pictures up on the wall?"

"I did," Louise said.

"I hate them."

"I'll take them down," Louise said.

"Leave them there. It gives me something to do in the afternoon. I can hate them." Darling took a long swallow. "Is that the way people paint these days?"

"Yes, Christian. Please don't drink any more."

"Do you like painting like that?"

"Yes, dear."

"Really?"

"Really."

Darling looked carefully at the prints once more. "Little Louise Tucker. The middle-western beauty. I like pictures with horses in them. Why should you like pictures like that?"

"I just happen to have gone to a lot of galleries in the last few years . . ."

"Is that what you do in the afternoon?"

"That's what I do in the afternoon," Louise said.

"I drink in the afternoon."

Louise kissed him lightly on the top of his head as he sat there squinting at the pictures on the wall, the glass of whisky held firmly in his hand. She put on her coat and went out without saying another word. When she came back in the early evening, she had a job on a woman's fashion magazine.

They moved downtown and Louise went out to work every morning and Darling sat home and drank and Louise paid the bills as they came up. She made believe she was going to quit work as soon as Darling found a job, even though she was taking over more responsibility day by day at the magazine, interviewing authors, picking painters for the illustrations and covers, getting actresses to pose for pictures, going out for drinks with the right people, making a thousand new friends whom she loyally introduced to Darling.

"I don't like your hat," Darling said, once, when she came in in the evening and kissed him, her breath rich with Martinis.

"What's the matter with my hat, Baby?" she asked, running her fingers through his hair. "Everybody says it's very smart."

"It's too damned smart," he said. "It's not for you. It's for a rich, sophisticated woman of thirty-five with admirers."

Louise laughed. "I'm practicing to be a rich, sophisticated woman of thirty-five with admirers," she said. He stared soberly at her. "Now, don't look so grim, Baby. It's still the same simple little wife under the hat." She took the hat off, threw it into a corner, sat on his lap. "See? Homebody Number One."

"Your breath could run a train," Darling said, not wanting to be mean, but talking out of boredom, and sudden shock at seeing his wife curiously a stranger in a new hat, with a new expression in her eyes under the little brim, secret, confident, knowing.

Louise tucked her head under his chin so he couldn't smell her breath. "I had to take an author out for cocktails," she said. "He's a boy from the Ozark Mountains and he drinks like a fish. He's a Communist."

"What the hell is a Communist from the Ozarks doing writing for a woman's fashion magazine?"

Louise chuckled. "The magazine business is getting all mixed up these days. The publishers want to have a foot in every camp. And anyway, you can't find an author under seventy these days who isn't a Communist."

"I don't think I like you to associate with all those people, Louise," Darling said. "Drinking with them."

"He's a very nice, gentle boy," Louise said. "He reads Ernest Dowson."

"Who's Ernest Dowson?"

Louise patted his arm, stood up, fixed her hair. "He's an English poet."

Darling felt that somehow he had disappointed her. "Am I supposed to know who Ernest Dowson is?"

"No, dear. I'd better go in and take a bath."

After she had gone, Darling went over to the corner where the hat was lying and picked it up. It was nothing, a scrap of straw, a red flower, a veil, meaningless on his big hand, but on his wife's head a signal of something . . . big city, smart and knowing women drinking and dining with men other than their husbands, conversation about things a normal man wouldn't know much about, Frenchmen who painted as though they used their elbows instead of brushes, composers who wrote whole symphonies without a single melody in them, writers who knew all about politics and women who knew all about writers, the movement of the proletariat, Marx, somehow mixed up with five-dollar dinners and the best-looking women in America and fairies who made them laugh and half-sentences immediately understood and secretly hilarious and wives who called their husbands "Baby." He put the hat down, a scrap of straw and a red flower, and a little veil. He drank some whisky straight and went into the bathroom where his wife was lying deep in her bath, singing to herself and smiling from time to time like a little girl, paddling the water gently with her hands, sending up a slight spicy fragrance from the bath salts she used.

He stood over her, looking down at her. She smiled up at him, her eyes half closed, her body pink and shimmering in the warm, scented water. All over again, with all the old suddenness, he was hit deep inside him with the knowledge of how beautiful she was, how much he needed her.

"I came in here," he said, "to tell you I wish you wouldn't call me 'Baby.' "

She looked up at him from the bath, her eyes quickly full of sorrow, half-understanding what he meant. He knelt and put his arms around her, his sleeves plunged heedlessly in the water, his shirt and jacket soaking wet as he clutched her wordlessly, holding her crazily tight, crushing her breath from her, kissing her desperately, searchingly, regretfully.

He got jobs after that, selling real estate and automobiles, but somehow, although he had a desk with his name on a wooden wedge on it, and he went to the office religiously at nine each morning, he never managed to sell anything and he never made any money.

Louise was made assistant editor, and the house was always full of strange men and women who talked fast and got angry on abstract subjects like mural painting, novelists, labor unions. Negro short-story writers drank Louise's liquor, and a lot of Jews, and big solemn men with scarred faces and knotted hands who talked slowly but clearly about picket lines and battles with guns and leadpipe at mine-shaft-heads and in front of factory gates. And Louise moved among them all, confidently, knowing what they were talking about, with opinions that they listened to and argued about just as though she were a man. She knew everybody, condescended to no one, devoured books that Darling had never heard of, walked along the streets of the city, excited, at home, soaking in all the million tides of New York without fear, with constant wonder.

Her friends liked Darling and sometimes he found a man who wanted to get off in the corner and talk about the new boy who played fullback for Princeton, and the decline of the double wingback, or even the state of the stock market, but for the most part he sat on the edge of things, solid and quiet in the high storm of words. "The dialectics of the situation . . . The theater has been given over to expert jugglers . . . Picasso? What man has a right to paint old bones and collect ten thousand dollars for them? . . . I stand firmly behind Trotsky . . . Poe was the last American critic. When he died they put lilies on the grave of American criticism. I don't say this because they panned my last book, but . . ."

Once in a while he caught Louise looking soberly and consideringly at him through the cigarette smoke and the noise and he avoided her eyes and found an excuse to get up and go into the kitchen for more ice or to open another bottle.

"Come on," Cathal Flaherty was saying, standing at the door with a girl, "you've got to come down and see this. It's down on Fourteenth Street, in the old Civic Repertory, and you can only see it on Sunday nights and I guarantee you'll come out of the theater singing." Flaherty was a big young Irishman with a broken nose who was the lawyer for a longshoreman's union, and he had been hanging around the house for six months on and off, roaring and shutting everybody else up when he got in an argument. "It's a new play, *Waiting for Lefty;* it's about taxi-drivers."

"Odets," the girl with Flaherty said. "It's by a guy named Odets."

"I never heard of him," Darling said.

"He's a new one," the girl said.

"It's like watching a bombardment," Flaherty said. "I saw it last Sunday night. You've got to see it."

"Come on, Baby," Louise said to Darling, excitement in her eyes already. "We've been sitting in the Sunday *Times* all day, this'll be a great change."

"I see enough taxi-drivers every day," Darling said, not because he meant that, but because he didn't like to be around Flaherty, who said things that made Louise laugh a lot and whose judgment she accepted on almost every subject. "Let's go to the movies."

"You've never seen anything like this before," Flaherty said. "He wrote this play with a baseball bat."

"Come on," Louise coaxed, "I bet it's wonderful."

"He has long hair," the girl with Flaherty said. "Odets. I met him at a party. He's an actor. He didn't say a goddam thing all night."

"I don't feel like going down to Fourteenth Street," Darling said, wishing Flaherty and his girl would get out. "It's gloomy."

"Oh, hell!" Louise said loudly. She looked coolly at Darling, as though she'd just been introduced to him and was making up her mind about him, and not very favorably. He saw her looking at him, knowing there was something new and dangerous in her face and he wanted to say something, but Flaherty was there and his damned girl, and anyway, he didn't know what to say.

"I'm going," Louise said, getting her coat. "I don't think Fourteenth Street is gloomy."

"I'm telling you," Flaherty was saying, helping her on with her coat, "it's the Battle of Gettysburg, in Brooklynese."

"Nobody could get a word out of him," Flaherty's girl was saying as they went through the door. "He just sat there all night."

The door closed. Louise hadn't said good night to him. Darling walked around the room four times, then sprawled out on the sofa, on top of the Sunday *Times*. He lay there for five minutes looking at the ceiling, thinking of Flaherty walking down the street talking in that booming voice, between the girls, holding their arms.

Louise had looked wonderful. She'd washed her hair in the afternoon and it had been very soft and light and clung close to her head as she stood there angrily putting her coat on. Louise was getting prettier every year, partly because she knew by now how pretty she was, and made the most of it.

"Nuts," Darling said, standing up. "Oh, nuts."

He put on his coat and went down to the nearest bar and had five drinks off by himself in a corner before his money ran out.

The years since then had been foggy and downhill. Louise had been nice to him, and in a way, loving and kind, and they'd fought only once, when he said he was going to vote for Landon. ("Oh, Christ," she'd said, "doesn't *anything* happen inside your head? Don't you read the papers? The penniless Republican!") She'd been sorry later and apologized for hurting him, but apologized as she might to a child. He'd tried hard, had gone grimly to the art galleries, the concert halls, the bookshops, trying to gain on the trail of his wife, but it was no use. He was bored, and none of what he saw or heard or dutifully read made much sense to him and finally he gave it up. He had thought, many nights as he ate dinner alone, knowing that Louise would come home late and drop silently into bed without explanation, of getting a divorce, but he knew the loneliness, the hopelessness, of not seeing her again would be too much to take. So he was good, completely devoted, ready at all times to go any place with her, do anything she wanted. He even got a small job, in a broker's office and paid his own way, bought his own liquor.

Then he'd been offered the job of going from college to college as a tailor's representative. "We want a man," Mr. Rosenberg had said, "who as soon as you look at him, you say, 'There's a university man.' " Rosenberg had looked approvingly at Darling's broad shoulders and well-kept waist, at his carefully brushed hair and his honest, wrinkle-less face.

"Frankly, Mr. Darling, I am willing to make you a proposition. I have inquired about you, you are favorably known on your old campus, I understand you were in the backfield with Alfred Diederich."

Darling nodded. "Whatever happened to him?"

"He is walking around in a cast for seven years now. An iron brace. He played professional football and they broke his neck for him."

Darling smiled. That, at least, had turned out well.

"Our suits are an easy product to sell, Mr. Darling," Rosenberg said. "We have a handsome, custom-made garment. What has Brooks Brothers got that we haven't got? A name. No more."

"I can make fifty, sixty dollars a week," Darling said to Louise that night. "And expenses. I can save some money and then come back to New York and really get started here."

"Yes, Baby," Louise said.

"As it is," Darling said carefully, "I can make it back here once a month, and holidays and the summer. We can see each other often."

"Yes, Baby." He looked at her face, lovelier now at thirty-five than it had ever been before, but fogged over now as it had been for five years with a kind of patient, kindly, remote boredom.

"What do you say?" he asked. "Should I take it?" Deep within him he hoped fiercely, longingly, for her to say, "No, Baby, you stay right here," but she said, as he knew she'd say, "I think you'd better take it."

He nodded. He had to get up and stand with his back to her, looking out the window, because there were things plain on his face that she had never seen in the fifteen years she'd known him. "Fifty dollars is a lot of money," he said. "I never thought I'd ever see fifty dollars again." He laughed. Louise laughed, too.

Christian Darling sat on the frail green grass of the practice field. The shadow of the stadium had reached out and covered him. In the distance the lights of the university shone a little mistily in the light haze of evening. Fifteen years. Flaherty even now was calling for his wife, buying her a drink, filling whatever bar they were in with that voice of his and that easy laugh. Darling half-closed his eyes, almost saw the boy fifteen years ago reach for the pass, slip the halfback, go skittering lightly down the field, his knees high and fast and graceful, smiling to himself because he knew he was going to get past the safety man. That was the high point, Darling thought, fifteen years ago, on an autumn afternoon, twenty years old and far from death, with the air coming easily into his lungs, and a deep feeling inside him that he could do anything, knock over anybody, outrun whatever had to be outrun. And the shower after and the three glasses of water and the cool night air on his damp head and Louise sitting hatless in the open car with a smile and the first kiss she ever really meant. The high point, an eighty-yard run in the practice, and a girl's kiss and everything after that a decline. Darling laughed. He had practiced the wrong thing, perhaps. He hadn't practiced for 1929 and New York City and a girl who would turn into a woman. Somewhere, he thought, there must have been a point where she moved up to me, was even with me for a moment, when I could have held her hand, if I'd known, held tight, gone with her. Well, he'd never known. Here he was on a playing field that was fifteen years away and his wife was in another city having dinner with another and better man, speaking with him a different, new language, a language nobody had ever taught him.

Darling stood up, smiled a little, because if he didn't smile he knew the tears would come. He looked around him. This was the spot. O'Connor's pass had come sliding out just to here . . . the high point. Darling put up his hands, felt all over again the flat slap of the ball. He shook his hips to throw off the halfback, cut back inside the center, picked his knees high as he ran gracefully over two men jumbled on the ground at the line of scrimmage, ran easily, gaining speed, for ten yards, holding the ball lightly in his two hands, swung away from the halfback diving at him, ran, swinging his hips in the almost girlish manner of a back in a broken field, tore into the safety man, his shoes drumming heavily on the turf, stiff-armed, elbow locked, pivoted, raced lightly and exultantly for the goal line.

It was only after he had sped over the goal line and slowed to a trot that he saw the boy and girl sitting together on the turf, looking at him wonderingly.

He stopped short, dropping his arms. "I . . ." he said, gasping a little though his condition was fine and the run hadn't winded him. "I—once I played here."

The boy and the girl said nothing. Darling laughed embarrassedly, looked hard at them sitting there, close to each other, shrugged, turned and went toward his hotel, the sweat breaking out on his face and running down into his collar.

Say Good-bye to Big Daddy

Randall Jarrell

Big Daddy Lipscomb, who used to help them up
After he'd pulled them down, so that "the children
Won't think Big Daddy's mean"; Big Daddy Lipscomb,
Who stood unmoved among the blockers, like the Rock

Of Gibraltar in a life insurance ad,
Until the ball carrier came, and Daddy got him;
Big Daddy Lipscomb, being carried down an aisle
Of women by Night Train Lane, John Henry Johnson,
And Lenny Moore; Big Daddy, his three ex-wives,
His fiancée, and the grandfather who raised him
Going to his grave in five big Cadillacs;
Big Daddy, who found football easy enough, life hard enough
To—after his last night cruising Baltimore
In his yellow Cadillac—to die of heroin;
Big Daddy, who was scared, he said: "I've been scared
Most of my life. You wouldn't think so to look at me.
It gets so bad I cry myself to sleep—" his size
Embarrassed him, so that he was helped by smaller men
And hurt by smaller men; Big Daddy Lipscomb
Has helped to his feet the last ball carrier, Death.

The big black man in the television set
Whom the viewers stared at—sometimes, almost were—
Is a blur now; when we get up to adjust the set,
It's not the set, but a NETWORK DIFFICULTY.
The world won't be the same without Big Daddy.
Or else it will be.

from University Days

James Thurber

I passed all the other courses that I took at my University, but I could never pass botany. This was because all botany students had to spend several hours a week in a laboratory looking through a microscope at plant cells, and I could never see through a microscope. I never once saw a cell through a microscope. This used to enrage my instructor. He would wander around the laboratory pleased with the progress all the students were making in drawing the involved and, so I am told, interesting structure of flower cells, until he came to me. I would just be standing there. "I can't see anything," I would say. He would begin patiently enough, explaining how anybody can see through a microscope, but he would always end up in a fury, claiming that I could *too* see through a microscope but just pretended that I couldn't. "It takes away from the beauty of flowers anyway," I used to tell him. "We are not concerned with beauty in this course," he would say. "We are concerned solely with what I may call the *mechanics* of flars." "Well," I'd say, "I can't see anything." "Try it just once again," he'd say, and I would put my eye to the microscope and see nothing at all, except now and again a nebulous milky substance—a phenomenon of maladjustment. You were supposed to see a vivid, restless clockwork of sharply defined plant cells. "I see what looks like a lot of milk," I would tell him. This, he claimed was the result of my not having adjusted the microscope properly, so he would readjust it for me, or rather, for himself. And I would look again and see milk.

I finally took a deferred pass, as they called it, and waited a year and tried again. (You had to pass one of the biological sciences or you couldn't graduate.) The professor had come back from vacation brown as a berry, bright-eyed, and eager to explain cell-structure again to his classes. "Well," he said to me, cheerily, when we met in the first laboratory hour of the semester, "we're going to see cells this time, aren't we?" "Yes, sir," I said. Students to right of me and to left of me and in front of me were seeing cells; what's more, they were quietly drawing pictures of them in their notebooks. Of course, I didn't see anything.

"We'll try it," the professor said to me, grimly, "with every adjustment of the microscope known to man. As God is my witness, I'll arrange this glass so that you see cells through it or I'll give up teaching. In twenty-two years of botany, I—" He cut off abruptly for he was beginning to quiver all over, like Lionel Barrymore, and he genuinely wished to hold onto his temper; his scenes with me had taken a great deal out of him.

So we tried it with every adjustment of the microscope known to man. With only one of them did I see anything but blackness or the familiar lacteal opacity, and that time I saw, to my pleasure and amazement, a variegated constellation of flecks, specks, and dots. These I hastily drew. The instructor, noting my activity, came back from an adjoining desk, a smile on his lips and his eyebrows high in hope. He looked at my cell drawing. "What's that?" he demanded, with a hint of a squeal in his voice. "That's what I saw," I said. "You didn't, you didn't, you *did*n't!" he screamed, losing control of his temper instantly, and he bent over and squinted into the microscope. His head snapped up. "That's your eye!" he shouted. "You've fixed the lens so that it reflects! You've drawn your eye!"

Another course that I didn't like, but somehow managed to pass, was economics. I went to that class straight from the botany class, which didn't help me any in understanding either subject. I used to get them mixed up. But not as mixed up as another student in my economics class who came there direct from a physics laboratory. He was a tackle on the football team, named Bolenciecwcz. At that time Ohio State University had one of the best football teams in the country, and Bolenciecwcz was one of its outstanding stars. In order to be eligible to play it was necessary for him to keep up in his studies, a very difficult matter, for while he was not dumber than an ox he was not any smarter. Most of his professors were lenient and helped him along. None gave him more hints, in answering questions, or asked him simpler ones than the economics professor, a thin, timid man named Bassum. One day when we were on the subject of transportation and distribution, it came Bolenciecwcz's turn to answer a question. "Name one means of transportation," the professor said to him. No light came into the big tackle's eyes. "Just any means of transportation," said the professor. Bolenciecwcz sat staring at him. "That is," pursued the professor, "any medium, agency, or method of going from one place to another." Bolenciecwcz had the look of a man who is being led into a trap. "You may choose among steam, horse-drawn, or electrically propelled vehicles," said the instructor. "I might suggest the one which we commonly take in making long journeys across land." There was a profound silence in which everybody stirred uneasily, including Bolenciecwcz and Mr. Bassum. Mr. Bassum abruptly broke this silence in an amazing manner. "Choo-choo-choo," he said, in a low voice, and turned instantly scarlet. He glanced appealingly around the room. All of us, of course, shared Mr. Bassum's desire that Bolenciecwcz should stay abreast of the class in economics, for the Illinois game, one of the hardest and most important of the season, was only a week off. "Toot, toot, too-tooooooot!" some student with a deep voice moaned, and we all looked encouragingly at Bolenciecwcz. Somebody else gave a fine imitation of a locomotive letting off steam. Mr. Bassum himself rounded off the little show. "Ding, dong, ding, dong," he said, hopefully. Bolenciecwcz was staring at the floor now, trying to think, his great brow furrowed, his huge hands rubbing together, his face red.

"How did you come to college this year, Mr. Bolenciecwcz?" asked the professor. "*Chuf*fa chuffa, *chuf*fa chuffa."

"M'father sent me," said the football player.

"What on?" asked Bassum.

"I git an 'lowance," said the tackle, in a low, husky voice, obviously embarrassed.

"No, no," said Bassum. "Name a means of transportation. What did you *ride* here on?"

"Train," said Bolenciecwcz.

"Quite right," said the professor. "Now, Mr. Nugent, will you tell us——"

If I went through anguish in botany and economics—for different reasons—gymnasium work was even worse. I don't even like to think about it. They wouldn't let you play games or join in the exercises with your glasses on and I couldn't see with mine off. I bumped into professors, horizontal bars, agricultural students, and swinging iron rings. Not being able to see, I could take it but I couldn't dish it out. Also, in order to pass gymnasium (and you had to pass it to graduate) you had to learn to swim if you didn't know how. I didn't like the swimming pool, I didn't like swimming, and I didn't like the swimming instructor, and after all these years I still don't. I never swam but I passed my gym work anyway, by having another student give my gymnasium number (978) and swim across the pool in my place. He was a quiet, amiable blonde youth, number 473, and he would have seen through a microscope for me if we could have got away with it, but we couldn't get away with it. Another thing I didn't like about gymnasium work was that they made you strip the day you registered. It is impossible for me to be happy when I am stripped and being asked a lot of questions. Still, I did better than a lanky agricultural student who was cross-examined just before I was. They asked each student what college he was in—that is, whether Arts, Engineering, Commerce, or Agriculture. "What college are you in?" the instructor snapped at the youth in front of me. "Ohio State University," he said promptly.

Superman

John Updike

I drive my car to supermarket,
  The way I take is superhigh,
A superlot is where I park it,
  And Super Suds are what I buy.

Supersalesmen sell me tonic—
  Super-Tone-O, for relief.
The planes I ride are supersonic
  In trains I like the Super Chief.

Supercilious men and women
  Call me superficial—*me*.
Who so superbly learned to swim in
  Supercolossality.

Superphosphate-fed foods feed me;
  Superservice keeps me new.
Who would dare to supersede me,
  Super-super-superwho?

Ace in the Hole

John Updike

The moment his car touched the boulevard heading home, Ace flicked on the radio. He needed the radio, especially today. In the seconds before the tubes warmed up, he said aloud, doing it just to hear a human voice, "Jesus. She'll pop her lid." His voice, though familiar, irked him; it sounded thin and scratchy, as if the bones in his head were picking up static. In a deeper register Ace added, "She'll murder me." Then the radio came on, warm and strong, so he stopped worrying. The Five Kings were doing "Blueberry Hill"; to hear them made Ace feel so sure inside that from the pack pinched between the car roof and the sun shield he plucked a cigarette, hung it on his lower lip, snapped a match across the rusty place on the dash, held the flame in the instinctive spot near the tip of his nose, dragged, and blew out the match, all in time to the music. He rolled down the window and snapped the match so it spun end over end into the gutter. "Two points," he said, and cocked the cigarette toward the roof of the car, sucked powerfully, and exhaled two plumes through his nostrils. He was beginning to feel like himself, Ace Anderson, for the first time that whole day, a bad day. He beat time on the accelerator. The car jerked crazily. "On Blueberry Hill," he sang, "my heart stood still. The wind in the wil-low tree"—he braked for a red light—"played love's suh-*weet* melodee—"

"Go, Dad, bust your lungs!" a kid's voice blared. The kid was riding in a '52 Pontiac that had pulled up beside Ace at the light. The profile of the driver, another kid, was dark over his shoulder.

Ace looked over at him and smiled slowly, just letting one side of his mouth lift a little. "Shove it," he said, good-naturedly, across the little gap of years that separated them. He knew how they felt, young and mean and shy.

But the kid, who looked Greek, lifted his thick upper lip and spat out the window. The spit gleamed on the asphalt like a half-dollar.

"Now isn't that pretty?" Ace said, keeping one eye on the light. "You miserable wop. You are *mis*erable." While the kid was trying to think of some smart comeback, the light changed. Ace dug out so hard he smelled burned rubber. In his rear-view mirror he saw the Pontiac lurch forward a few yards, then stop dead, right in the middle of the intersection.

The idea of them stalling their fat tin Pontiac kept him in a good humor all the way home. He decided to stop at his mother's place and pick up the baby, instead of waiting for Evey to do it. His mother must have seen him drive up. She came out on the porch holding a plastic spoon and smelling of cake.

"You're out early," she told him.

"Friedman fired me," Ace told her.

"Good for you," his mother said. "I always said he never treated you right." She brought a cigarette out of her apron pocket and tucked it deep into one corner of her mouth, the way she did when something pleased her.

Ace lighted it for her. "Friedman was O. K. personally," he said. "He just wanted too much for his money. I didn't mind working Saturdays, but until eleven, twelve Friday nights was too much. Everybody has a right to some leisure."

"Well, I don't dare think what Evey will say, but I, for one, thank dear God you had the brains to get out of it. I always said that job had no future to it—no future of any kind, Freddy."

"I guess," Ace admitted. "But I wanted to keep at it, for the family's sake."

"Now, I know I shouldn't be saying this, but any time Evey—this is just between us—any time Evey thinks she can do better, there's room for you *and* Bonnie right in your father's house." She pinched her lips together. He could almost hear the old lady think, There, I've said it.

"Look, Mom, Evey tries awfully hard, and anyway you know she can't work that way. Not that *that*—I mean, she's a realist, too . . ." He let the rest of the thought fade as he watched a kid across the street dribbling a basketball around a telephone pole that had a backboard and net nailed on it.

"Evey's a wonderful girl of her own kind. But I've always said, and your father agrees, Roman Catholics ought to marry among themselves. Now I know I've said it before, but when they get out in the greater world—"

"*No*, Mom."

She frowned, smoothed herself, and said, "Your name was in the paper today."

Ace chose to let that go by. He kept watching the kid with the basketball. It was funny how, though the whole point was to get the ball up into the air, kids grabbed it by the sides and squeezed. Kids just didn't think.

"Did you hear?" his mother asked.

"Sure, but so what?" Ace said. His mother's lower lip was coming at him, so he changed the subject. "I guess I'll take Bonnie."

His mother went into the house and brought back his daughter, wrapped in a blue blanket. The baby looked dopey. "She fussed all day," his mother complained. "I said to your father, 'Bonnie is a dear little girl, but without a doubt she's her mother's daughter.' You were the best-natured boy."

"Well I *had* everything," Ace said with impatience. His mother blinked like an owl. He nicely dropped his cigarette into a brown flowerpot on the edge of the porch and took his daughter into his arms. She was getting heavier, solid. When he reached the end of the cement walk, his mother was still on the porch, waving to him. He was so close he could see the fat around her elbow jiggle, and he only lived a half block up the street, yet here she was, waving to him as if he was going to Japan.

At the door of his car, it seemed stupid to him to drive the measly half block home. His old coach, Bob Behn, used to say never to ride where you could walk. Cars were the death of legs. Ace left the ignition keys in his pocket and ran along the pavement with Bonnie laughing and bouncing at his chest. He slammed the door of his landlady's house open and shut, pounded up the two flights of stairs, and was panting so hard when he reached the door of his apartment that it took him a couple of seconds to fit the key into the lock.

The run must have tuned Bonnie up. As soon as he lowered her into the crib, she began to shout and wave her arms. He didn't want to play with her. He tossed some blocks and a rattle into the crib and walked into the bathroom, where he turned on the hot water and began to comb his hair. Holding the comb under the faucet before every stroke, he combed his hair forward. It was so long, one strand curled under his nose and touched his lips. He whipped the whole mass back with a single pull. He tucked in the tufts around his ears, and ran the comb straight back on both sides of his head. With his fingers he felt for the little ridge at the back where the two sides met. It was there, as it should have been. Finally, he mussed the hair in front enough for one little lock to droop over his forehead, like Alan Ladd. It made the temple seem lower than it was. Every day, his hairline looked higher. He had observed all around him how blond men went bald first. He remembered reading somewhere, though, that baldness shows virility.

On his way to the kitchen he flipped the left-hand knob of the television. Bonnie was always quieter with the set on. Ace didn't see how she could understand much of it, but it seemed to mean something to her. He found a can of beer in the refrigerator behind some brownish lettuce and those hot dogs Evey never got around to cooking. She'd be home any time. The clock said 5:12. She'd pop her lid.

Ace didn't see what he could do but try and reason with her. "Evey," he'd say, "you ought to thank God I got out of it. It had no future to it at all." He hoped she wouldn't get too mad, because when she was mad he wondered if he should have married her, and doubting that made him feel crowded. It was bad enough, his mother always crowding him. He punched the two triangles in the top of the beer can, the little triangle first, and then the big one, the one he drank from. He hoped Evey wouldn't say anything that couldn't be forgotten. What women didn't seem to realize was that there were things you knew but shouldn't say.

He felt sorry he had called the kid in the car a wop.

Ace balanced the beer on a corner where two rails of the crib met and looked under the chairs for the morning paper. He had trouble finding his name, because it was at the bottom of a column on an inside sports page, in a small article about the county basketball statistics:

> "Dusty" Tremwick, Grosvenor Park's sure-fingered center, copped the individual scoring honors with a season's grand (and we do mean grand) total of 376 points. This is within eighteen points of the all-time record of 394 racked up in the 1949–1950 season by Olinger High's Fred Anderson.

Ace angrily sailed the paper into an armchair. Now it was Fred Anderson; it used to be Ace. He hated being called Fred, especially in print, but then the sportswriters were all office boys anyway, Behn used to say.

"Do not just ask for shoe polish," a man on television said, "but ask for *Emu Shoe Gloss*, the *only* polish that absolutely *guarantees* to make your shoes look shinier than new." Ace turned the sound off, so that the man moved his mouth like a fish blowing bubbles. Right away, Bonnie howled, so Ace turned it up loud enough to drown her out and went into the kitchen, without knowing what he wanted there. He wasn't hungry; his stomach was tight. It used to be like that when he walked to the gymnasium alone in the dark before a game and could see the people from town, kids and parents, crowding in at the lighted doors. But once he was inside, the locker room would be bright and hot, and the other guys would be there, laughing and towel-slapping, and the tight feeling would leave. Now there were whole days when it didn't leave.

A key scratched at the door lock. Ace decided to stay in the kitchen. Let *her* find *him*. Her heels clicked on the floor for a step or two; then the television set went off. Bonnie began to cry. "Shut up, honey," Evey said. There was a silence.

"I'm home," Ace called.

"No kidding. I thought Bonnie got the beer by herself."

Ace laughed. She was in a sarcastic mood, thinking she was Lauren Bacall. That was all right, just so she kept funny. Still smiling, Ace eased into the living room and got hit with, "What are *you* smirking about? Another question: What's the idea running up the street with Bonnie like she was a football?"

"You saw that?"

"Your mother told me."

"You saw her?"

"Of course I saw her. I dropped by to pick up Bonnie. What the hell do you think?—I read her tiny mind?"

"Take it easy," Ace said, wondering if Mom had told her about Friedman.

"Take it easy? Don't coach *me*. Another question: Why's the car out in front of her place? You give the car to her?"

"Look, I parked it there to pick up Bonnie, and I thought I'd leave it there."

"Why?"

"Whaddaya mean, why? I just did. I just thought I'd walk. It's not that far, you know."

"No, I don't know. If you'd be on your feet all day a block would look like one hell of a long way."

"Okay. I'm sorry."

She hung up her coat and stepped out of her shoes and walked around the room picking up things. She stuck the newspaper in the wastebasket.

Ace said, "My name was in the paper today."

"They spell it right?" She shoved the paper deep into the basket with her foot. There was no doubt; she knew about Friedman.

"They called me Fred."

"Isn't that your name? What *is* your name anyway? Hero J. Great?"

There wasn't any answer, so Ace didn't try any. He sat down on the sofa, lighted a cigarette, and waited.

Evey picked up Bonnie. "Poor thing stinks. What does your mother do, scrub out the toilet with her?"

"Can't you take it easy? I know you're tired."

"You should. I'm always tired."

Evey and Bonnie went into the bathroom; when they came out, Bonnie was clean and Evey was calm. Evey sat down in an easy chair beside Ace and rested her stocking feet on his knees."Hit me," she said, twiddling her fingers for the cigarette.

The baby crawled up to her chair and tried to stand, to see what he gave her. Leaning over close to Bonnie's nose, Evey grinned, smoke leaking through her teeth, and said, "Only for grownups, honey."

"Eve," Ace began, "there was no future in that job. Working all Saturday, and then Friday nights on top of it."

"I know. Your mother told *me* all that, too. All I want from you is what happened."

She was going to take it like a sport, then. He tried to remember how it *did* happen. "It wasn't my fault," he said. "Friedman told me to back this '51 Chevvy into the line that faces Church Street. He just bought it from an old guy this morning who said it only had thirteen thousand on it. So in I jump and start her up. There was a knock in the engine like a machine gun. I almost told Friedman he'd bought a squirrel, but you know I cut that smart stuff out ever since Palotta laid me off."

"You told me that story. What happens in this one?"

"Look, Eve. I *am* telling ya. Do you want me to go out to a movie or something?"

"Suit yourself."

"So I jump in the Chevvy and snap it back in line, and there was a kind of scrape and thump. I get out and look and Friedman's running over, his arms going like *this*"—Ace whirled his own arms and laughed—"and here was the whole back fender of a '49 Merc mashed in. Just looked like somebody took a planer and shaved off the bulge, you know, there at the back." He tried to show her with his hands. "The Chevvy, though, didn't have a dent. It even gained some paint. But *Friedman*, to *hear* him—Boy, they can rave when their pocketbook's hit. He said"—Ace laughed again—"never mind."

Evey said, "You're proud of yourself."

"No, listen. I'm not happy about it. But there wasn't a thing I could *do*. It wasn't my driving at all. I looked over on the other side, and there was just two or three inches between the Chevvy and a Buick. *Nobody* could have gotten into that hole. Even if it had hair on it." He thought this was pretty good.

She didn't. "You could have looked."

"There just wasn't the *space*. Friedman said stick it in, I stuck it in;"

"But you could have looked and moved the other cars to make more room."

"I guess that would have been the smart thing."

"I guess, too. Now what?"

"What do you mean?"

"I mean now what? Are you going to give up? Go back to the Army? Your mother? Be a basketball pro? What?"

"You know I'm not tall enough. Anybody under six-six they don't want."

"Is that so? Six-six? Well, please listen to this, Mr. Six-Foot-Five-and-a-Half: I'm fed up. I'm ready as Christ to let you run." She stabbed her cigarette into an ashtray on the arm of the chair so hard the ashtray jumped to the floor. Evey flushed and shut up.

What Ace hated most in their arguments was these silences after Evey had said something so ugly she wanted to take it back. "Better ask the priest first," he murmured.

She sat right up. "If there's one thing I don't want to hear about from you it's priests. You let the priests to me. You don't know a damn thing about it. Not a damn thing."

"Hey, look at Bonnie." he said, trying to make his tone easy.

Evey didn't hear him. "If you think," she went on, "if for one rotten moment you think, Mr. Fred, that the be-all and end-all of my life is you and your hot-shot stunts—"

"Look, Mother," Ace pleaded, pointing at Bonnie. The baby had picked up the ashtray and put it on her head for a hat.

Evey glanced down angrily. "Cute," she said. "Cute as her daddy."

The ashtray slid from Bonnie's head and she patted where it had been and looked around puzzled.

"Yeah, but watch," Ace said. "Watch her hands. They're really terrific hands."

"You're nuts," Evey said.

"No, honest. Bonnie's great. She's a natural. Get the rattle for her. Never mind, I'll get it." In two steps, Ace was at Bonnie's crib, picking the rattle out of the mess of blocks and plastic rings and beanbags. He extended the rattle toward his daughter, shaking it delicately. Made wary by this burst of attention, Bonnie reached with both hands; like two separate animals they approached from opposite sides and touched the smooth rattle simultaneously. A smile bubbled up on her face. Ace tugged weakly. She held on, and then tugged back. "She's a natural," Ace said, "and it won't do her any good because she's a girl. Baby, we got to have a boy."

"I'm not your baby," Evey said, closing her eyes.

Saying "Baby" over and over again, Ace backed up to the radio and, without turning around, switched on the volume knob. In the moment before the tubes warmed up, Evey had time to say, "Wise up, Freddy. What shall we do?"

The radio came in on something slow: dinner music. Ace picked Bonnie up and set her in the crib. "Shall we dance?" he asked his wife, bowing.

"I want to talk."

"Baby. It's the cocktail hour."

"This is getting us no place," she said, rising from her chair, though.

"Fred Junior. I can see him now," he said, seeing nothing.

"We will have no Juniors."

In her crib, Bonnie whimpered at the sight of her mother being seized. Ace fitted his hand into the natural place on Evey's back and she shuffled stiffly into his lead. When, with a sudden injection of saxophones, the tempo quickened, he spun her out carefully, keeping the beat with his shoulders. Her hair brushed his lips as she minced in, then swung away, to the end of his arm; he could feel her toes dig into the carpet. He flipped his own hair back from his eyes. The music ate through his skin and mixed with the nerves and small veins; he seemed to be great again, and all the other kids were around them, in a ring, clapping time.

The Jump Shooter

Dennis Trudell

The way the ball
hung there
against the blue or purple

one night last week
across town
at the playground where

I had gone to spare
my wife
from the mood I'd swallowed

and saw in the dusk
a stranger
shooting baskets a few

years older maybe
thirty-five
and overweight a little

beer belly saw him
shooting there
and joined him didn't

ask or anything simply
went over
picked off a rebound

and hooked it back up
while he
smiled I nodded and for

ten minutes or so we
took turns
taking shots and the thing

is neither of us said
a word
and this fellow who's

too heavy now and slow
to play
for any team still had

the old touch seldom
ever missed
kept moving further out

and finally his t-shirt
a gray
and fuzzy blur I stood

under the rim could
almost hear
a high school cheer

begin and fill a gym
while wooden
bleachers rocked he made

three in a row from
twenty feet
moved back two steps

faked out a patch
of darkness
arched another one and

the way the ball
hung there
against the blue or purple

then suddenly filled
the net
made me wave goodbye

breathe deeply and begin
to whistle
as I walked back home.

The Boxing Match

Virgil

from THE AENEID

They take their stand, each rising
On the balls of his feet, their arms upraised, and rolling
Their heads back from the punch. They spar, they lead,
They watch for openings. Dares, much the younger,
Is much the better in footwork; old Entellus
Has to rely on strength; his knees are shaky,
His wind not what it was. They throw their punches,
And many miss; and some, with a solid thump,
Land on the ribs or chest; temples and ears
Feel the wind of a miss, or the jaws rattle
When a punch lands. Entellus stands flat-footed,
Wasting no motion, just a slip of the body,
The watchful eyes alert. And Dares, feinting,
Like one who artfully attacks a city,
Tries this approach, then that, dancing around him
In varied vain attack. Entellus, rising,
Draws back his right (in fact, he telegraphs it),
And Dares, seeing it coming, slips aside;
Entellus lands on nothing but the wind
And, thrown off balance, heavily comes down
Flat on his face, as falls on Erymanthus
A thunder-smitten oak, and so on, and so on.
Roaring, the Trojans and Sicilians both

Rise to their feet; the noise goes up to heaven;
Acestes rushes in, to raise his comrade
In pity and sorrow. But that old-time fighter
Is not slowed down a bit, nor made more wary;
His rage is terrible, and his shame awakens
A consciousness of strength. He chases Dares
All over the ring, left, right, left, right, the punches
Rattle like hailstones on a roof; he batters Dares,
Spins him halfway around with one hand, clouts him
Straight with the other again. At last Aeneas
Steps in and stops it, with a word of comfort
For the exhausted Dares.

Translated by ROLFE HUMPHRIES

Crowd Pleaser

Budd Schulberg

The guy on my left was a regular. Every Friday night since I could remember, he had sat in that same seat on the aisle. He was broad and beefy-faced, with a high-blood-pressure complexion and a big mouth. He was powerfully built, despite the pot belly and spreading rump of middle age. The first night he sat next to me he bought me a beer, told me to keep him in mind next time I bought a new car, and handed me his card. Name was Dempsey. "Edward J. (Champ) Dempsey," it said on the card. "No, no relation to Jack," he chuckled. "We went to different schools together."

His voice, deep in his throat, always sounded as if he had a cold. The laughter with which he punctuated everything he said was open-mouthed and prolonged, loud and unmusical. He had a ridiculous pride in his ability to keep up a running patter of public speech throughout any fight. Years before he had appointed himself a sort of one-man claque to urge the fighters on to bloodier efforts, and whenever the boys in the ring decided to take it a little easy, coasting a round or feeling each other out, his throaty witticisms would pierce the dark and smoky silence: "Turn out the lights, they want to be alone!" or "Hey, girls, can I have the next dance?" Or if one of the boxers happened to be Jewish, he was quick to show what a linguist he was by yelling, "Hit him in the *kishges*," or display his knowledge of geography by shouting, "Send him back to Jerusalem!"

The fellow who always sat on my right was George Rogers, a big-money lawyer, but his seat was empty tonight. "Well, looks like our old friend George is playing hooky tonight, ha ha ha," Dempsey said. Rogers was a white-haired old-timer who hardly ever said a word to either of us. Dempsey had been trying to sell him a car since early last summer.

Just before the first preliminary boys climbed through the ropes, the usher led to Rogers' seat a fellow I had never seen before. He was short, thin, nervous, somewhere in his middle thirties, but already beginning to stoop from the waist like a much older man. His skin was pallid, he wore glasses, and he needed only the green eyeshade to become my stereotype of a bookkeeper.

"Excuse me, sir," he said as he squeezed by. "I am sorry to disturb you."

That wasn't what they usually said when they shoved past you at the Arena. Dempsey looked at him the way a gang leader eyes a new kid who has just moved into the block.

"Where's my old pal George tonight?" he wanted to know.

The man was shy and his answer came in a thin voice. "Mr. Rogers is out of town on business, sir. He was good enough to give me his ticket."

"You in Rogers' office?" Dempsey appraised him with salesman's eyes.

The newcomer said yes, not too encouragingly, but it was enough for Dempsey to lean across me and display his professional smile. "Dempsey's the name. What's yours, fella?"

"Glover," the fellow said, but he did not seem very happy about it.

"Glover!" Dempsey shuffled quickly through thousands of calling cards in his mind. "Used to know a Charley Glover back in K. C. fifteen years ago. Any relation to old Charley?"

"I've never had any relatives in the Middle West," Glover answered.

"Well, I won't hold it against you, ha ha ha," Dempsey said. "Here, have a cigar."

Dempsey leaned across me to hand it to him. He hadn't offered me a cigar since the night I told him to stop trying to sell me a car, and let him know why.

Glover said he didn't smoke cigars, and Dempsey lit his, igniting the match with a flick of his thumbnail. "So you work for Rogers, huh," he went on. "Well, George is a very, very good friend of mine. What are you, a junior partner?"

"Oh, no," Glover said, and something that was almost a smile lit his face for a moment, as if at the impossibility of such a suggestion. "I am a stenographer."

Dempsey's smile, or rather, his clever imitation of a smile, wiped from his face mechanically, like a lantern slide. When he abandoned it suddenly like that, his face looked even more bloated and aggressive than usual.

"A stenographer! Ha ha ha. Are you kidding?"

"Mr. Rogers has employed nothing but male stenographers for over thirty years."

Dempsey looked disgusted and turned away.

The boys in the curtain raiser were entering the ring. There was scattered applause for Sailor Gibbons, a rugged, battle-scarred veteran who had never graduated from the preliminary ranks. He bounded through the ropes with showy vigor and winked at a friend in the working press as he shuffled his feet in the rosin box. He was an old-timer getting ready to go to work, easy to hit but hard to stop, what the tub thumpers like to call a "crowd pleaser."

The boy who followed him through the ropes had the kind of figure and color that made everyone want to laugh. His 140 pounds were stretched over a six-foot frame and his skin was purple-black. His face was long and thin and solemn, and the ring-wise could detect nervousness in the way his muscles twitched in his legs as his handlers drew on his gloves. Over his shoulders was a bright orange bathrobe that identified him as a Golden Gloves Champion.

The moment Dempsey saw him, he began. "Ho ho! Look what we got with us tonight. A boogie! Boy, how I like to see them boogies get it!"

The announcer was introducing them ". . . and at one hundred thirty-nine and a half, just up from the amateur ranks, the Pride of Central Avenue, Young Joe Gans."

Dempsey cupped his hands around his mouth. "Come on, Sailor, send him back to Central Avenue—in sections." Then, like a professional comedian, he looked around for his laugh. He got it.

The stadium lights dimmed out and the ring lights came on, molding the ring and the fighters together in one intense glow. You could feel the nervous excitement in the hushed crowd, five thousand men and women crouching there in the darkness waiting for the blood.

In the white glare the fighters, the pale stocky one and the dark slender one, moved toward each other with animal caution and touched gloves in that empty gesture of sportsmanship. Gibbons was an in-fighter, strong-legged, thick-shouldered, crouching, weaving, willing to take one on the jaw to get inside and club and push and rough his man against the ropes. Young Gans was the duelist, jabbing with a long spidery left and dancing away.

"Come on, Sailor!" Dempsey bellowed. "Let's get home early. Down below. They can't take 'em there."

As if responding to Dempsey's instructions, Gibbons brought a wild right up from the floor in the general direction of the colored boy's stomach. But Gans swayed away from it with the graceful precision of a bullfighter.

Next to me a small voice spoke out in a conversational tone. "Nice work, Gans," Glover said.

Dempsey turned and frowned. "You pulling for the boogie? What you pulling for the boogie for? Betting his corner?"

"I like his style of fighting," Glover said.

"Fighting!" Dempsey said. "You call that fighting? The boogie is a hit-and-run driver, that's what he is. Ha ha ha." He liked it so well he cupped his hands to his mouth again and gave it to his public. "Hey, ref, how about giving that shine a ticket for hit-and-run driving?"

Some of Dempsey's fans in front of him turned around to show him they were laughing. Gibbons lunged at Gans again, and the Negro flicked his left in the white man's face half a dozen times and skittered sideways out of danger.

"Attaboy, Gans," Glover said. "Give him a boxing lesson."

He didn't say it loud enough for the fighters to hear; it was really intended as a little encouragement for himself, but Dempsey heard it and glared at Glover again. He opened his mouth to put Glover in his place but turned back and yelled at the fighters instead.

"Don't hit him in the head, Sailor. You'll break your hands. In the breadbasket. That's where they don't like it."

The Negro feinted with his left, pulling the slow-thinking Gibbons out of position, and scored with a short, fast right to the heart. Gibbons sagged, but his face spread in a big grin, and his legs pistoned rapidly up and down to show how light on his feet he was. He was hurt.

"He doesn't like them there, either," Glover said. "Nobody likes them there."

Dempsey was talking half to Glover and half to the fighters in the ring now. "But he took it. That's the way to take 'em, Sailor. Give the boogie some of that and watch him fold."

"I'm watching," Glover said. "All I can see is Gans's left in Gibbons' face." Suddenly he raised his voice, edged with excitement. "That's the way, Gans, jab him. Jab his head off." He was growing bolder as Gans piled up points.

Dempsey leaned forward, his fist tightly clenched, his shoulders moving in unison with Gibbons' as the Sailor tried to reach Gans with vicious haymakers; the colored fighter skillfully ducked and blocked and rolled until Gibbons was charging in with the crazed fury of a punished bull.

"Come on, eightball, why don't you fight?" Dempsey jeered.

"Good boy, Gans," Glover answered. "He hasn't hit you once this round."

When the bell rang, Gans dropped his hands automatically but Gibbons' right was cocked and while the sound of the bell was still *galong-galonging* through the arena, he let it go. You could see Gans stiffen and then sag as his body absorbed the pain for which it hadn't been prepared.

The blow made Dempsey laugh with excitement and relief. He always gave a short, nervous laugh when the fighter he was rooting against got hurt, but tonight he had someone special to laugh at. "That's the baby! What'd I tell you? He don't like 'em downstairs. Those boogies never do. One more like that and he'll quit cold."

"One more like that and Gibbons ought to be disqualified," Glover said.

"Aah, you nigger-lovers give me a pain," Dempsey said. "Always griping about those bastards getting gypped. That punch started before the bell."

"Well he'll have to wait three minutes before he can hit him again," Glover said. "The only time Gibbons can hurt him is when Gans isn't looking."

"Oh, is that so? What the hell do you know about it? I been sitting in this same seat for eight years. I'll bet you ain't even seen a fight before."

"Do you have to see a skunk to recognize its smell?"

Dempsey tensed himself to rise. "Listen, you little shrimp, if you're trying to call me a skunk . . ."

Glover looked frightened. Dempsey had at least fifty pounds on him, and Glover didn't look as if he had had too much experience with his dukes. But the bell saved him, in reverse timing. The ten-second warning buzzer for round two made fans around us say, "Sit down. Down in front! We wanna watch the fight in the ring."

The two fighters leaned toward each other from their stools, feet set for the spring at the bell. Dempsey and Glover anticipated the bell too, sliding forward to the edges of their seats, their legs tensing under them as if they also expected to leap up as the round started. Dempsey made his hands into fists again and they trembled with eagerness to begin punching. In the shadows just beyond range of the ring lights, Glover's face was white and drawn. His right hand was doubled against his mouth in a nervous gesture of apprehension.

"All right, Sailor, this is the round," Dempsey shouted. "In the belly. In the belly."

"Come on, Gans," Glover countered, "box his ears off again."

At the bell, Gibbons ran across the ring and tried to nail the Negro in his corner before he was set. Glover opened his mouth in fright, like a mother seeing her child run down in the street. "Look—look out!"

Without changing the solemn expression with which he had come into the ring, Young Gans stepped aside in what looked almost like a gesture of politeness—"please, after you"—and Gibbons plunged foolishly through the ropes.

"Where is he, Gibbons?" Glover said. "You can't even find him, much less hit him."

"Why don't you stand up and fight, you yellow bastard?" There was desperation in Dempsey's tone for the first time.

Glover's voice became shrill with combativeness. "That's the way to fight him, Gans. Keep that left in his face."

"Keep rushing him, Sailor. He can't hurt you. He couldn't break an egg."

"What are you blinking for, Sailor? What are you stopping for? I thought he couldn't hurt you."

"He's not hurt. A little nosebleed like that don't bother him. Keep after him, Sailor. Make the boogie fight!"

Young Gans was making a monkey out of Gibbons, but I was watching the fight between Glover and Dempsey now. They were talking at each other but looking straight ahead, straining forward for every movement and moment of the bout in the ring. I didn't have to watch the fight. There in the thin, hysterical voice of Glover and the bullfrog fury of Dempsey, it was more vivid than even Jimmy Powers or Bill Stern would have made it.

"How do you like that one? And that one? And that one?" Glover flicked the jabs in Dempsey's face.

Dempsey shook them off and laughed. "Powderpuff punches. All powderpuff punches. Hey! That's it! That's it! Break the boogie in two!"

Glover clinched a moment to ride out the pain and danced away again. "Who says you can't take 'em in the belly?"

Their voices rose as the tiring fighters fought harder, became more vulnerable now, more dangerous. But suddenly their shouting was lost in the giant roar that filled the place. The crowd was on its feet, screaming through its thousand wild mouths, screaming at the sight of a man, a black man, writhing convulsively on the canvas, bringing up his legs and clutching himself, twisting his long, serious face into a grotesque mask of agony.

Glover looked on in horror and futile anger. "Foul. Foul," he said. "He hit him low. I saw it. He hit him low."

There were others around him who saw it that way too and they took up the cry, "Foul, foul, foul . . ."

Dempsey was standing right next to me but his laughter sounded far away, as if the wave of voices breaking over us were carrying it off. "Ha ha ha ha ha," he said, and his face was distorted with terrible joy. "Foul, hell. Look at him dogging it. He wants to quit."

The referee had disregarded the cries of foul and taken up the count. Gans was fighting his sickness down, reaching out for a strand of the rope and clinging to it to keep the floor steady so he could rise from it again.

"Look at him dog it," Dempsey hollered. "He's yella. If that's a foul, he's got his crotch where his heart is."

A few people laughed and Dempsey winked at them. His sense of humor was coming back. He was feeling on top again. He looked over at Glover. Glover was badly shaken. Some of the strain of the Negro's torturous ascent had come into his face. "Well, wise guy, how do you like your nigger now?" Dempsey poured it on.

"All right, Gans," Glover pleaded, "coast through this round. You've won it on a foul anyway."

"Come on, Sailor, kill him, kill him, kill him!" Dempsey cheered.

The Negro was on his feet but he wasn't dancing around any more. It plainly hurt him to move now. His skin was a curious chalky color and his eyes turned toward his corner in distress.

Dempsey was laughing. "Look at him! he's so scared he's white! You're making a white man outa him, Sailor."

Gibbons rushed the crippled fighter into a corner and opened his cheek with a hard left hand.

"Ha ha ha. One more, Sailor. One more and he'll quit."

Glover was too full of injury to speak. Dempsey grinned over at him. "Wha'samatter, pal, lost your voice? Why, you was just full of chatter a minute ago." Glover did not seem to hear. He sat back in his seat and looked straight ahead. His fighter leaned wearily against the ropes, too weak to hold his man off any longer.

"Let him drop," Dempsey was shouting. "Stand back and let the boogie drop!"

Then there was a loud laugh, even louder than usual, and the Negro crumpled in the corner and lay still.

Dempsey stood up and pulled the seat of his pants away where it had creased into his buttocks. "What did I tell you? Didn't I tell you he'd dog it if he got hurt? I never saw a boogie yet that could take it in the belly."

The ring was being cleared for the next bout, the band was rendering *Stars and Stripes Forever* and the next pair of fighters was coming down the aisle. But Glover didn't seem to be hearing or seeing. He just hung his head and held his hands together in his lap. How long would it take him, I wondered, to recover from this pain in Young Gans's groin?

The Jockey

Carson McCullers

The jockey came to the doorway of the dining room, then after a moment stepped to one side and stood motionless, with his back to the wall. The room was crowded, as this was the third day of the season and all the hotels in the town were full. In the dining room bouquets of August roses scattered their petals on the white table linen and from the adjoining bar came a warm, drunken wash of voices. The jockey waited with his back to the wall and scrutinized the room with pinched, creepy eyes. He examined the room until at last his eyes reached a table in a corner diagonally across from him, at which three men were sitting. As he watched, the jockey raised his chin and tilted his head back to one side, his dwarfed body grew rigid, and his hands stiffened so that the fingers curled inward like gray claws. Tense against the wall of the dining room, he watched and waited in this way.

He was wearing a suit of green Chinese silk that evening, tailored precisely and the size of a costume outfit for a child. The shirt was yellow, the tie striped with pastel colors. He had no hat with him and wore his hair brushed down in a stiff, wet bang on his forehead. His face was drawn, ageless, and gray. There were shadowed hollows at his temples and his mouth was set in a wiry smile. After a time he was aware that he had been seen by one of the three men he had been watching. But the jockey did not nod; he only raised his chin still higher and hooked the thumb of his tense hand in the pocket of his coat.

The three men at the corner table were a trainer, a bookie, and a rich man. The trainer was Sylvester—a large, loosely built fellow with a flushed nose and slow blue eyes. The bookie was Simmons. The rich man was the owner of a horse named Seltzer, which the jockey had ridden that afternoon. The three of them drank whisky with soda, and a white-coated waiter had just brought on the main course of the dinner.

It was Sylvester who first saw the jockey. He looked away quickly, put down his whisky glass, and nervously mashed the tip of his red nose with his thumb. "It's Bitsy Barlow," he said. "Standing over there across the room. Just watching us."

"Oh, the jockey," said the rich man. He was facing the wall and he half turned his head to look behind him. "Ask him over."

"God no," Sylvester said.

"He's crazy," Simmons said. The bookie's voice was flat and without inflection. He had the face of a born gambler, carefully adjusted, the expression a permanent deadlock between fear and greed.

"Well, I wouldn't call him that exactly," said Sylvester. "I've known him a long time. He was O. K. until about six months ago. But if he goes on like this, I can't see him lasting out another year. I just can't."

"It was what happened in Miami," said Simmons.

"What?" asked the rich man.

Sylvester glanced across the room at the jockey and wet the corner of his mouth with his red, fleshy tongue. "A accident. A kid got hurt on the track. Broke a leg and a hip. He was a particular pal of Bitsy's. A Irish kid. Not a bad rider, either."

"That's a pity," said the rich man.

"Yeah. They were particular friends," Sylvester said. "You would always find him up in Bitsy's hotel room. They would be playing rummy or else lying on the floor reading the sports page together."

"Well, those things happen," said the rich man.

Simmons cut into his beefsteak. He held his fork prongs downward on the plate and carefully piled on mushrooms with the blade of his knife. "He's crazy," he repeated. "He gives me the creeps."

All the tables in the dining room were occupied. There was a party at the banquet table in the center, and green-white August moths had found their way in from the night and fluttered about the clear candle flames. Two girls wearing flannel slacks and blazers walked arm in arm across the room into the bar. From the main street outside came the echoes of holiday hysteria.

"They claim that in August Saratoga is the wealthiest town per capita in the world." Sylvester turned to the rich man. "What do you think?"

"I wouldn't know," said the rich man. "It may very well be so."

Daintily, Simmons wiped his greasy mouth with the tip of his forefinger. "How about Hollywood? And Wall Street——"

"Wait," said Sylvester. "He's decided to come over here."

The jockey had left the wall and was approaching the table in the corner. He walked with a prim strut, swinging out his legs in a half-circle with each step, his heels biting smartly into the red velvet carpet on the floor. On the way over he brushed against the elbow of a fat woman in white satin at the banquet table; he stepped back and bowed with dandified courtesy, his eyes quite closed. When he had crossed the room he drew up a chair and sat at a corner of the table, between Sylvester and the rich man, without a nod of greeting or a change in his set, gray face.

"Had dinner?" Sylvester asked.

"Some people might call it that." The jockey's voice was high, bitter, clear.

Sylvester put his knife and fork down carefully on his plate. The rich man shifted his position, turning sidewise in his chair and crossing his legs. He was dressed in twill riding pants, unpolished boots, and a shabby brown jacket—this was his outfit day and night in the racing season, although he was never seen on a horse. Simmons went on with his dinner.

"Like a spot of seltzer water?" asked Sylvester. "Or something like that?"

The jockey didn't answer. He drew a gold cigarette case from his pocket and snapped it open. Inside were a few cigarettes and a tiny gold penknife. He used the knife to cut a cigarette in half. When he had lighted his smoke he held up his hand to a waiter passing by the table. "Kentucky bourbon, please."

"Now, listen, kid," said Sylvester.

"Don't 'kid' me."

"Be reasonable. You know you got to behave reasonable."

The jockey drew up the left corner of his mouth in a stiff jeer. His eyes lowered to the food spread out on the table, but instantly he looked up again. Before the rich man was a fish casserole, baked in a cream sauce and garnished with parsley. Sylvester had ordered eggs Benedict. There were asparagus, fresh buttered corn, and a side dish of wet black olives. A plate of French-fried potatoes was in the corner of the table before the jockey. He didn't look at the food again but kept his pinched eyes on the centerpiece of full-blown lavender roses. "I don't suppose you remember a certain person by the name of McGuire," he said.

"Now, listen," said Sylvester.

The waiter brought the whisky, and the jockey sat fondling the glass with his small, strong, calloused hands. On his wrist was a gold link bracelet that clinked against the table edge. After turning the glass between his palms the jockey suddenly drank the whisky neat in two hard swallows. He set down the glass sharply. "No, I don't suppose your memory is that long and extensive, " he said.

"Sure enough, Bitsy," said Sylvester. "What makes you act like this? You hear from the kid today?"

"I received a letter," the jockey said. "The certain person we were speaking about was taken out from the cast on Wednesday. One leg is two inches shorter than the other one. That's all."

Sylvester clucked his tongue and shook his head. "I realize how you feel."

"Do you?" The jockey was looking at the dishes on the table. His gaze passed from the fish casserole to the corn and finally fixed on the plate of fried potatoes. His face tightened and quickly he looked up again. A rose shattered and he picked up one of the petals, bruised it between his thumb and forefinger, and put it in his mouth.

"Well, those things happen," said the rich man.

The trainer and the bookie had finished eating, but there was food left on the serving dishes before their plates. The rich man dipped his buttery fingers in his water glass and wiped them with his napkin.

"Well," said the jockey, "doesn't somebody want me to pass them something? Or maybe perhaps you desire to reorder. Another hunk of beefsteak, gentlemen, or——"

"Please," said Sylvester. "Be reasonable. Why don't you go on upstairs?"

"Yes, why don't I?" the jockey said.

His prim voice had risen higher and there was about it the sharp whine of hysteria.

"Why don't I go up to my god-damn room and walk around and write some letters and go to bed like a good boy? Why don't I just——" He pushed his chair back and got up. "Oh, foo," he said. "Foo to you. I want a drink."

"All I can say is it's your funeral," said Sylvester. "You know what it does to you. You know well enough."

The jockey crossed the dining room and went into the bar. He ordered a Manhattan, and Sylvester watched him stand with his heels pressed tight together, his body hard as a lead soldier's, holding his little finger out from the cocktail glass and sipping the drink slowly. "He's crazy," said Simmons. "Like I said."

Sylvester turned to the rich man. "If he eats a lamb chop, you can see the shape of it in his stomach a hour afterward. He can't sweat things out of him any more. He's a hundred and twelve and a half. He's gained three pounds since we left Miami."

"A jockey shouldn't drink," said the rich man.

"The food don't satisfy him like it used to, and he can't sweat it out. If he eats a lamb chop, you can watch it tooching out in his stomach and it don't go down."

The jockey finished his Manhattan. He swallowed, crushed the cherry in the bottom of the glass with his thumb, then pushed the glass away from him. The two girls in blazers were standing at his left, their faces turned toward each other, and at the other end of the bar two touts had started an argument about which was the highest mountain in the world. Everyone was with somebody else; there was no other person drinking alone that night. The jockey paid with a brand-new fifty-dollar bill and didn't count the change.

He walked back to the dining room and to the table at which the three men were sitting, but he did not sit down. "No, I wouldn't presume to think your memory is that extensive," he said. He was so small that the edge of the table top reached almost to his belt, and when he gripped the corner with his wiry hands he didn't have to stoop. "No, you're too busy gobbling up dinners in dining rooms. You're too——"

"Honestly," begged Sylvester. "You got to behave reasonable."

"Reasonable! Reasonable!" The jockey's gray face quivered, then set in a mean, frozen grin. He shook the table so that the plates rattled, and for a moment it seemed that he would push it over. But suddenly he stopped. His hand reached out toward the plate nearest to him and deliberately he put a few of the French-fried potatoes in his mouth. He chewed slowly, his upper lip raised, then he turned and spat out the pulpy mouthful on the smooth red carpet which covered the floor. "Libertines," he said, and his voice was thin and broken. He rolled the word in his mouth, as though it had a flavor and a substance that gratified him. "You libertines," he said again, and turned and walked with his rigid swagger out of the dining room.

Sylvester shrugged one of his loose, heavy shoulders. The rich man sopped up some water that had been spilled on the tablecloth, and they didn't speak until the waiter came to clear away.

To an Athlete Dying Young

A. E. Housman

The time you won your town the race
We chaired you through the market-place;
Man and boy stood cheering by,
And home we brought you shoulder-high.

Today, the road all runners come,
Shoulder-high we bring you home,
And set you at your threshold down,
Townsman of a stiller town.

Smart lad, to slip betimes away
From fields where glory does not stay
And early though the laurel grows
It withers quicker than the rose.

Eyes the shady night has shut
Cannot see the record cut,
And silence sounds no worse than cheers
After earth has stopped the ears;

Now you will not swell the rout
Of lads that wore their honour out,
Runners whom renown outran
And the name died before the man.

So set, before its echoes fade,
The fleet foot on the sill of shade,
And hold to the low lintel up
The still defended challenge-cup.

And round that early-laurelled head
Will flock to gaze the strengthless dead
And find unwithered on its curls
The garland briefer than a girl's.

The Capital of the World

Ernest Hemingway

Madrid is full of boys named Paco, which is the diminutive of the name Francisco, and there is a Madrid joke about a father who came to Madrid and inserted an advertisement in the personal columns of *El Liberal* which said: PACO MEET ME AT HOTEL MONTANA NOON TUESDAY ALL IS FORGIVEN PAPA and how a squadron of Guardia Civil had to be called out to disperse the eight hundred young men who answered the advertisement. But this Paco, who waited on table at the Pension Luarca, had no father to forgive him, nor anything for the father to forgive. He had two older sisters who were chambermaids at the Luarca, who had gotten their place through coming from the same small village as a former Luarca chambermaid who had proven hardworking and honest and hence given her village and its products a good name; and these sisters had paid his way on the auto-bus to Madrid and gotten him his job as an apprentice waiter. He came from a village in a part of Extramadura where conditions were incredibly primitive, food scarce, and comforts unknown and he had worked hard ever since he could remember.

He was a well built boy with very black, rather curly hair, good teeth and a skin that his sisters envied, and he had a ready and unpuzzled smile. He was fast on his feet and did his work well and he loved his sisters, who seemed beautiful and sophisticated; he loved Madrid, which was still an unbelievable place, and he loved his work which, done under bright lights, with clean linen, the wearing of evening clothes, and abundant food in the kitchen, seemed romantically beautiful.

There were from eight to a dozen other people who lived at the Luarca and ate in the dining room but for Paco, the youngest of the three waiters who served at table, the only ones who really existed were the bull fighters.

Second-rate matadors lived at that pension because the address in the Calle San Jeronimo was good, the food was excellent and the room and board was cheap. It is necessary for a bull fighter to give the appearance, if not of prosperity, at least of respectability, since decorum and dignity rank above courage as the virtues most highly prized in Spain, and bull fighters stayed at the Luarca until their last pesetas were gone. There is no record of any bull fighter having left the Luarca for a better or more expensive hotel; second-rate bull fighters never became first rate; but the descent from Luarca was swift since any one could stay there who was making anything at all and a bill was never presented to a guest unasked until the woman who ran the place knew that the case was hopeless.

At this time there were three full matadors living at the Luarca as well as two very good picadors, and one excellent banderillero. The Luarca was luxury for the picadors and the banderilleros who, with their families in Seville, required lodging in Madrid during the Spring season; but they were well paid and in the fixed employ of fighters who were heavily contracted during the coming season and the three of these subalterns would probably make much more apiece than any of the three matadors. Of the three matadors one was ill and trying to conceal it; one had passed his short vogue as a novelty; and the third was a coward.

The coward had at one time, until he had received a peculiarly atrocious horn wound in the lower abdomen at the start of his first season as a full matador, been exceptionally brave and remarkably skillful and he still had many of the hearty mannerisms of his days of success. He was jovial to excess and laughed constantly with and without provocation. He had, when successful, been very addicted to practical jokes but he had given them up now. They took an assurance that he did not feel. This matador had an intelligent, very open face and he carried himself with much style.

The matador who was ill was careful never to show it and was meticulous about eating a little of all the dishes that were presented at the table. He had a great many handkerchiefs which he laundered himself in his room and, lately, he had been selling his fighting suits. He had sold one, cheaply, before Christmas and another in the first week of April. They had been very expensive suits, had always been well kept and he had one more. Before he had become ill he had been a very promising, even a sensational, fighter and, while he himself could not read, he had clippings which said that in his debut in Madrid he had been better than Belmonte. He ate alone at a small table and looked up very little.

The matador who had once been a novelty was very short and brown and very dignified. He also ate alone at a separate table and he smiled very rarely and never laughed. He came from Valladolid, where the people are extremely serious, and he was a capable matador; but his style had become old-fashioned before he had ever succeeded in endearing himself to the public through his virtues, which were courage and a calm capability, and his name on a poster would draw no one to a bull ring. His novelty had been that he was so short that he could barely see over the bull's withers, but there were other short fighters, and he had never succeeded in imposing himself on the public's fancy.

Of the picadors one was a thin, hawk-faced, gray-haired man, lightly built but with legs and arms like iron, who always wore cattle-men's boots under his trousers, drank too much every evening and gazed amorously at any woman in the pension. The other was huge, dark, brown-faced, good-looking, with black hair like an Indian and enormous hands. Both were great picadors although the first was reputed to have lost much of his ability through drink and dissipation, and the second was said to be too headstrong and quarrelsome to stay with any matador more than a single season.

The banderillero was middle-aged, gray, cat-quick in spite of his years and, sitting at the table he looked a moderately prosperous business man. His legs were still good for this season, and when they should go he was intelligent and experienced enough to keep regularly employed for a long time. The difference would be that when his speed of foot would be gone he would always be frightened where now he was assured and calm in the ring and out of it.

On this evening every one had left the dining room except the hawk-faced picador who drank too much, the birthmarked-faced auctioneer of watches at the fairs and festivals of Spain, who also drank too much, and two priests from Galicia who were sitting at a corner table and drinking if not too much certainly enough. At that time wine was included in the price of the room and board at the Luarca and the waiters had just brought fresh bottles of Valdepeñas to the tables of the auctioneer, then to the picador and, finally, to the two priests.

The three waiters stood at the end of the room. It was the rule of the house that they should all remain on duty until the diners whose tables they were responsible for should all have left, but the one who served the table of the two priests had an appointment to go to an Anarcho-Syndicalist meeting and Paco had agreed to take over his table for him.

Upstairs the matador who was ill was lying face down on his bed alone. The matador who was no longer a novelty was sitting looking out of his window preparatory to walking out to the café. The matador who was a coward had the older sister of Paco in his room with him and was trying to get her to do something which she was laughingly refusing to do. This matador was saying "Come on, little savage."

"No," said the sister. "Why should I?"

"For a favor."

"You've eaten and now you want me for dessert."

"Just once. What harm can it do?"

"Leave me alone. Leave me alone, I tell you."

"It is a very little thing to do."

"Leave me alone, I tell you."

Down in the dining room the tallest of the waiters, who was overdue at the meeting, said "Look at those black pigs drink."

"That's no way to speak," said the second waiter. "They are decent clients. They do not drink too much."

"For me it is a good way to speak," said the tall one. "There are the two curses of Spain, the bulls and the priests."

"Certainly not the individual bull and the individual priest," said the second waiter.

"Yes," said the tall waiter. "Only through the individual can you attack the class. It is necessary to kill the individual bull and the individual priest. All of them. Then there are no more."

"Save it for the meeting," said the other waiter.

"Look at the barbarity of Madrid," said the tall waiter. "It is now half-past eleven o'clock and these are still guzzling."

"They only started to eat at ten," said the other waiter. "As you know there are many dishes. That wine is cheap and these have paid for it. It is not a strong wine."

"How can there be solidarity of workers with fools like you?" asked the tall waiter.

"Look," said the second waiter who was a man of fifty. "I have worked all my life. In all that remains of my life I must work. I have no complaints against work. To work is normal."

"Yes, but the lack of work kills."

"I have always worked," said the older waiter. "Go on to the meeting. There is no necessity to stay."

"You are a good comrade," said the tall waiter. "But you lack all ideology."

"*Mejor si me falta eso que el otro,*" said the older waiter (meaning it is better to lack that than work). "Go on to the *mitin.*"

Paco had said nothing. He did not yet understand politics but it always gave him a thrill to hear the tall waiter speak of the necessity for killing the priests and the Guardia Civil. The tall waiter represented to him revolution and revolution also was romantic. He himself would like to be a good catholic, a revolutionary, and have a steady job like this, while, at the same time, being a bullfighter.

"Go on to the meeting, Ignacio," he said, "I will respond for your work."

"The two of us," said the older waiter.

"There isn't enough for one," said Paco. "Go on to the meeting."

"*Pues, me voy,*" said the tall waiter. "And thanks."

In the meantime, upstairs, the sister of Paco had gotten out of the embrace of the matador as skilfully as a wrestler breaking a hold and said, now angry, "These are the hungry people. A failed bullfighter. With your ton-load of fear. If you have so much of that, use it in the ring."

"That is the way a whore talks."

"A whore is also a woman, but I am not a whore."

"You'll be one."

"Not through you."

"Leave me," said the matador who, now, repulsed and refused, felt the nakedness of his cowardice returning.

"Leave you? What hasn't left you?" said the sister. "Don't you want me to make up the bed? I'm paid to do that."

"Leave me," said the matador, his broad good-looking face wrinkled into a contortion that was like crying. "You whore. You dirty little whore."

"Matador," she said, shutting the door. "My matador."

Inside the room the matador sat on the bed. His face still had the contortion which, in the ring, he made into a constant smile which frightened those people in the first rows of seats who knew what they were watching. "And this," he was saying aloud. "And this. And this."

He could remember when he had been good and it had only been three years before. He could remember the weight of the heavy gold-brocaded fighting jacket on his shoulders on that hot afternoon in May when his voice had still been the same in the ring as in the café, and how he sighed along the point-dipping blade at the place in the top of the shoulders where it was dusty in the short-haired black hump of muscle above the wide, wood-knocking, splintered-tipped horns that lowered as he went in to kill, and how the sword pushed in as easy as into a mound of stiff butter with the palm of his hand pushing the pommel, his left arm crossed low, his left shoulder forward, his weight on his left leg, and then his weight wasn't on his leg. His weight was on his lower belly and as the bull raised his head the horn was out of sight in him and he swung over on it twice before they pulled him off it. So now when he went in to kill, and it was seldom, he could not look at the horns and what did any whore know about what he went through before he fought? And what had they been through that laughed at him? They were all whores and they knew what they could do with it.

Down in the dining room the picador sat looking at the priests. If there were women in the room he stared at them. If there were no women he would stare with enjoyment at a foreigner, *un inglés*, but lacking women or strangers, he now stared with enjoyment and insolence at the two priests. While he stared the birth-marked auctioneer rose and folding his napkin went out, leaving over half the wine in the last bottle he had ordered. If his accounts had been paid up at the Luarca he would have finished the bottle.

The two priests did not stare back at the picador. One of them was saying, "It is ten days since I have been here waiting to see him and all day I sit in the ante-chamber and he will not receive me."

"What is there to do?"

"Nothing. What can one do? One cannot go against authority."

"I have been here for two weeks and nothing. I wait and they will not see me."

"We are from the abandoned country. When the money runs out we can return."

"To the abandoned country. What does Madrid care about Galicia? We are a poor province."

"One understands the action of our brother Basilio."

"Still I have no real confidence in the integrity of Basilio Alvarez."

"Madrid is where one learns to understand. Madrid kills Spain."

"If they would simply see one and refuse."

"No. You must be broken and worn out by waiting."

"Well, we shall see. I can wait as well as another."

At this moment the picador got to his feet, walked over to the priests' table and stood, gray-headed and hawk-faced, staring at them and smiling.

"A torero," said one priest to the other.

"And a good one," said the picador and walked out of the dining room, gray-jacketed, trim-waisted, bow-legged, in tight breeches over his high-heeled cattleman's boots that clicked on the floor as he swaggered quite steadily, smiling to himself. He lived in a small, tight, professional world of personal efficiency, nightly alcoholic triumph, and insolence. Now he lit a cigar and tilting his hat at an angle in the hallway went out to the café.

The priests left immediately after the picador, hurriedly conscious of being the last people in the dining room, and there was no one in the room now but Paco and the middle-aged waiter. They cleared the tables and carried the bottles into the kitchen.

In the kitchen was the boy who washed the dishes. He was three years older than Paco and was very cynical and bitter.

"Take this," the middle-aged waiter said, and poured out a glass of the Valdepeñas and handed it to him.

"Why not?" the boy took the glass.

"Tu, Paco?" the older waiter asked.

"Thank you," said Paco. The three of them drank.

"I will be going," said the middle-aged waiter.

"Good night," they told him.

He went out and they were alone. Paco took a napkin one of the priests had used and standing straight, his heels planted, lowered the napkin and with head following the movement, swung his arms in the motion of a slow sweeping veronica. He turned and advancing his right foot slightly, made the second pass, gained a little terrain on the imaginary bull and made a third pass, slow, perfectly timed and suave, then gathered the napkin to his waist and swung his hips away from the bull in a media-veronica.

The dishwasher, whose name was Enrique, watched him critically and sneeringly.

"How is the bull?" he said.

"Very brave," said Paco. "Look."

Standing slim and straight he made four more perfect passes, smooth, elegant and graceful.

"And the bull?" asked Enrique standing against the sink, holding his wine glass and wearing his apron.

"Still has lots of gas," said Paco.

"You make me sick," said Enrique.

"Why?"

"Look."

Enrique removed his apron and citing the imaginary bull he sculptured four perfect, languid gypsy veronicas and ended up with a rebolera that made the apron swing in a stiff arc past the bull's nose as he walked away from him.

"Look at that," he said. "And I wash dishes."

"Why?"

"Fear," said Enrique."*Miedo.* The same fear you would have in a ring with a bull."

"No," said Paco. "I wouldn't be afraid."

"*Leche!*" said Enrique. "Every one is afraid. But a torero can control his fear so that he can work the bull. I went in an amateur fight and I was so afraid I couldn't keep from running. Every one thought it was very funny. So would you be afraid. If it wasn't for fear every bootblack in Spain would be a bullfighter. You, a country boy, would be frightened worse than I was."

"No," said Paco.

He had done it too many times in his imagination. Too many times he had seen the horns, seen the bull's wet muzzle, the ear twitching, then the head go down and the charge, the hoofs thudding and the hot bull pass him as he swung the cape, to re-charge as he swung the cape again, then again, and again, and again, to end winding the bull around him in his great media-veronica, and walk swingingly away, with bull hairs caught in the gold ornaments of his jacket from the close passes; the bull standing hypnotized and the crowd applauding. No, he would not be afraid. Others, yes. Not he. He knew he would not be afraid. Even if he ever was afraid he knew that he could do it anyway. He had confidence. "I wouldn't be afraid," he said.

Enrique said, "*Leche,*" again.

Then he said, "If we should try it?"

"How?"

"Look," said Enrique. "You think of the bull but you do not think of the horns. The bull has such force that the horns rip like a knife, they stab like a bayonet, and they kill like a club. Look," he opened a table drawer and took out two meat knives. "I will bind these to the legs of a chair. Then I will play bull for you with the chair held before my head. The knives are the horns. If you make those passes then they mean something."

"Lend me your apron," said Paco. "We'll do it in the dining room."

"No," said Enrique, suddenly not bitter. "Don't do it, Paco."

"Yes," said Paco. "I'm not afraid."

"You will be when you see the knives come."

"We'll see," said Paco. "Give me the apron."

At this time, while Enrique was binding the two heavy-bladed razor-sharp meat knives fast to the legs of the chair with two soiled napkins holding the half of each knife, wrapping them tight and then knotting them, the two chambermaids, Paco's sisters, were on their way to the cinema to see Greta Garbo in "Anna Christie." Of the two priests, one was sitting in his underwear reading his breviary and the other was wearing a nightshirt and saying the rosary. All the bullfighters except the one who was ill had made their evening appearance at the Café Fornos, where the big, dark-haired picador was playing billiards, the short, serious matador was sitting at a crowded table before a coffee and milk, along with the middle-aged banderillero and other serious workmen.

The drinking, gray-headed picador was sitting with a glass of cazalas brandy before him staring with pleasure at a table where the matador whose courage was gone sat with another matador who had renounced the sword to become a banderillero again, and two very houseworn-looking prostitutes.

The auctioneer stood on the street corner talking with friends. The tall waiter was at the Anarcho-Syndicalist meeting waiting for an opportunity to speak. The middle-aged waiter was seated on the terrace of the Café Alvarez drinking a small beer. The woman who owned the Luarca was already asleep in her bed, where she lay on her back with the bolster between her legs; big, fat, honest, clean, easy-going, very religious and never having ceased to miss or pray daily for her husband, dead, now, twenty years. In his room, alone, the matador who was ill lay face down on his bed with his mouth against a handkerchief.

Now, in the deserted dining room, Enrique tied the last knot in the napkins that bound the knives to the chair legs and lifted the chair. He pointed the legs with the knives on them forward and held the chair over his head with the two knives pointing straight ahead, one on each side of his head.

"It's heavy," he said. "Look, Paco. It is very dangerous. Don't do it." He was sweating.

Paco stood facing him, holding the apron spread, holding a fold of it bunched in each hand, thumbs up, first finger down, spread to catch the eye of the bull.

"Charge straight," he said. "Turn like a bull. Charge as many times as you want."

"How will you know when to cut the pass?" asked Enrique. "It's better to do three and then a media."

"All right," said Paco. "But come straight. Huh, torito! Come on, little bull!"

Running with head down Enrique came toward him and Paco swung the apron just ahead of the knife blade as it passed close in front of his belly and as it went by it was, to him, the real horn, white-tipped, black, smooth, and as Enrique passed him and turned to rush again it was the hot, blood-flanked mass of the bull that thudded by, then turned like a cat and came again as he swung the cape slowly. Then the bull turned and came again and, as he watched the onrushing point, he stepped his left foot two inches too far forward and the knife did not pass, but had slipped in as easily as into a wineskin and there was a hot scalding rush above and around the sudden inner rigidity of steel and Enrique shouting. "Ay! Ay! Let me get it out! Let me get it out!" and Paco slipped forward on the chair, the apron cape still held, Enrique pulling on the chair as the knife turned in him, in him, Paco.

The knife was out now and he sat on the floor in the widening warm pool.

"Put the napkin over it. Hold it!" said Enrique. "Hold it tight. I will run for the doctor. You must hold in the hemorrhage."

"There should be a rubber cup," said Paco. He had seen that used in the ring.

"I came straight," said Enrique, crying. "All I wanted was to show the danger."

"Don't worry," said Paco, his voice sounding far away. "But bring the doctor."

In the ring they lifted you and carried you, running with you, to the operating room. If the femoral artery emptied itself before you reached there they called the priest.

"Advise one of the priests," said Paco, holding the napkin tight against his lower abdomen. He could not believe that this had happened to him.

But Enrique was running down the Carrera San Jeromino to the all-night first-aid station and Paco was alone, first sitting up, then huddled over, then slumped on the floor, until it was over, feeling his life go out of him as dirty water empties from a bathtub when the plug is drawn. He was frightened and he felt faint and he tried to say an act of contrition and he remembered how it started but before he had said, as fast as he could, "Oh, my God, I am heartily sorry for having offended Thee who art worthy of all my love and I firmly resolve . . . ," he felt too faint and he was lying face down on the floor and it was over very quickly. A severed femoral artery empties itself faster than you can believe.

As the doctor from the first-aid station came up the stairs accompanied by a policeman who held on to Enrique by the arm, the two sisters of Paco were still in the moving-picture palace of the Gran Via, where they were intensely disappointed in the Garbo film, which showed the great star in miserable low surroundings when they had been accustomed to see her surrounded by great luxury and brilliance. The audience disliked the film thoroughly and were protesting by whistling and stamping their feet.

All the other people from the hotel were doing almost what they had been doing when the accident happened, except that the two priests had finished their devotions and were preparing for sleep, and the gray-haired picador had moved his drink over to the table with the two houseworn prostitutes. A little later he went out of the café with one of them. It was the one for whom the matador who had lost his nerve had been buying drinks.

The boy Paco had never known about any of this nor about what all these people would be doing on the next day and on other days to come. He had no idea how they really lived nor how they ended. He did not even realize they ended. He died, as the Spanish phrase has it, full of illusions. He had not had time in his life to lose any of them, nor even, at the end, to complete an act of contrition.

He had not even had time to be disappointed in the Garbo picture which disappointed all Madrid for a week.

A Caddy's Diary

Ring Lardner

Wed. Apr. 12.

I am 16 of age and am a caddy at the Pleasant View Golf Club but only temporary as I expect to soon land a job some wheres as asst pro as my game is good enough now to be a pro but to young looking. My pal Joe Bean also says I have not got enough swell head to make a good pro but suppose that will come in time, Joe is a wise cracker.

But first will put down how I come to be writeing this diary, we have got a member name Mr Colby who writes articles in the newspapers and I hope for his sakes that he is a better writer then he plays golf but any way I cadded for him a good many times last yr and today he was out for the first time this yr and I cadded for him and we got talking about this in that and something was mentioned in regards to the golf articles by Alex Laird that comes out every Sun in the paper Mr Colby writes his articles for so I asked Mr Colby did he know how much Laird got paid for the articles and he said he did not know but supposed that Laird had to split 50-50 with who ever wrote the articles for him. So I said don't he write the articles himself and Mr Colby said why no he guessed not. Laird may be a master mind in regards to golf he said, but that is no sign he can write about it as very few men can write decent let alone a pro. Writeing is a nag.

How do you learn it I asked him.

Well he said read what other people writes and study them and write things yourself, and maybe you will get on to the nag and maybe you wont.

Well Mr Colby I said do you think I could get on to it?

Why he said smileing I did not know that was your ambition to be a writer.

Not exactly was my reply, but I am going to be a golf pro myself and maybe some day I will get good enough so as the papers will want I should write them articles and if I can learn to write them myself why I will not have to hire another writer and split with them.

Well said Mr Colby smileing you have certainly got the right temperament for a pro, they are all big hearted fellows.

But listen Mr Colby I said if I want to learn it would not do me no good to copy down what other writers have wrote, what I would have to do would be write things out of my own head.

That is true said Mr Colby.

Well I said what could I write about?

Well said Mr Colby why don't you keep a diary and every night after your supper set down and write what happened that day and write who you cadded for and what they done only leave me out of it. And you can write down what people say and what you think and etc., it will be the best kind of practice for you, and once in a wile you can bring me your writeings and I will tell you the truth if they are good or rotten.

So that is how I come to be writeing this diary is so as I can get some practice writeing and maybe if I keep at it long enough I can get on to the nag.

Friday, Apr. 14.

We been haveing Apr. showers for a couple days and nobody out on the course so they has been nothing happen that I could write down in my diary but dont want to leave it go to long or will never learn the trick so will try and write a few lines about a caddys life and some of our members and etc.

Well I and Joe Bean is the 2 oldest caddys in the club and I been cadding now for 5 yrs and quit school 3 yrs ago tho my mother did not like it for me to quit but my father said he can read and write and figure so what is the use in keeping him there any longer as greek and latin dont get you no credit at the grocer, so they lied about my age to the trunce officer and I been cadding every yr from March till Nov and the rest of the winter I work around Heismans store in the village.

Dureing the time I am cadding I genally always manage to play at lease 9 holes a day myself on wk days and some times 18 and am never more then 2 or 3 over par figures on our course but it is a cinch.

I played the engineers course 1 day last summer in 75 which is some golf and some of our members who has been playing 20 yrs would give their right eye to play as good as myself.

I use to play around with our pro Jack Andrews till I got so as I could beat him pretty near every time we played and now he wont play with me no more, he is not a very good player for a pro but they claim he is a good teacher. Personly I think golf teachers is a joke tho I am glad people is suckers enough to fall for it as I expect to make my liveing that way. We have got a member Mr Dunham who must of took 500 lessons in the past 3 yrs and when he starts to shoot he trys to remember all the junk Andrews has learned him and he gets dizzy and they is no telling where the ball will go and about the safest place to stand when he is shooting is between he and the hole.

I dont beleive the club pays Andrews much salery but of course he makes pretty fair money giveing lessons but his best graft is a 3 some which he plays 2 and 3 times a wk with Mr Perdue and Mr Lewis and he gives Mr Lewis a stroke a hole and they genally break some wheres near even but Mr Perdue made a 83 one time so he thinks that is his game so he insists on playing Jack even, well they always play for $5.00 a hole and Andrews makes $20.00 to $30.00 per round and if he wanted to cut loose and play his best he could make $50.00 to $60.00 per round but a couple of wallops like that and Mr Perdue might get cured so Jack figures a small stedy income is safer.

I have got a pal name Joe Bean and we pal around together as he is about my age and he says some comical things and some times will wisper some thing comical to me wile we are cadding and it is all I can do to help from laughing out loud, that is one of the first things a caddy has got to learn is never laugh out loud only when a member makes a joke. How ever on the days when theys ladies on the course I dont get a chance to caddy with Joe because for some reason another the woman folks dont like Joe to caddy for them wile on the other hand they are always after me tho I am no Othello for looks or do I seek their flavors, in fact it is just the opp and I try to keep in the back ground when the fair sex appears on the seen as cadding for ladies means you will get just so much money and no more as theys no chance of them loosning up. As Joe says the rule against tipping is the only rule the woman folks keeps.

Theys one lady how ever who I like to caddy for as she looks like Lillian Gish and it is a pleasure to just look at her and I would caddy for her for nothing tho it is hard to keep your eye on the ball when you are cadding for this lady, her name is Mrs Doane.

Sat. Apr. 15.

This was a long day and am pretty well wore out but must not get behind in my writeing practice. I and Joe carried all day for Mr Thomas and Mr Blake. Mr Thomas is the vice president of one of the big banks down town and he always slips you a $1.00 extra per round but beleive me you earn it cadding for Mr Thomas, there is just 16 clubs in his bag includeing 5 wood clubs tho he has not used the wood in 3 yrs but says he has got to have them along in case his irons goes wrong on him. I dont know how bad his irons will have to get before he will think they have went wrong on him but personly if I made some of the tee shots he made today I would certainly considder some kind of a change of weppons.

Mr Thomas is one of the kind of players that when it has took him more than 6 shots to get on the green he will turn to you and say how many have I had caddy and then you are suppose to pretend like you was thinking a minute and then say 4, then he will say to the man he is playing with well I did not know if I had shot 4 or 5 but the caddy says it is 4. You see in this way it is not him that is cheating but the caddy but he makes it up to the caddy afterwards with a $1.00 tip.

Mr Blake gives Mr Thomas a stroke a hole and they play a $10.00 nassua and niether one of them wins much money from the other one but even if they did why $10.00 is chickens food to men like they. But the way they crab and squak about different things you would think their last $1.00 was at stake. Mr Thomas started out this A. M. with a 8 and a 7 and of course that spoilt the day for him and me to. Theys lots of men that if they dont make a good score on the first 2 holes they will founder all the rest of the way around and raze H with their caddy and if I was laying out a golf course I would make the first 2 holes so darn easy that you could not help from getting a 4 or better on them and in that way everybody would start off good natured and it would be a few holes at lease before they begun to turn sour.

Mr Thomas was beat both in the A. M. and P. M. in spite of my help as Mr Blake is a pretty fair counter himself and I heard him say he got a 88 in the P. M. which is about a 94 but any way it was good enough to win. Mr Blakes regular game is about a 90 takeing his own figures and he is one of these cocky guys that takes his own game serious and snears at men that cant break 100 and if you was to ask him if he had ever been over 100 himself he would say not since the first yr he begun to play. Well I have watched a lot of those guys like he and I will tell you how they keep from going over 100 namely by doing just what he done this P. M. when he come to the 13th hole. Well he missed his tee shot and dubbed along and finely he got in a trap on his 4th shot and I seen him take 6 wallops in the trap and when he had took the 6th one his ball was worse off then when he started so he picked it up and marked a X down on his score card. Well if he had of played out the hole why the best he could of got was a 11 by holeing his next niblick shot but he would of probly got about a 20 which would made him around 108 as he admitted takeing a 88 for the other 17 holes. But I bet if you was to ask him what score he had made he would say O I was terrible and I picked up on one hole but if I had of played them all out I guess I would of had about a 92.

These is the kind of men that laughs themselfs horse when they hear of some dub takeing 10 strokes for a hole but if they was made to play out every hole and mark down their real score their card would be decorated with many a big casino.

Well as I say I had a hard day and was pretty sore along towards the finish but still I had to laugh at Joe Bean on the 15th hole which is a par 3 and you can get there with a fair drive and personly I am genally hole high with a midiron, but Mr Thomas topped his tee shot and dubbed a couple with his mashie and was still quiet a ways off the green and he stood studing the situation a minute and said to Mr Blake well I wonder what I better take here. So Joe Bean was standing by me and he said under his breath take my advice and quit you old rascal.

Mon. Apr. 17.

Yesterday was Sun and I was to wore out last night to write as I cadded 45 holes. I cadded for Mr Colby in the A. M. and Mr Langley in the P. M. Mr Thomas thinks golf is wrong on the sabath tho as Joe Bean says it is wrong any day the way he plays it.

This A. M. they was nobody on the course and I played 18 holes by myself and had a 5 for a 76 on the 18th hole but the wind got a hold of my drive and it went out of bounds. This P. M. they was 3 of us had a game of rummy started but Miss Rennie and Mrs Thomas come out to play and asked for me to caddy for them, they are both terrible.

Mrs Thomas is Mr Thomas wife and she is big and fat and shakes like jell and she always says she plays golf just to make her skinny and she dont care how rotten she plays as long as she is getting the exercise, well maybe so but when we find her ball in a bad lie she aint never sure it is hers till she picks it up and smells it and when she puts it back beleive me she don't cram it down no gopher hole.

Miss Rennie is a good looker and young and they say she is engaged to Chas Crane, he is one of our members and is the best player in the club and dont cheat hardly at all and he has got a job in the bank where Mr Thomas is the vice president. Well I have cadded for Miss Rennie when she was playing with Mr Crane and I have cadded for her when she was playing alone or with another lady and I often think if Mr Crane could hear her talk when he was not around he would not be so stuck on her. You would be surprised at some of the words that falls from those fare lips.

Well the 2 ladies played for 2 bits a hole and Miss Rennie was haveing a terrible time wile Mrs Thomas was shot with luck on the greens and sunk 3 or 4 putts that was murder. Well Miss Rennie used some expressions which was best not repeated but towards the last the luck changed around and it was Miss Rennie that was sinking the long ones and when they got to the 18th tee Mrs Thomas was only 1 up.

Well we had started pretty late and when we left the 17th green Miss Rennie made the remark that we would have to hurry to get the last hole played, well it was her honor and she got the best drive she made all day about 120 yds down the fair way. Well Mrs Thomas got nervous and looked up and missed her ball a ft and then done the same thing right over and when she finely hit it she only knocked it about 20 yds and this made her lay 3. Well her 4th went wild and lit over in the rough in the apple trees. It was a cinch Miss Rennie would win the hole unless she dropped dead.

Well we all went over to hunt for Mrs Thomas ball but we would of been lucky to find it even in day light but now you could not hardly see under the trees, so Miss Rennie said drop another ball and we will not count no penalty. Well it is some job any time to make a woman give up hunting for a lost ball and all the more so when it is going to cost her 2 bits to play the hole out so there we stayed for at lease 10 minutes till it was so dark we could not see each other let alone a lost ball and finely Mrs Thomas said well it looks like we could not finish, how do we stand? Just like she did not know how they stood.

You had me one down up to this hole said Miss Rennie.

Well that is finishing pretty close said Mrs Thomas.

I will have to give Miss Rennie credit that what ever word she thought of for this occasion she did not say it out loud but when she was paying me she said I might of give you a quarter tip only I have to give Mrs Thomas a quarter she dont deserve so you dont get it.

Fat chance I would of had any way.

Thurs. Apr. 20.

Well we been haveing some more bad weather but today the weather was all right but that was the only thing that was all right. This P. M. I cadded double for Mr Thomas and Chas Crane the club champion who is stuck on Miss Rennie. It was a 4 some with he and Mr Thomas against Mr Blake and Jack Andrews the pro, they was only playing best ball so it was really just a match between Mr Crane and Jack Andrews and Mr Crane win by 1 up. Joe Bean cadded for Jack and Mr Blake. Mr Thomas was terrible and I put in a swell P. M. lugging that heavy bag of his besides Mr Cranes bag.

Mr Thomas did not go off of the course as much as usual but he kept hitting behind the ball and he run me ragged replacing his divots but still I had to laugh when he was playing the 4th hole which you have to drive over a ravine and every time Mr Thomas misses his tee shot on this hole why he makes a squak about the ravine and says it ought not to be there and etc.

Today he had a terrible time getting over it and afterwards he said to Jack Andrews this is a joke hole and ought to be changed. So Joe Bean wispered to me that if Mr Thomas kept on playing like he was the whole course would be changed.

Then a little wile later when we come to the long 9th hole Mr Thomas got a fair tee shot but then he whiffed twice missing the ball by a ft and the 3d time he hit it but it only went a little ways and Joe Bean said that is 3 trys and no gain, he will have to punt.

But I must write down about my tough luck, well we finely got through the 18 holes and Mr Thomas reached down in his pocket for the money to pay me and he genally pays for Mr Crane to when they play together as Mr Crane is just a employ in the bank and dont have much money but this time all Mr Thomas had was a $20.00 bill so he said to Mr Crane I guess you will have to pay the boy Charley so Charley dug down and got the money to pay me and he paid just what it was and not a dime over, where if Mr Thomas had of had the change I would of got a $1.00 extra at lease and maybe I was not sore and Joe Bean to because of course Andrews never gives you nothing and Mr Blake dont tip his caddy unless he wins.

They are a fine bunch of tight wads said Joe and I said well Crane is all right only he just has not got no money.

He aint all right no more than the rest of them said Joe.

Well at lease he dont cheat on his score I said.

And you know why that is said Joe, neither does Jack Andrews cheat on his score but that is because they play to good. Players like Crane and Andrew that goes around in 80 or better cant cheat on their score because they make the most of the holes around 4 strokes and the 4 strokes includes their tee shot and a couple of putts which everybody is right there to watch them when they make them and count them right along with them. So if they make a 4 and claim a 3 why people would just laugh in their face and say how did the ball get from the fair way on to the green, did it fly? But the boys that takes 7 and 8 strokes to a hole can shave their score and you know they are shaveing it but you have to let them get away with it because you cant prove nothing. But that is one of the penaltys for being a good player, you cant cheat.

To hear Joe tell it pretty near everybody are born crooks, well maybe he is right.

Wed. Apr. 26.

Today Mrs Doane was out for the first time this yr and asked for me to caddy for her and you bet I was on the job. Well how are you Dick she said, she always calls me by name. She asked me what had I been doing all winter and was I glad to see her and etc.

She said she had been down south all winter and played golf pretty near every day and would I watch her and notice how much she had improved.

Well to tell the truth she was no better then last yr and wont never be no better and I guess she is just to pretty to be a golf player but of course when she asked me did I think her game was improved I had to reply yes indeed as I would not hurt her feelings and she laughed like my reply pleased her. She played with Mr and Mrs Carter and I carried the 2 ladies bags wile Joe Bean cadded for Mr Carter. Mrs Carter is a ugly dame with things on her face and it must make Mr Carter feel sore when he looks at Mrs Doane to think he married Mrs Carter but I suppose they could not all marry the same one and besides Mrs Doane would not be a sucker enough to marry a man like he who drinks all the time and is pretty near always stood, tho Mr Doane who she did marry aint such a H of a man himself tho dirty with money.

They all gave me the laugh on the 3d hole when Mrs Doane was makeing her 2d shot and the ball was in the fair way but laid kind of bad and she just ticked it and then she asked me if winter rules was in force and I said yes so we teed her ball up so as she could get a good shot at it and they gave me the laugh for saying winter rules was in force.

You have got the caddys bribed Mr Carter said to her.

But she just smiled and put her hand on my sholder and said Dick is my pal. That is enough of a bribe to just have her touch you and I would caddy all day for her and never ask for a cent only to have her smile at me and call me her pal.

Sat. Apr. 29.

Today they had the first club tournament of the year and they have a monthly tournament every month and today was the first one, it is a handicap tournament and everybody plays in it and they have prizes for low net score and low gross score and etc. I cadded for Mr. Thomas today and will tell what happened.

They played a 4 some and besides Mr Thomas we had Mr Blake and Mr Carter and Mr Dunham. Mr Dunham is the worst man player in the club and the other men would not play with him a specialy on a Saturday only him and Mr Blake is partners together in business. Mr Dunham has got the highest handicap in the club which is 50 but it would have to be 150 for him to win a prize. Mr Blake and Mr Carter has got a handicap of about 15 a piece I think and Mr Thomas is 30, the first prize for the low net score for the day was a dozen golf balls and the second low score a ½ dozen golf balls and etc.

Well we had a great battle and Mr Colby ought to been along to write it up or some good writer. Mr Carter and Mr Dunham played partners against Mr Thomas and Mr Blake which ment that Mr Carter was playing Thomas and Blakes best ball, well Mr Dunham took the honor and the first ball he hit went strate off to the right and over the fence outside of the grounds, well he done the same thing 3 times. Well when he finely did hit one in the course why Mr Carter said why not let us not count them 3 first shots of Mr Dunham as they was just practice. Like H we wont count them said Mr Thomas we must count every shot and keep our scores correct for the tournament.

All right said Mr Carter.

Well we got down to the green and Mr Dunham had about 11 and Mr Carter sunk a long putt for a par 5, Mr Blake all ready had 5 strokes and so did Mr Thomas and when Mr Carter sunk his putt why Mr Thomas picked his ball up and said Carter wins the hole and I and Blake will take 6s. Like H you will said Mr Carter, this is a tournament and we must play every hole out and keep our scores correct. So Mr Dunham putted and went down in 13 and Mr Blake got a 6 and Mr Thomas missed 2 easy putts and took a 8 and maybe he was not boiling.

Well it was still their honor and Mr Dunham had one of his dizzy spells on the 2d tee and he missed the ball twice before he hit it and then Mr Carter drove the green which is only a midiron shot and then Mr Thomas stepped up and missed the ball just like Mr Dunham. He was wild and yelled at Mr Dunham no man could play golf playing with a man like you, you would spoil anybodys game.

Your game was all ready spoiled said Mr Dunham, it turned sour on the 1st green.

You would turn anybody sour said Mr Thomas.

Well Mr Thomas finely took a 8 for the hole which is a par 3 and it certainly looked bad for him winning a prize when he started out with 2 8s, and he and Mr Dunham had another terrible time on No 3 and wile they was messing things up a 2 some come up behind us and hollered fore and we left them go through tho it was Mr Clayton and Mr Joyce and as Joe Bean said they was probly disappointed when we left them go through as they are the kind that feels like the day is lost if they cant write to some committee and preffer charges.

Well Mr Thomas got a 7 on the 3d and he said well it is no wonder I am off of my game today as I was up ½ the night with my teeth.

Well said Mr Carter if I had your money why on the night before a big tournament like this I would hire somebody else to set up with my teeth.

Well I wished I could remember all that was said and done but any way Mr Thomas kept getting sore and sore and we got to the 7th tee and he had not made a decent tee shot all day so Mr Blake said to him why dont you try the wood as you cant do no worse?

By Geo I beleive I will said Mr Thomas and took his driver out of the bag which he had not used it for 3 yrs.

Well he swang and zowie away went the ball pretty near 8 inchs distants wile the head of the club broke off clean and saled 50 yds down the course. Well I have got a hold on myself so as I dont never laugh out loud and I beleive the other men was scarred to laugh or he would of killed them so we all stood there in silents waiting for what would happen.

Well without saying a word he came to where I was standing and took his other 4 wood clubs out of the bag and took them to a tree which stands a little ways from the tee box and one by one he swang them with all his strength against the trunk of the tree and smashed them to H and gone, all right gentlemen that is over he said.

Well to cut it short Mr Thomas score for the first 9 was a even 60 and then we started out on the 2d 9 and you would not think it was the same man playing, on the first 3 holes he made 2 4s and a 5 and beat Mr Carter even and followed up with a 6 and a 5 and that is how he kept going up to the 17th hole.

What has got in to you Thomas said Mr Carter.

Nothing said Mr Thomas only I broke my hoodoo when I broke them 5 wood clubs.

Yes I said to myself and if you had broke them 5 wood clubs 3 yrs ago I would not of broke my back lugging them around.

Well we come to the 18th tee and Mr Thomas had a 39 which give him a 99 for 17 holes, well everybody drove off and as we was following along why Mr Klabor come walking down the course from the club house on his way to the 17th green to join some friends and Mr Thomas asked him what had he made and he said he had turned in a 93 but his handicap is only 12 so that give him a 81.

That wont get me no wheres he said as Charley Crane made a 75.

Well said Mr Thomas I can tie Crane for low net if I get a 6 on this hole.

Well it come his turn to make his 2d and zowie he hit the ball pretty good but they was a hook on it and away she went in to the woods on the left, the ball laid in behind a tree so as they was only one thing to do and that was waste a shot getting it back on the fair so that is what Mr Thomas done and it took him 2 more to reach the green.

How many have you had Thomas said Mr Carter when we was all on the green.

Let me said Mr Thomas and then turned to me, how many have I had caddy?

I dont know I said.

Well it is either 4 or 5 said Mr Thomas.

I think it is 5 said Mr Carter.

I think it is 4 said Mr Thomas and turned to me again and said how many have I had caddy?

So I said 4.

Well said Mr Thomas personly I was not sure myself but my caddy says 4 and I guess he is right.

Well the other men looked at each other and I and Joe Bean looked at each other but Mr Thomas went ahead and putted and was down in 2 putts.

Well he said I certainly come to life on them last 9 holes.

So he turned in his score as 105 and with his handicap of 30 why that give him a net of 75 which was the same as Mr Crane so instead of Mr

Crane getting 1 dozen golf balls and Mr Thomas getting ½ a dozen golf balls why they will split the 1st and 2d prize makeing 9 golf balls a piece.

Tues. May 2.

This was the first ladies day of the season and even Joe Bean had to carry for the fair sex. We cadded for a 4 some which was Miss Rennie and Mrs Thomas against Mrs Doane and Mrs Carter. I guess if they had of kept their score right the total for the 4 of them would of ran well over a 1000.

Our course has a great many trees and they seemed to have a traction for our 4 ladies today and we was in amongst the trees more then we was on the fair way.

Well said Joe Bean theys one thing about cadding for these dames, it keeps you out of the hot sun.

And another time he said he felt like a boy scout studing wood craft.

These dames is always up against a stump he said.

And another time he said that it was not fair to charge these dames regular ladies dues in the club as they hardly ever used the course.

Well it seems like they was a party in the village last night and of course the ladies was talking about it and Mrs Doane said what a lovely dress Miss Rennie wore to the party and Miss Rennie said she did not care for the dress herself.

Well said Mrs Doane if you want to get rid of it just hand it over to me.

I wont give it to you said Miss Rennie but I will sell it to you at ½ what it cost me and it was a bargain at that as it only cost me $100.00 and I will sell it to you for $50.00.

I have not got $50.00 just now to spend said Mrs Doane and besides I dont know would it fit me.

Sure it would fit you said Miss Rennie, you and I are exactly the same size and figure, I tell you what I will do with you I will play you golf for it and if you beat me you can have the gown for nothing and if I beat you why you will give me $50.00 for it.

All right but if I loose you may have to wait for your money said Mrs Doane.

So this was on the 4th hole and they started from there to play for the dress and they was both terrible and worse then usual on acct of being nervous as this was the biggest stakes they had either of them ever played for tho the Doanes had got a bbl of money and $50.00 is chickens food.

Well we was on the 16th hole and Mrs Doane was 1 up and Miss Rennie sliced her tee shot off in the rough and Mrs Doane landed in some rough over on the left so they was clear across the course from each other. Well I and Mrs Doane went over to her ball and as luck would have it it had come to rest in a kind of a groove where a good player could not hardly make a good shot of it let alone Mrs Doane. Well Mrs

Thomas was out in the middle of the course for once in her life and the other 2 ladies was over on the right side and Joe Bean with them so they was nobody near Mrs Doane and I.

Do I have to play it from there she said. I guess you do was my reply.

Why Dick have you went back on me she said and give me one of her looks.

Well I looked to see if the others was looking and then I kind of give the ball a shove with my toe and it come out of the groove and laid where she could get a swipe at it.

This was the 16th hole and Mrs Doane win it by 11 strokes to 10 and that made her 2 up and 2 to go. Miss Rennie win the 17th but they both took a 10 for the 18th and that give Mrs Doane the match.

Well I wont never have a chance to see her in Miss Rennies dress but if I did I aint sure that I would like it on her.

Fri. May 5.

Well I never thought we would have so much excitement in the club and so much to write down in my diary but I guess I better get busy writeing it down as here it is Friday and it was Wed. A. M. when the excitement broke loose and I was getting ready to play around when Harry Lear the caddy master come running out with the paper in his hand and showed it to me on the first page.

It told how Chas Crane our club champion had went south with $8000 which he had stole out of Mr Thomas bank and a swell looking dame that was a stenographer in the bank had elloped with him and they had her picture in the paper and I will say she is a pip but who would of thought a nice quiet young man like Mr Crane was going to prove himself a gay Romeo and a specialy as he was engaged to Miss Rennie tho she now says she broke their engagement a month ago but any way the whole affair has certainly give everybody something to talk about and one of the caddys Lou Crowell busted Fat Brunner in the nose because Fat claimed to of been the last one that cadded for Crane. Lou was really the last one and cadded for him last Sunday which was the last time Crane was at the club.

Well everybody was thinking how sore Mr Thomas would be and they would better not mention the affair around him and etc. but who should show up to play yesterday but Mr Thomas himself and he played with Mr Blake and all they talked about the whole P. M. was Crane and what he had pulled.

Well Thomas said Mr Blake I am curious to know if the thing come as a surprise to you or if you ever had a hunch that he was libel to do a thing like this.

Well Blake said Mr Thomas I will admit that the whole thing come as a complete surprise to me as Crane was all most like my son you might say and I was going to see that he got along all right and that is what makes me sore is not only that he has proved himself dishonest but that he could be such a sucker to give up a bright future for a sum of money like $8000 and a doll face girl that cant be no good or she would not of let him do it. When you think how young he was and the carreer he might of had why it certainly seems like he sold his soul pretty cheap.

That is what Mr Thomas had to say or at lease part of it as I cant remember a ½ of all he said but any way this P. M. I cadded for Mrs Thomas and Mrs Doane and that is all they talked about to, and Mrs Thomas talked along the same lines like her husband and said she had always thought Crane was to smart a young man to pull a thing like that and ruin his whole future.

He was getting $4000 a yr said Mrs Thomas and everybody liked him and said he was bound to get ahead so that is what makes it such a silly thing for him to of done, sell his soul for $8000 and a pretty face.

Yes indeed said Mrs Doane.

Well all the time I was listening to Mr Thomas and Mr Blake and Mrs Thomas and Mrs Doane why I was thinking about something which I wanted to say to them but it would of ment me looseing my job so I kept it to myself but I sprung it on my pal Joe Bean on the way home tonight.

Joe I said what do these people mean when they talk about Crane selling his soul?

Why you know what they mean said Joe, they mean that a person that does something dishonest for a bunch of money or a gal or any kind of a reward why the person that does it is selling his soul.

All right I said and it dont make no differents does it if the reward is big or little?

Why no said Joe only the bigger it is the less of a sucker the person is that goes after it.

Well I said here is Mr Thomas who is vice president of a big bank and worth a bbl of money and it is just a few days ago when he lied about his golf score in order so as he would win 9 golf balls instead of a ½ a dozen.

Sure said Joe.

And how about his wife Mrs Thomas I said, who plays for 2 bits a hole and when her ball dont lie good why she picks it up and pretends to look at it to see if it is hers and then puts it back in a good lie where she can sock it.

And how about my friend Mrs Doane that made me move her ball out of a rut to help her beat Miss Rennie out of a party dress.

Well said Joe what of it?

Well I said it seems to me like these people have got a lot of nerve to pan Mr Crane and call him a sucker for doing what he done, it seems to me like $8000 and a swell dame is a pretty fair reward compared with what some of these other people sells their soul for, and I would like to tell them about it.

Well said Joe go ahead and tell them but maybe they will tell you something right back.

What will they tell me?

Well said Joe they might tell you this, that when Mr Thomas asks you how many shots he has had and you say 4 when you know he has had 5, why you are selling your soul for a $1.00 tip. And when you move Mrs Doanes ball out of a rut and give it a good lie, what are you selling your soul for? Just a smile.

O keep your mouth shut I said to him.

I am going to said Joe and would advice you to do the same.

A Mighty Runner (Variation of a Greek Theme)

E. A. Robinson

The day when Charmus ran with five
In Arcady, as I'm alive,
He came in seventh.—"Five and one
Make seven, you say? It can't be done."—
Well, if you think it needs a note,
A friend in a fur overcoat
Ran with him, crying all the while,
"You'll beat 'em, Charmus, by a mile!"
And so he came in seventh.
Therefore, good Zoilus, you see
The thing is plain as plain can be;
And with four more for company,
He would have been eleventh.

Runner

W. H. Auden

All visible, visibly
Moving things
Spin or swing,
One of the two,
Move as the limbs
Of a runner do,
To and fro,
Forward and back,
Or, as they swiftly
Carry him,
In orbit go
Round an endless track:
So, everywhere, every
Creature disporting
Itself according
To the Law of its making,
In the rivals' dance
Of a balanced pair
Or the ring-dance
Round a common centre,
Delights the eye
By its symmetry
As it changes place,
Blessing the unchangeable
Absolute rest
Of the space they share.

. . . .

The camera's eye
Does not lie,
But it cannot show
The life within,
The life of a runner
Or yours or mine,
That race which is neither

Fast nor slow
For nothing can ever
Happen twice,
That story which moves
Like music when
Begotten notes
New notes beget,
Making the flowing
Of time a growing,
Till what it could be
At last it is
Where fate is freedom,
Grace and surprise.

part 2

First Person Singular: The Athlete Speaks

Considering the long history of sports, it is remarkable that so few athletes have written about their experiences. Indeed, it is only recently that the player on the field has taken to the pen or the typewriter, as the case may be. Athlete-writers, though, have at least one advantage over nonathletes who have written about sports. Athletes can convey with immediacy the experience of a sports activity, whether it is the private experience of a Mike Spino or the public one of a Jesse Owens. Even when describing the meaning sports has for someone else, as Jerry Kramer did for Vince Lombardi, the athlete's writing has a directness generally lacking in the sports writing of others.

Writing from the vantage point of their own experience, athletes have probed the emotions, motivations, and meanings of their activities. They have described the exhilaration felt in performing well and the despair felt in performing poorly; they have explored the drive to succeed and the factors that have inhibited it; and they have related what they do to larger concerns. Athletes have discussed, from various viewpoints, many of the issues facing our society, such as racism, sexism, exploitation, the economics of sports, and conflicting value systems and life styles. But above all, athletes are concerned with the integrity of their sport. All else is subordinate to the view of sports as a genuine contest, the classical *agon* between athlete and athlete or athlete and nature.

Open Letter to a Young Negro

Jesse Owens and Paul G. Neimark

"Tell them how the good times between us were."
—Luz Long

"All black men are insane. . . . Almost any living thing would quickly go mad under the unrelenting exposure to the climate created and reserved for black men in a white racist society. . . . I am secretly pleased about the riots. Nothing would please the tortured man inside me more than seeing bigger and better riots every day."

Those words were spoken by Bob Teague to his young son in *Letters to a Black Boy*. He wrote these letters to "alert" his son to "reality" so that the boy wouldn't "be caught off guard—unprepared and undone."

Are his words true?

Does a black man have to be just about insane to exist in America?

Do all Negroes feel a deep twinge of pleasure every time we see a white man hurt and a part of white society destroyed?

Is reality something so stinking terrible that it'll grab your heart out of your chest with one hand and your manhood with the other if you don't meet it armed like a Nazi storm trooper?

Bob Teague is no "militant." He's a constructive, accomplished journalist with a wife and child. If he feels hate and fear, can *you* ever avoid feeling it?

Whether it's Uncle Tom or ranting rioter doing the talking today, you're told that you'll have to be afraid and angry. The only difference is that one tells you to hold it in and the other tells you to let it out. Life is going to be torture because you're a Negro, they all say. They only differ on whether you should grin and bear it or take it out on everyone else. But National Urban League official, Black Panther leader or any of the in-betweens all seem to agree on one thing today: "We must organize around our strongest bond—our blackness."

Is that really our strongest bond? Isn't there something deeper, richer, better in this world than the color of one's skin?

Let me tell you the answer to that. Let me prove it to you so strong and deep that you'll taste it for all the days to come. Let me throw my arm around your shoulder and walk you to where so much good is and where the only blackness worth fearing is the black they're trying to color your soul.

Even though you weren't born for ten, maybe twenty years after, you've probably heard the story—the story of the 1936 Olympics and how I managed to come out with four gold medals. A lot of words have been written about those medals and about the one for the broad jump in particular. Because it was during that event that Hitler walked out on me and where, in anger, I supposedly fouled on my first two jumps against his prize athlete, Luz Long. The whole Olympics for me and, symbolically, for my country, seemed to rest on that third jump.

Yes, a lot of words have been written about that day and the days that followed. And they've almost been true, just as it's almost true that sometimes every black man weakens a little and does hate the white man, just as it's almost true that reality is tough at times and does make you want to weaken.

Yet, just like *those* "truths," what was written about me was only a half-truth without some other more important words. I want to say them to you now.

I *was* up against it, but long before I came to the broad jump. Negroes had gone to the Olympics before, and Negroes had won before. But so much more was expected of me. Because this was the time of the most intense conflict between dictatorship and freedom the world had ever known. Adolf Hitler was arming his country against the entire world, and almost everyone sensed it. It was ironic that these last Olympic Games before World War II was to split the earth were scheduled for Berlin, where he would be the host. From the beginning, Hilter had perverted the games into a test between two forms of government, just as he perverted almost everything else he touched.

Almost everything else.

The broad jump preliminaries came before the finals of the other three events I was in—the hundred-meter and two-hundred-meter dashes and the relay. How I did in the broad jump would determine how I did in the entire Olympics. For here was where I held a world record that no one had ever approached before except one man: Luz Long, Hitler's best athlete.

Long, a tall, sandy-haired, perfectly built fellow (the ideal specimen of Hitler's "Aryan supremacy" idea), had been known to jump over twenty-six feet in preparing for the Games. No one knew for sure what he could really do because Hitler kept him under wraps. But stories had filtered out that he had gone as far as I had, farther than anyone else in the world. I was used to hearing rumors like that and tried not to think too much about it. Yet the first time I laid eyes on Long, I sensed that the stories hadn't been exaggerated. After he took his first jump, I knew they hadn't. This man was something. I'd have to set an Olympic record and by no small margin to beat him.

It would be tough. August in Berlin was muggier than May in Ann Arbor or Columbus. Yet the air was cool, and it was hard getting warmed up. The ground on the runway to the broad jump pit wasn't the same consistency as that at home. Long was used to it. I wasn't.

His first jump broke the Olympic record. In the trials!

Did it worry me a little? More than a little. He was on his home ground and didn't seem susceptible to the pressure. In fact, he'd already done one thing I always tried to do in every jumping event and race I ran: discourage the competition by getting off to a better start.

Well, there was only one way to get back the psychological advantage. Right off the bat I'd have to make a better jump than he did. I didn't want to do it that way—it wasn't wise to use up your energy in preliminaries. Long could afford to showboat in the trials. This was his only event, the one he'd been groomed for under Hitler for years. I had to run three races besides, more than any other athlete on either team.

But I felt I had to make a showing right then. I measured off my steps from the takeoff board and got ready. Suddenly an American newspaperman came up to me. "Is it true, Jesse?" he said.

"Is what true?" I answered.

"That Hitler walked out on you? That he wouldn't watch you jump?"

I looked over at where the German ruler had been sitting. No one was in his box. A minute ago he had been there. I could add two and two. Besides, he'd already snubbed me once by refusing the Olympic Committee's request to have me sit in that box.

This was too much. I was mad, hate-mad, and it made me feel wild. I was going to show him. He'd hear about this jump, even if he wouldn't see it!

I felt the energy surging into my legs and tingling in the muscles of my stomach as it never had before. I began my run, first almost in slow motion, then picking up speed, and finally faster and faster until I was moving almost as fast as I did during the hundred-yard dash. Suddenly the takeoff board was in front of me. I hit it, went up, up high—so high I knew I was outdoing Long and every man who ever jumped.

But they didn't measure it. I heard the referee shout "Foul!" in my ears before I even came down. I had run too fast, been concentrating too much on a record and not enough on form. I'd gone half a foot over the takeoff board.

All the newspaper stories and books I've ever seen about that Olympic broad jump had me fouling on the next of my three tries, because the writers felt that made the story more dramatic. The truth is I didn't foul at all on my second jump.

I played it safe. Too safe. I was making absolutely sure I didn't foul. All right, I said to myself. Long had won his point. But who would remember the preliminaries tomorrow? It was the finals that counted. I had to make sure I got into those finals. I wasn't going to let him psyche me out of it. I wasn't going to let Hitler anger me into throwing away what I'd worked ten years for.

So I ran slower, didn't try to get up as high during my jump. Hell, I said to myself, if I can do twenty-six feet trying my best, I sure ought to be able to do a foot less without much effort. That would be enough to qualify for the finals, and there I'd have three fresh jumps again. That's where I'd take apart Luz Long.

It's funny how sometimes you can forget the most important things. I forgot that I wasn't the kind of guy who could ever go halfway at anything. More than that, no sprinter or jumper can really take just a little bit off the top. It's like taking a little bit off when you're working a mathematical equation or flying an airplane through a storm. You need the total concentration and total effort from beginning to end. One mistake and you're dead. More than that, my whole style was geared to giving everything I had, to using all my speed and energy every second of what I was doing. Once or twice I'd tried a distance race just for kicks. I was miserable at it. If I couldn't go all out all the time, I was no good.

So my second jump was no good.

I didn't foul. But I didn't go far enough to qualify, either. It wasn't just Long and Owens in the event anymore. There were dozens of other participants from other counties, and a bunch of them—too many—were now ahead of me.

I had one jump left.

It wasn't enough.

I looked around nervously, panic creeping into every cell of my body. On my right was Hitler's box. Empty. His way of saying I was a member of an inferior race who would give an inferior performance. In back of that box was a stadium containing more than a hundred thousand people, almost all Germans, all wanting to see me fail. On my right was the broad jump official. Was he fair? Yeah. But a Nazi. If it came to a close call, a hairline win-or-lose decision, deep down didn't he, too, want to see me lose? Worst of all, a few feet away was Luz Long, laughing with a German friend of his, unconcerned, confident, *Aryan.*

They were against me. Every one of them. I was back in Oakville again. I was a nigger.

Did I find some hidden resource deep within me, rise to the occasion and qualify for the finals—as every account of those Olympics says?

The hell I did.

I found a hidden resource, but it wasn't inside of me. It was in the most unlikely and revealing place possible.

Time was growing short. One by one the other jumpers had been called and taken their turns. What must have been twenty minutes or half an hour suddenly seemed like only seconds. I was going to be called next. I wasn't ready. I wanted to shout it—*I wasn't ready!*

Then the panic was total. I had to walk in a little circle to keep my legs from shaking, hold my jaw closed tight to stop my teeth from chattering. I didn't know what to do. I was lost, with no Charles Riley to turn to. If

I gave it everything I had, I'd foul again. If I played it safe, I wouldn't go far enough to qualify. *And this is what it all comes down to,* I thought to myself. *Ten years and 4,500 miles to make a nigger of myself and not even reach the finals!*

And then I couldn't even think anymore. I started to feel faint, began to gasp for breath. Instinctively, I turned away from everyone so they couldn't see me. But I couldn't help hearing them. The thousands of different noises of the stadium congealed into one droning hum—*ch-ch-ch-ch ch-ch-ch-ch,* louder and louder in my ears. It was as though they were all chanting it. Hatefully, gleefully. *Ch-ch-ch-ch. Ch-ch-ch-ch. CH-CH-CH-CH.*

Suddenly I felt a firm hand on my arm. I turned and looked into the sky-blue eyes of my worst enemy.

"Hello, Jesse Owens," he said. "I am Luz Long."

I nodded. I couldn't speak.

"Look," he said. "There is no time to waste with manners. What has taken your goat?"

I had to smile a little in spite of myself—hearing his mixed-up American idiom.

"Aww, nothing," I said. "You know how it is."

He was silent for a few seconds. "Yes," he said finally, "I know how it is. But I also know you are a better jumper than this. Now, *what has taken your goat?*"

I laughed out loud this time. But I couldn't tell him, him above all. I glanced over at the broad jump pit. I was about to be called.

Luz didn't waste words, even if he wasn't sure of which ones to use.

"Is it what Reichskenzler Hitler did?" he asked.

I was thunderstruck that he'd say it. "I—" I started to answer. But I didn't know what to say.

"I see," he said "Look, we talk about that later. Now you must jump. And you must qualify."

"But how?" I shot back.

"I have thought," he said. "You are like I am. You must do it one hundred percent. Correct?" I nodded. "Yet you must be sure not to foul." I nodded again, this time in frustration. And as I did, I heard the loudspeaker call my name.

Luz talked quickly. "Then you do both things, Jesse. You remeasure your steps. You take off six inches behind the foul board. You jump as hard as you can. But you need not fear to foul."

All at once the panic emptied out of me like a cloudburst.

Of course!

I jogged over to the runway. I remeasured my steps again. Then I put a towel parallel to the place half a foot before the takeoff board from where I wanted to jump.

I walked back to the starting spot. I began my run, hit the place beside the towel, shot up into the air like a bird and qualified by more than a foot.

The next day I went into the finals of the broad jump and waged the most intense competition of my life with Luz Long. He broke his own personal record and the Olympic record, too, and then I—thanks to him—literally flew to top that. Hours before I had won the hundred meters in 10.3, and then afterward the 200 meters in 20.7 and helped our team to another gold medal and record in the relay.

During the evenings that framed those days, I would sit with Luz in his space or mine in the Olympic village, and we would form an even more intense friendship. We were sometimes as different inside as we looked on the outside. But the things that were the *same* were much more important to us.

Luz had a wife and a young child, too. His was a son. We talked about everything from athletics to art, but mostly we talked about the future. He didn't say it in so many words, but he seemed to know that war was coming and he would have to be in it. I didn't know then whether the United States would be involved, but I did realize that this earth was getting to be a precarious place for a young man trying to make his way. And, like me, even if war didn't come, Luz wasn't quite sure how he would make the transformation from athletics to life once the Olympics were over.

We talked, of course, about Hitler and what he was doing. Luz was torn between two feelings. He didn't believe in Aryan supremacy any more than he believed the moon was made of German cheese, and he was disturbed at the direction in which Hitler was going. Yet he loved his country and felt a loyalty to fight for it if it came to that, if only for the sake of his wife and son. I couldn't understand how he could go along with Hitler under any circumstances, though, and I told him so.

He wasn't angry when I said it. He just held out his hands and nodded. He didn't explain because he didn't understand completely himself, just as I couldn't explain to him how the United States tolerated the race situation. So we sat talking about these things, some nights later than two Olympic performers should have. We didn't come up with any final answers then, only with a unique friendship. For we were simply two uncertain young men in an uncertain world. One day we would learn the truth, but in the meantime, we would make some mistakes. Luz's mistake would cost him too much.

Yet we didn't make the mistake of not seeing past each other's skin color to what was within. If we couldn't apply that principle to things on a world scale, we still could live it fully in our own way in the few days we had together, the only days together we would ever have.

We made them count. We crammed as much understanding and fun as we could into every hour. We didn't even stop when we got out on the track. Luz was at my side cheering me on for every event, except the broad jump, of course. There he tried to beat me for all he was worth, but nature had put just a little more spring into my body and I went a handful of inches farther.

After he failed in his last attempt to beat me, he leaped out of the pit and raced to my side. To congratulate me. Then he walked toward the stands pulling me with him while Hitler was glaring, held up my hand and shouted to the gigantic crowd, "Jesse Owens! Jesse Owens!"

The stadium picked it up. "Jesse Owens!" they responded—though it sounded more like *Jaz-eee-ooh-wenz.* Each time I went for a gold medal and a record in the next three days, the crowd would greet me with "*Jaz-eee-ooh-wenz! Jaz-eee-ooh-wenz!*"

I'd had people cheering me before, but never like this. Many of those men would end up killing my countrymen, and mine theirs, but the truth was that they didn't want to, and would only do it because they "had" to. Thanks to Luz, I learned that the false leaders and sick movements of this earth must be stopped in the beginning, for they turn humanity against itself.

Luz and I vowed to write each other after the Games, and we did. For three years we corresponded regularly, though the letters weren't always as happy as our talks at the Olympics had been. Times were hard for me and harder for Luz. He had had to go into the German army, away from his wife and son. His letters began to bear strange postmarks. Each letter expressed more and more doubt about what he was doing. But he felt he had no other choice. He was afraid for his family if he left the army. And how could they leave Germany? It was Luz's world, just as the South had been the only world for so many Negroes.

The last letter I got from him was in 1939. "Things become more difficult," he said, " and I am afraid, Jesse. Not just the thought of dying. It is that I may die for the wrong thing. But whatever might become of me, I hope only that my wife and son will stay alive. I am asking you who are my only friend outside of Germany, to someday visit them if you are able, to tell them about why I had to do this, and how the good times between us were. Luz."

I answered right away, but my letter came back. So did the next, and the one after. I inquired about Luz through a dozen channels. Nothing. A war was on. Finally, when it was over, I was able to get in touch with Luz's wife and find out what had happened to him. He was buried somewhere in the African desert.

Luz Long had been my competition in the Olympics. He was a white man—a Nazi white man who fought to destroy my country.

I loved Luz Long, as much as my own brothers. I still love Luz Long.

I went back to Berlin a few years ago and met his son, another fine young man. And I told Karl about his father. I told him that, though fate may have thrown us against one another, Luz rose above it, rose so high that I was left with not only four gold medals I would never have had, but with the priceless knowledge that the only bond worth anything between human beings is their humanness.

Today there are times when that bond doesn't seem to exist. I know. I felt the same way before my third jump at the 1936 Olympics, as well as a thousand other times. There've been many moments when I did feel like hating the white man, all white men, felt like giving in to fearful reality once and for all.

But I've learned those moments aren't the real me. And what's true of me is true of most men I've met. My favorite speech in a movie is the scene in *High Noon* when Gary Cooper, alone and hunted by the four sadistic killers, momentarily weakens and saddles a horse to get out of town. Like everyone else, his deputy wants him to do it and helps him. But Cooper finally won't get up on the horse.

"Go on!" his deputy shouts. "Do it!"

"I can't do it," Cooper says.

"You were going to a minute ago!"

"I was tired," Cooper tells him. "A man thinks a lotta things when he's tired. But I *can't do it.*"

We all get tired. But know yourself, know your humanness, and you'll know why you can never finally throw in with the bigotry of blackthink. You must not be a Negro. You must be a human being first and last, if not always.

Reach back, Harry Edwards. Reach back inside yourself and grapple for that extra ounce of guts, that last cell of manhood even you didn't know you had, that something that lets you stand the pain and beat the ghetto and go on to break the records. Use it now to be totally honest with yourself.

For when the chips are really down, you can either put your skin first or you can go with what's inside it.

Sure, there'll be times when others try to keep you from being human. But remember that prejudice isn't new. It goes way back, just as slavery goes way back, to before there ever was an America. Men have always had to meet insanity without losing their own minds.

That doesn't mean you should stand still for bigotry. Fight it. Fight it for all you're worth. But fight your *own* prejudice, too. Don't expect perfection in your white brother until there's not an ounce of blackthink left in you. And remember that the hardest thing for all of us isn't to fight, but to stop and think. *Black, think* . . . is the opposite of . . . *blackthink.*

I'm not going to play any Establishment games with you. My way isn't its own reward. Self-knowledge, getting rid of the bitterness, a better life are the rewards.

So be a new kind of "militant," an *immoderate moderate,* one hundred percent involved, but as a man, not a six-foot hunk of brown wrapping paper, be an extremist when it comes to your ideals, a moderate when it comes to the raising of your fist.

Live every day deep and strong. Don't pass up *your* Olympics and *your* Luz Long. Don't let the blackthinkers sell you out for a masquerade rumble where the real you can never take off the mask.

You see, black *isn't* beautiful.

White isn't beautiful.

Skin-deep is *never* beautiful.

Testament of a Samurai

Yukio Mishima

If there has ever been anything that has set me apart from other people, it was the inferiority complex about my own physique that I developed as a young boy. I was weak and frail, and there was nothing at all about my body I could be happy about or take pride in. To make matters worse, my youthful environment had none of the literary atmosphere that would have pampered my weakness but was conditioned by the background of World War II. Every day offered me countless examples that one had to be strong because there was no pity to waste upon the weak. And the harshness of my environment persisted in altered form even after the war was over, with the added element of American sensuality that deepened my inferiority complex and made my misery more acute.

I was not deformed or especially prone to sickness. It was mainly a matter of my being skinny and having a bad stomach. Soon after I had started to make my way as a writer I became painfully aware that this unnatural and unhealthy pursuit was going to make my plight still worse. I began to have a keen sense of mortality, fearing I might become a total wreck before I reached 30. I had done some horseback riding in school, and now my concern caused me to take this up again and also to set up a crossbar in my backyard, from which I duly swung. Neither effort did me much good.

In the summer of my 30th year I discovered the discipline of body building. During the course of a trip to the United States I had heard something about the sport, but I was sure it was a technique that would never be of any use to me. In that not-to-be-forgotten summer of 1955, however, I came across a picture in a magazine of the physical culture club of Waseda University, with an accompanying sentence that riveted my attention: "Anyone at all could develop a similar physique." I quickly got in touch with Hitoshi Tamari, the Waseda coach.

We had our first conversation in the lobby of the Nikkatsu Hotel, where Tamari was able to astound me with the feat of so rippling his chest muscles that their activity was apparent even beneath his shirt. And when he insisted that "you yourself will be able to do the same thing someday," I put myself under his guidance.

Tamari came to my house three times a week. I bought some barbells and an exercise bench, and so began unwittingly to amuse my friends and provide cartoonists with material for years to come. Though I by no means overdid my exercises, during this first period all sorts of physical disabilities came along to aggravate the normal pain that was part of the initiation. My tonsils became chronically swollen and a light fever persisted. I even went in for X rays. Some friends, at my eager urging, embarked on body building with me at this time, but all of them gave it up before the first month was over, precisely because of this initial agony that had to be undergone. What sustained me was the realization that day by day I was growing in strength. It is a kind of joy that is peculiarly elemental.

If one takes up body building at about 20, when the muscles are most suited for development and the bones themselves have not reached their maximum growth, the results can be spectacular. At 30, however, I had a massive handicap to overcome. Nonetheless, after no more than a year my body had so developed that I could hardly believe my eyes. I saw the apparently miraculous proof of what the flesh, which had seemed in my youth so unresponsive to the spirit in which all my dependence lay, had now been able to accomplish under the force of that spirit. And after a full year had passed, I suddenly realized one day that the stomach disorder that had harassed me for so long was gone, like something I had put down somewhere and forgotten.

Before this year was over I had come under the tutelage of a remarkable man named Tomoo Suzuki. He was middle-aged and had been a gym instructor in the navy. His vocabulary was strikingly colorful, and he was ever buoyant and exuberant. He was also intensely didactic, and he would brook no word that ran counter to his somewhat heretical dogma of physical culture. According to Suzuki, one should avoid any exercise that tightened the muscles, concentrating on those that stretched them and made them limber. And so it was that in Suzuki's gym I found myself confronted with the Imperial Navy exercises I had once suffered through in high school. But now when I performed these calisthenics, I felt—if I might boast just a little—tears of joy in my eyes. Suzuki's influence upon me was profound. His slogan of "exercises for everyday life" became mine.

Suzuki made much of his belief in the link between body and spirit. He had an instructor assisting him at the gym, and as this young man was leading a group in calisthenics one day Suzuki pointed at him and admonished me in these terms: "See, Mr. Mishima, take a good look. In a sound body you'll find a sound spirit. Look at the perfect suppleness of his body, the dexterity of his movements. There's a real human person for you."

As it happened, the model youth later absconded with the weekly receipts of the gym. Even now I have to smile every time I recall Suzuki's sour expression when I joked with him afterward about a sound body ensuring a sound mind.

Nevertheless, I have done a great deal of thinking about the interrelationship of body and mind. As a writer I really must have a mind that is not altogether healthy in order to produce my books. And yet could I not best safeguard this necessary disorder by keeping my flesh in the best possible shape? I must delve into elements of the human condition that are unpleasant in every way. So, perhaps, just as when one lowers himself down into the depths of a well, he is relatively safe only if the sides of that well are hewed from good, solid stone.

In the course of this first year of training, then, the confidence I had in my own body increased immeasurably. I was sure I had succeeded in smashing through the barrier that had for so long cut me off from the world of sport. I was now ready to plunge into it, beside myself with eagerness. I finally decided to take up boxing.

Tomoo Kojima, the coach of the Nippon University boxing team, was the man I went to in the early autumn of 1956, a year after my athletic career had begun. Kojima's character was quite different from Suzuki's. He was sincere and quietly earnest, shunning all verbal display. His life was dedicated to boxing. He did not drink. He did not smoke. He cherished his family. And he allowed himself nothing that he forbade the young men who trained under his care. In the literary world I had the reputation of being rather severe with myself, but compared to the preternatural austerity practiced by Kojima, I conducted myself like an unbridled wastrel.

I joined the training camp of the Nippon University boxing team to work out with them, and while at camp I kept up my weight lifting to maintain the tone of my arm and chest muscles.

We were housed in an old and dirty building. The odor of the toilet encroached upon the shower room. Trunks and sweatshirts were draped over the ring ropes. Torn punching bags hung from the ceiling. Of such stuff, I reflected, were sports epics made. All these props symbolized a kind of barbaric elegance I had not previously experienced.

Once training began, there was no time for elegance of any sort. The rounds were three minutes, with a 30-second rest period, and the student boxers had to spar for at least nine rounds in accordance with Kojima's training program. And then the remainder of the time was devoted to jumping rope, working out with the medicine ball, punching the heavy bag and shadowboxing. During the first day of this I thought every minute my breath was going to give out, but my earlier training had taught me I would become used to this sort of hardship, too. By the third day I felt myself starting to become accustomed to the rigorous drills.

I will never forget the excitement I felt the first time I entered the ring for a sparring session. The truth was that my first adversary was Kojima himself, and he took it extremely easy on me. Though I was formidable enough to look at, stepping into the ring, I took little pride in the headgear, which felt so strange, and the heavy gloves, which stirred so odd a sensation. After I put them on I gave my chin a light tap, and the coach laughed beside me. "That's what everybody does the first time," he said. When I heard this I felt an extravagant happiness at the thought that I had become, after all, without my realizing it, not too much different from other men who liked sports.

Once the sparring began, the three-minute round seemed to stretch on into eternity. Kojima pressed his attack, and in sidestepping and retreating, my legs quickly lost their response and dragged leadenly. At the first session one round completely finished me. The second time I lasted two rounds, but in the course of the second my knee gave way beneath me, and down I went. I had begun to realize what were the limits to the endurance of my 30-year-old body. But I took satisfaction in being able to learn them on my own.

During my first or my second sparring session a novelist friend visited the camp with an eight-millimeter movie camera and captured my wretched performance on film. Sometime later, when the literary crowd gathered at my house, he showed his film to a mambo accompaniment, to the hilarity of all. And, indeed, my on-screen figure making its desperate evasive actions to the Latin rhythm seemed like something out of a cartoon.

In the course of the next few weeks I gradually got to know various men in the boxing world, and Kojima would sometimes take me to the gyms of professional boxers for workouts. On one of these occasions a sportswriter made a proposal to Kojima: "Why not enter Mishima in a preliminary bout?" Kojima, who had admonished me never to box in a serious bout, vehemently refused. But even now the memory of that invitation rests in my mind, together with an invitation made to me right after the war to join the Communist Party. These are the two most dazzlingly seductive, if unlikely, temptations ever put before me.

I tasted the rigors of boxing for a year before giving it up. My main reason for so doing at last was the realization that the thoroughgoing practice of this sport was beyond me. What I practice now is kendo, the form of samurai swordsmanship involving the use of the blunt Japanese lance known as the *shinai.* The combatants, in their formal armor and with their cries echoing back through the centuries, are symbols of an era now gone. Because I have not had opportunity enough to master its fine points, I acknowledge that my kendo form leaves much to be desired, but it is the sport most suited to me and one that has brought me a deep serenity of spirit. Kendo is bound up intimately with what makes me what I am. In it the ideal harmony between the body and the spirit is realized. And its practice has finally satisfied that nostalgic yearning that I have so long felt toward athletics.

I use the word "nostalgic" in a highly personal sense, by no means wanting to imply a relationship with some event in my past. I have, for example, felt my heart swell with nostalgia in places throughout the world I had never visited before, such as, for example, when I stood beneath the palm trees of the West Indies or walked through the streets of Lisbon. So it is with sports, a feeling that for long years had lain deep within me. And now at age 45, with this yearning at last satisfied, my impression is that this has come about not through my own efforts but through the working of fate.

Though it was just 12 years ago that I took up kendo in earnest, the truth of the matter is that I encountered it earlier as part of my middle-school curriculum. In my school such sports as kendo, judo, archery and riding were required subjects, and so I hated all of them. I felt a hot flush of special mortification whenever I heard the rude, barbaric, threatening cries of kendo. My boyish sensibility was affronted by their gross shamelessness, their animality. They threatened culture. They threatened civilization. Whenever I heard them I wanted to cover my ears.

Now, 30 years later, I feel quite otherwise. The sound is pleasant to me: I have fallen in love with it. This sound is the cry of Nippon itself buried deep within me, a circumstance which I have at last recognized, and to which I have responded. It is a cry that present-day Nippon is ashamed of and desperately tries to suppress, but it breaks out, shattering all pretense. It is something bound up with memories that are dark, something that recalls the flow of new-shed blood. But whatever the recollections it provokes, they are ones that most truthfully recall our nation's past. It is the cry of our race bursting through the shell of modernization. This ghost of Nippon Past has been long confined in chains, denied sustenance and so reduced to weak groans. But in the kendo drill halls we lend it our throats to come alive, giving it its chance to break free.

When I hear the kendo cry issue from my own throat and from the throats of others, I sometimes look out the window of the small drill hall in downtown Tokyo where I practice. And as I look up at the new elevated freeways cutting across the sky, I say to myself that there lies mere phenomena while here below, the substance of things cries out, and I am happy. Yet, at the same time, how well aware I am that the happiness that comes of incarnating the force behind these cries is a happiness fraught with danger. For my part, I hope that kendo never becomes the international sport redolent of good fellowship that judo has. I never want it to lose the quality that sets it against the spirit of the modern age.

My instructor was Masami Yoshikawa, a man whose character much impressed me. His manner was calm and deferential, and he had none of that somewhat haughty bearing that some kendoists affect. Furthermore, he was not at all moralistic nor did he insist upon the slavish submission of his students. He was, in short, free of those overbearing characteristics that have done such harm to kendo's reputation.

Kendo in the summer, a mask over my face, the sweat pouring from me so I feel every drop of energy is draining out of me—at such times I think. "This is too much," yet I love every moment. Kendo is no ordinary sport, I realize, and one of its unusual characteristics is that, quite different even from other sports whose basis is one-to-one combat, a large number of older men are still active competitors. And never in kendo drill halls do you find that exaggerated regard for seniority that in other sports in Nippon causes younger athletes to so defer to their elders that they let them win.

As I look back upon my own athletic history, I am struck by how much it differs from that of other men. I began at an age when most men had long before passed their peak of active participation. Part of my early problem, I realize now, was the approach toward sport followed in Japanese schools during the war. The situation now is somewhat better than during that period, when the emphasis was upon military drills. But even today it is still a matter of the weak losing out to the strong. The boy who is not naturally endowed with strength and agility can do nothing but resign himself as best he can to being a sports dropout. Although school days are the time when sports participation should be enjoyed to the full, varsity teams and clubs tend to preempt all the facilities. The boy who has no talent for athletics then must turn to the arts to see if he has any talent that might be cultivated there, and the result is the rigid structuring that has so compartmentalized our society. Even today my memory is fresh with the sorrow I felt as a boy because I thought my not having been endowed with athletic skill or strength shut me out forever from the world of sport. How fine it would be if there were even one school that did away with all varsity competition and instead so improved the status of its athletic clubs that they embraced everyone and were so run that the particular capabilities of each student were given the proper scope for development.

Finally, let me conclude with a few words on the problem of sports and the ordinary workman and white-collar man. The situation is such that most men in modern society have been reduced willy-nilly to the status of spectators. And such are the stresses of our modern world, getting worse each day, that the marks of age already begin to appear upon more and more men when they are no more than 30. Excess weight brings on cholesterol disorders and weakens the heart of modern urban man. Too much drinking ravages his liver. The pressure of nervous tension gives him stomach ulcers. And how pitiful a spectacle is the thriving business our drugstores do, crowded as they are with men seeking some alleviation for their ills. Though these men realize that sports participation would benefit them immensely, their work affords them neither the necessary leisure nor opportunity. And though sometimes it may happen that there is a drill hall or gym furnished by their companies, such facilities are usually taken up by the company-sponsored teams. Thus the frustration of their school days persists.

I have an ideal that I have been dreaming about for some time: gymnasiums standing in every section of our cities, open to all, without qualification, who are willing to pay a very small membership fee. These would be open late every night and equipped with everything necessary to facilitate a member's participation in whatever sport he likes. There would be directors who would give understanding guidance suited to the age and experience of each member. Those just beginning a particular sport would be grouped together so they could learn from each other's mistakes and good efforts alike. And as for exhibitions, it would not be a matter of letting only the best participate, but everyone would get his place in the sun no matter how awkward and inexperienced he was.

Athletics exert a man's strength to the utmost. To run and leap, to dart about with sweat pouring from your body, to expend your last ounce of energy and afterward to stand beneath a hot shower—how few things in life can give such enjoyment!

When I was going through my boxing phase the mambo fad had seized Tokyo, and once, when I was showering after a hard workout, a young boxer turned to me with a grin beneath the hot spray and said: "The ones going crazy over the mambo, they'll never know what it's like to stand under a shower like this."

I will never forget this boy's naive boast. He was not being pedantic but merely speaking the truth as he knew it. The feel of a hot shower after vigorous exercise—surely this must be one of the elements essential to a man's happiness. No matter how much power a man may amass, no matter how much he outdoes himself in dissipation, if he never experiences the feel of such a shower, how far is he from knowing the real joy of being alive?

Translated by MICHAEL GALLAGHER

Adventures of a Y.M.C.A. Lad

H. L. Mencken

When I reach the shades at last it will no doubt astonish Satan to discover, on thumbing my *dossier*, that I was once a member of the Y.M.C.A. Yet a fact is a fact. What is more remarkable, I was not recruited by a missionary to the heathen, but joined at the suggestion of my father, who enjoyed and deserved the name of an infidel. I was then a little beyond fourteen years old, and a new neighborhood branch of the Y, housed in a nobby pressed-brick building, had just been opened in West Baltimore, only a few blocks from our home in Hollins street. The whole upper floor was given over to a gymnasium, and it was this bait, I gathered, that fetched my father, for I was already a bookworm and beginning to be a bit round-shouldered, and he often exhorted me to throw back my shoulders and stick out my chest.

Apparently he was convinced that exercise on the wooden horse and flying rings would cure my scholarly stoop, and make a kind of grenadier of me. If so, he was in error, for I remain more or less Bible-backed to this day, and am often mistaken for a Talmudist. All that the Y.M.C.A.'s horse and rings really accomplished was to fill me with an ineradicable distaste, not only for Christian endeavor in all its forms, but also for every variety of callisthenics, so that I still begrudge the trifling exertion needed to climb in and out of a bathtub, and hate all sports as rabidly as a person who likes sports hates common sense. If I had my way no man guilty of golf would be eligible to any office of trust or profit under the United States, and all female athletes would be shipped to the white-slave corrals of the Argentine.

Indeed, I disliked that gymnasium so earnestly that I never got beyond its baby-class, which was devoted to teaching freshmen how to hang their clothes in the lockers, get into their work-suits, and run around the track. I was in those days a fast runner and could do the 100 yards, with a fair wind, in something better than fourteen seconds, but how anyone could run on a quadrangular track with sides no more than fifty feet long was quite beyond me. The first time I tried it I slipped and slid at all four corners, and the second time I came down with a thump that somehow contrived to skin both my shins. The man in charge of the establishment—the boys all called him Professor—thereupon put me to the punching-bag, but at my fourth or fifth wallop it struck back, and I was floored again. After that I tried all the other insane apparatus in the place, including the horizontal bars, but I always got into trouble very quickly, and never made enough progress to hurt myself seriously, which might have been some comfort, at least on the psychological side. There were other boys who fell from the highest trapezes, and had to be sent home in hacks, and yet others who broke their arms or legs and were heroic figures about the building for months afterward, but the best I ever managed was a bloody nose, and that was caused, not by my own enterprise, but by another boy falling on me from somewhere near the roof. If he had landed six inches farther inshore he might have fractured my skull or broken my neck, but all he achieved was to scrape my nose. It hurt a-plenty, I can tell you, and it hurt still worse when the Professor doused it with arnica, and splashed a couple of drops into each of my eyes.

Looking back over the years, I see that that ghastly gymnasium, if I had continued to frequent it, might have given me an inferiority complex, and bred me up a foe of privilege. I was saved, fortunately, by a congenital complacency that has been a godsend to me, more than once, in other and graver situations. Within a few weeks I was classifying all the boys in the place in the inverse order of their diligence and prowess, and that classification, as I have intimated, I adhere to at the present moment. The youngsters who could leap from bar to bar without slipping and were facile on the trapeze I equated with simians of the genus *Hylobates*, and convinced myself that I was surprised when they showed a capacity for articulate speech. As for the weight-lifters, chinners, somersaulters, leapers and other such virtuosi of striated muscle, I dismissed them as *Anthropoidea* far inferior, in all situations calling for taste or judgment, to schoolteachers or mules.

I should add that my low view of these prizemen was unaccompanied by personal venom; on the contrary, I got on with them very well, and even had a kind of liking for some of them—that is, in their private capacities. Very few, I discovered, were professing Christians, though the Y.M.C.A., in those days even more than now, was a furnace of Protestant divinity. They swore when they stubbed their toes, and the older of them entertained us youngsters in the locker-room with their adventures in amour. The chief free-and-easy trysting-place in West Baltimore, at the time, was a Baptist church specializing in what was called "young people's work." It put on gaudy entertainments, predominantly secular in character, on Sunday nights, and scores of the poor working girls of the section dropped in to help with the singing and lasso beaux. I gathered from the locker-room talk that some of those beaux demanded dreadful prices for their consent to the lassoing. Whether this boasting was true or not I did not know, for I never attended the Sabbath evening orgies myself, but at all events it showed that those who did so were of an antinomian tendency, and far from ideal Y.M.C.A. fodder. When the secretaries came to the gymnasium to drum up customers for prayer-meetings downstairs the Lotharios always sounded razzberries and cleared out.

On one point all hands were agreed, and that was on the point that the Professor was what, in those days, was called a pain in the neck. When he mounted a bench and yelled "Fellows!" my own blood always ran cold, and his subsequent remarks gave me a touch of homicidal mania. Not until many years afterward, when a certain eminent politician in Washington took to radio crooning, did I ever hear a more offensive voice. There were tones in it like the sound of molasses dripping from a barrel. It was not at all effeminate, but simply saccharine. Had I been older in worldly wisdom it would have suggested to me a suburban curate gargling over the carcass of a usurer who had just left the parish its richest and stupidest widow. As I was, an innocent boy, I could only compare it to the official chirping of a Sunday-school superintendent. What the Professor had to say was usually sensible enough, and I don't recall him ever mentioning either Heaven or Hell; it was simply his tone and manner that offended me. He is now dead, I take it, for many years, and I only hope that he has had good luck *post mortem*, but while he lived his harangues to his students gave me a great deal of unnecessary pain, and definitely slanted my mind against the Y.M.C.A. Even when, many years later, I discovered as a newspaper correspondent that the Berlin outpost thereof, under the name of the *christliche Verein junger Männer*, was so enlightened that it served beer in its lamissary, I declined to change my attitude.

But I was driven out of the Y.M.C.A. at last, not by the Professor nor even by his pupils in the odoriferous gymnasium—what a foul smell, indeed, a gymnasium has! how it suggests a mixture of Salvation Army, elephant house, and county jail!—but by a young member who, so far as I observed, never entered the Professor's domain at all. He was a pimply, officious fellow of seventeen or eighteen, and to me, of course, he seemed virtually a grown man. The scene of his operations was the reading-room, whither I often resorted in self-defense when the Professor let go with "Fellows!" and began one of his hortations. It was quiet there, and though most of the literature on tap was pietistic I enjoyed going through it, for my long interest in the sacred sciences had already begun. One evening, while engaged upon a pamphlet detailing devices for catching boys and girls who knocked down part of their Sunday-school money, I became aware of the pimply one, and presently saw him go to a bookcase and select a book. Dropping into a chair, he turned its pages feverishly, and presently he found what he seemed to be looking for, and cleared his throat to attract attention. The four or five of us at the long table all looked up.

"See here, fellows," he began—again that ghastly "fellows!"—"let me have your ears for just a moment. Here is a book"—holding it up—"that is worth all the other books ever written by mortal man. There is nothing like it on earth except the One Book that our Heavenly Father Himself gave us. It is pure gold, pure meat. There is not a wasted word in it. Every syllable is a perfect gem. For example, listen to this—"

---

christliche Verein junger Männer: Christlike fraternity of young men; Christian club of young men, Y.M.C.A.

What it was he read I don't recall precisely, but I remember that it was some thumping and appalling platitude or other—something on the order of "Honesty is the best policy," "A guilty conscience needs no accuser," or "It is never too late to mend." I guessed at first that he was trying to be ironical, but it quickly appeared that he was quite serious, and before his audience managed to escape he had read forty or fifty such specimens of otiose rubbish, and following nearly every one of them he indulged himself in a little homily, pointing up its loveliness and rubbing in its lesson. The poor ass, it appeared, was actually enchanted, and wanted to spread his joy. It was easy to recognize in him the anti-social animus of a born evangelist, but there was also something else—a kind of voluptuous delight in the shabby and preposterous, a perverted aestheticism like that of a latter-day movie or radio fan, a wild will to roll in and snuffle balderdash as a cat rolls in and snuffles catnip. I was, as I have said, less than fifteen years old, but I had already got an overdose of such blah in the McGuffey Readers and penmanship copybooks of the time, so I withdrew as quickly as possible, unhappily aware that even the Professor was easier to take than this jitney Dwight L. Moody. I got home all tuckered out, and told my father (who was sitting up reading for the tenth or twentieth time a newspaper account of the hanging of two labor leaders) that the Y.M.C.A. fell a good deal short of what it was cracked up to be.

He bade me go back the next evening and try again, and I did so in filial duty. Indeed, I did so a dozen or more nights running, omitting Sundays, when the place was given over to spiritual exercises exclusively. But each and every night that imbecile was in the reading-room, and each and every night he read from that revolting book to all within ear-shot. I gathered gradually that it was having a great run in devotional circles, and was, in fact, a sort of moral best-seller. The author, it appeared, was a Methodist bishop, and a great hand at inculcating righteousness. He not only knew by heart all the immemorial platitudes, stretching back to the days of Gog and Magog; he had also invented many more or less new ones, and it was these novelties that especially aroused the enthusiasm of his disciple. I wish I could recall some of them, but my memory has always had a humane faculty for obliterating the intolerable, and so I can't. But you may take my word for it that nothing in the subsequent writings of Dr. Orison Swett Marden or Dr. Frank Crane was worse.

In a little while my deliverance was at hand, for though my father had shown only irritation when I described to him the pulpit manner of the Professor, he was immediately sympathetic when I told him about the bishop's book, and the papuliferous exegete's laboring of it. "You had better quit," he said, "before you hit him with a spittoon, or go crazy. There ought to be a law against such roosters." *Rooster* was then his counter-word, and might signify anything from the most high-toned and elegant Shriner, bank cashier or bartender to the most scurvy and abandoned Socialist. This time he used it in its most opprobrious sense, and so my career in the Y.M.C.A. came to an end. I carried away from it, not only an indelible distrust of every sort of athlete, but also a loathing of Methodist bishops, and it was many years afterward before I could bring myself to admit any such right rev. father in God to my friendship. I have since learned that some of them are very pleasant and amusing fellows, despite their professional enmity to the human race, but the one who wrote that book was certainly nothing of the sort. If, at his decease, he escaped Hell, then moral theology is as full of false alarms as secular law.

Mind over Water

Diana Nyad

I have been working on swimming since I was ten, four hours a day or more, every day, skipping the greater part of my social life, not a huge sacrifice, but something. I have put more grueling hours into it than someone like Jimmy Connors will ever know in a lifetime. I don't begrudge him his talent in that particular sport. There is simply no way he could comprehend the *work* that goes into marathon swimming.

What I do is analogous to other long-distance competitions: running, cycling, rowing, those sports where training time far exceeds actual competition time. But swimming burns more calories per minute than anything else. The lungs, heart and muscles must all be working at peak efficiency for this sport, which doesn't require brute strength but rather the strength of endurance. I can do a thousand sit-ups in the wink of an eye—and I never do sit-ups on a regular basis. I've run the mile in 5:15, not exactly Olympic caliber, but better than most women can do. My lung capacity is six point one liters, greater than a lot of football players. My heartbeat is forty-seven or forty-eight when I am at rest, this is compared to the normal seventy-two for other people. A conditioned athlete usually has a heartbeat of sixty plus. These characteristics are not due to genetics—I attained them by swimming hour after hour, year after year.

My first marathon, the ten-miler at Hamilton, Ontario, scared me to death. Judith De Nijs, the best in the world throughout the Sixties, was there, saying that if a woman ever beat her she would retire from the sport. She came over to me and said, "Vell, I hear you're a very good svimmer. Vell, you are not going to beat me." She put on her cap and walked away. I thought, whew. I swam the race and beat her by about fifteen minutes, which is a lot for a ten-miler. Judith De Nijs never swam again.

Greta Andersen was the same way. She swam the Channel I don't know how many times, as well as the Juan de Fuca Strait, and sixty miles across Lake Michigan. She beat every man she swam against at least once. She could have gone on forever. But she said that if another woman ever beat her, she'd quit. When Marty Sinn beat her, Andersen kept her word.

I'm not like that. Sandra Bucha has beaten me a couple of times in individual swims. I've been beaten by Corrie Dixon. They were better than me on those days.

Because I'm interested in people who are involved in exploring their potential, there is no one group I can respect more than marathon swimmers. When I'm in a hospital bed in La Tuque, for instance, after swimming in a twenty-four-hour team race, weak from exposure and nearly having frozen to death, and next to me is the guy I passed at three in the morning, we look at each other as if we're kings of the mountain. We have a love for each other, a close camaraderie.

There is considerable anxiety before a swim. I don't know until the day of the race whether the wind will be whipping up fifteen-foot waves or whether the surface will be glass. On the morning of a swim, our trainers wake us at around three a. m. for breakfast. We see the press, we eat. Nobody talks. The tension in the room is amazing. I never look at the swimmers; I look out at the lake and wonder what it will do to me, whether I'll be able to cross it. The race is more than me versus my competition. There is always the risk that I may not conquer the water.

At breakfast I have five or six raw eggs, a lot of cereal, toast and jam, juice. For my feedings during the race from the boat, I drink a hot powdered liquid that provides me with thirteen hundred calories and more protein per tablespoon than a four-ounce steak. It gets my blood sugar back up. In a race my blood sugar drops below metabolism level in three minutes. A cup of this stuff every hour barely helps. Before the hour's up my sugar is way down. I can feel it. I feel depressed. But if my protein level stays high, I'm not really in trouble.

I would say that eighty percent of success in a race is due to mind. Before starting, all natural reserves are working for me, my adrenaline, everything. Once out there, it's a matter of mental guts. After twelve hours in cold water, my blood sugar down, I'm seventeen pounds lighter, exhausted, it takes more than knowing I've trained hard for this. I have to dig down deep.

I've done some marathon running, but the isolation in long-distance swimming is more extreme. I'm cut off physically from communication. The water sloshing over my cap leaves me virtually deaf. I wear tiny goggles that fit just over my eyes—they're always foggy, so I can't see very well. I turn my head to breathe on every stroke, sixty times a minute, six hundred strokes every mile for hours and hours. As I turn my head I see the blur of the boat and some people on it.

These countless rhythmic hours make marathon swimming unique. John Lilly, the dolphin experimenter, has found that a subject floating in a tank with eyes and ears covered becomes disoriented, slipping into a near dream state. During a long swim I'm left with my own thoughts. My mind drifts in a mesmerized world. It's hypnotic. My subconscious comes to the fore. I have sexual fantasies and sometimes flashbacks to my childhood. It's dreaming hours on end. All I hear is the water slapping and my arms whishing through water. All I see is fog. It is extremely lonely.

I'm strong at the beginning of a swim, then I have low points. I know the pain in my shoulders will be bad all the way. I've rolled over on my back, thinking this body will not do another stroke. Sometimes at a low point a swimmer will get out. In ten minutes he's saying to himself, "Why didn't I stick it out? I could have made it. I could have come back around." That's happened to me, too, when I couldn't get back into it.

In rough ocean, I have thrown up from beginning to end of a thirteen-hour swim, swishing around like a cork, violently sick to my stomach. I would do anything to stop this feeling—and the only thing that will is to be on dry land. But I can put up with it—I have to. In my first year of marathon swimming, I got out because of seasickness. Now I get just as seasick and stick it.

Fatigue, pain, and huge waves are manageable. The toughest condition is cold water. Cliff Lumsdon, my trainer since 1972, swam in the Canadian Nationals in 1955. Lake Ontario was forty-five degrees. The life expectancy for a normal-weight person in forty-five-degree water is something like forty minutes. A marathon swimmer has only a film of grease for insulation, which wears off after a little while. After one hour, everyone was out of the water but Lumsdon. The temperature simply couldn't be handled. But Cliff stayed in for the entire fifteen miles, finishing in nineteen hours, eighteen minutes. He went through a substantial recovery period but was never hospitalized.

My coldest time was training on Ontario for the Capri to Naples race in 1974. I was supposed to leave later that day for Europe, but thought, why waste the time? Why not swim for an hour, just to loosen up? I did a thousand strokes out, then stopped to turn around, empty my goggles, get a sighting onshore. But I realized I hadn't been feeling my legs. I couldn't bring them to the surface. My skin was lobster red. My breath stuck in my throat. I tried to scream to some boys onshore, but nothing came out. I started to swim a slow breaststroke. My hands were so cold I couldn't close my fingers. People onshore finally saw I was in trouble. By now I was onto shallow rocks. A man waded out and grabbed me under my arms to lift me out of the water. His hands, his ninety-eight-point-six-degree hands, burned my skin. They took me to the hospital and put me in a warmer. I had severe burns all the way through the Capri-Naples race.

The temperature that day in Ontario was forty. I'd been in the water an hour. It freaks me out when I think Cliff lasted nineteen hours in forty-five-degree water. I just couldn't do it. My body weight is less than his, but still. . . . I really have to psych myself up for cold water.

There are still a few bodies of water I want to conquer. I'm considering all of the five Great Lakes in the summer of '76. Each lake is a different challenge.

The lakes are pretty cold. Superior is so cold I'd have to cross it at the shortest point. A legal marathon may be undertaken only in a regular racing suit, cap, goggles, and grease—no flotation devices, no insulating suit. Even at the shortest crossing, Superior may be impossible, given these requirements.

I've found suitable start and finish options for each lake. I could swim from Michigan City to Chicago, for instance, which is thirty miles; or from Benton Harbor to Chicago, which is sixty. My route will depend on how cold the water is. Distance doesn't mean anything to me; it's the condition of the water that counts.

Marathon swimming will never be as popular as other sports for obvious reasons. Spectators can only watch the finish, not the whole process. It's like the Tour de France—the most popular cycling race in the country and you can't see anything. But there is empathy among the spectators when the contestants stop for the night. You see their huge legs, muscular bodies dust-covered and sweaty, their power exhausted.

There is the same empathy at the end of a marathon swim. People have spent the whole day waiting. From a mile out I can hear clapping and screaming. The people realize I swam from a place they couldn't see on the clearest day. They know I may faint when I arrive. They share with me the most extreme moment of all—for after the pain, the cold, the hours, the distance, after the fatigue and the loneliness, after all this comes my emergence. And my emergence is what it's all about.

from Instant Replay

Jerry Kramer and Dick Schaap

July 29

Lombardi's lungs were going all day long today. "This is a game of abandon," he told the backs, "and you run with complete abandon. You care nothing for anybody or anything, and when you get close to the goal line, your abandon is intensified. Nothing, not a tank, not a wall, not a dozen men, can stop you from getting across that goal line." He stared at the backs hard. "If I ever see one of my backs get stopped a yard from the goal line," he said, "I'll come off that bench and kick him right in the can."

Vince was a little gentler on the rookies; he knows exactly who can take what. "Some of you boys are having trouble picking up your assignments," he said. "It's a tough task. You've got so many plays to learn, so many moves to learn. If you make a mistake, if you drop a pass or miss a block, anything like that, hell, forget it. If we had a defensive back here who felt bad every time he got beat on a pass pattern, he wouldn't be worth a damn. Take an education, but don't dwell on it. Don't let it affect your play. You will drop passes. You will make mistakes." Then he added, "But not very many if you want to play for the Green Bay Packers."

Vince found time to discuss the singing in the dining room, too. "The singing absolutely stinks," he said. "It's lousy. I don't give a damn what you sing, but I want to hear you. I want to see what kind of a man you are." He does, too. He can judge a man by his singing performance. If a man has the guts to stand up in front of fifty or sixty guys and try to carry a tune, especially if he's got a bad voice, the same man is likely to handle himself well in a crucial situation in a ball game. At least he's got poise.

August 9

Coach Lombardi gave us one of his periodic lectures today on life and football. "Winning is not a sometime thing here," he said. "It is an all-the-time thing. You don't win once in a while, you don't do things right once in a while, you do them right all the time.

"There is no room for second place here. There's only one place here, and that's first place. I've finished second twice in my time here, and I don't ever want to finish second again. There's a second-place bowl game, and it's a hinky-dinky football game, held in a hinky-dinky town, played by hinky-dinky football players. That's all second place is: Hinky-dinky.

Vince has got to be the only person I've ever met who could use a word like "hinky-dinky," talking to football players, and get away with it.

He reminded us, for maybe the hundredth time, that professional football is not a nice game. "Some of our offensive linemen," he said, "are too nice sometimes. This is a violent sport. That's why the crowds love it, that's why people love it, because it's a violent sport, a body-contact sport. We're a little too nice. We've got to get a little meaner."

Then he made his regular speech about outside interests. "I want every minute of your day to be devoted to football," he said. "This is the only thing you're here for." He looked straight at me, with my bow-and-arrow factory and my diving business, and straight at Fuzzy, with his restaurants, and he was dying to say something. But he can't be as strict as he used to be about outside interests, now that he's got so many of them himself.

After dinner, Coach was still steaming, and when a few guys got up to leave, he said, "What the hell is going on here? Sit down. Let's have some singing." Everybody was kind of down, kind of beat. Then a couple of us veterans got up and sang, and then we had the rookies sing, and then all the veterans, and then just the veterans over thirty, and Max got up and said, 'How 'bout the veterans over thirty-five?"

So Max and Zeke sang by themselves, and then all the coaches sang, and then the trainers, and finally we all sang together, making a horrible racket, and the whole atmosphere changed, the whole mood of depression lifted. We were a team again.

October 3

Coach Lombardi seemed more disturbed than angry during our meeting this morning. He said there's a general lack of enthusiasm on the club, a lack of desire, something he can't quite put his finger on. He said that sometimes he would rather lose and have everybody play a perfect game than win and have everybody look sloppy. My immediate reaction is to say that's crazy, that's ridiculous, he couldn't really mean that, but, somehow, I suspect he does, at least in theory. His desire for perfection is immense, and he's been very unhappy with our habit of doing only as much as we have to do to win.

Then Vince talked about Bart. He told us that Bart's been playing with injuries ever since the season began and as he spoke, he got very emotional. "I don't know if you guys know it or not," Lombardi said, "but this guy's been hurt and he's been in pain, and he's been playing hurt, and he's been——" And Vince couldn't finish the sentence. He got all choked up and misty-eyed, and he looked like he was going to start crying, and he just motioned to another coach to turn the lights off and start the projector. He was sort of quiet while we suffered through the movies of the Atlanta game.

After the movies, we played our regular touch game, and I intercepted four passes, an all-time Tuesday morning record. The guys awarded me the game ball, and I just hope this is an omen of the game to come. There's been a lot of stuff in the papers about Alex Karras and how great he is. I guess it's been a while since the writers could find anything to zing Green Bay, and Alex's been giving them a mouthful. I'd like to give him a mouthful—of my shoe.

November 26

At our devotional service this morning we had a guest speaker, a retired doctor who spends his time traveling around the country talking to athletes about Christ. He gave us copies of his booklet *Athletes in Action,* and I began thinking about people who never make decisions about their own lives.

The other day, I saw a film called *Cool Hand Luke,* and Paul Newman played a wild character who courted disaster all his life. He had no goal, no fear, and toward the end of his life he escaped from prison two or three times. The last time he escaped, he came upon a church and went in and got on his knees and said something like, "Old Man, whadaya got planned for me? What's next, Old Man? Whadaya want me to do? What did you put me on earth for, Old Man?"

I ask the same questions. I often wonder where my life is heading, and what's my purpose here on earth besides playing the silly games I play every Sunday. I feel there's got to be more to life than that. There's got to be some reason to it.

Many people never take control of their own lives, never say this is the way it's going to be, and maybe I'm one of them. I didn't come up with any answers this morning. I just thought about it for a while.

When we got to the stadium everything was pretty tense, pretty tight. Our people seemed nervous; this was the most we'd been up for a game, physically and emotionally, in some time. It's another reflection of Coach Lombardi's brilliance, I guess. Several times during the season I felt we were low, we were dead, and perhaps it was all deliberate, all part of Lombardi's scheme to bring us along gradually. Beyond any question, we were up today.

There's a danger of getting too high, to the point where you're ineffective. Inexperienced ballplayers are especially vulnerable to this. They get so emotional they can't do anything right. We've got a lot of young boys, and today, before the game, Vince was kind of gauging them, trying to measure their emotions. "How you feel, Jerry?" he asked me. "You think everybody's ready?"

"I don't know about the rest of them, Coach," I said, "but I sure as hell am ready."

Lombardi called us together, and we were all jumping around, hopped up, chattering, tight as drums.

"OK, boys," Coach said, in a calm voice. "I want to tell you a little story." He paused, and we waited, very quietly, to hear what he had to say. "Did you ever hear," Vince said, "about why Belgians are so strong?"

In Green Bay, we tell Belgian jokes, the same jokes people in some areas tell about Italians and people in other areas tell about Poles.

"No," one of the guys said.

"'Cause they raise dumbbells," said Lombardi.

That was his whole pregame speech. It was a silly, asinine little joke, but it worked. It took the edge off the tension. Most of the guys giggled, and we all loosened up. We went out and beat the Bears 17-13.

January 14

When we got to the Orange Bowl in Miami I dropped my stuff in the locker room and strolled out to the field for a little look at the pregame festivities. I saw the two big statues, one marked Oakland, the other marked Green Bay, breathing smoke. I just wanted to kill a little time, settle down a little.

In the locker room, for the first time all season I decided to leave my tape recorder running during the pregame talks. If I got caught by Lombardi, I didn't think he'd suspend me at this stage of the year.

Bob Skoronski spoke first. "Let's not waste any time, boys," he said. "Let's go out there from the opening play. They're a good football team, boys. If we lose, boys, we've lost everything we ever worked for. Everything. I don't have any damn intention of losing this ball game, and I don't think anybody else here does."

"Fellas," said Willie Davis, "you know as well as I do that when we went to camp in July, this is what we had in mind. This game. This game is going to determine what's said about the Packers tomorrow. Fellas, in another sixty minutes, we can walk in here with another world championship. Fellas, it's recognition, it's prestige, and, fellas, it's money. So let's go out and have fun. Let's go out and just hit people. Let's just go out and play football the way we can.

"My impression of this ball club," Forrest Gregg said, "is that they're the type of people who like to intimidate you. Watch those linebackers, those linemen, the way they're hitting people late. No sense getting upset about it. They're gonna do some pass interference and holding and stuff like that, but let's not get upset about it. Let's go out there and play our brand of football. Let's face it. They're a little bit afraid of us right now. Let's put it to them from the very first whistle and put it to them every play."

"It's the last game for some of us," said Max, "and we sure don't want to go out of here and live the rest of our lives letting these guys beat us."

"Let's play with our hearts," said Nitschke.

Then Carroll Dale led us in the Lord's Prayer, and we broke up with whoops and hollers, and we ran out on the field and loosened up, and then we came back inside for our pads and our helmets and a few words from Coach Lombardi.

"It's very difficult for me to say anything," Vince said. "Anything I could say would be repetitious. This is our twenty-third game this year. I don't know of anything else I could tell this team. Boys, I can only say this to you: Boys, you're a good football team. You are a proud football team. You are the world champions. You are the champions of the National Football League for the third time in a row, for the first time in the history of the National Football League. That's a great thing to be proud of. But let me just say this: All the glory, everything that you've had, everything that you've won is going to be small in comparison to winning this one. This is a great thing for you. You're the only team maybe in the history of the National Football League to ever have this opportunity to win the Super Bowl twice. Boys, I tell you I'd be so proud of that I just fill up with myself. I just get bigger and bigger and bigger. It's not going to come easy. This is a club that's gonna hit you. They're gonna try to hit you and you got to take it out of them. You got to be forty tigers out there. That's all. Just hit. Just run. Just block and just tackle. If you do that, there's no question what the answer's going to be in this ball game. Keep your poise. Keep your poise. You've faced them all. There's nothing they can show you out there you haven't faced a number of times. Right?"

"Right!"

"RIGHT!"

"Let's go. Let's go get 'em."

The game ended 33–14, with Oakland in possession of the ball. We had been planning for the co-captains, Skoronski and Davis, to carry Vince off the field, but Willie was playing when the gun went off, so Gregg and I, the two men closest to Coach, just lifted him up and started running out on the field. He was grinning at us and slapping us and he hollered, "Head for the dressing room, boys," and we headed for the dressing room, clutching the man who'd made us the Super Bowl champions for the second year in a row.

When we had all reached the dressing room, Vince gathered us together. "This has to be one of the great, great years," he said. "I think it's something you'll always remember. You know everything happened to us. We lost a lot of people. Thank goodness we had the boys who could replace them and did a helluva job. And those who were not hurt played a little bit better. Boys, I'm really proud of you. We should all be very, very thankful."

We got down on our knees, and we began, in unison, "Our Father, Who art in Heaven, hallowed be Thy name . . ."

We finished the Lord's Prayer and we all began slapping each other on the back and hugging each other, and, once again, the cameramen and reporters poured in.

I sat in front of my locker, and I talked and talked and talked. I talked about the mistakes we made during the first half. I talked about the spirit of our team. I talked about Lombardi. I saw the fellow who wrote the article in *Esquire* about Lombardi, and I cussed him out a bit. I told anecdotes and I told my opinion of just about everything, and after a while I noticed that most of my teammates were dressed and were starting to leave the locker room. I was still in my uniform, still perched in front of my locker. I really didn't want to get up.

I wanted to keep my uniform on as long as I possibly could.

First Practice

Gary Gildner

After the doctor checked to see
we weren't ruptured,
the man with the short cigar took us
under the grade school,
where we went in case of attack
or storm, and said
he was Clifford Hill, he was
a man who believed dogs
ate dogs, he had once killed
for his country, and if
there were any girls present
for them to leave now.
                                        No one
left. OK, he said, he said I take
that to mean you are hungry
men who hate to lose as much
as I do. OK. Then
he made two lines of us
facing each other,
and across the way, he said,
is the man you hate most
in the world,
and if we are to win
that title I want to see how.
But I don't want to see
any marks when you're dressed,
he said. He said, *Now.*

My Fights with Jack Dempsey

Gene Tunney

At the Dempsey-Carpentier fight, I had seen one other thing. Another angle flashed, as at a corner of the ring I watched and studied. Famous in those days was the single dramatic moment, the only moment when the Orchid Man seemed to have a chance. That was when, in the second round, Carpentier lashed out with a right-hand punch. He was renowned for his right, had knocked out English champions with it. He hit Dempsey high on the jaw with all his power.

I was in a position to see the punch clearly and note how Carpentier threw it. He drew back his right like a pitcher with a baseball. The punch was telegraphed all over the place. Yet it landed on a vulnerable spot. How anybody could be hit with a right launched like that was mystifying to one who understood boxing. Dempsey went back on his heels, jarred. Carpentier couldn't follow up, and in a moment Jack was again on the relentless job of wrecking the Orchid Man with body blows. But it was a vivid demonstration that the champion could be hit with a right.

Dempsey was no protective boxer. He couldn't do defensive sparring. He relied on a shifty style, his own kind of defense, and couldn't be hit just any way. His weakness was that he could be nailed with a straight right. Later on, I saw this confirmed in other Dempsey battles. It was dramatized sensationally at the Polo Grounds when the powerful but clumsy Firpo smashed him with a right at the very beginning of the first round, and later blasted Dempsey out of the ring with right-hand punches—the Wild Bull of the Pampas almost winning the championship.

To me it signified that the strategy of defensive boxing might be supplemented by a right-hand punch—everything thrown into a right. It would never do for me to start mixing with the Champ in any knock-down, drag-out exchange of haymakers. He'd knock me out. It would have to be a surprise blow, and it could easily be that. Both Carpentier and Firpo, who had nailed the Champ, were noted for their right—all they had. But Jack would never suspect a Sunday punch from me, stepping in and trying to knock him out with a right.

I was catalogued not only as a defensive boxer but also as a light hitter, no punch. I might wear an opponent down and cut him to pieces, but I couldn't put him to sleep with a knockout slam. That had been true—previously. I had been going along with the handicap of bad hands. I could hit hard enough, but didn't dare for fear of breaking my hands. So I was a comparatively light hitter—and typed as one.

Finally, in desperation, I had to do something about my fragile hands. I went to a lumber camp in Canada for one winter and worked as a woodsman, chopping down trees. The grip of the ax was exercise for my damaged mitts. Months of lumber camp wood chopping and other hand exercises worked a cure. My hands grew strong and hard, my fists rugged enough to take the impact of as powerful a blow as I could land. In subsequent bouts I had little trouble with my hands. This I knew, and others might have been aware of the change, but I was tagged as a feather duster puncher—and that was that. The old philosophy of giving a dog a bad name.

Prizefight publicity often resorts to the ballyhoo of a secret punch, a surprise blow, nearly always a fraud—but I really had the chance. At the beginning of the first round I would step in and put everything I had in a right-hand punch, every ounce of strength. I might score a knockout, or the blow would daze the champion sufficiently to make it easier to outbox him the rest of the way.

I was, meanwhile, fighting my way to the position of challenger. I won the light heavyweight championship from Battling Levinsky and subsequently fought Carpentier, the Orchid Man, and went through a series of savage bouts with Harry Greb, one of the greatest of pugilists. In our first bout, Greb gave me a murderous mauling. In our last, I beat him almost as badly. After a long series of matches with sundry light heavies and heavies I went on to establish myself as heavyweight contender by defeating Tom Gibbons. It was dramatic irony that I earned my shot at the title at the expense of Tom, brother of my model, Mike.

Public opinion of my prospects with Dempsey was loud and summary. The champion is always the favorite, and Dempsey was one of the greatest champions, as destructive a hitter as the prize ring has ever known. He was considered unbeatable, and I was rated as a victim peculiarly doomed to obliteration, pathetic, absurd.

It was argued that I was a synthetic fighter. That was true. As a kid prelim battler, my interest had been in romantic competition and love of boxing, while holding a job as a shipping clerk with a steamship company. As a marine in France, my love of boxing and a distaste for irksome military duties after the armistice brought me back as a competitor in A.E.F. boxing tournaments. We gave our best to entertain our buddies and, incidentally, to avoid guard duty. After the war, when I had grown up, my purpose simply was to develop the sparring ability I had as a means of making money—seeing in the heavyweight championship a proud and profitable eminence.

They said I lacked the killer instinct—which was also true. I found no joy in knocking people unconscious or battering their faces. The lust for battle and massacre was missing. I had a notion that the killer instinct was really founded in fear, that the killer of the ring raged with ruthless brutality because deep down he was afraid.

Synthetic fighter, not a killer! There was a kind of angry resentment in the accusation. People might have reasoned that, to have arrived at the position of challenger, I must have won some fights. They might have noted that, while the champion had failed to flatten Tom Gibbons I had knocked him out. But then the Dempsey-Gibbons bout was ignored as rather mystifying, one of "those things."

The prizefight "experts" were almost unanimous in not giving me a chance. The sports writers ground out endless descriptions of the doleful things that would happen to me in the ring with Dempsey. There were, so far as I know, only a few persons prominent in sports who thought I might win, and said so. One was Bernard Gimbel, of the famous mercantile family, a formidable amateur boxer and a student of ring strategy. The others included that prince of sports writers, the late W. O. McGeehan, and a few lesser lights in the sports-writing profession. They picked me to win, and were ridiculed. The consensus of the experts was echoed by the public, though with genuine sadness on the part of some.

Suspicion of a hoax started following a visit by a newspaperman to my training camp at Speculator, New York. Associated Press reporter Brian Bell came for an interview. He noticed a book lying on the table next to my bed. Books were unexpected equipment in a prizefight training camp. He was curious and took a look at the volume—*The Way of All Flesh.* That surprised him. The Samuel Butler opus was, at that time, new in its belated fame, having been hugely praised by George Bernard Shaw as a neglected masterpiece. It was hardly the thing you'd expect a prizefighter to be reading, especially while training for a bout with Jack Dempsey.

Brian Bell knew a story when he saw one. He later became one of the chief editors of the Associated Press. Instead of talking fight, he queried me about books. I told him I liked to read Shakespeare. That was the gag. That was the pay-off. The A.P. flashed the story far and wide—the challenger, training for Jack Dempsey, read books, literature—Shakespeare. It was a sensation. The Shakespeare-Tunney legend was born.

The story behind it all went back to a day in 1917 when a young marine named Gene Tunney was getting ready to embark with his company bound for the war in France. We were stowing things in our kits, when I happened to glance at the fellow next to me. I noticed that among the belongings he was packing were two books. That surprised me.

In the marines you kept the stuff you took to the minimum. You carried your possessions on your back in the long marches favored by the Marine Corps. Every ounce would feel like a ton. Yet here was a leatherneck stowing away two books to add to his burden. I was so curious that I sneaked a look at the two books and saw—Shakespeare. One was *Julius*

Ceasar, the other, *A Winter's Tale.* He must be a real professor, I thought.

The leatherneck in question was the company clerk. I had known him when in recruit camp—a young lawyer in civilian life, quiet and intelligent. Now, my respect for him went up many notches. He must be educated indeed to be taking two volumes of Shakespeare to carry on his back on the long marches we would have in France.

We sailed in the usual transport style, piled in bunks in a stuffy hold. The weather was rough, and virtually the whole division of marines became seasick. The few good sailors poked unmerciful fun at their seasick comrades. I happened to be one of the fortunate, and joined in the ridicule of the miserable sufferers.

Sickest of all was the company clerk. He writhed in misery. He would lie on deck all day, an object of groaning filth. At night he was equally disgusting in his bunk. This was the tier next to mine, and I saw more of him than most. The high respect I had formed for him went down those many notches. He might be educated, he might take Shakespeare to war with him, but he was a mess at sea.

We put in at Brest, and promptly the order came—prepare to march. We were to put on a show at the dock for inspection by the brass hats. I started to get ready, and then came the appalling discovery. I couldn't find the tunic of my uniform. I knew I had stowed it in my kit, but it was gone. I hunted everywhere. In the Marine Corps it was practically a capital offense for a leatherneck to be without an article of issue, and here I was without my tunic for the long march upon arrival in France.

I heard a marine asking: "Whose is this?" He was on a cleaning job, and was holding up a disreputable object that he had fished from under the bunks. "Somebody's blouse," he announced with a tone of disgust, "and look at it."

I did—it was my blouse, a mess of seasick filth.

The explanation was easy to guess. The company clerk in the tier of bunks next to mine had done it. Having befouled all of his clothes, he had, in his dumb misery, reached into my bunk and taken my blouse. He had worn it until it was too filthy to wear—after which he had chucked it under the bunks.

There was nothing I could do. There was no time to get the blouse cleaned, and there was no use blaming it on the company clerk. It was strictly up to me to have possession of every article of issue in good shape. I could only inform our company commander that I didn't have my tunic—and take the penalty, extra guard duty and kitchen police.

When, ashore, the company clerk came out of his seasickness and realized what had happened, he was duly remorseful. He was a decent fellow, his only real offense having been seasickness. He told me how sorry he was, and asked what he could do to make up for the trouble he had got me into. What could he give me? That was the way things were requited among the marines—handing something over to make up for something. What did he have that I might want? He hadn't anything I could take, except those two books. I told him, "Give me one of them and call things square." He did. He retained *Julius Caesar* and gave me *A Winter's Tale.* He knew what he was about, as anyone who knows Shakespeare will attest.

Having the book, I tried to read it but couldn't make any sense of it. I kept on trying. I always had a stubborn streak, and figured the book must mean something. But it didn't, so far as I could make out. I went to the company clerk. He had given me the book, and it might mean something to him. It did, and he proceeded to explain.

He coached me, led me through *A Winter's Tale,* which turned out to be interesting. That was practically my introduction to Shakespeare—the hard way. After training on *A Winter's Tale,* I read such works as *Hamlet, Macbeth, Othello,* with ease.

I had always liked reading—and this had a practical side. I found that books helped in training for boxing bouts. One of the difficulties of the prizefight game is that of relieving tension in training camp, getting one's mind off the fight. The usual training camp devices were jazz phonograph records and the game of pinochle. I didn't like jazz, and the mysteries of pinochle were too deep for me. So I resorted to reading as a way to ease the dangerous mental strain during training. I found that books were something in which I could lose myself and get my mind off the future fight—like *The Way of All Flesh,* which Brian Bell of the Associated Press found me reading while training for Dempsey.

Hitherto, as just another prizefighter, my personal and training camp habits had been of little news interest, and nobody had bothered to find out whether I read books or not. Now, as the challenger for the heavyweight title, I was in a glare of publicity, and the disclosure that I read books, literature, Shakespeare, was a headline. The exquisite twist was when one of Dempsey's principal camp followers saw the newspaper story. He hurried to Jack with a roar of mirth. "It's in the bag, Champ. The so-and-so is up there reading a book!"

The yarn grew with the telling—training for Dempsey on Shakespeare. It simplified itself down to the standing joke—Tunney, the great Shakespearean. This put the finishing touch to the laugh over my prospects in the ring with Dempsey.

It made me angry and resentful. I was an earnest young man with a proper amount of professional pride. The ridicule hurt. It might have injured my chances. To be consigned so unanimously to certain and abject defeat might have been intimidating, might have impaired confidence. What saved me from that was my stubborn belief in the correctness of my logic. The laugh, in fact, helped to defeat itself and bring about the very thing that it ridiculed. It could only tend to make the champion overconfident.

For a boxer there's nothing more dangerous than to underestimate an opponent. Jack Dempsey was not one to underestimate. It was not his habit of mind to belittle an antagonist. He was far too intelligent for that. In fact, Jack rather tended to underestimate himself. With all his superb abilities in the ring, he was never arrogant or cocky, never too sure of himself. But not even Jack Dempsey could escape the influence of opinion so overwhelming, such mockery as "It's in the bag, Champ. The so-and-so is up there reading a book." That could help my strategy of a surprise blow to knock him out or daze him for the rest of the fight.

When we finally got into the ring at Philadelphia things went so much according to plan that they were almost unexciting to me. During the first minute of sparring, I feinted Dempsey a couple of times, and then lashed out with the right-hand punch, the hardest blow I ever deliberately struck. It failed to knock him out. Jack was tough, a hard man to flatten. His fighting style was such that it was difficult to tag him on the jaw. He fought in a crouch, with his chin tucked down behind his left shoulder. I hit him high, on the cheek. He was shaken, dazed. His strength, speed, and accuracy were reduced. Thereafter it was a methodical matter of outboxing him, foiling his rushes, piling up points, clipping him with repeated, damaging blows, correct sparring.

There was an element of the unexpected—rain. It drizzled and showered intermittently throughout the fight. The ring was wet and slippery, the footing insecure. That was bad for a boxer like me, who depended on speed and sureness of foot for maneuvering. One false step with Jack Dempsey might bring oblivion. On the other hand, the slippery ring also worked to the disadvantage of the champion. A hitter needs secure footing from which to drive his punches, and any small uncertainty underfoot may rob him of his power. So the rain was an even thing except that it might have the therapeutic value of a shower for a dazed man, and Dempsey was somewhat dazed during the ten rounds. Jack was battered and worn out at the end, and I might have knocked him out if the bout had gone a few rounds more. The decision was automatic, and I was heavyweight champion of the world.

The real argument of the decade grew out of my second bout with Dempsey at Chicago, the following year—the "long count" controversy. It produced endless talk, sense and nonsense, logic and illogic. To this day in any barroom you can work up a wrangle on the subject of the long count. How long was Tunney on the floor after Dempsey knocked him down? Could he have got up if the count had been normal?

To me the mystery has always been how Dempsey contrived to hit me as he did. In a swirl of action, a wild mix-up with things happening fast, Jack might have nailed the most perfect boxer that ever blocked or side-stepped a punch, he was that swift and accurate a hitter. But what happened to me did not occur in any dizzy confusion of flying fists. In an ordinary exchange Dempsey simply stepped in and hit me with a left hook.

It was in the seventh round. I had been outboxing Jack all the way. He hadn't hurt me, hadn't hit me with any effect. I wasn't dazed or tired. I was sparring in my best form, when he lashed out.

For a boxer of any skill to be hit with a left swing in a commonplace maneuver of sparring is sheer disgrace. It was Dempsey's most effective blow, the one thing you'd watch for—you'd better, for the Dempsey left, as prize-ring history relates, was murder. I knew how to evade it, side-step or jab him with a left and beat him to the punch. I had been doing that all along.

I didn't see the left coming. So far as I was concerned, it came out of nowhere. That embarrassed me more than anything else—not to mention the damage done. It was a blow to pride as well as to the jaw. I was vain of my eyesight. My vision in the ring was always excellent. I used to think I could see a punch coming almost before it started. If there was anything I could rely on, it was my sharpness of eye—and I utterly failed to see that left swing.

The only explanation I have ever been able to think of is that in a training bout I had sustained an injury to my right eye. A sparring partner had poked me in the eye with thumb extended. I was rendered completely blind for an instant, and after some medical treatment was left with astigmatism which could easily have caused a blind spot, creating an area in which there was no vision. Our relative positions, when Dempsey hit me, must have been such that the left swing came up into the blind spot, and I never saw it.

With all his accuracy and power Dempsey hit me flush on the jaw, the button. I was knocked dizzy. Whereupon he closed for the kill, and that meant fighting fury at its most destructive. When Dempsey came in for a knockout he came with all his speed and power. I didn't know then how many times he slugged me. I had to look at the motion pictures the next day to find out. There were seven crashing blows, Dempsey battering me with left and right as I fell against the ropes, collapsing to a sitting position on the canvas.

Of what ensued during the next few seconds, I knew nothing. I was oblivious of the most debated incident of the long count and had to be told later on what happened.

The story went back to the Dempsey-Firpo fight, to that wild first round during which Firpo hit the floor in one knock-down after another. This was in New York, where the rule was that a boxer scoring a knock-down must go to a neutral corner and remain there until the referee had completed the count. In the ring with the Wild Bull of the Pampas, Dempsey undoubtedly through excitement of battle violated that rule, as the motion pictures showed clearly afterward.

Jack confesses he remembers nothing that took place during that entire fight. Firpo landed a terrific first blow. Dempsey, after suffering a first-blow knock-down, apparently jumped up to the fray by sheer professional instinct—the fighting heart of a true champion. Instead of going to a corner, Jack would stand over Firpo and slug him as he got up. After one knock-down, Jack stepped over his prostrate opponent to the other side, to get a better shot at him—the referee was in the way. After another knock-down, Dempsey slugged Firpo before the South American had got his hands off the floor, when he was still technically down. The Champ might well have been disqualified for that—not to mention the fact that he was pushed back into the ring when Firpo battered him out. The referee, however, in his confusion permitted all the violations.

The Dempsey-Firpo brawl aroused a storm of protest and brought about a determination that in the future Dempsey should be kept strictly to the rules. In our Chicago bout the regulation applied—go to a neutral corner upon scoring a knock-down. The refereee had been especially instructed to enforce this. He was told that, in case of a knock-down, he was not to begin a count until the boxer who had scored the knock-down had gone to a neutral corner.

This was the reason for the long count. Dempsey, having battered me to the canvas, stood over me to hit me the moment I got up—if I did get up. The referee ordered him to a neutral corner. He didn't go. The referee, in accordance with instructions, refrained from giving count until he did go. That imposed on Jack a penalty of four seconds. It was that long before he went to the corner and the referee began the count.

When I regained full consciousness, the count was at two. I knew nothing of what had gone on, was only aware that the referee was counting two over me. What a surprise! I had eight seconds in which to get up. My head was clear. I had trained hard and well, as I always did, and had that invaluable asset—condition. In the proverbial pink, I recovered quickly from the shock of the battering I had taken. I thought—what now? I'd take the full count, of course. Nobody but a fool fails to do that. I felt all right, and had no doubt about being able to get up. The question was what to do when I was back on my feet.

I never had been knocked down before. In all the ring battles and training bouts I had engaged in, I had never previously been on the canvas. But I had always thought about the possibility, and had always planned before each bout what to do if I were knocked down, what strategy to use upon getting up. That depended on the kind of opponent.

I had thought the question out carefully in the case of Jack Dempsey. If he were to knock me down, he would, when I got up, rush me to apply the finisher. He would be swift and headlong about it. Should I try to clinch and thus gain some seconds of breathing space? That's familiar strategy for a boxer after a knock-down. Often it's the correct strategy—

but not against Dempsey, I figured. He hit too hard and fast with short punches for it to be at all safe to close for a clinch. He might knock me out.

Another possibility was to get set and hit him as he rushed. That can be effective against a fighter who, having scored a knock-down, comes tearing in wide open, a mark for a heavy blow. If you are strong upon getting to your feet, you can sometimes turn the tables by throwing everything into a punch. Bob Fitzsimmons often did it. But that wouldn't do against Dempsey, I reckoned. He was too tough and hit too hard. He would welcome a slugging match. After having been knocked down, I might not be in any shape to take the risk of stepping in and hitting him.

For my second bout with Dempsey the plan that I decided upon, in case I was knocked down, was based on the thing I had learned about Jack. Word from his training camp had indicated that his legs were none too good. I had learned that his trainers had been giving him special exercises for footwork, because he had slowed down in the legs. That was the cue—match my legs against his, keep away from him, depend on speed of foot, let him chase me until I was sure I had recovered completely from the knock-down.

The plan would work if my own legs were in good shape, after the battering I had taken. That was what I had to think about on the floor in Chicago. My legs felt all right. At the count of nine I got up. My legs felt strong and springy.

Jack came tearing in for the kill. I stepped away from him, moving to my left—circling away from his left hook. As I side-stepped swiftly, my legs had never been better. What I had heard about Dempsey's legs was true. As I circled away from him, he tried doggedly, desperately, to keep up with me—but he was slow. The strategy was okay—keep away from him until I was certain that all the effects of the knockdown had worn off. Once, in sheer desperation, Jack stopped in his tracks and growled at me to stand and fight.

I did—but later, when I knew that my strength, speed, and reflexes were complete normal. I started to close with him and hit him with the encyclopedia of boxing. Presently Dempsey's legs were so heavy that he couldn't move with any agility at all, and I was able to hit him virtually at will. He was almost helpless when the final bell rang—sticking it out with stubborn courage.

I have often been asked—could I have got up and carried on as I did without those extra four seconds on the long count? I don't know. I can only say that at the count of two I came to, and felt in good shape. I had eight seconds to go. Without the long count, I would have had four seconds to go. Could I, in that space of time, have got up? I'm quite sure that I could have. When I regained consciousness after the brief period of black-out, I felt that I could have jumped up immediately and matched my legs against Jack's, just as I did.

The long count controversy, with all the heated debate, produced a huge public demand for another Dempsey-Tunney fight, number three. Tex Rickard was eager to stage it. He knew, as everybody else did, that it would draw the biggest gate ever. The first Dempsey-Tunney fight grossed over a million seven hundred thousand; the second, over two million and a half. Rickard was sure a third would draw three million. I was willing, eager. I planned to retire after another championship bout, wanted to get all that I could out of it.

But Jack refused. He was afraid of going blind. The battering he had taken around the eyes in his two fights with me alarmed him. The very thing that kept him from being hit on the jaw, his style of holding his chin down behind his shoulder, caused punches to land high. He dreaded the horror that has befallen so many ring fighters and is the terror of them all—the damage that comes from too many punches around the eyes, blindness.

Jack Dempsey was a great fighter—possibly the greatest that ever entered a ring. Looking back objectively, one has to conclude that he was more valuable to the sport or "The Game" than any prizefighter of his time. Whether you consider it from his worth as a gladiator or from the point of view of the box office, he was tops. His name in his most glorious days was magic among his people, and today, twenty years after, the name Jack Dempsey is still magic. This tells a volume in itself. As one who has always had pride in his profession as well as his professional theories, and possessing a fair share of Celtic romanticism, I wish that we could have met when we were both at our unquestionable best. We could have decided many questions, to me the most important of which is whether "a good boxer can always lick a good fighter."

I still say yes.

Running as a Spiritual Experience

Mike Spino

Weather is different every day; running has its shades of sunshine and rain. At Syracuse I ran daily in the worst weather imaginable. Because of the hard winter, my running mate and I had an agreement that we would never talk while running. Snow covered many of the roads, so out of convenience, with only slight variation, we ran the same course almost every day. After classes we would return to our rooms and prepare to run. To watch us get ready, you would have thought us looney. First, there was long underwear, shorts, and hood. Next socks for hands and feet and navy caps. The run was always better because you could think of a warm shower, and know that the nervous feeling preceding the daily task of running would be gone.

Eastern winters linger into spring, but one day the sun shone in a different way. Snow still curbing the road, but the inside pavement, where the black-brown dirt met cement, looked almost bounceable. Earlier in the day the spirit of approaching spring made us, my coach, my running mate, and I decide on a formidable venture. At a place beginning in the mountains and ending in a valley near the city, we had a six mile stretch which was part of a longer, twenty mile course. We decided to run the six miles as fast as possible. The plan was for Jack, our coach, to trail us with his car, and sound his horn as we passed each mile. Marty, my running mate, was to run the first three miles, jump in the car for the next two, and finish the last mile with me. We traveled to the starting point which was out of the sunshine into the late afternoon mist. Jack suggested a time schedule he thought we could run. I was sure I couldn't keep the pace; Marty said nothing, taking an "if you think you can do it I'll try, since I'm not running the whole way" attitude.

Almost even before we started, cars began to back up behind Jack's car, but he continued to drive directly behind us, and the cars soon tired of sounding horns and drove around all three of us. From my first step I felt lighter and looser than ever before. My thin shirt clung to me, and I felt like a skeleton flying down a wind tunnel. My times at the mile and two miles were so fast that I almost felt I was cheating, or had taken some unfair advantage. It was like getting a new body that no one else had heard about. My mind was so crystal clear I could have held a conversation. The only sensation was the rhythm and the beat; all perfectly natural, all and everything part of everything else. Marty told me later that he could feel the power I was radiating. He said I was frightening.

Marty jumped back into the car. There were three miles to go; it was still pure pleasure. A car darted from a side street, I had to decide how to react, and do it, both at the same time. I decided to outrun the car to the end of the intersection. The car skidded and almost hit Jack's car, but somehow we got out of danger and had two miles to run. The end of the fourth and the start of the fifth mile was the beginning of crisis. My legs lost their bounce: I struggled to keep my arms low, so they wouldn't swing across my chest and cut off the free passage of air. My mind concentrated on only one thing: to keep the rhythm. If I could just flick my legs at the same cadence for a few more minutes I would run a fast time.

Slowly I realized I was getting loose again. I knew then I could run the last mile strongly. Perhaps, there is such a thing as second wind. Whatever, Marty jumped from the car when a mile remained, but after a few hundred yards he couldn't keep pace, so he jumped back in.

In the last half mile something happened which may have occurred only one or two times before or since. Furiously I ran; time lost all semblance of meaning. Distance, time, motion were all one. There were myself, the cement, a vague feeling of legs, and the coming dusk. I tore on. Jack had planned to sound the horn first when a quarter mile remained, and then again at the completion of the six miles. The first sound barely reached my consciousness. My running was a pouring feeling. The final horn sounded. I kept on running. I could have run and run. Perhaps I had experienced a physiological change, but whatever, it was magic. I came to the side of the road and gazed, with a sort of bewilderment, at my friends. I sat on the side of the road and cried tears of joy and sorrow. Joy at being alive; sorrow for a vague feeling of temporalness, and a knowledge of the impossibility of giving this experience to anyone.

We got back into the car and drove. Everyone knew something special, strange, and mystically wonderful had happened. At first no one spoke. Jack reminded us that the time I had run was phenomenal compared to my previous times. At first we thought Jack's odometer might be incorrect, so we drove to a local track and measured a quarter mile. It measured correctly. On the way home, I asked Jack if he would stop at a grass field, near our house. I wanted to savor the night air; I wanted to see if the feeling remained. It did, and it didn't. I have never understood what occurred that late afternoon: whether it was just a fine run, combined with dusk, as winter was finally breaking, or finding out who and what I was through a perfect expression of my own art form. It still remains a mystery.

part 3

Sideline Boos and Cheers: Social and Cultural Criticism

The role of the athlete in society has been controversial from the Golden Age of Greece to the present. In general, arguments have centered on the question of emphasis: whether society should stress mind over body or the reverse. Specific arguments have been concerned with amateurism versus professionalism, women in sports, athletics as part of the educational process, the athlete and the state, racism in sports, and sport as an art form. All of these are dealt with in the essays that follow. Like fiction, nonfiction has reflected the nature and direction of sports in society. It has also, from time to time, exerted an influence that has shaped social attitudes toward sports. Baldassare Castiglione's advice to a Renaissance courtier, for instance, was instrumental in defining the sports suitable for gentlemen. To choose a more contemporary instance, Theodore Roosevelt's ringing defense of the strenuous life helped to preserve college football, which at the time was threatened because of excessive violence and laxity in the enforcement of rules. The question of violence in sports is again raised by Norman Mailer in "The Death of Benny Paret." Regardless of the issues, the ceaseless boos and cheers from the sidelines leave little doubt that sports are a microcosm of the larger world in which we all function.

Wisdom over Strength

Xenophanes

But even if one should win a victory by swiftness of foot, or in the pentathlon, there where is the precinct of Zeus beside the streams of the fountain of Pisa in Olympia, or in wrestling, or in painful boxing, or in the dread struggle which men call the pancratium, and should become a more glorious spectacle for his fellow citizens to behold, and should win a conspicuous seat of honor in athletic contests, and should receive his food at public expense, and a gift which would be a treasure to him; yes, even if he won a victory with racehorses . . . though he should gain all this, yet would he not be as worthy as I. For our wisdom is a better thing than strength of men and of horses. But this is a most unreasonable custom, and it is not right to honor strength above excellent wisdom. For even if there should be a good boxer among the folk, or a champion in the pentathlon, or in wrestling, or in swiftness of foot, which is the most honored exhibition of strength among all the contests of men in games, the state would not on that account be any the more law-abiding. But little would be the state's joy, if a man should win a victory in athletics by the banks of Pisa; for these things do not make rich the store chambers of a state.

Translated by W. A. OLDFATHER

Female Athletes

Juvenal

from SATIRE VI

And what about female athletes, with their purple
Track-suits, and scented oils? Not to mention our lady-fencers—
We've all seen *them*, stabbing the stump with a foil,
Shield well advanced, going through the proper motions:
Just the right training needed to blow a matronly horn
At the Floral Festival—unless they have higher ambitions,
And the goal of all their practice is the real arena.
But then, what modesty can be looked for in some
Helmeted hoyden, a renegade from her sex,
Who thrives on masculine violence—yet would not prefer
To *be* a man, since the pleasure is so much less?
What a fine sight for some husband—*it might be you*—his wife's
Equipment put up at auction, baldric, armlet, plumes
And one odd shinguard! Or if the other style
Of fighting takes her fancy, imagine your delight when
The dear girl sells off her greaves! (And yet these same women
Have such delicate skins that even sheer silk chafes them;
They sweat in the finest chiffon.) Hark how she snorts
At each practice thrust, bowed down by the weight of her helmet;
See the big coarse puttees wrapped round her ample hams—
Then wait for the laugh, when she lays her weapons aside
And squats on the potty! Tell me, you noble ladies,
Scions of our great statesmen—Lepidus, blind Metellus,
Fabius the Guzzler—what gladiator's woman
Ever rigged herself out like this, or sweated at fencing-drill?

Translated by PETER GREEN

Cheerleader

Jim Wayne Miller

Seventeen and countless times french-kissed,
her body marbled milk and honey, bread
and wine on tongues at half-time Eucharist,
she takes the floor to be distributed.

Jammed bleachers all at once are smitten dumb
Deliciously she sways; her metered cheers
ricochet off girders in the gym;
they fall like sibyls' leaves over the tiers.

She spins; her skirt, gathering speed, whirls,
floats off her dimpled knees slender thighs
snug red panties—stands, falls.
The sweating crowd speaks tongues and prophecies.

from The Book of the Courtier

Baldassare Castiglione

The Count now paused a little, and messer Bernardo Bibbiena said, laughing:

"I remember what you said earlier, that this Courtier of ours must be endowed by nature with beauty of countenance and person, and with a grace that shall make him so agreeable. Grace and beauty of countenance I think I certainly possess, and this is the reason why so many ladies are ardently in love with me, as you know; but I am rather doubtful as to the beauty of my person, especially as regards these legs of mine, which seem to me decidedly less well proportioned than I should wish: as to my bust and other members however, I am quite content. Pray, now, describe a little more in particular the sort of body that the Courtier is to have, so that I may dismiss this doubt and set my mind at rest."

After some laughter at this, the Count continued:

"Of a certainty that grace of countenance can be truly said to be yours, nor need I cite further example than this to show what manner of thing it is, for we unquestionably perceive your aspect to be most agreeable and pleasing to everyone, albeit the lineaments of it are not very delicate. Still it is of a manly cast and at the same time full of grace; and this characteristic is to be found in many different types of countenance. And of such sort I would have our Courtier's aspect; not so soft and effeminate as is sought by many, who not only curl their hair and pluck their brows, but gloss their faces with all those arts employed by the most wanton and unchaste women in the world; and in their walk, posture and every act, they seem so limp and languid that their limbs are like to fall apart; and they pronounce their words so mournfully that they appear about to expire upon the spot: and the more they find themselves with men of rank, the more they affect such tricks. Since nature has not made them women, as they seem to wish to appear and be, they should be treated not as good women but as public harlots, and driven not merely from the courts of great lords but from the society of honest men.

"Then coming to the bodily frame, I say it is enough if this be neither extremely short nor tall, for both of these conditions excite a certain contemptuous surprise, and men of either sort are gazed upon in much the same way that we gaze on monsters. Yet if we must offend in one of the two extremes, it is preferable to fall a little short of the just measure of height than to exceed it, for besides often being dull of intellect, men thus huge of body are also unfit for every exercise of agility, which thing I should much wish in the Courtier. And so I would have him well built and shapely of limb, and would have him show strength and lightness and suppleness, and know all bodily exercises that befit a man of war; whereof I think the first should be to handle every sort of weapon well on foot and on horse, to understand the advantages of each, and especially to be familiar with those weapons that are ordinarily used among gentlemen; for besides the use of them in war, where such subtlety in contrivance is perhaps not needful, there frequently arise differences between one gentleman and another, which afterwards result in duels often fought with such weapons as happen at the moment to be within reach: thus knowledge of this kind is a very safe thing. Nor am I one of those who say that skill is forgotten in the hour of need; for he whose skill forsakes him at such a time, indeed gives token that he has already lost heart and head through fear.

"Moreover I deem it very important to know how to wrestle, for it is a great help in the use of all kinds of weapons on foot. Then, both for his own sake and for that of his friends, he must understand the quarrels and differences that may arise, and must be quick to seize an advantage, always showing courage and prudence in all things. Nor should he be too ready to fight except when honour demands it; for besides the great danger that the uncertainty of fate entails, he who rushes into such affairs recklessly and without urgent cause, merits the severest censure even though he be successful. But when he finds himself so far engaged that he cannot withdraw without reproach, he ought to be most deliberate, both in the preliminaries to the duel and in the duel itself, and always show readiness and daring. Nor must he act like some, who fritter the affair away in disputes and controversies, and who, having the choice of weapons, select those that neither cut nor pierce, and arm themselves as if they were expecting a cannonade; and thinking it enough not to be defeated, stand ever on the defensive and retreat,—showing therein their utter cowardice. And thus they make themselves a laughing-stock for boys, like those two men of Ancona who fought at Perugia not long since, and made everyone laugh who saw them."

"And who were they?" asked my lord Gaspar Pallavicino.

"Two cousins," replied messer Cesare.

Then the Count said:

"In their fighting they were as like as two brothers;" and soon continued: "Even in time of peace weapons are often used in various exercises, and gentlemen appear in public shows before the people and ladies and great lords. For this reason I would have our Courtier a perfect horseman in every kind of seat; and besides understanding horses and what pertains to riding, I would have him use all possible care and diligence to lift himself a little beyond the rest in everything, so that he may be ever recognized as eminent above all others. And as we read of Alcibiades that he surpassed all the nations with whom he lived, each in their particular province, so I would have this Courtier of ours excel all others, and each in that which is most their profession. And as it is the especial pride of the Italians to ride well with the rein, to govern wild horses with consummate skill, and to play at tilting and jousting,—in these things let him be among the best of the Italians. In tourneys and in the arts of defence and attack, let him shine among the best in France. In stick-throwing, bull-fighting, and in casting spears and darts, let him excel among the Spaniards. But above everything he should temper all his movements with a certain good judgment and grace, if he wishes to merit that universal favour which is too greatly prized.

"There are also many other exercises, which although not immediately dependent upon arms, yet are closely connected therewith, and greatly foster manly sturdiness; and one of the chief among these seems to me to be the chase, because it bears a certain likeness to war: and truly it is an amusement for great lords and befitting a man at court, and furthermore it is seen to have been much cultivated among the ancients. It is fitting also to know how to swim, to leap, to run, to throw stones, for besides the use that may be made of this in war, a man often has occasion to show what he can do in such matters; whence good esteem is to be won, especially with the multitude, who must be taken into account withal. Another admirable exercise, and one very befitting a man at court, is the game of tennis, in which are well shown the disposition of the body, the quickness and suppleness of every member, and all those qualities that are seen in nearly every other exercise. Nor less highly do I esteem vaulting on horse, which although it be fatiguing and difficult, makes a man very light and dexterous more than any other thing; and besides its utility, if this lightness is accompanied by grace, it is to my thinking a finer show than any of the others.

"Our Courtier having once become more than fairly expert in these exercises, I think he should leave the others on one side: such as turning summersaults, rope-walking, and the like, which savour of the mountebank and little befit a gentleman.

"But since one cannot devote himself to such fatiguing exercises continually, and since repetition becomes very tiresome and abates the admiration felt for what is rare, we must always diversify our life with various occupations. For this reason I would have our Courtier sometimes descend to quieter and more tranquil exercises, and in order to escape envy and to entertain himself agreeably with everyone, let him do whatever others do, yet never departing from praiseworthy deeds, and governing himself with that good judgment which will keep him from all folly; but let him laugh, jest, banter, frolic and dance, yet in such fashion that he shall always appear genial and discreet, and that everything he may do or say shall be stamped with grace."

Translated by Leonard Eckstein Opdycke

Value of an Athletic Training

Theodore Roosevelt

One of the many strong points in General Francis Walker's admirable Harvard address was the stress he laid upon the immense benefit conferred by the practice of athletics, whether in football, baseball, rowing, or on the track, on college students (and of course on boys and young men generally) who do not stand in the first rank as champions. No persons are more benefited by athletic sports than those men who never attain to the first rank in them; who may try for class crew, a class eleven, or a class nine, but who do not get on save possibly in an emergency as a substitute; and who, when they take part in running or jumping, wrestling or boxing contests, now and then win a trial, but hardly ever a final, heat.

General Walker's address is good reading just at this time in view of the noisy crusade which is being carried on against athletic sports generally and football in particular. Most sane persons are agreed as to the great good conferred by these sports, both upon the average man taking part in them and upon the community at large. Very emphatically we do not approve of brutality of any kind. We firmly believe, for instance, that the present football rules should be amended at two or three important points so as to reduce the danger in the game. Moreover, we believe that the students themselves, and if they refuse, then the graduates and the faculties of the different colleges, should insist upon the umpires putting a peremptory stop to any kind of slugging or kindred brutality in the game. Any man who has had experience in umpiring a game like polo, for instance, is able to guarantee that a resolute umpire can immediately stop reckless and brutal playing, or the efforts of a player to damage an opponent, by the simple exercise of wise and prompt severity, ruling the offender off the field at once and penalizing heavily the side on whose behalf the offense is committed. In the same way there is no difficulty whatever in making athletes study. All faculties should insist upon the students who take part in athletic games not neglecting their studies, and if there is any tendency toward this neglect, it is perfectly simple to stop it immediately by refusing to allow a man to play on an eleven if he does not reach a certain standard in his marks.

However, while thus utterly opposed to certain of the tendencies that have crept into our athletics, and notably into the game of football, we are equally emphatic in our belief that these sports are good things for the men taking part in them, and for our people generally, and that in particular it would be a real misfortune to lose the game of football. Much of the feeling against the game, and against athletics too, has been stirred up by the persistent and very foolish attacks upon them made by various newspapers, the *Evening Post* being the chief, and, on the whole, the least rational offender. Such attacks as those in the *Post* are in part due to ignorance, and in part to the fact that some persons who are by nature timid, shrink from the exercise of manly and robust qualities if there is any chance of its being accompanied by physical pain. They are also due in part to that striving after sensationalism, that spirit of breezy, enterprising journalism, which is so unwholesome a characteristic of a portion of our press.

It is perfectly true that our young men should not go to college merely to get their bodies trained, but it is also true that they should not go there merely to get their intellects trained. Far above bodily strength, far above mere learning comes character. No soundness of body and limb, no excellence of mental training—admirable though each of these is—can atone for the lack of what in old fashioned phrase would be called the virtues;

for the lack of courage, of honesty, of self control, of temperance, of steadfast resolution, of readiness to stand up for one's rights, and carefulness not to infringe on the rights of others. Now of course many of these qualities are not conferred by athletic exercises any more than they are conferred by the study of Latin or Greek; but there are others which certain courses of study do tend to bring out, and yet others which are most undoubtedly strengthened and developed by the demands made upon them in playing the rougher and manlier sports, especially outdoor sports. In a perfectly peaceful and commercial civilization such as ours there is always a danger of laying too little stress upon the more manly virtues—upon the virtues which go to make up a race of statesmen and soldiers, of pioneers and explorers by land and sea, of bridge-builders and road-makers, of commonwealth builders—in short, upon those virtues for the lack of which, whether in an individual or in a nation, no amount of refinement and learning, of gentleness and culture, can possibly atone. These are the very qualities which are fostered by vigorous, manly out of door sports, such as mountaineering, big game hunting, riding, shooting, rowing, football, and kindred games.

Of course if these sports are carried to an excess they do harm exactly as excessive study or excessive devotion to business does harm; and equally, of course, they are beneficial very largely in proportion to the extent to which they are followed and shared in by the classes of our population which must feel their need. Professional sports are of small consequence, and, in so far as they have any consequence at all, are good merely in that they excite those who look on and admire the performances to try to take part in similar ones of their own. It is a good thing that the young merchant or lawyer, young bank clerk or dry goods clerk, should belong to a local baseball nine, and should have a chance now and then for an hour or two's brisk exercise. This will give tone both to his body and his mind, and will offset the evil consequences of a merely sedentary occupation. But the only good resulting from seeing a battle between two paid professional nines is the emulation excited in the minds of the younger portion of the onlookers to try their own hands at the bat.

The great development and wide diffusion and practice of athletic exercises among our people during the last quarter of a century (this diffusion taking place precisely among those classes where the need of it was greatest) has been a very distinct advantage to our national type. Only the other day Mr. John Burroughs, in speaking upon this very point, dwelt upon the improved physique of the young American of the present day as compared with his predecessor of twenty-five years back. This is as it should be. It would be an ill thing for this republic if we developed on the lines of the Byzantine and Bengalese, if our mercantile men learned nothing but how to make money, and our lawyers, students, and men of trained intellects generally, grew to unite "the heads of professors with the hearts of hares."

Turn for a moment to the colleges, and especially to the college of the ordinary type, where men are taught the classics, mathematics, etc., rather than to the purely professional schools for lawyers, doctors, and civil engineers. It is rather amusing to see athletics objected to on what are in part the same grounds as those held by the people who object to collegiate education in toto—on the theory that it is not fitted to make men succeed better in after-life. As a matter of fact, only a limited number of the men who study classics and mathematics, philosophy, history, and modern languages, in our undergraduate academic departments, ever have the chance in after-life to turn the knowledge thus acquired to their own direct pecuniary advantage. Yet who can measure the inestimable benefit these studies confer? The average graduate makes no more use in his regular business of Latin and Greek than of football or rowing. The exceptions to this are of course those men who intend to become specialists in some branch of study, and pass a life as students of history, literature, or science, of Greek or Latin, or as professors and school teachers. Of course, to these men the knowledge gained in college is of direct pecuniary benefit, while whatever they did in athletic sports might not be, though even for these men the benefit resulting from athletic sports would be very great. Exactly as Parkman could not possibly have written history as he did had he not been himself fond of and familiar with the wild life he portrayed, so, apart from the benefit to the health of the professor or school teacher who has taken part in athletic work and appreciates its importance, there is also a very real benefit to those who come under him. Other things being equal, boys will be taught best by and will receive most benefit from their intercourse with professors and principals at schools and at colleges who in addition to being students are also men who have a hearty love for life, who are strong as well as gentle, and brave and tender and honest as well as learned.

For the great bulk of the boys in college, then, there is almost as little direct pecuniary benefit to be obtained from the lectures and recitations as from the sports. The effect to be looked for is the indirect effect upon the boy's character. Most assuredly he should be made to study well, and should be turned out of college if he won't study. He should be made as familiar as possible with the great literature—the Greek and the English or, if his tastes lie that way, with the lesser literatures such as the Latin, the Italian, the French, the Spanish, or the German. He should be taught the histories of the great peoples—the Romans, for instance, and the men of English stock who have risen to the foremost places for the deeds they have done in conquest and in government, in politics, in war, and in jurisprudence. Every effort should be made to develop the intellectual side of the boy's character. No one can more strenuously insist upon this than we do. But we believe also that we should try to develop the boy's body, and, above all, should try to develop the simple but all-essential traits which go to make up manliness.

Even if we look at the question only from the standpoint of the student it is probable that there is no just ground for the complaints against athletics. Investigation of the records made by athletes at Harvard a few years ago disclosed the fact that their average standing was above that of the rest of the class. My own observation leads me to believe that this will hold true as a general rule, for though athletes may stand below the hard-working men who know nothing but study, they usually stand well above the men of vicious or fibreless character, who naturally fall to the foot of the class.

If, on the other hand, we adopt the standpoint of the man who looks to the results in after-life, the athlete appears to even better advantage. The men who take part in vigorous sports, whether they attain to the first rank, or merely stand among those who get no particular honor at the time, but have nearly as much fun and just as much ultimate benefit, are apt in after-life to do rather better in the rough work of the world than those of their fellows who had no taste for athletic work. Of course there are exceptions to this, and it does not apply at all to those who follow sport for their business.

One very great benefit of athletic sports arises from their tendency to minimize dissipation. They have been very potent allies in the fight against debauchery. Another good thing is that they tend to lessen the importance of the merely social clubs, and of "popular" leaders in the different colleges. If the victorious athlete sometimes eclipses the glory that rightfully belongs to the hard student, it is yet true, on the other hand, that he also throws into the shade the old time college hero who strove to obtain leadership by his wealth, his social position, or his prominence in fast life. This is, of course, an unadulterated benefit, especially to the boy's after-career. Looking over the men whom I knew in my day at college, it is noteworthy that those who then were leaders in athletic sports, now, twelve or fifteen years afterwards, stand on the average above rather than below their fellows who did not take part in manly exercises; just exactly as on the average the men who stood well in their studies then now occupy a position, as a rule, rather better than that of those who did not. There are many exceptions to both rules, of course, and it is a very melancholy thing to see a man who in middle life rests his sole title to consideration upon the fact that he was once a member of a university team, or was once a man who was marked highest in his Latin courses; but these are exceptions only, and they are not much more exceptional among the athletes than among the hard students. To take the sports which it is at present the fashion most to decry, football and rowing, among my friends I happen to number several ex-captains of football teams and of crews, and they are, as a whole, decidedly above, not below, the ordinary standard of college graduates; they are men who do their duty well, both to the State and to their own families—men who are, in short, good American citizens.

Of course there is a real danger just at present in the exaggerated regard felt by the public generally for the athletic hero of the moment. The captain of a successful football team or a winning crew is in danger of having his head turned. The year after graduation is rather a hard one for a young fellow, who may be a very decent young fellow, but who, because he happens to have been captain of a winning team, has shared newspaper prominence with Senators and members of the President's cabinet. He has got to drop, and drop hard, before he becomes of any use in the world; and having the "tuck" taken out of him will not prove pleasant—it never does prove pleasant. If in this process he succumbs, and if he does nothing in later life, and lives on the memories of the past, and fails to realize that an admirable exercise for a boy must under no circumstances be made the main business of a man, why, then he becomes a mere useless cumberer of the world's surface, and the sooner he is removed the better. Ordinarily, however, he goes through the disagreeable process all right, although with more or less discomfort to himself and to his friends, and comes out at the end a better man than if he had never had the experience.

Athletic sports, then, are of great benefit not only to the student as a student, but to the college graduate who wants to play a man's part in life, provided, always, that he does not fall into the foolish mistake of confounding that healthful play which best fits a man for serious work with the serious work itself. He will do well to keep in mind the career of Washington, who was a devoted fox hunter, and whose fox hunting doubtless helped to make him a good general in after-life, but who never for a moment sought to carry on fox hunting to the damage of any serious business, whether of war, of politics, or of his private affairs.

Granting that athletic sports do good, it remains to be considered what athletic sports are the best. The answer to this is obvious. They are those sports which call for the greatest exercise of fine moral qualities, such as resolution, courage, endurance, and capacity to hold one's own and to stand up under punishment. For this reason out-of-door sports are better than gymnastics and calisthenics. To be really beneficial the sport must be enjoyed by the participator. Much more health will be gained by the man who is not always thinking of his health than by the poor being who is forever wondering whether he has helped his stomach or his lungs, or developed this or that muscle. Laborious work in the gymnasium, directed towards the fulfilling of certain tests of skill or strength, is very good in its way; but the man who goes through it does not begin to get the good he would in a season's play with an eleven or a nine on the gridiron field or the diamond. The mere fact that the moral qualities are not needed in the one case, but are all the time called into play in the other, is sufficient to show the little worth of the calisthenic system of gymnastic development when compared with rough outdoor games. The other day there was published in the papers a list of the twenty-five strongest men in Harvard, as shown by tests used in the gymnasium, together with a casual mention of the fact that not one of the crew of the football eleven was included in these twenty-five. This fact, if true, was sufficient to destroy much of the value of such a table. There is little point in the mere development of strength. The point lies in developing a man who can do something with his strength, who not only has the skill to turn his muscles to advantage, but the heart and the head to direct that skill, and to direct it well and fearlessly. Gymnastics and calisthenics are very well in their way as substitutes when nothing better can be obtained, but the true sports for a manly race are sports like running, rowing, playing football and baseball, boxing and wrestling, shooting, riding, and mountain-climbing.

Of all these sports there is no better sport than football. A particularly silly argument advanced against it is that put forward by various people, including, to their discredit, some medical men, to the effect that it is not "Greek." These estimable gentlemen apparently think that the Greek athletes resembled the marble statues we now see of them, even to the extent of not winning their victories by blood and sweat, as all mere human beings must win them. If these gentlemen would study the Greek games, including the chariot races and the *pankration,* and then with equal disinterestedness study those of our modern American colleges, they could not help coming to the conclusion that the latter are immeasurably ahead of the former not only in the qualities of manliness and fair play, but especially in those of courtesy and generosity to the vanquished. As for the chatter about our football games being like the Roman gladiatorial shows, it is not worth discussion.

But in closing I wish to say one word very seriously to the men who have influence in athletic sports, and who share my belief in them. What I have to say with reference to all sports refers especially to football. The brutality must be done away with and the danger minimized. If necessary the college faculties must take a hand, and those of the different colleges must cooperate. The rules for football ought probably to be altered so as to do away with the present mass play, and, I think, also the present system of interference, while the umpires must be made to prevent slugging or any kind of foul play by the severest penalties. Moreover, professionalism must be stopped outright. It should be distinctly understood among the academics and colleges that no team will have anything to do with another upon which professionals are employed. If it be true that one of the Exeter teams of schoolboys has played this year with three professionals, grown men, admitted to the school for the sole purpose of playing football, then this team and academy should be cut off from all

---

pankration: a combination of wrestling and boxing, the objective of which was to force the opponent to admit defeat.

athletic intercourse with every other team and academy, and any games that have been won with these professionals on the team should in the record be declared forfeited to the other side. This is not the place in which to go into the minutiae of changing the rules so as to do away with brutality, foul play, and professionalism but every honest believer in manly sport must make war on them without ceasing.

One final word as to the element of danger. By the methods spoken of above this element of danger will be minimized, but that it will always obtain to a slight extent cannot be denied. There are very few sports, indeed, where it does not exist. Under a proper system of rules it is doubtful whether football is as dangerous as mountaineering or as the better kinds of sport on horseback, such as riding across country and playing polo. No untrained boy or man unfit to take part in the game and unacquainted with the rules should be allowed to play. If he does he is liable to meet with fatal accidents, precisely as a man would be who, with no knowledge of horsemanship, mounted a spirited horse and tried to ride him over fences. But after every precaution has been taken, then it is mere unmanliness to complain of occasional mishaps. Among my many friends who have played football I know of few who have met with serious, and none who have met with fatal, accidents; but more than one has been killed, and many have been injured, in riding to hounds, in polo, and in kindred pastimes. The sports especially dear to a vigorous and manly nation are always those in which there is a certain slight element of risk. Every effort should be made to minimize this risk, but it is mere unmanly folly to try to do away with the sport because the risk exists.

Athletics: " . . . Unquenchably the Same"?

Byron R. White

Speakers normally either entertain or they educate, educate in the sense that they review the old or instruct in the new, arouse or reassure, criticize or reaffirm. But sometimes the speaker's main function is merely to satisfy a curiosity by appearing, showing himself and making a noise or two. A college dean told me a short while ago that the students probably didn't care at all what I said; they were simply curious to see and make sure that people from the bench were human too.

What all this does to clarify my mission here is difficult to tell. Entertainment is not my line and I cannot hope to educate you experts and specialists in the areas with which you are concerned at this annual meeting. Nor am I so sure that many of you are so very curious about Justices of the Supreme Court.

Nevertheless, here I am; in any event you have the comfort of knowing that I have only a one night stand and the truth is that in accepting your invitation I acted rather impulsively. A moment of reflection would have suggested that I should not preempt this podium and deny it to others who might contribute more to your meeting. But organizations like yours, to say nothing of Williamsburg, have an hydraulic attraction for me. I knew my family and I would have a good time and we truly have.

Ladies and gentlemen, it is said in the books that Darius, the Persian king in the sixth and fifth centuries B.C., determined to conquer the Greeks, considering them to be an inferior race. He accordingly sent a spy among them to see how they trained for battle and to determine their capabilities. This spy disguised himself as a merchant and infiltrated the Greek army. What he saw was Greek soldiers, their bodies naked and oiled, practicing a variety of athletics. They did much dancing, too, clad only in a bronze shield. And they walked together, arm in arm, hand in hand. These soldiers seemed strong enough, but they sat and paid close attention when Greek poets were read aloud to them. The spy reported to Darius that the Greeks spent their time cavorting around in the nude or sitting, partially clothed, while listening to idiots propound ridiculous ideas about freedom and equality for the individual citizen.

Darius and his luxurious court were greatly amused and thought conquest of Greece would be a terribly easy job. What a rude shock it was when at Marathon the Persian army was driven out to sea. All of this was beyond the comprehension of the powerful emperor.

The same can be said of his son, Xerxes, who succeeded his father and also tried to conquer Greece. The night before his naval forces were to battle the Greeks at Salamis, word came to Xerxes that Themistocles, aboard his flagship, was in a deep discussion about certain passages in a Pindar ode. Xerxes, like his father had been, was amused. But the next day he wept when he saw his naval forces routed by the art loving Greeks whose only weapons were their virile bodies and steel minds.

I don't know how much fact or myth these stories contain but they do express a basic idea about the Greeks: For them, intellectual power and physical vigor were not incompatible but were natural allies; together they counted for much more than either one alone and even more than the sum of the individual parts.

The ancient Greeks made what were probably history's greatest contributions to philosophy, government and the arts. But at the same time, athletics were an essential part of education and training, and no other nation has ever produced so high an average of physical development as the Greeks did in the classic period. The result was a standard of athletic excellence perhaps never again equaled.

The historian Isocrates expressed the idea well when he said this: ". . . certain of our ancestors, long before our time, invented and bequeathed to us two disciplines: physical training for the body, of which gymnastics is a part, and for the mind, philosophy. These twin arts are parallel and complementary, by which their masters prepare the mind to become more intelligent and the body to become more serviceable, nor separating sharply the two kinds of education, but using similar methods of instruction, exercise and discipline."

For the Greeks, a strong body was not only of great utility for simple survival. Athletics were a joy in themselves. Strong and graceful performance was inherently satisfying. A vigorous body did much for personality and much for the mind. Moreover, physical training and competitive sports were thought productive of that sound character and noble vision so essential to wise government which was a central concern of the serious minded Greek.

The representative nature of the Panhellenic athlete and the connection of the games with the national religion perhaps explain the great honor which came to winning athletes. Whole cities turned out to welcome the returning heroes. Songs were composed and their exploits recorded on pillars of stone. Athletic poetry and art were common. Statues were raised in some public places. It became common to give substantial prizes to winning athletes, and they also enjoyed important public privileges. They were even exempted from taxation at a later date. It is probably true that the victorious athlete in Greece enjoyed a distinction such as he has never had, before or since.

But the sad story is that Greek athletes destroyed themselves. Even in those ancient days, sports without serious competition became meaningless. Competition begat specialization, trainers, coaches and winners who had time for little else. Professionalism followed, with excessive prizes and the accompanying corruption.

Even in Socrates' day, many youths were turning from sport. He once lectured a young man for his poor physical condition. The youth haughtily said he was not competing because he was an amateur. Socrates replied that there was no such thing as an amateur as far as physical condition was concerned and that it was the young man's duty to be strong and healthy.

Plato and Aristotle decried the trend. Euripides, himself fond of athletics, said, "Of all the countless evils throughout Hellas, there is none worse than the race of athletes. . . . In youth they strut about in splendor, the pride of their city, but when bitter old age comes upon them, they are cast aside like threadbare garments."

Xenophanes added these words about the athlete: "Yet he is not so worthy as I, and my wisdom is better than the strength of men and horse. Nay, this is a foolish custom, nor is it right to honor strength more than wisdom."

The historian Isocrates, whom I have quoted before, lucidly posed the problem, and he might well have written some of the speeches which are given today. "Many times," he said, "have I wondered at those who first convoked the national assemblies and established the athletic games, amazed that they should have thought the powers of men's bodies to be deserving of so great bounties, while to those who had toiled in private for the public good and trained their own minds so as to be able to help also their fellowmen, they apportioned no reward whatsoever, when in all reason they ought rather to have made provision for the latter, for if all the athletes would acquire twice the strength they now possess, the rest of the world would not be better off, but let a single man attain to wisdom and all men will reap the benefit who are willing to share his insight."

The first case of bribery in Greek athletics was reported in 388 B.C., when one boxer bribed another to give the match away. Other instances followed. It took some time, but in a span of 100 years athletics had fallen into a corrupt and deplorable state, and the country had developed into an unathletic nation of spectators. The glory and value of athletics were dead.

All of this has a familiar ring. Neither the fascination with athletics nor the problems which beset them are unique to the Greeks. Many other countries in many other periods have become heavily involved with sports, which in some instances have entered into the very social fabric of the community. The British, for example, have an old and solid commitment to athletics. Indeed, among their most valuable exports in the eighteenth and nineteenth centuries were their athletic games and all that the idea of sports implied. This tradition is very much alive today. On July 17, 1956, at the Guildhall in London in the presence of Her Majesty the Queen, the Lord Mayor interrupted the city's reception for King Faisal of Iraq to announce the score in the cricket match with Australia. And in January, 1957, there was widespread surprise, disappointment and anger that the famous football player, Stanley Matthews, had not been knighted. The New Statesman went so far as to say that Sir Anthony Eden would lose more votes over this than over the Suez Canal or petrol rationing. English athletics, of course, have their problems but their rather firm tradition of amateurism has not yet been seriously eroded by the overlay of their immensely popular professional sports.

As for ourselves, massive involvement in athletics is an obvious aspect of our culture. Our investments in facilities and manpower are astronomical at both the amateur and professional levels. Millions are engaged in some form of athletic recreation each week and millions more are spectators. Interschool and intercollege competitions are of consuming interest to large groups of people. The current group of heroes always includes a number of athletes. The professional games have grown enormously and promise great financial return. Professional football has even revolutionized family life on Sundays.

I would hesitate to assess the total picture in America. Others have tried and I refer you to them. A much narrower focus is the situation in the high schools and colleges, indeed in the handling of athletics and sports in any of our schools as part of the educational process. Here the debate has been intense and continues to be so.

The basic question, I suppose, is why we put up with physical training or athletics in any form in any of our schools or colleges. But I think this is primarily a rhetorical inquiry, for I doubt that any significant number of thinking people would advocate excising from the schools any and all forms of physical education and training. This is so for a number of reasons.

In the first place, athletic games are immense fun. Young people, given a little room, the opportunity and a minimum of intelligent supervision, can easily have an exhilarating time. And this, I must confess, I consider to be a worthy end in itself, at least for those children who live in the predominantly gray atmosphere of our great cities. Secondly, there is the matter of health and physical fitness, which are also seminal values and which need no further justification. Our gigantic health programs aimed at curing disease are perhaps limited only by the preventive measures which the young should learn at an early age, including as a primary matter the whole process of physical training and conditioning. The immediate and practical benefits of a strong and healthy body—and I am not talking here of those who make a fetish of their physiques—are very great indeed. There is a considerable difference between health on the one hand and strength and vigor on the other. I am sure you can count among your friends many who are perfectly healthy but not very energetic; who are seldom sick but tire easily; who don't seem to need a doctor but who do seem to need a rest, a nap or a coffee break; or who appear perfectly normal but wear out in the middle of that sustained, emergency effort which everyone of us has from time to time, whatever our line of work.

Appearance, demeanor and personality are equally basic considerations in pleasant and effective living and each, more often than not, is subject to measurable improvement by significant involvement in some form of vigorous athletic or recreational activity.

It is also said, and I am one of those who believe it, that our athletics afford one of the few opportunities for our youth to nourish and develop those important qualities of character which are absolutely essential to the great performances required of this Nation in the next few decades. Native ability plus formal education may be an inadequate formula to produce the excellence we so urgently require. We need those mysterious and elusive qualities of courage, determination, presence of mind, self-control and concentration upon a given task—these are the traits which we hope will be inevitably developed when the athlete is repeatedly confronted with situations demanding them and which he will carry with him to his other endeavors.

The late President Kennedy said all this in these few well chosen words which I will quote: " . . . the physical vigor of our citizens is one of America's most precious resources . . . [It] is not only one of the most important keys to a healthy body; it is the basis of dynamic and creative intellectual activity. The relationship between the soundness of the body and the activities of the mind is subtle and complex. Much is not yet understood. But we do know what the Greeks knew; that intelligence and skill can only function at the peak of their capacity when the body is healthy and strong; that hardy spirits and tough minds usually inhabit sound bodies.

"In this sense," he went on, "physical fitness is the basis of all the activities of our society. And if our bodies grow soft and inactive, if we fail to encourage physical development and prowess, we will undermine our capacity for thought, for work and for the use of those skills vital to an expanding and complex America.

"Thus," he concluded, "the physical fitness of our citizens is a vital prerequisite to America's realization of its full potential as a nation, and to the opportunity of each individual citizen to make full and fruitful use of his capacities."

But with all this undergirding for our athletic programs, there are troublesome areas left to consider. Of course, the schools should concern themselves with the body as well as the mind, for it is the schools who have the only really consistent access to our youth and, if room for recreation is not available in the schools, it will not be available at all. But all this may be admitted without accepting the validity of our existing athletic system. Perceptive critics argue that a physical fitness program can produce a strong and healthy youth without the elaborate overlay of competitive athletics on an interscholastic basis. The system of school against school, it is said, inevitably has unfortunate consequences for a truly comprehensive program: energy and effort are concentrated upon producing the school team; it is an exclusive system which leaves all but the chosen few sitting in the grandstands to cheer; the participants themselves are so pressured into peak performance and pushed to such limits that they neglect their minds and overtax their bodies, the very antithesis of a sound program. Moreover, if these unfortunate conditions exist in the high schools, it is said that the colleges are even worse, much worse.

To what extent these criticisms are true, you know better than I. Certainly, in some schools and in some areas they have considerable validity. And wherever valid, they prove what history has taught before—that athletics carry the seeds of their own destruction and without sound direction the suicide will most surely occur.

No one can justify a school program which benefits only the few and neglects the many. No one can defend a system which discourages the many who cannot compete with the best and see no reason, therefore, to compete at all. No one can fairly close his eyes to those many young people who do not put athletic skill high on their priority list, but who urgently need and would enjoy athletic participation, given more inviting conditions. Is it really necessary for the schools to choose between the school team on the one hand and no athletics and no physical fitness programs on the other?

The answer is clearly in the negative. There is no incompatibility between a broadly focused physical education program and the team sports. There is no necessity to discard either. On the contrary, there is ample justification for both. Such a program presents few problems that able management and direction cannot cure, particularly when it is tied to the schools, which have the responsibility of producing whole men and women who are stunted in neither mind nor body, who are neither mental nor physical cripples and who must be willing and able to face the rigors of the future.

This is familiar territory to all of you and to your organization. The basic criteria under which you operate reveal your awareness of these problems and of the goals for which you strive. Your handbook says that athletics are to be an integral part of the secondary school program; that athletics are for the benefit of all youths; that the aim is maximum participation in a well balanced intramural and interscholastic program with emphasis on safe and healthful standards of competition; and that your task is concerned primarily with extending benefits of athletics to all participants and to spreading these benefits to constantly increasing numbers.

There is, as I have said, no mystery about what your problems are; and your goals are reasonably clear. The difficulties lie more in day-to-day performance and in closing the gap between principle and practice, between theory and reality in everyday life. I have no illusions, and I am sure you don't either, about the difficulties which you consistently encounter in implementing admittedly sound ideas. Solving public problems in a democracy is not an easy task, nor should it be. It is a job for the patient and the hardy and a job that deserves doing, not for some impersonal notions about athletics, but for the generation of the young.

There is not a shadow of a doubt these days as to our need for men and women of intellect, energy and character. Since its very beginning, this country, along with others, has been in constant change and flux. The rate of change has been steadily increasing and there is every indication that the trend will continue. Change in our country has ridden on an unfolding technology which has left nothing untouched, on a rapidly growing population and on a socio-economic system which has emphasized shared values. With rapid change has come a vast complexity and the imposition of almost an absolute demand for not only an adequate but an extended education. Whatever the unemployment figures seem to indicate, there is today, and there will be, an almost inexhaustible demand for talent to manage the private business world, to man essential government positions and to devote itself to solving the critical problems swirling around our position in what we sometimes call the family of nations.

But this kind of talent must prove itself and this process of proof which goes on in our schools all across the land can be an unnerving thing to the average young person who has begun to think and ask questions about his future. There seems to be that rather awesome necessity to shape up and measure up, and the entrance requirements to any kind of meaningful life are constantly on the rise. Energy, brains, character and motivation seem basic ingredients for a successful formula.

Unquestionably, difficult demands are imposed on the young. But the rate of obsolescence of their elders is very high indeed and for the young who want it, there is almost unlimited opportunity in the challenges which lie ahead.

Herein, I suppose, lies the importance of organizations like yours, which are tied to the overall academic institution but are dedicated to producing those nonacademic consequences which bear so heavily on achievement and the way a young man makes his peace with the world.

Substantially, you are dealing with human nature in a specialized context. This, as was said by Dr. George Norlin, long-time president of the University of Colorado, is a very old problem. Using his words, "Lo, all these centuries human nature remains unchanged. . . . Perhaps we had better accept this unflattering fact and make the best of it. Perhaps the time may come when college students will hold pep meetings to stir the philosophy department to do or die or will root with enthusiasm when the department of chemistry discovers a new element, but that time has not come nor will the Carnegie report on athletics (or others like it) bring it about in our day or our generation."

Human nature and athletics, as Shelley said about another subject, are "through time and change, unquenchably the same."

We have our peculiar problems in the judiciary, ladies and gentlemen, but your distinctive tasks involve the management of the young and their athletics. Fortunately, I can leave these tasks with you during the forthcoming week and I wish you the very best of things.

Now I Went Down to the Ringside and Little Henry Armstrong Was There

Kenneth Patchen

They've got some pretty horses up in the long dark mountains.
Get him, boy!

They've got some nifty riders away yonder on that big sad road.
Get him, boy!

They've got some tall talk off in that damn fine garden.
Get him, boy!

When you can't use your left, then let the right go.
When your arms get tired, hit him with a wing.
When you can't see very good, smell where he is.

They've got some juicy steaks in that nice sweet by-and-by.
Get him, boy!

They've got a lot of poor black lads in that crummy old jail-
house.
Get him, boy!

O they've got a lot of clean bunks up in their big wide blue sky.
That's his number, boy!

The Death of Benny Paret

Norman Mailer

On the afternoon of the night Emile Griffith and Benny Paret were to fight a third time for the welterweight championship, there was murder in both camps. "I hate that kind of guy," Paret had said earlier to Pete Hamill about Griffith. "A fighter's got to look and talk and act like a man." One of the Broadway gossip columnists had run an item about Griffith a few days before. His girl friend saw it and said to Griffith, "Emile, I didn't know about you being that way." So Griffith hit her. So he said. Now at the weigh-in that morning, Paret had insulted Griffith irrevocably, touching him on the buttocks, while making a few more remarks about his manhood. They almost had their fight on the scales.

The accusation of homosexuality arouses a major passion in many men; they spend their lives resisting it with a biological force. There is a kind of man who spends every night of his life getting drunk in a bar, he rants, he brawls, he ends in a small rumble on the street; women say, "For God's sakes, he's homosexual. Why doesn't he just turn queer and get his suffering over with." Yet men protect him. It is because he is choosing not to become homosexual. It was put best by Sartre who said that a homosexual is a man who practices homosexuality. A man who does not, is not homosexual—he is entitled to the dignity of his choice. He is entitled to the fact that he chose not to become homosexual, and is paying presumably his price.

The rage in Emile Griffith was extreme. I was at the fight that night, I had never seen a fight like it. It was scheduled for fifteen rounds, but they fought without stopping from the bell which began the round to the bell which ended it, and then they fought after the bell, sometimes for as much as fifteen seconds before the referee could force them apart.

Paret was a Cuban, a proud club fighter who had become welterweight champion because of his unusual ability to take a punch. His style of fighting was to take three punches to the head in order to give back two. At the end of ten rounds, he would still be bouncing, his opponent would have a headache. But in the last two years, over the fifteen-round fights, he had started to take some bad maulings.

This fight had its turns. Griffith won most of the early rounds, but Paret knocked Griffith down in the sixth. Griffith had trouble getting up, but made it, came alive and was dominating Paret again before the round was over. Then Paret began to wilt. In the middle of the eighth round, after a clubbing punch had turned his back to Griffith, Paret walked three

---

The title has been supplied by the editors for this excerpt from *The Presidential Papers*.

disgusted steps away, showing his hindquarters. For a champion, he took much too long to turn back around. It was the first hint of weakness Paret had ever shown, and it must have inspired a particular shame, because he fought the rest of the fight as if he were seeking to demonstrate that he could take more punishment than any man alive. In the twelfth, Griffith caught him. Paret got trapped in a corner. Trying to duck away, his left arm and his head became tangled on the wrong side of the top rope. Griffith was in like a cat ready to rip the life out of a huge boxed rat. He hit him eighteen right hands in a row, an act which took perhaps three or four seconds, Griffith making a pent-up whimpering sound all the while he attacked, the right hand whipping like a piston rod which has broken through the crankcase, or like a baseball bat demolishing a pumpkin. I was sitting in the second row of that corner—they were not ten feet away from me, and like everybody else, I was hypnotized. I had never seen one man hit another so hard and so many times. Over the referee's face came a look of woe as if some spasm had passed its way through him, and then he leaped on Griffith to pull him away. It was the act of a brave man. Griffith was uncontrollable. His trainer leaped into the ring, his manager, his cut man, there were four people holding Griffith, but he was off on an orgy, he had left the Garden, he was back on a hoodlum's street. If he had been able to break loose from his handlers and the referee, he would have jumped Paret to the floor and whaled on him there.

And Paret? Paret died on his feet. As he took those eighteen punches something happened to everyone who was in psychic range of the event. Some part of his death reached out to us. One felt it hover in the air. He was still standing in the ropes, trapped as he had been before, he gave some little half-smile of regret, as if he were saying, "I didn't know I was going to die just yet," and then, his head leaning back but still erect, his death came to breathe about him. He began to pass away. As he passed, so his limbs descended beneath him, and he sank slowly to the floor. He went down more slowly than any fighter had ever gone down, he went down like a large ship which turns on end and slides second by second into its grave. As he went down, the sound of Griffith's punches echoed in the mind like a heavy ax in the distance chopping into a wet log.

Paret lay on the ground, quivering gently, a small froth on his mouth. The house doctor jumped into the ring. He knelt. He pried Paret's eyelid open. He looked at the eyeball staring out. He let the lid snap shut. He reached into his satchel, took out a needle, jabbed Paret with a stimulant. Paret's back rose in a high arch. He writhed in real agony. They were calling him back from death. One wanted to cry out, "Leave the man alone. Let him die." But they saved Paret long enough to take him to a hospital where he lingered for days. He was in coma. He never came out of it. If he lived, he would have been a vegetable. His brain was smashed. But they held him in life for a week, they fed him chemicals, and made exploratory operations into his skull, and fed details of his condition to

The Goat. And The Goat kicked clods of mud all over the place, and spoke harshly of prohibiting boxing. There was shock in the land. Children had seen the fight on television. There were editorials, gloomy forecasts that the Game was dead. The managers and the prizefighters got together. Gently, in thick, depressed hypocrisies, they tried to defend their sport. They did not find it easy to explain that they shared an unstated view of life which was religious.

It was of course not that religion which is called Judeo-Christian. It was an older religion, a more primitive one—a religion of blood, a murderous and sensitive religion which mocks the effort of the understanding to approach it, and scores the lungs of men like D. H. Lawrence, and burns the brain of men like Ernest Hemingway when they explore out into the mystery, searching to discover some part of the secret. It is the view of life which looks upon death as a condition which is more alive than life or unspeakably more deadening. As such it is not a very attractive notion to the Establishment. But then the Establishment has nothing very much of even the Judeo-Christian tradition. It has a respect for legal and administrative aspects of justice, and it is devoted to the idea of compassion for the poor. But the Establishment has no idea of death, no tolerance for Heaven or Hell, no comprehension of bloodshed. It sees no logic in pain. To the Establishment these notions are a detritus from the past.

Like a patient submerged beneath the plastic cover of an oxygen tent, boxing lives on beneath the cool, bored eyes of the doctors in the Establishment. It would not take too much to finish boxing off. Shut down the oxygen, which is to say, turn that switch in the mass media which still gives sanction to organized pugilism, and the fight game would be dead.

But the patient is permitted to linger for fear the private detectives of the Establishment, the psychiatrists and psychoanalysts, might not be able to neutralize the problem of gang violence. Not so well as the Game. Of course, the moment some piece of diseased turnip capable of being synthesized cheaply might prove to have the property of tranquilizing a violent young man for a year, the Establishment would wipe out boxing. Every time a punk was arrested, the police would prescribe a pill, and violence would walk the street sheathed and numb. Of course the Mob would lose revenue, but then the Mob is also part of the Establishment, it, and the labor unions and the colleges and the newspapers and the corporations are all part of the Establishment. The Establishment is never simple. It needs the Mob to grease the chassis on its chariot. Therefore, the Mob would be placated. In a society with strong central government, it is not so difficult to turn up a new source of revenue. What is more difficult is to enter the plea that violence may be an indispensable element of life. This is not the place to have the argument: it is enough to say that if the liberal Establishment is right in its unstated credo that death is a void, and man leads out his life suspended momentarily above that void, why then there is no argument at all. Whatever shortens life is monstrous. We have not the right to shorten life, since life is the only possession of the psyche, and in death we have only nothingness. What then can there be said in defense of sports-car racing, war, or six-ounce gloves?

But if we go from life into a death which is larger than our life has been, or into a death which is small, if death comes to nothing for one man because he swallowed his death in his life, and if for another death is alive with dimension, then the certitudes of the Establishment lose power. A drug which offers peace to a pain may dull the nerve which could have taught the mind how to carry that pain into the death which comes on the next day or on the decades that follow. A tranquilizer gives coma to an anxiety which may later smell of the dungeon, beneath the ground. If we are born into life as some living line of intent from an eternity which may have tortured us or nurtured us in death, then we may be obliged to go back to death with more courage and art than we left it. Or face the dim end of going back with less.

That is the existential venture, the unstated religious view of boxers trying to beat each other into unconsciousness or, ultimately, into death. It is the culture of the killer who sickens the air about him if he does not find some half-human way to kill a little in order not to deaden all. It is a defense against the plague, against that plague which comes from violence converted into the nausea of all that nonviolence which is void of peace. Paret's death was with horror, but not all the horror was in the beating, much was in the way his death was cheated. Which is to say that his death was twice a nightmare. I knew that something in boxing was spoiled forever for me, that there would be a fear in watching a fight now which was like the fear one felt for any *novillero* when he was having an unhappy day, the bull was dangerous, and the crowd was ugly. You knew he would get hurt. There is fascination in seeing that the first time, but it is not as enjoyable as one expects. It is like watching a novelist who has written a decent book get run over by a car.

Something in boxing was spoiled. But not the principle, not the right for one man to try to knock another out in the ring. That was perhaps not a civilized activity, but it belonged to the tradition of the humanist, it was a human activity, it showed a part of what man was like, it belonged to his ability to create art and artful movement on the edge of death or pain or danger or attack, and it had much to say about the subtleties of human style. For there are boxers whose bodies move like a fine brain, and there are others who pound the opposition down with the force of a trade-union leader, there are fools and wits and patient craftsmen among boxers, wild men full of a sense of outrage, and steady oppressive peasants, clever spoilers, dogged infantrymen who walk forward all night, hypno-

---

novillero: a minor bullfighter who fights young bulls; a novice bullfighter.

tists (like Liston), dancers, lovers, mothers giving a scolding, horsemen high on their legs. There is knowledge to be found about our nature, and the nature of animals, of big cats, lions, tigers, gorillas, bears, walruses (Archie Moore), birds, elephants, jackals, bulls. No, I was not down on boxing, but I loved it with freedom no longer. It was more like somebody in your family was fighting now. And the feeling one had for a big fight was no longer clear of terror in its excitement. There was awe in the suspense.

An Innocent at Rinkside

William Faulkner

The vacant ice looked tired though it shouldn't have. They told him it had been put down only a few minutes ago following a basketball game and after the hockey match it would be taken up again to make room for something else. But it looked not expectant but resigned, like the mirror simulating ice in the Christmas store window, not before the miniature fir trees and reindeer and cosy lamplit cottage were arranged upon it, but after they had been dismantled and cleared away.

Then it was filled with motion, speed. To the innocent, who had never seen it before, it seemed discorded and inconsequent, bizarre and paradoxical like the frantic darting of the weightless bugs which run on the surface of stagnant pools. Then it would break, coalesce through a kind of kaleidoscopic whirl like a child's toy, into a pattern, a design almost beautiful, as if an inspired choreographer had drilled a willing and patient and hard-working troupe of dancers—a pattern, design which was trying to tell him something, say something to him urgent and important and true in that second before, already bulging with the motion and the speed, it began to disintegrate and dissolve.

Then he learned to find the puck and follow it. Then the individual players would emerge. They would not emerge like the sweating bare-handed behemoths from the troglodyte mass of football, but instead as fluid and fast and effortless as rapier thrusts or lightning—Richard with something of the passionate glittering fatal alien quality of snakes, Geoffrion like an agile ruthless precocious boy who maybe couldn't do anthing else but then he didn't need to; and others—the veteran Laprade, still with the know-how and the grace. But he had time too now, or rather time had him, and what remained was no longer expendable that recklessly, heedlessly, successfully; not enough of it left now to buy fresh passion and fresh triumph with.

Excitement: men in rapid, hard, close physical conflict, not just with bare hands, but armed with the knife blades of skates and the hard, fast, deft sticks which could break bones when used right. He had noticed how many women were among the spectators, and for just a moment he thought that perhaps this was why—that here actual male blood could flow, not from the crude impact of a heavier fist but from the rapid and delicate stroke of weapons, which, like the European rapier or the frontier pistol, reduced mere size and brawn to its proper perspective to the passion and the will. But only for a moment because he, the innocent, didn't like that idea either. It was the excitement of speed and grace, with the puck for catalyst, to give it reason, meaning.

He watched it—the figure-darted glare of ice, the concentric tiers rising in sections stipulated by the hand-lettered names of the individual fan-club idols, vanishing upward into the pall of tobacco smoke trapped by the roof—the roof which stopped and trapped all that intent and tense watching, and concentrated it downward upon the glare of ice frantic and frenetic with motion; until the byproduct of the speed and the motion—their violence—had no chance to exhaust itself upward into space and so leave on the ice only the swift glittering changing pattern. And he thought how perhaps something is happening to sport in America (assuming that by definition sport is something you do yourself, in solitude or not, because it is fun), and that something is the roof we are putting over it and them. Skating, basketball, tennis, track meets and even steeplechasing have moved indoors; football and baseball function beneath covers of arc lights and in time will be rain- and coldproofed too. There still remain the proper working of a fly over trout water or the taking of a rise of birds in front of a dog or the right placing of a bullet in a deer or even a bigger animal which will hurt you if you don't. But not for long: in time that will be indoors too beneath lights and the trapped pall of spectator tobacco, the concentric sections bearing the name and device of the lion or the fish as well as that of the Richard or Geoffrion of the scoped rifle or four-ounce rod.

But (to repeat) not for long, because the innocent did not quite believe that either. We—Americans—like to watch, we like the adrenalic discharge of vicarious excitement or triumph or success. But we like to do also: the discharge of the personal excitement of the triumph and the fear to be had from actually setting the horse at the stone wall or pointing the overcanvased sloop or finding by actual test if you can line up two sights and one buffalo in time. There must have been little boys in that throng too, frantic with the slow excruciating passage of time, panting for the hour when they would be Richard or Geoffrion or Laprade—the same little Negro boys whom the innocent has seen shadowboxing in front of a photograph of Joe Louis in his own Mississippi town, the same little Norwegian boys he watched staring up the snowless slope of the Holmenkollen jump one July day in the hills above Oslo.

Only he (the innocent) did wonder just what a professional hockey-match, whose purpose is to make a decent and reasonable profit for its owners, had to do with our National Anthem. What are we afraid of? Is it our national character of which we are so in doubt, so fearful that it might not hold up in the clutch, that we not only dare not open a professional athletic contest or a beauty-pageant or a real-estate auction, but we must even use a Chamber of Commerce race for Miss Sewage Disposal or a wildcat land-sale, to remind us that liberty gained without honor and sacrifice and held without constant vigilance and undiminished honor and complete willingness to sacrifice again at need, was not worth having to begin with? Or, by blaring or chanting it at ourselves every time ten or twelve or eighteen or twenty-two young men engage formally for the possession of a puck or a ball, or just one young woman walks across a lighted platform in a bathing-suit, do we hope to so dull and eviscerate the words and tune with repetition, that when we do hear it we will not be disturbed from that dream-like state in which "honor" is a break and "truth" an angle?

"Perfect Day—A Day of Prowess"

Robert Frost

Americans would rather watch a game than play a game. Statement true or false? Why, as to these thousands here today to watch the game and not play it, probably not one man-jack but has himself played the game in his athletic years and got himself so full of bodily memories of the experience (what we farmers used to call kinesthetic images) that he can hardly sit still. We didn't burst into cheers immediately, but an exclamation swept the crowd as if we felt it all over in our muscles when Boyer at third made the two impossible catches, one a stab at a grounder and the other a leap at a line drive that may have saved the day for the National League. We all winced with fellow feeling when Berra got the foul tip on the ungloved fingers of his throwing hand.

As for the ladies present, they are here as next friends to the men, but even they have many of them pitching arms and batting eyes. Many of them would prefer a league ball to a pumpkin. You wouldn't want to catch them with bare hands. I mustn't count it against them that I envision one in the outfield at a picnic with her arms spread wide open for a fly ball as for a descending man-angel. Luckily it didn't hit her in the mouth which was open too, or it might have hurt her beauty. It missed her entirely.

How do I know all this and with what authority do I speak? Have I not been written up as a pitcher in *The New Yorker* by the poet, Raymond Holden?—though the last full game I pitched in was on the grounds of Rockingham Park in Salem, New Hampshire, before it was turned into a race track. If I have shone at all in the all-star games at Breadloaf in Vermont it has been as a relief pitcher with a soft ball I despise like a picture window. Moreover I once took an honorary degree at Williams College along with a very famous pitcher, Ed Lewis, who will be remembered and found in the record to have led the National League in pitching quite a long time ago. His degree was not for pitching. Neither was mine. His was for presiding with credit over the University of New Hampshire and the Massachusetts College of Agriculture. He let me into the secret of how he could make a ball behave when his arm was just right. It may sound superstitious to the uninitiated, but he could push a cushion of air up ahead of it for it to slide off from any way it pleased. My great friendship for him probably accounts for my having made a trivial 10¢ bet on the National League today. He was a Welshman from Utica who, from having attended eisteddfods at Utica with his father, a bard, had like another Welsh friend of mine, Edward Thomas, in England, come to look on a poem as a performance one had to win. Chicago was my first favorite team because Chicago seemed the nearest city in the league to my original home town, San Francisco. I have conquered that prejudice. But I mean to see if the captain of it, Anson my boyhood hero, is in the Hall of Fame at Cooperstown where he belongs.

May I add to my self-citation that one of my unfulfilled promises on earth was to my fellow in art, Alfred Kreymborg, of an epic poem some day about a ball batted so hard by Babe Ruth that it never came back, but got to going round and round the world like a satellite. I got up the idea long before any artificial moon was thought of by the scientists. I meant to begin something like this:

> It was nothing to nothing at the end of the tenth
> And the prospects good it would last to the nth.

It needs a lot of work on it before it can take rank with *Casey at the Bat*.

In other words, some baseball is the fate of us all. For my part I am never more at home in America than at a baseball game like this in Clark Griffith's gem of a field, gem small, in beautiful weather in the capital of the country and my side winning. Here Walter Johnson flourished, who once threw a silver dollar across the Potomac (where not too wide) in emulation of George Washington, and here Gabby Street caught the bulletlike ball dropped from the top of George Washington's monument. It is the time and the place. And I have with me as consultant the well-known symbolist, Howard Schmitt of Buffalo, to mind my baseball slang and interpret the incidentals. The first player comes to the bat, Temple of the Redlegs, swinging two bats as he comes, the meaning of which or moral of which, I find on application to my consultant, is that we must always arrange to have just been doing something beforehand a good deal harder than what we are just going to do.

But when I asked him a moment later what it symbolized when a ball got batted into the stands and the people instead of dodging in terror fought each other fiercely to get and keep it and were allowed to keep it, Howard bade me hold on; there seemed to be a misunderstanding between us. When he accepted the job it was orally; he didn't mean to represent himself as a symbolist in the high-brow or middle-brow sense of the word, that is as a collegiate expounder of the double entendre for college classes; he was a common ordinary cymbalist in a local band somewhere out on the far end of the Eeryie Canal. We were both honest men. He didn't want to be taken for a real professor any more than I wanted to be taken for a real sport. His utmost wish was to contribute to the general noise when home runs were made. He knew they would be the most popular hits of the day. And they were—four of them from exactly the four they were expected from, Musial, Williams, Mays and Mantle. The crowd went wild four times. Howard's story would have been more plausible if he had brought his cymbals with him. I saw I would have to take care of the significances myself. This comes of not having got it in writing. The moral is always get it in writing.

Time was when I saw nobody on the field but the players. If I saw the umpire at all it was as an enemy for not taking my side. I may never have wanted to see bottles thrown at him so that he had to be taken out by the police. Still I often regarded him with the angry disfavor that the Democratic Party showed the Supreme Court in the '30s and other parties have shown it in other crises in our history. But now grown psychological, shading 100, I saw him as a figure of justice, who stood forth alone to be judged as a judge by people and players with whom he wouldn't last a week if suspected of the least lack of fairness or the least lack of faith in the possibility of fairness. I was touched by his loneliness and glad it was relieved a little by his being five in number, five in one so to speak, *e pluribus unum.* I have it from high up in the judiciary that some justices see in him an example to pattern after. Right there in front of me for reassurance is the umpire brought up perhaps in the neighborhood of Boston who can yet be depended upon not to take sides today for or against the American League the Boston Red Sox belong to. Let me celebrate the umpire for any influence for the better he may have on the Supreme Court. The justices suffer the same predicaments with him. I saw one batter linger perceptibly to say something to the umpire for calling him out on a third strike. I didn't hear what the batter said. One of the hardest things to accept as just is a called third strike.

It has been a day of prowess in spite of its being a little on the picnic side and possibly not as desperately fought as it might be in a World Series. Prowess, prowess, in about equal strength for both sides. Each team made 11 hits, two home runs and not a single error. The day was perfect, the scene perfect, the play perfect. Prowess of course comes first, the ability to perform with success in games, in the arts and, come right down to it, in battle. The nearest of kin to the artists in college where we all become bachelors of arts are their fellow performers in baseball, football and tennis. That's why I am so particular college athletics should be kept from corruption. They are close to the soul of culture. At any rate the Greeks thought so. Justice is a close second to prowess. When displayed toward each other by antagonists in war and peace, it is known as the nobility of noble natures. And I mustn't forget courage, for there is neither prowess nor justice without it. My fourth, if it is important enough in comparison to be worth bringing in, is knowledge, the mere information we can't get too much of and can't ever get enough of, we complain, before going into action.

As I say, I never feel more at home in America than at a ball game be it in park or in sandlot. Beyond this I know not. And dare not.

Baseball and Writing

Marianne Moore

Suggested by post-game broadcasts.

Fanaticism? No. Writing is exciting
and baseball is like writing.
  You can never tell with either
    how it will go
    or what you will do;

generating excitement—
a fever in the victim—
pitcher, catcher, fielder, batter.
Victim in what category?
*Owl*man watching from the press box?
To whom does it apply?
Who is excited? Might it be I?

It's a pitcher's battle all the way—a duel—
a catcher's, as, with cruel
puma paw, Elston Howard lumbers lightly
back to plate. (His spring
de-winged a bat swing.)
They have that killer instinct;
yet Elston—whose catching
arm has hurt them all with the bat—
when questioned, says, unenviously,
"I'm very satisfied. We won."
Shorn of the batting crown, says, "We";
robbed by a technicality.

When three players on a side play three positions
and modify conditions,
the massive run need not be everything.
"Going, going . . ." Is
it? Roger Maris
has it, running fast. You will
never see a finer catch. Well . . .
"Mickey, leaping like the devil"—why
gild it, although deer sounds better—
snares what was speeding towards its treetop nest,
one-handing the souvenir-to-be
meant to be caught by you or me.

Assign Yogi Berra to Cape Canaveral;
he could handle any missile.
He is no feather. "Strike! . . . Strike *two!*"
Fouled back. A blur.
It's gone. You would infer
that the bat had eyes.
He put the wood to that one.

Praised, Skowron says, "Thanks, Mel.
I think I helped a *little* bit."
All business, each, and modesty.
Blanchard, Richardson, Kubek, Boyer.
In that galaxy of nine, say which
won the pennant? *Each.* It was he.

Those two magnificent saves from the knee—throws
by Boyer, finesses in twos—
like Whitey's three kinds of pitch and pre-
diagnosis
with pick-off psychosis.
Pitching is a large subject.
Your arm, too true at first, can learn to
catch the corners—even trouble
Mickey Mantle. ("Grazed a Yankee!
My baby pitcher, Montejo!"
With some pedagogy,
you'll be tough, premature prodigy.)

They crowd him and curve him and aim for the knees. Trying
indeed! The secret implying:
"I can stand here, bat held steady."
One may suit him;
none has hit him.
Imponderables smite him.
Muscle kinks, infections, spike wounds
require food, rest, respite from ruffians. (Drat it!
Celebrity costs privacy!)
Cow's milk, "tiger's milk," soy milk, carrot juice,
brewer's yeast (high-potency)—
concentrates presage victory

sped by Luis Arroyo, Hector Lopez—
deadly in a pinch. And "Yes,
it's work; I want you to bear down,
but enjoy it
while you're doing it."
Mr Houk and Mr. Sain,
if you have a rummage sale,

don't sell Roland Sheldon or Tom Tresh.
Studded with stars in belt and crown,
the Stadium is an adastrium.
O flashing Orion,
your stars are muscled like the lion.

Some Questions on Sports

Marianne Moore and George Plimpton

GEORGE PLIMPTON *Did you ever watch James Thorpe play football? Was he idolized in the school?*

MARIANNE MOORE He was liked by all—*liked* in italics, rather than venerated or idolized—unless perhaps privately admired by "Pop" Warner, he was such an all-round phenomenon—"Jim." He was off-hand, modest, casual about anything in the way of fame or eminence achieved. This modesty, with top performance, was characteristic of him, and no back-talk. The charge of professionalism was never popular in the Olympic world; everyone felt it should not be held against him, since any violation was accidental rather than intentional.

I used to watch football practice on the field after school sometimes; signals for passes; little starts with the ball; kicks for goal; and often watched track sports in spring—throwing the hammer, at which James was adept, taking hurdles—the jump. He had a kind of ease in his gait that is hard to describe. Equilibrium with no strictures; but crouched in the lineup for football he was the epitome of concentration, wary, with an effect of plenty in reserve. I never saw him irascible, sour, or primed for vengeance. In the classroom he was a little laborious, but dependable; took time—head bent earnestly over the paper; wrote a fine even clerical hand—every character legible; every terminal curving up—consistent and generous. I don't mention team trips away for I know nothing about them; but celebrations involving liquor (reputedly) can't be good for any athlete.

G. P. *Could you say something about* style *and the athlete?*

M. M. An animal—also an athlete—in command of a skill should glory in it; but the manner, probably, is inadvertent. To attain nicety, deliberateness at some point in performance is obligatory. The halves of the body should have some practice in compensating for each other. Then when experience has lent confidence, opportunity seems like destiny.

A sense of ability and prime strength safeguarded by caution—with a recollection of success—a Goliath-like brashness tamed by near-misses—should, I feel, conduce to form. Not knowing how to hold back by perhaps a second seems to account for many a failure—many a ball in tennis, shot into the net, resulting in the cheerful insult "too anxious" or "still with you." Taking a Blue Ridge bus from Washington to Hagerstown one time, I saw through the window a handful of boys taking turns swinging on a rope from a tree branch over a creek—each letting go the rope exactly at the right moment to hit the pool like a cast at a trout. And in San Francisco once, I saw from a window overlooking a backyard a cat—black Siamese—catching hummingbirds. From a motionless crouch on a fence half-shaded by flowers, the body lunged in a long horizontal pounce—a kind of long chameleon-tongue striking a fly.

Restraint seems to be the key to form as equilibrium. The most spectacular instance of equilibrium that I recall was a slack-rope walker in the Great Sensational Swedish Circus shown on International Showtime television, January 30, 1964. The performer, gliding forward in long slow strides without parasol or wand, rested his head on the wire, raising his legs till vertical, stood on his head for some time, supported by a tip of a forefinger on the wire at each side of the head, then sprang lightly down. Also, I have seen a girl ascend a tall ladder with a glass of wine balanced on her forehead. On the glass rested an oblong parallelogram tray on which six small-stemmed glasses of wine stood. She descended the ladder, without having spilled a drop, and in conclusion before bowing, took one glass up and drank the wine. The pleasantest instance of dexterity to watch that I have seen recently was the jumping of a horse with a name like Exceptional (no mention of it in the *Times* the next day, that I could find) by a girl in the International Contest at Madison Square Garden. Launched for the jump, the horse looked self-automated as it floated up out over the barrier, with ease as if liking the airlift—forelegs flattened to the body but with no rectangular carousel bend of the knee. Seurat's "Standing Horse" in the Guggenheim Museum has a stance that says it all—ears forward, legs sloping almost imperceptibly forward, and level back.

G. P. *And now perhaps something of the relationship between the athlete and the animal?*

M. M. I am sure that stricture interferes with form, and with dexterity. A gibbon in a flying leap seems to have no joints; and an orangoutang can lie stretched out, high up on a level pipe, with one arm under its head, eating an orange with the other hand, and a knee drawn up as a man might lie on a couch. The little gray poodle in *Flipper* (Walt Disney) before his dive into the pool, straining up erect on thin hind legs, jubilant to go, and otters shown at the top of a snow-slide, were not afflicted with muscle kinks. Aptitude without zeal is not much. Next to the manse we lived in, in Chatham, New Jersey, a small brindled bulldog had ears fringed with scars; staggering from a last encounter, if he saw a sizable dog across the street, he had to be forcibly restrained from limping out to fight—as Cassius Clay in being reminded of Sonny Liston, said, "I can't wait to get at him; it took two policemen to keep me off him. Don't mention him no more."

Manipulating an implement involves nicety. It seems to me that aptitude for mobility is at a peak in the elephant. I have seen in a movie an Asian elephant edging a lawn beside a pavement, using the finger of its proboscis as daintily as if it were a razor; have also seen an elephant slowly push flat a good-sized tree, as in pulling and piling teak.

Mrs. Thrale, with friends comparing people and their likeness to some animal or other said, "We pitched upon the elephant for his resemblance" (Dr. Johnson's)—adding that "the proboscis of that creature was like his mind, most exactly strong to buffet even the tiger and pliable to pick up even the pin."

G. P. *Why is baseball the particular sport that has held your interest as a poet? Or have others? Football?*

M. M. Roy Campanella roused, I should say revived, my interest in baseball in 1953 or 1954, at Ebbets Field. Karl Spooner was pitching. Roy Campanella, who was catching, walked out to the mound, and after a few earnest words to Karl came briskly back to the plate after a parting encouraging slap or pat on Karl's rear. His brisk, confident little roll was very prepossessing and I thought, "I guess I'll have to keep an eye on him." His experienced crouch with no sign of reluctance, and the fact that he never missed a foul, corroborated the pleasing impression. But the notable thing about him was his vim. It belongs with the remark in his book, *It's Good to Be Alive,* that he enjoyed the game so much, he would gladly play even if he didn't get paid.

Football seems scientifically tactical nowadays—not so conglomerate as fifty years ago, with fewer mounds of bodies, and victims exanimately breathless at the bottom of the pile.

Tennis is the game that I liked from the first and always have. We played on a dirt court by a giant willow belonging to the school we attended till grammar-school age and I till entering college. My brother is tall and hard to get past, playing net. I am no athlete, tire soon, seldom achieve a decisive shot, have no whirlwind serve, but can place the ball "where they ain't."

One day a youngster, a great-nephew of the principal of the school, arrived for a visit and had a new racquet. He magnanimously lent it to me while waiting a turn—a Harry C. Lee Dreadnaught Driver, strung in red and blue gut (rather gaudy, I thought). It had a slotted throat, disparaged by some as a sales feature, but it lightened the grip and weighted the top in my opinion. I improved so that I could think of nothing else; my mother got me one, and from then on my brother and I considered any day wasted when we did not play. Thanks to the new weapon, we welcomed adversaries but seldom could beat two men (friends who lived nearby—older than we—one of whom reclusively read the *Figaro* by the willow when not playing). Twenty-five or so years later, for me an accidental thrill came in a small tennis competition in which Personnel in the Puget Sound Navy Yard entered my brother and me in 1924. The score was 3-6, 7-5, 6-3. Seven pairs. A tough hand-ornamented score-sheet was thumbtacked to a tree. The final set of a three-set series with the finalists went to seven deuces. My face began to burn and I could hardly swallow but dared not fail my brother. It was my serve. I heard a murmur—a curious battle cry. "Now cuckoo; together," caught a fractional glance back, fortunately took my opponent off-balance; and the feeble return, my brother angled out of our competitor's reach. Our matching opponent sprang over the net, shook hands, and said, "Well—I guess that's curtains."

Much later—in Brooklyn—I had no one to play, selected a boy and got him a racquet at Davega's. He took no interest and had no ability. Another boy who had sat at our door in aggrieved disgust as the recruit accompanied me to the courts, came to the rescue and had everything but experience. We had to procure permits from Lefferts Mansion—some distance away—but nothing deterred two more boys from joining us, and a benevolent Park man winked at interlopers, one of whom owned a bicycle entitled Colleen in bold script along the back of the saddle, with foxtails flowing from the handlebars. The boys are now in the Coast Guard, Air Force, or thriving businessmen (married to Yvonne, or Betty, or Helene).

G. P. *Have you met, or known, many athletes? McGraw? Or Mack?*

M. M. Near the Fence, on my first visit to Yale, I met Ray Biglow (Lucius Horatio Biglow), Captain of 1907's football team. He was All-American right tackle, and Varsity Captain in 1907. Yale never lost a game to Harvard or Princeton while he was right tackle; also had a Y for rowing. He was commensurately modest. He never went on the field loaded with pads and armor—was the picture of solid know-how; had not much to say but spoke with great exactness and sensibility—with no self-consciousness; no affectations. Professor Jack Read said he was the only member of his class in Nineteenth Century Poets to hand in the written assignment the day before his last game against Harvard.

My brother—John Warner Moore (Captain, Chaplain Corps, USN, Ret.) was sailing officer on each of the ships on which he served, and crews trained by him for Fleet Regattas consistently won. My nephew, John Warner Moore, was a Yale Varsity swimmer for three years.

One of my pleasantest memories of Harvard was meeting—in November 1962—members of Lowell House who are athletes: Jamie Hoyt '65—a middleweight boxer and football player; Eugene Kinasewich, Varsity and all-Ivy League hockey player from Alberta; and John Carroll, Varsity Lacrosse player who has taught in Tanganyika, as surgical assistant and assistant in carpenter work with natives. "Tanganyikan soccer," he says, "is the most agreeable integration of sport with daily life I have ever witnessed. At all levels soccer is played in one's street clothes—bare feet, baggy shorts, and tattered undershirt—and they can really boom the ball on their bare calloused feet. Pickup games spread like fire. Schoolboys, washing their only clothes in the icy stream, race naked after a floppy rag against a raw wind from the high mountains. Nothing can express the exultation that comes with sport played like this."

When teaching at the Carlisle Indian School, Charles (Chief) Bender, the pitcher, was a respected figure whom I often saw—the perfect model of a pitcher, proportioned much like Ty Cobb but taller; and anything but common property, his patrician aspect modified by the fact that he was not so lofty as to despise chewing gum. I had in my department, besides James Thorpe, Joel Wheelock, Gus Welsh, Alex Arcasa—all indispensable on the football team.

John McGraw and Connie Mack? I used to thrust John McGraw's *How to Play Baseball* on little boys in the Hudson Park Branch of the New York Public Library when they came asking what they should read. Connie Mack went to Buckhorn, Kentucky, looking for a left-handed pitcher. Dr. Elmer Gabbard was showing him the Buckhorn School—a magnificent effort in compensating for broken homes, feuding fathers, and moonshiners—when they met a boy who had a string of squirrels he had stoned for the family dinner—stoned, he said, with his left hand. Connie Mack hired him, but on the mound the boy used his right hand. Asked why he had stoned the squirrels with his left hand instead of his right, the boy said, "If I used my right hand, I was afraid I might bruise them."

G. P. *What are the aspects of baseball that particularly appeal to you?*

M. M. Dexterity—with a logic of memory that makes strategy possible. Phil Rizzuto observed that for Elston Howard, not just any ball would do—that he could have had the batting crown if it hadn't been for a regulation: "You have to pitch him in tight, so he can't get the best part of the bat on it." And Mudcat (Jimmy) Grant's apparent ferocity and abandon are worth watching—seeing him leap up to pull down a speedy liner hit over the mound. I admire, too, Minnie Minoso's fury; and certainly the Yankee pitcher Al Downing (Alphonse Erwin Downing) had (as Arthur Daley says) "all the ingredients." His left arm goes up in a jug-handle curve, his right lies across him like a barrel stave—left leg trailing to right, kneeling—the right leg as prop—so he can't fall. In 1961 against the Senators, Arthur Daley says, "he struck out two, walked batters, hit batters, batters hit him, so that after an inning and a third, Ralph Houk, the manager, saved him further embarrassment and took him out." But as Elston Howard says, "He has the best arm on the ball field. He has been close to no-hitters and has got to make it sometime. Curves and fancy pitches can be learned, but no one can teach a man how to throw a fast ball." Hope of scoring seems focused in the pitcher, and I think a "pleasant" mound may have something to do with inducing an intimation of triumph.

One of the handsomest things about the game, I think, is accuracy that looks automatic in fielding fast balls. I never tire of a speedy ball from the catcher finding the glove of the pitcher, when half the time he isn't even looking at it.

A record, it seems to me, doesn't compare with "from-time-to-time good plays by uncelebrities." I went to the Yankee Stadium one time to see Babe Ruth. He could bat, but his pigeon-toed, stubbed little trot lacked beauty. The batter I like to watch is Willie Mays. Vim marks every action—an effect of knowing he has what it takes, without being conceited. Responsibility and talent; calling it enough. There's a moral to it. I can always last in a drawn-out game—to wait for Elston Howard at bat. Two little boys, perhaps taking him for an umpire, detained my brother one time and said, "Did you see that home run? My Daddy did that."

A thing I don't like about baseball is the veteran who hazes the rookie—such as nailing Ty Cobb's spikes to the clubhouse floor, and sawing his bat through. It's not funny, but a heavy thought to me that when Honus Wagner was asked why he smiled happily after saying, "Nice hit," to Cobb and being told to "Go to hell," he said: "I liked that remark. He was the first major leaguer ever to speak to me."

Roger Maris, in being victim of the batting competition, suffered in being a cause of worry it seemed to me—while in people's concept of him, he was a star; then revealed a touch of embarrassment in being party to a commercial. Infrarub shouldn't harm him but it doesn't lend a ball player luster exactly. He then regained my sympathy by admitting that the only privacy he could count on was when taking his place on the ball field.

We like home runs but Mickey Mantle is a beautiful outfielder and I think I like him catching flies better than I like him hitting them. Some of his spectacular incalculable catches do not fade from the mind. In any case, it is most pleasing that two such batting fielders as Roger Maris and Mickey Mantle have at no time been diminished by internecine jealousies. Their series of ailments by no means estrange one—at least not me, who am prone to any impairment—sprained a right middle finger playing basketball, I was hit on the eye at close range by a tennis ball, made only second teams in hockey and Lacrosse in college, and was in momentary danger of being spilled, when two or three classmates and I rented polo ponies from an ex-army-officer and would dash about the lanes and woodlands of Bryn Mawr.

Prize Fighters and Authors

Sherwood Anderson

Why do intellectual men, writers, painters, *etc.*, often have such a passion for prize fighters, or, for that matter, for bull fighters? A short time ago a great fuss was being made about Mr. Gene Tunney's mind. He probably hadn't too much. A working mind leaves its marks on the face. There was nothing particularly sensitive about Mr. Tunney's face. It was not the face of a bruiser nor yet the face of a thinker. On the whole, it was a placid face. Mr. Dempsey, when champion, was more popular. He was more a creature of impulse. I saw him once and immediately took to him. We were in the studio of a New York photographer. He took me into a corner of the room. "You are a writer, eh?" "Yes," I said.

He told me that he had been acting in the movies. "I hate it," he said. He made no pretense of having a mind, but I felt at once that he had one, and a good one too. "I enjoy fighting," he said. He meant that he enjoyed the rush of it, the plunge, the excitement. He was no cold, calculating fellow—this Dempsey.

Before a fight the man was all nerves. He walked restlessly up and down the room that day when I saw him. It was just before the fight in which he lost his championship. Tunney had been in the same place the day before. The photographer, after Dempsey had left, showed me several photographs he had taken of the man Tunney. Beside Dempsey he seemed to me a dilettante, a dilettante with his fists, with his mind, with his feelings.

"He would be self-conscious." I thought. This man is no plunger. He would be a man always thinking, "Now, as I am a prize fighter, I must look fierce." He would be a gentleman. "I must develop my mind."

I could imagine Dempsey going off on almost any sort of angle. He might get drunk, get into a saloon brawl. He might take a sudden and violent fancy for some woman. He might do any generous thing.

Mr. Tunney went off to Europe. He went on a walking trip with a writer. I could fancy them going along the road together. They were both thinking. One was thinking, "Here am I, a man of the mind. I have a close friend who is a prize fighter. How wonderful!" And there was the other thinking, "I am a prize fighter, but I am no brute. I am a man of mind. My being with this writer proves it."

There was a great deal of newspaper talk about all this.

It is true that the man of the mind has always a liking for the man of action. Primitive, simple people appeal to him. He is trying to understand human nature. These self-conscious calculating men do not appeal to him. They are too much like himself.

And he is himself a man of action—in the true sense. The painter, at his easel, when he is really painting, is an excited man. All of his nerves are on edge. I have watched painters at work who were like Dempsey about to enter the prize ring. One man I knew swore violently sometimes when he was painting. If you had interrupted him at such a time he might well have hit you with his fist. He might have beaten you brutally. "Get out of here!"

He was trying to catch some delicate thing. Thoughts and feeling elude like a fast opponent in the ring. You rush at your opponent—the mood. "Oh, if I could only hit it squarely, send it sprawling!"

I remember going once into an apartment in New York. A man I knew lived there, a writer friend. He had invited me to come and dine with him.

I went in the late afternoon. The place was quiet. I went through his workroom. He was in his bedroom, lying on his bed.

He told me later that he had been working for two years trying to get just the feeling he wanted in a certain piece of work. That morning he had got up feeling ill. However, as he sat at breakfast, what he wanted came clear at last. He had written some twelve thousand words during the day. The twelve thousand words were the very heart of a long book. After he wrote them that day he never changed a word. It was marvelous writing.

And what a physical task! All day he had been hitting and hitting. There was perfect timing of the sentences. They rang like bells. I have read over what the man wrote that day a hundred times. I can see no flaw in it.

He told me that on the particular day of which I am now speaking he was so exhausted that by noon he could hardly sit in his chair. He sent out and got a quart of whiskey. During the afternoon he drank it all. "I was drunk later—when I had finished the thing," he told me. "While I worked I was not drunk."

It was a physical test. When I saw him he was so exhausted he could scarcely raise his head from the bed. He was as a prize fighter might have been after a marvelous fight.

As for the Tunney, he was always a bit too patronizing about his trade. He profited by the prize-fighting thing and yet spoke of it with contempt. The being intellectual was a bit too obvious. On my life, Mr. Jack Dempsey, or before him the Negro Jack Johnson, had each of them a better mind.

There is too much of this bunk about a man having a mind because he has read the classics. It was not Mr. Will Shakespeare's fault that Mr. Tunney, after he had retired from the ring with his million, began delivering lectures about Mr. Will Shakespeare's plays.

Gene Tunney

William Lyon Phelps

from AUTOBIOGRAPHY WITH LETTERS

On Thursday 22 December 1927, while we were staying at the house of Mr. William Matheson at Coconut Grove, Florida, I went over to Miami Beach and had a long talk with the champion heavy-weight boxer of the world, Joseph J. Tunney of New York, universally known as Gene Tunney. I knew he was fond of reading Shakespeare. I told him that I was teaching Shakespeare at Yale, and that during the coming Spring term I should be very glad to have him address my class. He immediately agreed.

When this was announced in the newspapers, I was called up on the telephone by a reporter and asked "Can Tunney really talk in public on Shakespeare, or is this just part of the ballyhoo for the next fight?" I replied that if we should change places, Mr. Tunney would look much better lecturing on Shakespeare than I should in the ring with Jack Dempsey.

Mr. Matheson invited Tunney to meet the Bishop of Florida and Mrs. Mann, together with Ruth Bryan Owen, and several others, at lunch. Although Tunney is a big man and weighed two hundred pounds, his hands and feet are small. He stood beside Mrs. Owen, a tall woman, and we found her hands were longer, though not as broad as his. Tunney and the Bishop carried on a spirited conversation; and Tunney told us how he came to enjoy Shakespeare. It was when he was a private soldier in the

World War. There was a comrade who was always talking about Shakespeare; and Tunney, becoming interested, made up his mind he would read him. He had the bad luck to begin with *Winter's Tale.* He read it through from beginning to end and it made no impression. I think most adventurers would have stopped there. Not so Tunney. *He read through Winter's Tale ten times.*

After the tenth reading, he felt he had mastered it. He then went on to read the other plays. In a similar manner, by concentrating his listening powers, he became a passionate lover of the best symphonic music and of the operas of Wagner.

On 23 April Tunney addressed my Shakespeare class. The large auditorium was jammed, with crowds standing up. Tunney used no notes. He spoke informally for three-quarters of an hour. He told the students they had had every educational advantage and he had had none. "But when you are graduated and out in the world, then your case will be like mine. Your professors will not be able to help you; you will have to do it all for yourself. If you succeed, it will be because you have had the necessary will-power and perseverance." He said perhaps his favourite play of Shakespeare was *Troilus and Cressida.* For it applied exactly to his own case. "Why have I been invited to speak at Yale? Surely not because I have anything important to say about Shakespeare. I have been invited because I am the champion boxer of the world. I am that *now,* and there is great interest in everything I do and say. I am followed around by crowds. But how long do you suppose that will last? It will last just as long as I am heavy-weight champion. Ten years from now nobody will care what I do or what I say. It is important for me therefore to make the most of the present moment, for the present moment is all I have."

He said Shakespeare understood that situation perfectly. Hector was the heavy-weight champion of the Trojans and the only man among the Greeks who could stand up to him was Achilles. But Achilles would not fight. He sulked in his tent. And yet he was very angry when Ulysses and the other Greeks put up Ajax to fight Hector; and all their cheers were for Ajax. "Now Ajax," said Mr. Tunney, "was a big powerful man without much brains, just like Jack Sharkey."

The next day a reporter called up Sharkey at his training-camp and said "Tunney says you are like Ajax." It is possible that Mr. Sharkey thought Ajax was some kind of a disease, for he responded, "You can tell Tunney there is nothing the matter with me at all."

I believe every newspaper in the world contained some kind of report of Tunney's address. Press cuttings were sent me from India, New Zealand, Alaska, Japan—indeed from everywhere. For the moment, Tunney found himself more famous for having lectured at Yale than for having defeated Dempsey; and I found myself more famous for having invited him than for any book I had written or any professional work I had done. . . .

About thirty years before this occasion, when on St. Patrick's Day, 1897, Jim Corbett fought Fitzsimmons at Carson City, Nevada, several prominent undergraduates at Yale had sent a small Yale flag for Corbett to place in his corner as a talisman during the fight. Although Corbett did not do this, the fact that the flag had been sent got into the newspapers, and the result was a scandal. Hundreds of persons insisted that these students be expelled, and I well remember that there was a long and exciting Faculty meeting, and that they were saved only by a close vote. One of the students was Payne Whitney.

Suppose the Faculty could have known that in thirty years the champion boxer of the world would lecture at Yale on Shakespeare!

That summer of 1928 Tunney was in the island of Brioni in the Mediterranean; there he was joined by the most famous literary man in the world and by the most famous musical composer—Bernard Shaw and Richard Strauss. The three men took long walks together. Mr. Shaw told me. "The newspaper men kept coming over from the mainland; they cared nothing whatever for anything I said or that Strauss could say; our opinions did not interest them. But the moment Tunney opened his mouth the reporters took down every word. They wished to know his opinions on every subject."

Some literary man, I have forgotten which, said he would rather be champion boxer of the world than a great poet. "For how wonderful it must be to go to any city in the world and know that you can lick any man in that town."

When one considers the number of strong fellows in every city, it seems incredible that any one man can feel certain of whipping them. I asked Tunney about that, and he replied "Well, there is room for only one champion at a time. The place is free and open to any man who can take and hold it." Then, after some reflexion, he said, "There are five qualities necessary if one wishes to be champion of the world, and all five are seldom found in one man."

The candidate for the championship must possess great strength; he must have a body far stronger than that of the average healthy young man. Of course there are thousands of whom this is true; there are any number of powerful young men. The second qualification is panther-like agility, speed, and nimbleness; this quality, when it is combined with immense weight and strength, is not so common. The man must be like an elephant in solid strength and like a leopard in ease and grace of movement. Still, while the combination is not so common as either quality taken singly, there are plenty of young men who are both strong and fast. The third quality is courage, the foundation of all virtues for any ambitious man, no matter where his ambition may lie. Many men are secretly afraid, no matter how confident their bearing, or how assured their speech. The successful fighter must either be without fear or succeed in overcoming it. Tunney told me (and without a shade of conceit) that he was not afraid of anybody or anything.

The fourth quality must be the ability to take punishment without becoming disabled. This is different from courage. Just as the bravest man may be seasick, or dizzy at a great height, so the bravest man in the ring may receive a blow either so powerful or so well directed that he cannot go on, and the fight is lost. This was the case with Corbett in his memorable contest with Fitzsimmons. He had courage, confidence, and will power; but when Fitzsimmons hit him in the solar plexus, he was like a man paralysed; he was through. If he had been able to endure that blow, he could have gone on and probably won. "Now," said Tunney, "if I had received that particular blow, it would have hurt, I should have felt the terrible impact, but I should not have become disabled. In Chicago, Dempsey repeatedly hit me fearful blows; they were like the shock of a pile-driver; every one of those blows hurt; yet I was able to go on. One reason was that whether I am in training or not, I keep my body, by the proper exercises every day, in such condition that it can successfully withstand almost any human blow."

And he explained how, on rising from bed every morning, he sat down, put his feet under the radiator, and bent over backward, keeping the abdominal muscles hard as steel. Should the ordinary healthy man try that motion just once, the result would be hernia.

The fifth, last, and by no means least of the qualifications is perfect control of the nerves; for strange as it may seem in the case of professional boxers, all of whom are of exceptional strength and bodily vigour, more men fail to reach the championship through bad nerves than through any other defect. Prizefighters suffer from insomnia even more than brain workers, and it is easy to see why. The ordinary prizefighter is not a man of many intellectual resources; he cannot divert his mind with a variety of things. Thus, when he is in training for a contest and the day of doom draws near, he becomes more and more nervous. He cannot exercise every moment, and when he is not in full bodily activity, he finds it difficult to relax and feel cheerful, because he is thinking all the time of the great day. Finally, when he steps into the ring, his nerves are in a frazzle.

I envy Gene Tunney his nerve control more than his strength or agility. On the day before his contests and on the morning thereof, he was as calm and self-possessed as if nothing unusual were going on.

He said something of value to every man and woman without regard to the nature of their work. He regarded it as fortunate that he loved good books and music, etc., quite apart from the intrinsic value of such things; because, during his weeks of active training, he could at any moment divert his mind by reading a good book or listening to the piano. It is not healthy for any man or woman to be obsessed by one thought; the mind becomes hag-ridden, and the nerves go to pieces. The brain needs variety; thus the more avocations a man has outside of his work, the more efficiently he will do that work, and the fresher and healthier his mind will be.

Thus all the five qualities enumerated by Gene Tunney are very seldom found in any one man. 1. Strength. 2. Supple agility and speed. 3. Courage. 4. Ability to take punishment. 5. Complete control of the nerves.

The ideal element in Tunney's nature enabled him to see the goal long before he reached it, as one sees the towers and pinnacles of a city from afar. He has all along been aided by sensitiveness to beauty, which has found expression and which has brought him refreshment and inspiration in poetry and music. Stephen Phillips's poem, *Marpessa,* is one of his favourites, and he carried it everywhere. Another of his best-loved poets is Francis Thompson, original, imaginative, and spiritual. In music, the *études* of Chopin move him more deeply than anything else. Among novelists, his most intimate friend is Thornton Wilder.

Unlike many self-made men, he has allowed neither success nor flattery to turn his head. He is not conceited; yet in his ring contests and in his preparation for them he was filled with confidence. His nature illustrates the difference between confidence and conceit.

This cheerful confidence did not make him careless, either in the ring or out of it. He made his own training rules and never departed from them. And even when he was not in training, he kept himself in condition by neither smoking nor drinking, by being careful in diet, *and by not getting excited.* On the day he fought Dempsey at Chicago, he had a good dinner at three o'clock, then read Somerset Maugham's novel *Of Human Bondage* for an hour and a half, and actually forgot he was to fight that evening!

Confidence means two things; it means that one is certain of one's abiltiy to perform the assigned task, certain of being equal to the situation; and secondly, it means that one enjoys the work in the assurance that one can do it well. The great surgeon goes to the hospital, not with fear and trembling, but with the certainty that he will perform the operation as it should be performed; so he is happy in his work.

The Myth of the Racially Superior Athlete

Harry Edwards

While there can be little argument with the obvious fact that black performances in sports have been and continue to be superior, on the whole, to those of whites, there is room for considerable debate over the identity and character of the factors that have determined that superiority and contributed to its perpetuation.

The myth of the black male's racially determined, inherent physical and athletic superiority over the white male rivals the myth of black sexual superiority in antiquity. While both are well fixed in the Negrolore and folk beliefs of American society, in recent years the former has been subject to increasing emphasis due to the overwhelmingly disproportionate representation of black athletes on all-star rosters, on Olympic teams, in the various "most valuable player" categories, and due to the black athletes' overall domination of the highly publicized or so-called "major sports"—basketball, football, baseball, track and field. But seldom in recent times has the myth of racially linked black athletic prowess been subject to so explicit a formulation and presentation as in the January 18, 1971 issue of *Sports Illustrated* magazine.

In an article entitled "An Assessment of 'Black is Best' " by Martin Kane, one of the magazine's senior editors, several arguments are detailed, discussed and affirmed by a number of widely known medical scientists, athletic researchers, coaches and black athletes. In essence, the article constitutes an attempt to develop a logical and scientifically defensible foundation for the assertion that black athletic superiority in sports is due to racial characteristics indigenous to the black population in America but not generally found within the white population.

Clearly there is no argument that black society is contributing more than its 11% share of athletes and star-status performers to professional sports. And where blatant racism and discrimination do not keep blacks from participation almost completely—such as in the Southeastern Conference—a similar pattern of black domination prevails in colleges and at other amateur levels where major sports endeavors are pursued.

Attempting to explain this disproportionate representation, Kane mentions, almost in passing, the probable influences of contemporary societal conditions and then launches into a delineation and discussion of the major factors giving rise to black athletic superiority. They are:

Racially linked physical and psychological characteristics:

1. Proportionately longer leg lengths, narrower hips, wider calf bones and greater arm circumference among black athletes than among whites.

2. A greater ratio of tendon to muscle among blacks, giving rise to a condition typically termed "double jointedness," a relatively dense bone structure.

3. A basically elongated body structure among black athletes enabling them to function as more efficient heat dissipaters relative to whites.

Race-related psychological factors:

1. The black athlete's greater capacity for relaxation under pressure relative to the capacity of the white athlete.

Racially specific historical occurrences:

1. The selectivity of American slavery in weeding out the hereditarily and congenitally weak from among those who came to be the forebears of today's black population.

Let us now turn to a general consideration of these major factors.

RACIALLY LINKED PHYSICAL AND PHYSIOLOGICAL CHARACTERISTICS

Kane's attempt to establish the legitimacy of this category of factors as major contributions to the emergence of black athletic superiority suffers from two basic maladies—one methodological, the other arising from a dependence upon scientifically debatable assumptions and presumptions concerning differences between the "races" of men and the impact of these differences upon capacity for physical achievement.

Simply stated, one grossly indefensible methodological tactic is obvious in virtually every case of "scientific" evidence presented in support of a physical or physiological basis for black athletic superiority. *In no case was the evidence presented gathered from a random sample of subjects selected from the black population at large in America.* Thus, supporting data, for the most part, were taken from black athletes of already proven excellence or from blacks who were availabe due to other circumstances reflective of some degree of uncontrolled social, political, or otherwise contrived selectivity. Therefore, the generalization of the research findings on these subjects to the black population as a whole—even assuming the findings to be valid—constitutes a scientific blunder of the highest magnitude and invalidates the would-be scientific foundations of this component of the author's argument.

With regard to the alleged physical traits supposedly characteristic of black athletes, the question can justifiably be posed. "What two outstanding black athletes look alike or have identical builds?" One of Kane's resource persons answers this question: "Lloyd C. 'Bud' Winter makes it quite obvious that black athletes differ from each other physically quite as much as whites do." He notes that Ray Norton, a sprinter, was tall and slender with scarcely discernible hips, that Bobby Painter, a sprinter, was squat and dumpy with a swayback and a big butt, that Dennis Johnson was short and wiry, that Tommy Smith was tall and wiry, and so on.

Further evidence is plentiful: What physical characteristics does Lew Alcindor have in common with Elgin Baylor, or Wilt Chamberlain with Al Attles, etc? The point is simply that Wilt Chamberlain and Lew Alcindor have more in common physically with Mel Counts and Henry Finkel, two seven-foot white athletes, than with most of their fellow black athletes.

Even excepting the hyperbolic illustrations just documented, what emerges from any objective analysis of supposed physical differences between so-called races is the undeniable fact that there exist more differences between individual members of any one racial group than between any two groups as a whole.

Recognition of this essential fact precludes the type of incredible qualification that Kane is forced to make when faced with exceptions that do not fit the framework he has developed. A case in point is his assertion that the physical differences between white and black racial groupings predispose blacks to dominate the sports requiring speed and strength while whites, due to racially linked physical traits, are predestined to prevail in those sporting events requiring endurance. When confronted with the fact that black Kenyans won distance races and defeated highly touted and capable whites in the 1968 Olympic Games, the author makes the ridiculous post hoc assertion that (the Kenyans) Keino and Bikila have black skin but a number of white features.

RACE-RELATED PSYCHOLOGICAL FACTORS

The academic belief in the existence of a national or a racial "character" was supposedly disposed of by scholars decades ago. Their persistence among the ranks of coaches and other segments of the American population only indicates the difficulty with which racial stereotypes and caricatures are destroyed or altered to comply with prevailing knowledge. Kane and his resource persons, mostly coaches, recreate a portrait of the black athlete as the happy-go-lucky, casual, "What—me worry?" Negro made so familiar to Americans through history books, Stepin Fetchit movies and other societal outlets. But besides the fact that the overall portayal is inappropriate, not even the psychological traits attributed to black athletes are substantiated.

Kane quotes Lloyd C. Winter, former coach of a long line of successful black track and field athletes, as stating: "A limber athlete has body control, and body control is part of skill. It is obvious that many black people have some sort of head-start motor in them, but for now I can only theorize that their great advantage is relaxation under stress. As a class, the black athletes who have trained under me are far ahead of whites in that one factor—relaxation under pressure. It's their secret."

In data collected by Bruce C. Ogilvie and Thomas A. Tutko, two athletic psychologists whose work was ironically featured in the same issue of *Sports Illustrated* in which Kane's article appears, a strong case is made for the fact that black athletes are significantly less relaxed than white athletes in the competitive situation. (I am intimately familiar with this data as a result of my Ph.D. dissertation, *Sport in America: Its Myths and Realities.*) Using an Institute for Personality and Ability Testing (IPAT) test that is generally considered to have a high degree of reliability in both cross-cultural and simple comparative investigations, the following findings emerged when the psychological orientations of successful black and white athletes were compared:

1. On an IPAT test, successful black athletes showed themselves to be considerably more serious, concerned and "uptight" than their white counterparts as indicated by their relative scores on the item "Sober/Happy-go-lucky." Blacks had a mean stern score of 5.1 as compared to a mean score for whites of 5.5 (level of significance of differences between scores is .01; N = 396 whites, 136 blacks).
2. On the IPAT item of "Casual/Controlled," successful black athletes indicated a more controlled orientation. Blacks had a mean stern score of 6.6 as compared with the whites' mean score of 6.2 (level of significance of differences is .01; N = 396 whites, 136 blacks).

Sociologically, this pattern of differences among black athletes is perhaps to be expected, given the fact that they are aware that they operate at a decided disadvantage competing against whites for highly valued positions and rewards in an admittedly white racist society. Furthermore, sports participation holds the greatest promise of escape from the material degradation of oppressed black society. Thus, the assertion that black athletes are more "relaxed" than white not only lacks scientific foundation but is ludicrous as even a commonsense assumption.

RACIALLY SPECIFIC HISTORICAL OCCURRENCES

Kane states that "it might be that without special breeding the African has a superior physique." The statements of Kane and his resource persons evidence confusion as to the scope of characteristics involved in the selectivity process as it has affected mankind. Natural selection or "the survival of the fittest" has been predicated upon relative strength and physical attributes to a lesser degree in mankind than in any other form of animal life. This has been due largely to man's tremendously developed mental capabilities. The same would have held for the slave. While some may have survived as a result of greater physical strength and toughness, many undoubtedly also survived due to their shrewdness and thinking abilities.

The major implication of Kane's argument for the black population at large is that it opens the door for at least an informal acceptance of the idea that whites are *intellectually* superior to blacks. Blacks, whether athletes or nonathletes, must not give even this passing credence to the possibility of white intellectual superiority. By a tempered or even enthusiastic admission of black physical superiority, the white population of this racist society loses nothing. For it is a simple fact that a multitude of even lower animals are physically superior, not only to whites, but to mankind as a whole: gorillas are physically superior to whites, leopards are physically superior to whites, as are lions, walruses and elephants. So by asserting that blacks are physically superior, whites at best reinforce some old stereotypes long held about Afro-Americans—to wit, that they are little removed from the apes in their evolutionary development.

On the other hand, intellectual capability is the highest-priced commodity on the world market today. If in a fit of black identity, or simple stupidity, we accept the myth of innate black superiority, we could be inadvertently recognizing and accepting an ideology which has been used as the justification for black slavery, segregation and general oppression.

What then are the major factors underlying black athletic superiority? They emerge from a complex of societal conditions. These conditions instill a heightened motivation among black male youths to achieve success in sports; thus, they channel a proportionately greater number of talented black people than whites into sports participation. Our best sociological evidence indicates that capacity for physical achievement (like other common human traits such as intelligence, artistic ability, etc.) is evenly distributed throughout any population. Thus, it cuts across class, religious, and, more particularly, racial lines. For race, like class and religion, is primarily a culturally determined classification. *The simple fact of the matter is that the scientific concept of race has no proven biological or genetic validity.* As a cultural delineation, however, it does have a social and political reality. This social and political reality of race is the primary basis of stratification in this society and the key means of determining the priority of who shall have access to means and thus, valued goods and services.

Blacks are relegated in this country to the lowest priority in terms of access to valued goods and services. This fact, however, does not negate the equal and proportionate distribution of talent across both black and white populations. Hence, a situation arises wherein whites, being the dominant group in the society, have access to *all* means toward achieving desirable valuables defined by the society. Blacks, on the other hand, are channeled into the one or two endeavors open to them—sports, and to a lesser degree, entertainment.

Bill Russell once stated that he had to work as hard to achieve his status as the greatest basketball player of the last decade as the president of General Motors had to work to achieve his position. The evidence tends to indicate that Russell is quite correct. In short, it takes just as much talent, perseverance, dedication and earnest effort to succeed in sports as to become a leading financier, business executive, attorney or doctor. Few occupations (music and art being perhaps the exceptions) demand more time and dedication than sports. A world-class athlete will usually have spent a good deal of his youth practicing the skills and techniques of his chosen sport.

The competition for the few positions is extremely keen and if he is fortunate he will survive in that competition long enough to become a professional athlete or an outstanding figure in one of the amateur sports. For as he moves up through the various levels of competition, fewer and fewer slots or positions are available and the competition for these becomes increasingly intense because the rewards are greater. Since the talents of 25 million Afro-Americans have a disproportionately higher concentration in sports, the number of highly gifted whites in sports is proportionately less. Under such circumstances, black athletes naturally predominate. Further, the white athletes who do participate in sports operate at a psychological disadvantage because they believe blacks to be inherently superior as athletes. Thus, the white man has become the chief victim of his own lie.

On Hurricane Jackson

Alan Dugan

Now his nose's bridge is broken, one eye
will not focus and the other is astray;
trainers whisper in his mouth while one ear
listens to itself, clenched like a fist;
generally shadow-boxing in a smoky room,
his mind hides like the aching boys
who lost a contest in the Pan-Hellenic games
and had to take the back roads home,
but someone else, his perfect youth,
laureled in newsprint and dollar bills,
triumphs forever on the great white way
to the statistical Sparta of the champs.

The Chinese Boxes of Muhammad Ali

Budd Schulberg

Cassius Marcellus Clay was minus six when quietly invincible Joe Louis was demolishing Max Schmeling and sending him back on his shield to the land of the self-styled master race. The Joe Louis of Clay's childhood was another man, a balding, overweight ex-champion getting a boxing lesson from Ezzard Charles and a pathetic thumping from Marciano. Manager-trainer Angelo Dundee, a fixture in Cassius's corner from the first fight to the last, remembers Clay as a bubbling sixteen-year-old bouncing into the Louisville gym and begging to put on the gloves with Angelo's flashy light heavyweight Willie Pastrano. Flying up from Ali's training quarters last March for the latest and greatest Fight of the Century, Angelo reminisced about his champion. In his voice was the awe one reserves for first meetings with the gods.

"There was something special about him even then," Dundee remembered. "Something about the way he moved, like the song says. Something about the way he talked. He's learned a lot, traveling around the world, being with people—he really feeds off people—little people, big people—that's his college. He doesn't learn from books—truth is he never really learned to read, but he sucks up knowledge, information, ideas like an elephant sucks up water. And he trumpets it all out just like an elephant too."

"Do you go along with Ali's description of Ali? Is he the most unusual fighter you ever handled?"

Over the big Cuban cigar in the small Groucho Marx-like face the answer poured forth without a second's hesitation. "Not just a fighter, he's the most unusual human being, the most fascinating person I ever met—period."

In those hectic days before and after "The Fight"—the most widely attended single event in the history of the world—we were to enjoy an intimate look at the man who created the first $20-million rumble through the force of two unique qualities: his physical coordination and his metaphysical personality. A personality as changeable as a March weather report, a psyche simple one moment, complex the next, loving, suspicious, overgenerous, self-protective, with flashes of brilliance lighting a dense thunder sky. We were privileged to sit with him in his introspective moments, get caught with him in the midst of crowds that threatened to crush him to death with their love, watch him handle rival hangers-on with the delicacy of a born diplomat, and see him swing from playful child to a man under all the pressures our hyped-up sports world and superstate Pentagon can bring to bear on a quixotic and sensitive nature.

We have said with conceit (in the old-fashioned sense) and also with conviction that, just as a people get the government they deserve, so each period in our history seems to create the heavyweight champion it needs to express itself on the platform where body language and social currents fuse. This seems to have been true of every true knight we have studied in the lists from American slavery's heavyweight champion Tom Molineaux upward. But never has there been a prize fighter who seemed so to our manner born as Cassius Marcellus Clay a.k.a. Muhammad Ali. His career began, appropriately, in 1960, in the Camelot days, in the time of the Kennedys that welcomed the decade, promised it hope, and asked for sacrifices in exchange for solutions. The New Frontier. Already antique, the words ring with the sound of pewter respectfully aged and polished for Sunday visitors. Imagine a time before the Bay of Pigs, before Dallas, before Watts, before the attempted Americanization of Indochina, before assassination became an annual horror, Medgar Evers, John Kennedy, Malcolm X, Martin Luther King, Bobby Kennedy. . . . Before the credibility gap of LBJ. Before the Chicago Convention, before Kent State and Jackson State. Before Nixon promised to get us out of the war by invading Cambodia and Laos and North Vietnam.

As our only world-famous athlete of the Shook-Up Decade just past, C. M. C. a.k.a. M. A. received into his beautiful black body every one of the poisoned arrows mentioned above. Wounded by all those arrows of our social misfortune, he refused to die. Hate him for this or despise him for that, he is still our youth, our conscience, our Mark Twain of bitterness and laughter. Of all our champions, gloved and bareknuckled, from the end of the eighteenth century to the dawn of the twenty-first, he is, in his own words, "the most unusual." Taunted by the ofays, Jack Johnson taunted back. Accepted by whites who offered him the national laurels and social responsibilities that came with the championship, Joe Louis accepted back. Never quite an Uncle Tom, he was the Good Joe who knew his place. He was the hero but never the author of his allegory.

But the Sixties were a whole different number. In a time of prodigies turning on their dads—or rather, tuning out their daddies—ready for the bell, ready to take on all comers in and out of the ring, was that prodigious brown descendant of Henry Clay: Cassius Marcellus Clay, the Fifth Beatle. Before we were prepared for the impact—but what were we prepared for in innocent 1960?—the loud laughing mouth in the handsome Greek god of a head was shouting, "Here I come, ready or not!" And who except his fellow teen-agers could have been ready for the innovative style that was to revolutionize not only the heavyweight division but the heavy social order that it entertained?

Watching him dance around the best and biggest of the amateurs on his way to AAU and Golden Gloves titles, *cognoscenti* of the game were more amused than impressed. A heavyweight who prances around the ring like a lightweight? Look at the way he bends his dancer's waist backward to avoid being hit! A tough pro would move in and break his back when he pulled that kid stuff. That just ain't the way a heavyweight fights. But this was more than fast tactical footwork; it was excessive mobility, sometimes physically unnecessary, a new psychological weapon—hit and run, jab and dance, befuddle, frustrate, and tire the enemy before zeroing in.

Beatle V had begun to create his own pop culture in the ring. Archetype of the young athlete in the Age of Aquarius, he bounced happily to Rome for the 1960 Olympics, dazzling foreign challengers who could not believe a six-foot-three-inch will-o'-the-wisp. Or a bronze Mercury, for the eighteen-year-old original convinced an adoring audience that he was that earlier Roman deity incarnate, combining speed and grace with eloquence, wit, and a mysterious elegance.

Home to Louisville he came wearing his gold medal and his boyish grin, and the white world seemed united with the black in agreement with his own efflorescent image of himself: the prettiest, the wittiest, the greatest. He strutted the streets of his hometown and paused to admire his reflection in store-front windows. "Look at me—I'm beautiful! An' I'm gonna stay pretty cuz there ain't a fighter on earth fast enought t' hit me!" Then he would dance and throw his lightning combinations into the air, or in the direction of a half-scared, half-awed ten-year-old black brother—he has always been drawn to kids, and especially black kids, though this was still 1960 and the pattern was all ego-popping ebullience, a narcissism that might have been irritating but that was instead irresistible because it was so utterly without guile, because it spoke to you with the directness of the wild rose who says, "Look at me, am I not beauty? Inhale me, am I not perfume?" You could no more resent the natural arrogance of the rose than you could the insouciant "Look Ma, I'm dancin'!" of young Cassius Marcellus. Of course a rose also has thorns, weapons concealed for its protection. That might have been a warning as to the deeper nature of the brown deity preparing for his pivotal role in the epic drama of the Sixties.

Scene 1, Act I, was deceptively harmonious, as truly made epic dramas demand, festooned with integrated hero worship and gratitude seemingly requited.

A group of well-to-do Louisville sports put their money where their local pride is and set up a syndicate to sponsor Cassius's professional career. In return for half the anticipated profits, they pay him a comfortable weekly salary, with a down payment on a tangerine-colored Cadillac, the first of a long line of exotic chariots. His first pro test is a win over a tough white sheriff, Tunney Hunsaker. Clay's fights are performances—put-ons with blood. As he moves up into the big time, he rhymes his predictions—"Archie Moore will fall in four"—and the ancient light heavyweight, almost thirty years older than the quickfooted bard, suffers the prophecy.

Next we see Clay at, of all places, The Bitter End, a hip Greenwich Village launching pad for avant-garde talent, where he sports a new tuxedo to engage in poetry competition with a lineup of ezra-pounded bards, grooving to his impending Garden bout with tough and highly rated Doug Jones. In a style all his own—call it an infectious boxing supplement to the anti-over-thirty spirit of the oncoming youth style—he laughs off all the old champions. Who's Liston? Louis who? To a generation splitting from its elders and their traditions, he's "The Greatest." Under that title he cuts a record of chatter, doggerel, and song, and long before the hard-eyed experts of the ring think he's championship material or ready for Terrible Sonny Liston, his LP is discovered by teen-agers, including my sons, who find in his uninhibited ego-tripping nonsense that indescribable pleasure of being different from us, yes, and better than us. When my younger son was playing Clay's platter for the third consecutive time, I tried to cross-examine him as to what was so great about "The Greatest."

Across the generation net the answer was slapped back into my court in impatient monosyllables, "I dunno, Pop. I jus' dig 'im. I think he's cool. I dig the way he dances around those older fighters and makes 'em miss. And the way he rhymes and picks the round. He makes it more fun than in your day. And he's not a hypocrite. He knows he's 'The Greatest.' So why not say it? Why be a hypocrite? Be honest."

We retreated strategically, doing a verbal imitation of Cassius's defensive backbend, sensing the chronological lightning crackling in the atmosphere. We closed his bedroom door, and he went on singing along with Clay. The message was clear: The jib of "our" athletic heroes was cut to modesty. To every age its style, and "ours" (if we had to be consigned to the past) was for winners to hang their heads in mock self-deprecation. "Well, those guys in front of me opened up a pretty good hole and I just ran to daylight and got lucky, I guess." Did we ever hear a broken-field runner telling the press, "Look, I'm so shifty and so fast, it's impossible for the defense to lay a hand on me"? It's true that Joe Louis was asked one too many times how he expected to handle Billy Conn's speed and boxing ability and came up with the mot, "He c'n run, but he can't hide." But when the fight was over, and the job accomplished, it simply wasn't Louis's or "our" style to speak the exuberant truth: "Look, I tried to tell you how great I was, and you chumps wouldn't listen. There's never been anything like me in the history of the world."

Truth, man. Don't hide behind a lot of well-gee-whizzes like your daddies. Come to think of it, a whole new generation coming of age in the early Sixties thought of the preceding generation as slower, dumber, less musical, less honest, more hung-up, less where-it's-at. Every generation wants to devour its predecessor, and we have only to go back two generations to conjure the Jazz Age of Fitzgerald and College Humor when bare knees, rumble seats, ukuleles, bathtub gin, wild parties, and free verse were creating a new life-style almost as horrifying to the people who grew up in the nineteenth century as the present youth culture is to the parents of Woodstock Nation. The key to that sentence is almost. Maybe it's because we're still going through it, but the intensity with which that Now generation wants to rip off daddy and mommy (*vide:* the latest "youth-oriented" epic at your neighborhood moviehouse) makes the Scott-Zelda rebellion seem as dangerous as a game of post office.

If the child of our times carries a flower in one hand and a stick of dynamite in the other, it is because he is an Oedipus who has read one book too many of Marcuse (or Che or Fanon) and is ready to lay down his guitar and his strobe light to fight for something he defines dimly, but deafeningly demands—a better world, an environment that will contain and harmonize our nuclear genius.

And where does this bring Cassius Clay (as he still called himself in his antechampion days)? To Las Vegas in the hot July of 1963. President Kennedy is still safely in the White House. There are some 15,000 U.S. Army "advisers" still noncombat in Vietnam. Sonny Liston, first a homeless St. Louis waif, then a tough old jailbird, later a Teamster goon, is heavyweight champion of the world. Yet to burst on the American consciousness is a black intelligence burning with scorn for "the collective white men" and "the so-called American Negro"—Malcolm X.

Cassius Clay has come to Vegas as the heir-apparent to the heavyweight throne. He has just butchered the British and Empire champion, Henry Cooper, in five rounds after having been saved by the bell himself at the end of four. Proximity to disaster hasn't dampened Cassius Clay's love affair with Cassius Clay. "He thrives on the precipice," says faithful Angelo Dundee. "He could give Norman Vincent Peale lessons on the power of positive thinking." And it's true that the clout of the Cooper hook that put him down has served only to convince young Clay that the most powerful punch in the world can deflect him but momentarily from his climb to the top of the mountain. He is twenty-one years old, and one of his roommates is Destiny. The other is his brother Rudolph Valentino Clay.

When David Brinkley and his TV producer, Stuart Schulberg, call on the Clay brothers, they find them stretched out on their luxurious beds, barechested and barefooted, wearing expensive slacks. "Da-vid Brinkley!" Cassius cries out, in that natural comedy style that makes his emphatic pronunciation of names laugh-provoking without being insulting, "Da-vid Brinkley, you're my man!" Cassius is on the phone to room service ordering breakfast. "Orange juice, a couple of jugs, a box of corn flakes. And milk. Can you send three quarts? And eggs—scramble up a nice batch for us, say about two dozen? Two or three rashers of bacon and a loaf of toast. What, service for six? No, ma'am, this is breakfast for two!" The recent conqueror of the British Empire and his brother Rudolph Valentino fill the room with their laughter. Then Cassius turns to Brinkley with those large eyes framed like a movie star's between butterfly brows and high cheeckbones. "Say, David, will you do me a favor, let's do the 'good nights' together." And the supercharged contender lapses into a more than passable imitation of Chet Huntley. "This is Cassius Marcellus Clay in Las Vegas. Good night, David." And Brinkley responds in his patented sign-off. "And this is David Brinkley. Good night, Cassius." Clay breaks up. He pounds his brother in joy. "Hey, David, that's out of sight!"

Watching him roll his marvelous brown body and bark with laughter like a frolicking young sea lion, who would guess that this would be the same man who was soon to frighten, infuriate, and finally confront the white power structure of America? But looking back on the twenty-one-year-old Cassius with the hindsight gained from observing and visiting with the twenty-nine-year-old Ali, we now know that within the beamish boy who bantered with Brinkley lurked the racial anxiety, producing anger as causatively as boiling water releases steam. We follow joyously flamboyant Cassius Clay through his visit to Vegas for the Liston-Patterson "fight." And since everything about the transformation of Cassius the Caterpillar into Muhammad the Butterfly is instructive, we wonder at the meaning of his existential acts. He invades the casino where Liston is playing blackjack, calls him an ugly bear, invites him to an impromptu match to settle the title here and now, laughs at the scowl that had frozen the blood of men who had thought themselves brave.

Onlookers were merely amused by the brash kid with the big mouth who seemed to have borrowed his publicity buildups from the wrestlers' division of the classical school of acting. What was dangerous about Cassius was not immediately appreciated: the intensity, the concentration, the determination with which he played. It was this that separated the fools of Shakespeare from mere Middle Ages merrymakers. Wise kings listened to inspired fools while foolish kings laughed at the exterior apparatus of their jokes.

The best of fools was a set of delicate Chinese boxes, and just such a fool was Brother Malcolm's "so-called American Negro," a series of ingeniously fitted personalities, each larger one concealing and protecting a smaller one within until you finally come to the true resilient core. Many hundreds of years of slavery and now more than a century of hypocritical "freedom"—a democracy with the black man still locked into the steaming cities while the white man retreats from his day's work to the flowering suburbs—this is the historical imbalance that conditions all but the most profoundly integrated (or whitened, Ali might say today) black man to take refuge in his Chinese boxes as a fox hides in the hedge from the hounds.

I may have more black friends than 95 per cent of white Americans, and sometimes I feel I have succeeded in reaching the box within the box within the box—but I never leave the room without a feeling that the brothers left together will now continue to remove black Chinese box after Chinese box until at last they are left sitting around in their naked souls, like a game of spiritual strip poker that reveals all to each, an exclusive deal played in a private club off limits even to sympathetic white players who would join the game.

What has all this to do with Cassius Clay in pursuit of Liston's title and his subsequent odyssey? To our minds, a great deal. We are preparing ourselves not to be surprised when a young man, making of each boxing bout his parable, exchanges one image for another as dramatically but also as easily as an actor changes costumes between scenes.

And make no mistake about it, they were scenes in a drama that young Cassius knew he was playing, an allegory in the Brechtian manner that he was consciously authoring and acting out. On many different levels—the physical, the psychical, the religio-political. From his training camp for the first Liston fight Cassius waged an intense campaign of psychological warfare. The old bus Cassius had bought to move with his entourage was painted red and white with "World's Most Colorful Fighter" emblazoned across the top, and covered with signs broadcasting his low opinion of the champion: Bear Hunting Season. Liston Will Fall in Eight. Big Ugly Bear. . . . Cassius would invade Liston's training camp, hose him with a torrent of insults and threats—poetically alone in America in thinking he could supplant the brooding, dangerous Sonny, who was expected to spank the obstreperous Cassius as a stern papa would whup a wayward son. The odds on Liston were eight to one. Of the press who were on the scene from every continent, we remember not one who gave the strident challenger a chance.

But Angelo Dundee, who somehow managed to remain uninvolved in the psychological high jinks and the gathering morality play, had warned us that Cassius had the style to outbox and defeat the ponderous, aging Liston. An odd group had believed in Cassius Clay. Our teen-aged son David, who sent me twenty-five dollars he had saved from allowances to bet on youth vs. age; Drew "Bundini" Brown, an ancient mariner and saloon-keeper with a gift of gab, almost as seven-tongued as Cassius, who was called "assistant trainer" but was really the guru-in-residence; and an unobtrusive black man who was guite possibly the most remarkable man, black or white, then living in America. This was the acknowledged spokesman for blackness in Harlem, the scourge of Uncle Toms and Negro civil rights leaders who spoke of integration and gradual improvements. This was the rising star of black militancy, the ex-hoodlum, thief, dope peddler, and pimp who finally, through the teaching of Elijah Muhammad, had come to understand his life of ghetto hustling as the painful preparation for his eventual role as liberator of his more than twenty million brothers suffering a living genocide in white America. Born Malcolm

Little, he was known in the street as Big Red before he became even better known as Malcolm X.

In tracing two centuries of major prize fights, we can see how inextricably they are woven into our social fabric. From Molineaux to Louis, our champions were heroes of related acts that served as parables of cultural change. But B.C., Before Clay, they had only dimly recognized their roles. Now it was A.D., After Dallas, which Malcolm X had called "America's chickens come home to roost." There was a keen black hatred of all white institutions in Malcolm's mind when he made the statement that Elijah used as the official reason for silencing him, pending his excommunication from the Black Church. The headline, seemingly a crass postmortem on the catastrophe in Dallas, had been taken from a context in which Malcolm had been discussing the atmosphere of racial hatred and social violence that the white man had created in America, a rabid intolerance that finally had struck down the Chief of State himself. This was too tragically true. A liberal white President had no business driving in an open car through a hate-filled Texas city where his enemies were articulate and armed. Camelot was in ruins, the boiling volcano in Harlem was getting ready to erupt again, and Malcolm X, in the moment of greatest travail in a life that sensitively reflected all the nightmare distortions of the American dream, was counseling the challenger along lines either totally unfamiliar or anathema to the sports world.

Malcolm was not a fight fan; indeed he hardly knew who Cassius was when he met him and Rudolph at the Detroit mosque several years before. Cassius impressed him then simply as a likable, friendly, clean-cut, down-to-earth youngster with a contagious quality.

But in The Fight of 1964, Malcolm was convinced that Cassius had invited him to Miami to help the young fighter prove to the world the superiority of Islam over a white Christianity that had brainwashed the Negro community to accept inferior status and servitude. Molineaux had fought merely with his fists. Johnson had fought with his mocking smile and his wicked tongue. Cassius would fight with weapons never before carried into an American ring, his faith in a non-Western religion, as well as his growing awareness that, while he might be part of a minority 10 per cent in the United States, he was also part of a global family of nonwhites among whom Caucasians were in turn a minority doomed to eventual defeat. While Cassius was rattling his bear trap and playing the loudmouthed fool, while white Miami was either disgusted or entertained by this shrill showboating, a new philosophical and social confrontation was taking place that would prove as crucial to the middle Sixties as was the Louis-Schmeling debate to the late Thirties.

"This fight is the truth," Malcolm told Cassius. "It's the Cross and the Crescent fighting in a prize ring—for the first time. It's a modern crusade—a Christian and a Muslim facing each other with television to beam it off Telstar for the whole world to see what happens." The mystical reformed master hustler with the razor-blade mind was convinced that Allah had brought Cassius to this moment in order to prove something to black men with stunted egos who thought they needed white spiritual advisors.

Those who attended the wildest weigh-in in the history of the heavyweight division thought that Cassius was more in need of psychiatric than spiritual assistance. Minutes before he burst into the ring at the Miami Beach auditorium we could hear the threatened promise of his arrival, like thunder before a storm. Then he and Bundini exploded into view, furiously pounding canes in angry rhythms on the floor and shouting their tribal slogan, "We're coming to rumble. . . . Float like a butterfly—sting like a bee! Where's the ugly bear? . . ." For an hour the demonstration went on, with Cassius screaming, lunging at Liston, shaking his fists, bulging his eyes. Cool and seasoned Jesse Abramson of the New York *Herald Tribune*, trained to report without involving his emotions, was for the first time shaken at a weigh-in. "I think they should call it off," he said to us. "He's in no condition to fight tonight." Most experts decided that Cassius was terrified and suffering from manic hysteria at the prospect of having to enter the ring with the dour-faced champion. Liston did his best to fix him with "the look," a baleful stare he had perfected during many years in prison. But Cassius would not be transfixed like Floyd Patterson. Screaming like a banshee, pounding the stage with his feet as if possessed, he kept up this bizarre performance until his blood pressure had bubbled over the 200 mark and observers were convinced that the next stop was the psychiatric ward.

While reporters were asking the local boxing commissioners if they were considering calling off this unequal contest between a seasoned old champion and this hysterical boy, Cassius was back at his motel being examined by Dr. Ferdie Pacheco, who found his blood pressure miraculously normal. "A case of self-induced hysteria," diagnosed Pacheco. As Malcolm said, it was a case of mind over matter. There wasn't a man in the world Sonny Liston was afraid of. But was this towering dark screamer a human being or a whirling dervish?

What we were seeing, along with all the other innovations Cassius was bringing to the climactic ritual of the heavyweight championship, were the new tactics of confrontation politics. Already a cult figure to the young, he was applying to the traditional ceremony of the ring the outlandish behavior of an Abbie Hoffman, a "crazy," against which the old-fashioned prison aggression of Sonny Liston could not aim its cold inner fire. Old-time boxing purists were disgusted, but there was Muslim method in his madness. In that hour of simulated rage he had cried, "You're the chump and I'm the champ! It is prophesied for me to win! I cannot be beaten!"

In the fight that night, a macabre affair haunted by goblins and doubting Thomases, Cassius confounded his army of skeptics by making Sonny

Liston suddenly look very slow and very tired. The old bull was winded after two rounds, punching ponderous gloves into the spaces that Cassius had occupied a moment before. At the end of seven rounds Liston hulked in his corner like a rejected Buddha, a worn-out god with a hole in his cheek toppled from his throne by a new religion—while the irrepressible standard-bearer of this new religion leaped around the ring proclaiming to the world he had just conquered symbolically for Islam, for Harlem, for Birmingham, for South Chicago, for a billion dark-skinned rooters around the globe, "I am the king! I am the king!"

Next morning at the press conference we discovered another of the Chinese boxes that make up the complex called Cassius Clay. Or so he had been called until that morning when he announced, in a voice with the volume now turned so low he was barely audible, that he was giving up his "slave name" and from now on would be known as Cassius X.

He chided the reporters for almost unanimously picking against him and informed them that he believed in the religion of Islam, that he believed Elijah Muhammad was his apostle, and that this was the religion believed in by more than seven hundred million people throughout Africa and Asia. Now reporters in the back of the room were calling "Louder," whereas the day before they had feared that Cassius's vocal gymnastics might burst their eardrums. When he stepped down from the platform we asked him about his immediate plans, and he told us he thought he would travel to Africa, the Middle East, and Asia. "They will all want to see the new champion of the world who believes the way they do," he said so quietly you had to lean toward him to hear it all. "And I will talk with the leaders and the wise men of those countries."

Of the past eight heavyweight champions, six had been Negro, but this was the first black champion to proclaim his blackness, to say to the white world, "I don't have to be what you want me to be," the ideal practitioner to tap out on the heads and bodies of his opponents the message: Black Is Beautiful.

400-meter Freestyle

Maxine W. Kumin

THE GUN full swing the swimmer catapults and cracks
s
i
x

feet away onto that perfect glass he catches at
a
n
d
throws behind him scoop after scoop cunningly moving
t
h
e
water back to move him forward. Thrift is his wonderful
s
e
c
ret; he has schooled out all extravagance. No muscle
r
i
p
ples without compensation wrist cock to heel snap to
h
i
s
mobile mouth that siphons in the air that nurtures
h
i
m
at half an inch above the sea level so to speak.
T
h
e
astonishing whites of the soles of his feet rise
a
n
d
salute us on the turns. He flips, converts, and is gone
a
l
l
in one. We watch him for signs. His arms are steady at
t
h
e
catch, his cadent feet tick in the stretch, they know
t
h
e
lesson well. Lungs know, too; he does not list for

a
i
r
he drives along on little sips carefully expended
b
u
t
that plum red heart pumps hard cries hurt how soon
i
t
s
near one more and makes its final surge TIME: 4:25:9

Symbolic Forms of Movement: The Feminine Image in Sports

Eleanor Metheny

The issues debated in this paper have a very long history. They were raised as early as 776 B.C. by the custom of excluding women from the sacred precincts of Olympia. They were raised in 1896 when women were admitted to competition in some events in the modern Olympic Games, but excluded from others. They are being argued around the world today as every national Olympic Committee makes its own decisions about the inclusion of women in the lists of competitors. This paper is not an attempt to resolve all of these long-standing issues; rather it is an attempt to inquire into the underlying nature of these controversies.

In an earlier paper—"Symbolic Forms of Movement: The Olympic Games"—I have interpreted the Olympic events as symbolic formulations of man's conception of himself as a consequential force within the universe of space, time, mass, and energy. In the present paper I shall pursue that interpretation with reference to some conceptions of roles appropriate for women.

THE BIOLOGICAL BASIS OF THE FEMALE ROLE

At the biological level, arguments about appropriate roles for men and women must be pursued in terms of differences in anatomical structure and function. These sexually significant differences are too well known to need explication here. With reference to sports competition, the important question is: How are these differences related to the ability to overcome the inertia of mass?

In terms of averages, it is a truism that men are larger and stronger than women; but this generalization does not hold for individual representatives of the two sexes. Some women may be very large and strong, and their ability to overcome the inertia of mass may be far greater than that of the majority of men. Similarly, some men may be smaller and less muscular than many women, and in any contest with the inertia of mass they may make a very poor showing—and may, in fact, be bested by the majority of the opposite sex.

To some extent these relationships may be modified by pregnancy, the demands of infant care, and possibly menstruation; and all of these episodes may serve to limit a woman's interest in the kind of training men may undergo in preparation for international competition. But they do not vitiate the biological fact that women appear to be fully competent to engage in a contest with the inertia of mass. In terms of averages, women's achievements may be less spectacular than those of men; in terms of individual achievement, some women may well excel most of the male competitors in any athletic event.

It would seem then that the age-old arguments about whether or not women should be admitted to competition in the Olympic events cannot be pursued in meaningful terms at the strictly biological level of anatomical structure and function.

THE MYTHOLOGICAL IMAGE OF THE FEMALE ROLE

In every culture, men and women play different roles within the social organization. In part, these roles are defined by the relative contribution each sex makes to the reproduction of the species—a biologically-determined contribution which is the same in all cultures. But in larger terms, these roles are established by some less well-defined set of factors not directly related to these biological differences, as evidenced by the fact that they differ from culture to culture. This complex of factors serves to determine the *masculine image* of behaviors appropriate to males and the corresponding *feminine image* of behaviors appropriate to females in each social group.

At the time of the early Olympic Festivals, which date back beyond the first recorded games of 776 B.C., the images of masculinity and femininity within the emerging culture of ancient Greece were clearly delineated. These early Greeks envisioned their gods as persons very like themselves, differing from human beings only in the extent of their personal powers over the natural forces of the universe. Thus, they assigned to their male gods all of the behaviors appropriate to their own image of supermasculinity, while the behaviors of superfemininity were assigned to the female goddesses. A brief review of the characteristics of these gods and goddesses may give us some insight into the fact that women were excluded from the sacred precincts of Olympia.

Among the male gods, Zeus, the hurler of thunderbolts, had dominion over all the forces of earth; and his messenger, Hermes, could overcome both space and time with winged feet. Poseidon, the earth-shaker, had similar dominion over the forces of the sea. Ares, the god of war, was a powerful destructive force; and Hephaestus, the god of the metal workers, could subdue the materials of earth with one powerful blow of his hammer and shape them into forms of his own choosing. Even Apollo, who epitomized the intellectual powers of reason and logic, was pictured as an athlete, well able to overcome the forces of earth by skillful use of his bodily strength as well as by his intellectual prowess.

What an Olympic team the gods would have been! How they would have excelled in every contest in the early Olympic Festivals! And it may be noted that the Olympic Games in which men strove to overcome the forces of the earth in symbolic contests were held in honor of Zeus, the all-powerful father of the gods.

In contrast, the image projected by the female goddesses is almost totally devoid of any suggestion of physical strength that might be used to overcome the forces of earth—or of men.

Demeter, the Earth Mother, is envisioned as the ground in which all life is bred and nurtured. Hera, the wife of Zeus, is pictured as his helpmate, whose own will must ever be subordinated to the desires of her husband. (It may be noted, however, that Hera is never wholly resigned to this role and at times she used her own female resources to seduce Zeus into doing her will rather than his.) Aphrodite, born of the foam of the sea, has none of these homely virtues. She is the goddess of beauty, infinitely desirable to all men. But if she delights in arousing their sexual desires, she can also be cruel and treacherous. In return for her favors, she demands tribute from her admirers, and men may well be fearful of her vengeance when her need of adoration is not satisfied. We are told that she was an accomplished swimmer, but she appears to have used this skill largely to display her lovely body in attractive poses that lured men to their own destruction.

The fact that these early Greeks could not reconcile feminine desirability with athletic prowess is underlined in the legends of Artemis and Athena. Artemis, the beautiful goddess of the hunt, was fleet of foot, and none excelled her in the use of bow and arrow—but men did not find her lovely body desirable. Or perhaps it was the other way around. At any rate, legend relates that Artemis and her followers rejected the love of men and found delight in the companionship of women. Athena, a goddess of wisdom, and of all goddesses the most respected, carried her own spear as she led men into battle, and her most famous statue shows her in full fighting array. But, alas, she too was denied the love of men, her perpetual virginity being commemorated in the Temple of the Maiden called the Parthenon.

Perhaps Artemis might have entered the foot races in the earliest games at Olympia; perhaps Athena might have thrown the javelin as well as the spear—and in fact there were some limited competitions of this type for maidens in some of the festivals attended by women. But even in Sparta, where young girls were encouraged to develop both strength and skill, marriage put an end to such competitive endeavours. For adult women, the virtues demanded were those of Demeter, Hera, and Aphrodite—and the strength, skill and intellect of Athena and Artemis did not fit in this image of feminine desirability.

These are the elements of which the prototypes of masculinity and femininity were compounded by the early ancestors of Western civilization. But these images were never wholly static. As men learned increasingly to control the stuff of their universe with skill and intellect, rather than with sheer strength of muscle, the masculine image reflected this evolving interpretation of man's role as a consequential force within the grand design. So, too, the feminine image began to change—albeit much more slowly.

The shift from muscle to skill and intellect may be seen in the contrast between Heracles, the legendary hero of pre-Homeric Greece, and Theseus, the later hero who made Athens into the most powerful of all Greek cities.

Heracles, who is sometimes credited with founding the earliest form of the Olympic Games, was a man of incredible strength. Certainly he would have been a formidable competitor in all of the early Olympic events, for no man could excel him in size or in strength of muscle. In all truth, however, he was not very bright, and his great strength led him into all sorts of trouble. He suffered great pangs of remorse for the damage caused by his own ineptitude, but he did not seem to learn much from these destructive episodes.

Theseus, who comes along much later in the story of Greece, presents quite a different picture. He is smaller than Heracles, and has less strength, but he uses that strength with far greater skill—and is more disposed to forethought than to remorse and vain regret. He is the first king to establish and maintain his right to rule largely by force of intellect, and in his story we find the first recognition of the virtues of cooperation among men and cities. Heracles might well have bested Theseus in the pancratium and other weight events in the Olympic arena, but Theseus would have excelled in any contest demanding skill and strategy in the use of the lighter implements, and probably in the team games—which were later to demand cooperation as well as competition.

In the time of Heracles, the feminine image projected by Demeter, Hera and Aphrodite was embodied in the legendary first woman, Pandora. She was lovely to behold, her name means "all joys," and she was welcomed as a helpmate—but, alas, she was really very stupid. Allowing her curiosity to overcome her caution, she opened the box that contained all the evils and sorrows of mankind, and let them loose in the world—where they plague men to this very day. But in her one display of good sense, she did slam the lid down just in time to preserve woman's greatest gift to man—the gift of hope.

In the picture of Pandora, there is little to suggest an interest in overcoming the inertia of mass. But Hippolyta, Queen of the Amazons, who won the enduring love of Theseus many centuries later, presents quite a different image.

As a ruler of her own kingdom, Hippolyta was the equal of Theseus in intelligence and skill, although smaller in size and of lesser strength. As they confronted each other in mortal combat at their first meeting, her courage matched his, and she fought bravely and well, neither asking nor offering advantage. In the eyes of Theseus she was both beautiful and desirable, and when he had won her he found new joy in the sexual embrace, for her ardor and skill matched his own. In marriage, she was a faithful helpmate and a devoted mother, and equally she was a good companion, both at home and in the hunt. In the end, she proved her love for Theseus by offering up her own life to save his—and it is said that he mourned her unceasingly for the rest of his days.

The legendary Hippolyta seems to have combined in her own person the skill and intellect of Artemis and Athena, the homely virtues of Demeter and Hera, and the beauty and desirability of Aphrodite. Surely, to Theseus, she was everything a man might hope to find in a woman. Had she been admitted to the lists of the Olympic Games, it seems likely that she would have earned her laurels proudly—not in the pancratium or weight-events, perhaps, but surely in the foot races and the javelin throw. And it seems likely that Theseus would have found pride in her achievements. But for the citizens of Athens, the time for recognition of such womanly feats had not yet come.

Hippolyta was cruelly rejected by the Athenians, both male and female. They could not reconcile intellect, skill and strength with their image of adult female sexuality. In her own life, however, Hippolyta proved them wrong—and they never forgave her for this. To this day, her name evokes suspicion in the minds of many men and women. Nonetheless, she left her own bright legend for future generations—the legend of a woman who delighted in using *all* of her own personal powers, a woman far ahead of her own time who won and held the love of the most eminent and farseeing man among the citizens of early Athens.

The gods and goddesses of ancient Greek myth have long departed from their home on Mt. Olympus, but their images are still reflected in the connotations of the words *masculine* and *feminine* as we use them today. Historically, as men have moved forward on the path of skill and intellect pointed out by Theseus, they have tended to devalue the virtues of sheer muscular power—but the term *masculine* still suggests the image of Heracles. So, too, it is Pandora's image that is suggested by the term *feminine.* And many of the arguments about the appropriateness of sports competition for women hinge on those connotations.

However, when the modern Olympic Games were established in 1896, the image of Hippolyta was partially cleansed of the slurs that have tarnished it through the years, and women were at long last permitted to seek their own laurels in some events. Today the image of the feminine athlete is still somewhat blurred, but its modern outlines now seem to be emerging in currently sanctioned patterns of sports competition for women. . . .

SPORT AS A SYMBOLIC FORMULATION OF SOCIALLY SANCTIONED FEMALE ROLES

Within the context of the biological, mythological, and social interpretations of the nature of females, we may now examine the theory that the sports in which women compete serve to formulate some conception of the female's role as a consequential force within the universe of space, time, mass, and energy.

At the international level, as represented by the Olympic Games, women are categorically prohibited from any attempt to overcome an opponent by direct application of bodily force. Since this prohibition cuts across all cultural lines, it would seem to be traceable to some biologically-defined difference common to the men and women of all social groups. The clue may lie in the differences between the ways in which males and females may use their own bodily forces in the mutual act of procreation.

For the male, the procreative act may be construed in terms of direct application of bodily forces subject to the male's control. Conversely, the female role must be construed in passive terms as the act of receiving and nurturing new life rather than creating it by personal intent expressed in terms of bodily force. Thus, the male may use his own muscular powers to coerce the female and force her to submit to his will, but the female cannot similarly coerce the male. By extension, then, it may well seem biologically appropriate for the male to force another person to submit to his will by direct application of muscular powers through bodily contact; conversely, it would be biologically inappropriate for the female to coerce or subdue another person by use of the muscular powers of her own body.

This interpretation may be further extended in the roles assigned to men and women in the mortal combat of war. Here, men have long found it possible to justify their own attempts to coerce other men into submission by threat of death; but men have seldom permitted their women to engage in such direct forms of mortal combat. Athena may have carried her spear as she led men into battle, but, insofar as legend relates, she did not personally use her own body to wrestle with the enemy. Hippolyta and her Amazons did, on occasion, engage in hand-to-hand combat—but the most severe charge made against Hippolyta by the Athenians was that she had "fought like a man."

When the resistance to be overcome in a contest is centered in an *object*, rather than in the body of another *person*, the prohibitions against use of bodily force by women are stated in relative, rather than in categorical, terms. Here the issue seems to be: *How much force* may a woman appropriately apply to an object?

At the Olympic level, women are not permitted to lift heavy weights or to throw the hammer. They are, however, permitted to put the shot, hurl the discus, and throw the javelin. Similarly, they are barred from the pole vault, the high jump, the high hurdles, and the longer foot races, but they are permitted to compete in the long jump, the low hurdles, and the shorter races. They are also barred from the more strenuous team games, but in 1964 they were permitted to compete in the milder game of volleyball—the only team game in which there is no possibility of direct body contact between opponents.

The facets of biology provide no logical basis of support for these relative distinctions. The number of women competent to perform in the excluded events may be small—but so is the comparable number of men: and this is generally true for all of the events included on the women's list, with the numbers increasing as the events become less physically demanding.

Socially, however, there appears to be a relationship between participation in such strenuous events and the kinds of work commonly done by the performer's parents. Women from homes in which both the father and mother are commonly employed in some form of manual labor may seemingly use their own muscular forces in athletics without impairing their own marriageability. Here the old fallacy of associating displays of strength with sexual inadequacy seems to be greatly weakened—although it still cannot be wholly dismissed as a factor in the determination of social approval. It must also be noted that even within the manual laborer group social approval tends to decrease as the muscular forces demanded by the events increase.

Within the category of fully-approved events in which the contestant attempts to overcome the resistance of an object, strength is generally far less important than skill. The contested objects in such games as golf, archery, tennis, badminton, and squash are essentially weightless, and the objective of the contest is to move these objects through space by manipulating a light instrument with skill and speed. (The heaviest such instrument is probably the bowling ball, which even very small women can lift without difficulty.) This emphasis on instrumental manipulation is further emphasized in the face-to-face games by either nets or rules that prohibit bodily contact. (Even in fencing, in which the body of the opponent is touched by the instrument, the touch is symbolic rather than forceful.)

All of these games were developed in the later years of human history by men called "gentle"—men whose personal status rested on the presumption of superiority in intellect and skill rather than of their muscular powers. But women did not participate in the early forms of these games. Not until the Industrial Revolution had created new forms of employment for women in industry, and not until women in the more socially-favored classes had begun to claim some measure of personal equality with their husbands, did women begin to participate in these sports reserved for gentlemen.

Significantly, these sports pioneers seldom competed with men directly in any of these games, and there is still strong aversion to this form of competition. Today, the socially-approved forms of competition in tennis, for example, are still man-man, woman-woman, and mixed doubles—in which the marriage relationship is symbolized by a partnership in which a man and woman combine their forces in a contest with another partnership team. Today, styles in double play are changing—but the most common strategy still emphasizes the man's strength of arm, while the woman uses her skill to support his efforts within a smaller part of their common court area.

Thus, in mixed doubles the woman still tends to play the role appropriate to Hera, the helpmate, as she uses the skills of Artemis and Athena and Hippolyta to support the efforts of her male partner, reinforcing his attempts to win the contest rather than threatening his mastery over their common environment. However, it must be noted that side-by-side play is now frequently seen in mixed doubles, particularly when both of the partners are superior players. So it would seem that men who are sure of their own strength and skill are not offended by displays of strength and skill in their mates—particularly when these female forces are combined with their own male forces to their mutual advantage.

Within the category of socially approved events in which the contestant attempts to project her body into or through space, women display a high degree of muscular strength as well as great skill and daring. In swimming, they propel themselves through the water with great speed, but they seldom compete in the longer distances. As Aphrodite noted, however, the water-supported movements of swimming display the female body to advantage, and it is noteworthy that the aesthetically pleasing patterns of synchronized swimming were developed by women, rather than by men. Similarly, women in gymnastics and free exercise have developed their own movement patterns, which emphasize grace and beauty to a far greater extent than do the standard events for men.

Diving, figure-skating, and skiing are also classed as graceful forms of movement, and in these sports personal velocity is greatly facilitated by the use of such manufactured devices as springboards, skates, and skis.

The management of the high velocities produced by these devices requires both strength and skill, but it is skill that is emphasized rather than strength.

Today, in the United States, the image of femininity projected by college women and endorsed by their potential mates is a "double image"—with one aspect identified as "woman at work" and the other identified as "woman at home."

As workers, these college women see themselves dealing with the forces of the universe in consequential ways, even as their men do. But neither the men nor the women picture themselves overcoming the resistance of mass, or of other persons, by sheer muscular force of bodily contact. Rather, they are prepared to use their wits in the realm of ideas, and they are adept in the use of lightweight equipment and manufactured devices that call for dexterity and skill rather than strength. On occasion, the men may still feel called upon to demonstrate the age-old conception of masculinity by performing feats of strength; but few college women seek this expression of their own human powers.

As potential wives and mothers, the college women are concerned with expressing their femininity in quite different ways. Recognizing their own biologically-based need for dependence on the male wage-earner, they modify their behavior in ways designed to enhance their own sexual desirability. They may also, on occasion, conceal their own abilities as workers lest the man of their choice might feel belittled by their competence.

Both sides of the image are evidenced in the socially approved list of sports for women. Strength and bodily contact are de-emphasized in favor of skill and grace; force is applied to weightless objects with lightweight implements; and velocity is attained by use of manufactured devices. And there is no serious competition in which women are matched against men. Rather, in those sports in which men and women participate together, they play as partners, with women generally accepting the supporting rather than the dominant role.

Thus, in our own time, it would seem that the college women of the United States have found it possible to combine the sexually-based image of Aphrodite, Hera and Demeter with the personal powers of Athena, Artemis, and Hippolyta, without doing violence to either, within the realm of sports competition. Thus, too, the forms of competition they have chosen may be construed as a dramatic formulation of their conception of the complex roles females may play as consequential forces within the grand design of the universe. Perhaps Heracles and Pandora might have been dismayed by this interpretation of what a woman is and what she can do—but let it be said to the credit of Theseus that he foresaw this picture some three thousand years ago when he described Hippolyta as everything a man might hope to find in a woman—and let us remember, too, that the legend of his love for her has endured, time without end, through the long years of human history.

The Stadium

William Heyen

The stadium is filled,
for this is the third night the moon
has not appeared as even a thin sickle.

We light the candles we were told to bring.
The diamond is lit red with torches.
Children run the bases.

A voice, as though from a tomb,
leads us to the last amen of a hymn.
Whole sections of the bleachers begin to moan.

The clergy files from the dugouts
to the makeshift communion rails
that line the infield grass.

We've known, all our lives,
that we would gather here in the stadium
on just such a night,

that even the bravest among us
would weep softly in the dark aisles,
catching their difficult breath.

Sport and Society: USSR vs. U.S.

Henry W. Morton

The sport program has been a great success from the Party's point of view and a positive achievement in the eyes of the world. With sport in the USSR organized in the form of a pyramid, along which by periodic competitions the best rise to higher levels and the cream become Olympic and international competitors, the Soviet Union has a very effective method of selection from the entire reserve of physical culturists in the country. One of its greatest gains has been increased opportunity in sport for women, who contribute greatly to Russia's supremacy at the Olympic Games. In terms of Communist goals, it has aided in the military preparedness of the nation, has helped to raise labor productivity, has increased Soviet international prestige, and has served as a means of social control in attracting and directing individuals in Party-sponsored activities.

Sport in Soviet society is enjoyed and appreciated by a citizenry which is attracted to athletic activity and thrilled by national and international sport competitions. That the Soviet people are sport enthusiasts is evidenced not only by the rapidly increasing number of sport participants, and by accounts of foreign visitors returned from the USSR, but also by depositions made by former Soviet citizens. When the latter were asked what aspect of present Soviet life they would not change, one answer often given was: The present system of sport and physical culture under government sponsorship. Why? They said that those in the Soviet Union who wanted to engage in athletics—children, adolescents, adults—had the opportunity to do so and had certain (if not always the best) facilities and equipment placed at their disposal for a nominal membership fee, facilities which they felt were only sometimes available to the individual in the West, and at a much higher admission fee. Many held the opinion that the state alone has the necessary resources to provide for a comprehensive sport program at a minimal cost to the citizen.

Yet in spite of a good deal of Marxian rhetoric, the system is geared to favoring the gifted and potential athlete while the average participant is short-changed, and it has spawned a number of abuses from which the socialist camp is no more immune than the Western nations it so frequently attacks. In many respects, the Soviet world of sport is a microcosm of Soviet society, mirroring the Party's success in transforming Russia into a leading power and at the same time its frustration in modeling the New Soviet Man.

The Soviet sport movement has great imitative appeal, understandably, within the Communist orbit, where similar sport administrations have been adopted, even in those bloc countries (Hungary, Czechoslovakia) whose sport tradition and achievements much predate Soviet Russia's. Its appeal is also strong to emerging nations, where the state is looked upon as the natural initiator of any program which requires the marshaling of people and resources. Leaders of these countries are well aware of the attractiveness of sport, and the Soviets are now in a position to send coaches to any country that requests aid in this area. With Russian help Indonesia built a huge sport stadium in Jakarta for the Asiatic Games of 1962.

I should like to consider briefly the American position in the international sport picture. Traditionally the United States participated only intermittently in international contests. Yet we held the world leadership, even though it is only for the quadrennial Olympic festivals that we have marshalled our athletic forces to compete abroad. In the interim period the United States still practices an isolationist policy regarding the great number of championships and international athletic events held on the European continent. America's sport parochialism stems from the nature of our favorite pastimes—baseball, football, golf, and bowling—which do not have universal appeal, while the internationally popular sports—soccer, bicycle-racing, volleyball, and so on—hold little interest for the American sport fan. In areas where a community of interest does exist, in track and field, in tennis, and in basketball, we are often negligent in exploiting the possibilities of international exchange. Very few foreign track and basketball teams have visited the United States.

A major difference in our approach from the Soviet attitude toward sport is that we are not dominated by an ideological system which determines the perspective for all our actions, nor do our sport directives flow from a central source or are our athletes committed to serving the state above their individual interests. On the contrary, our tradition of autonomous organizations independent of state interference permits instances like the following: The Brockton team which captured the United States Amateur Hockey Championship in 1959 lost all of its five games in the USSR by appalling scores because the majority of the original players could not make the trip owing to personal commitments. In the 1961 dual track meet between the USSR and the United States, ten American track champions refused to compete because of differences they had with AAU (Amateur Athletic Union) officials, thereby weakening their team. Charles McKinley, the leading American tennis player in 1961, did not play against Italy in the Davis Cup Zonal Competition of that year because his college informed him that further absences from classes would adversely affect his grades. Against lesser American opposition, Italy defeated the United States.

There is little doubt that ideally the chief merit of athletics is that it provides a healthy outlet for youthful energies; record-breaking and international performances should be secondary considerations. On the other hand, top athletic performances serve as strong magnets in attracting young people to sport. We have, however, not followed in the English tradition which emphasizes playing the game above victory, having our own form of winning mania. Still we as a nation have not the desire, nor do we feel the urgency, to spend huge sums of money to compete with the Communists in this area. Many Americans share the view of former President Eisenhower, expressed at his February 3, 1960, press conference, in which he stated that it was not necessary to keep up with the Russians in all areas, including sport, and that the United States could achieve a greater tempo only "if you take our country and make it into an armed camp and regiment it."

Need the alternatives rest at either extreme, state regimentation or haphazard organization? Could not our governmental agencies responsible for foreign policy and the various sport federations coordinate their efforts more efficiently to effect a better image of America abroad? United States prestige will not necessarily suffer if we act responsibly by sending representative players to foreign competitions, even if they do not win. We only lose face if we show indifference towards foreign athletes and fans by sending inferior teams. We must see our athletes abroad as what they really are, cultural diplomats—an aspect of sports which the Soviets have exploited very well.

Our international sport reputation can best be served by applying more efficiently the vast resources available to us. Advances could be made particularly in the area of financing. Often teams and athletes, in the less money-drawing sports of skiing, wrestling, weight lifting, gymnastics, and so forth, are not sent in sufficient numbers because of the lack of available funds. In time, it may be necessary to ask for federal contributions to help ease the financial burden. Such organizations as the People-to-People Sports Committee, composed of civic-minded, sports-interested citizens, whose object is to bring foreign players to the United States, need greater support from sport bodies as well as from the public.

In the Soviet Union, Party-directed policy goes to the extreme in its wholesale export of Soviet athletes as cultural ambassadors. We, on the other hand, largely unaware of the political repercussions of sport, have barely begun to subject our international sport participation to a much-needed reappraisal.

The Importance of Participation

John F. Kennedy

I want to express my thanks to you for this award. Politics is an astonishing profession—it has permitted me to go from being an obscure lieutenant serving under General MacArthur to Commander in Chief in fourteen years, without any technical competence whatsoever; and it's also enabled me to go from being an obscure member of the junior varsity at Harvard to being a honorary member of the Football Hall of Fame.

Actually, there are not so many differences between politics and football. Some Republicans have been unkind enough to suggest that my election, which was somewhat close, was somewhat similar to the Notre Dame-Syracuse game. But I'm like Notre Dame; we just take it as it comes and we're not giving it back.

I'm proud to be here tonight. I think General MacArthur, when he was Superintendent, really spoke about football in the classic way, because on so many occasions, in war and peace, I have seen so many men who participated in this sport—some celebrated and some obscure—who did demonstrate that the seeds had been well sown.

I am delighted to be here tonight and participating with you. This is a great American game. It has given me, personally, some of the most pleasant moments of my life—from last Saturday when I had a chance to see the Army-Navy game to a Harvard-Yale game I saw forty years before.

And I'm also glad to be here tonight with some men who also gave me some of the most exciting moments of my life. Clint Frank, who I understand is sitting down there, whom I saw score 5 touchdowns against Princeton. Tom Harmon who scored 21 points on my twenty-first birthday in the first half of a game against California. Cliff Battles who made George Marshall look good at Boston way back in the thirties. And Jay Berwanger who's here tonight, who, when Chicago was tenth in the Big Ten, was on everyone's All-American. And Sam Huff, who campaigned with me through the coal mines of West Virginia—and he's even better at that than he is on Sunday.

So I'm like a good many other Americans who never quite made it—but love it.

I do see a close relationship between sports and our national life and I sometimes wonder whether those of us who love sports have done as much as we should in maintaining sports as a constructive part of this country's existence.

I will not enter into a debate about whether football or baseball is our national sport. The sad fact is that it looks more and more as if our national sport is not playing at all—but watching. We have become more and more not a nation of athletes but a nation of spectators.

Professional athletes—professional athletics—I believe has a great place in our national life, but I must confess that I view the growing emphasis on professionalism and specialization in amateur sports without great enthusiasm. Gibbon wrote two centuries ago that professionalism in amateur sports was one of the early evidences of the decline and fall of the Roman Empire.

Football today is far too much a sport for the few who can play it well. The rest of us—and too many of our children—get our exercise from climbing up to seats in stadiums, or from walking across the room to turn on our television sets. And this is true for one sport after another, all across the board.

The result of this shift from participation to, if I may use the word "spectation," is all too visible in the physical condition of our population.

Despite our much-publicized emphasis on school athletics, our own children lag behind European children in physical fitness. And astonishingly enough, when Dr. Kraus and Dr. Weber recently went back, after ten years, to Europe they found a sharp decline in the physical fitness of European children, because in the last decade mechanization had begun to get at them too.

It's no wonder that we have such a high proportion of rejections for physical reasons in our Selective Service. A short time ago General Hershey told me that since October of 1948, of some six million young men examined for military duty, more than a million were rejected as physically unfit for military service. A good many of these men would not have been rejected if they had had an opportunity, when younger, to take part in an adequate physical development program.

To get two men today, the United States Army must call seven men. Of the five rejected, three are turned down for physical reasons and two for mental disabilities. To get the 196 thousand additional men that we needed for Berlin, the government had to call up, therefore, 750 thousand men—and the rejection rate is increasing each year.

I find this situation disturbing. We are underexercised as a nation. We look, instead of play. We ride, instead of walk. Our existence deprives us of the minimum of physical activity essential for healthy living. And the remedy, in my judgment, lies in one direction; that is, in developing programs for broad participation in exercise by all of our young men and women—all of our boys and girls.

I do not say this in order to decry excellence in sports or anywhere else. But excellence emerges from mass participation. This is shown by the fact that in some areas of our Olympic Games, we have steadily fallen behind those nations who have stressed broad participation in a great variety of sports.

I believe that as a nation we should give our full support, for example, to our Olympic development program. We will not subsidize our athletes as some nations do, but we should as a country set a goal, not in the way the Soviet Union or the Chinese do, but in the kind of way that Australia and other countries do—perhaps in our own way, to emphasize this most important part of life, the opportunity to exercise, to participate in physical activity, and generally to produce a standard of excellence for our country which will enable our athletes to win the Olympics—but more importantly than that, which will give us a nation of vigorous men and women.

There are more important goals than winning contests, and that is to improve on a broad level the health and vitality of all of our people.

We have begun this year to make progress toward this goal with the new President's Council on Youth Fitness. The idea behind our youth fitness program is to give as many American boys and girls as possible a chance for a healthy physical development.

Coach Bud Wilkinson and the Council staff, in cooperation with the Nation's leading educators and medical organizations, have worked out a basic physical fitness program for our elementary and secondary schools. Pilot projects have been set up in a number of cities.

The results so far show the effectiveness of what can be done and the extent of the need. In Muskogee, Oklahoma, for example, a city which prides itself on athletic achievement, which has had seven All-Americans in recent years, forty-seven per cent of the students failed a minimum physical fitness test. Only a fraction of those who qualified could pass the more comprehensive test of physical capability. Yet only six weeks of participation in a daily fifteen-minute program of vigorous exercise brought about a twenty-four per cent improvement among those who failed the first test.

Throughout the country we have found equally discouraging examples of deficiency—and equally encouraging examples of progress. I hope that every school district in this country will adopt our minimum program. I urge every parent to support the program and his own children's participation in it. I urge our colleges and universities to lay down basic standards of physical fitness. I urge the Nation's community recreation centers to provide more opportunity for those who are no longer attending school. And finally, I urge organizations such as this, with all of the prestige and influence which you bring to American life, to help establish more programs for participation by American boys and girls—by Americans young and old. In short, what we must do is literally change the physical habits of millions of Americans—and that is far more difficult than changing their tastes, their fashions, or even their politics.

I do not suggest that physical development is the central object of life, or that we should permit cultural and intellectual values to be diminished, but I do suggest that physical health and vitality constitute an essential element of a vigorous American community.

No one knew this better than the men of Greece, to whom our civilization owes so much. The Greeks sought excellence not only in philosophy and drama and sculpture and architecture, but in athletics. The same people who produced the poetry of Homer, the wisdom of Plato and Aristotle—they also produced the Olympic Games. The Greeks understood that mind and body must develop in harmonious proportion to produce a creative intelligence. And so did the most brilliant intelligence of our earliest days, Thomas Jefferson, when he said, "Not less than two hours a day should be devoted to exercise." If a man who wrote the Declaration of Independence, was Secretary of State, and twice President could give it two hours, our children can give it ten or fifteen minutes.

There's no reason in the world—and we've seen it tonight—why Americans should not be fine students and fine athletes. When I was young, Barry Wood used to play with Ben Ticknor football for Harvard—and hockey and baseball and tennis. He was a ten-letter man—and also the First Marshal of Phi Beta Kappa. And since then he has combined a life of leadership in the medical profession.

I have in Washington, as you know—and he is a friend of many of you—the Deputy Attorney General, Byron White, who was simultaneously a Rhodes scholar and a halfback for the Detroit Lions, and the year that he led the league in ground gained rushing, was also number one man in his class at the Yale Law School. We can combine and must combine intellectual energy and physical vitality.

Theodore Roosevelt once said, "The credit belongs to the man who is actually in the arena—whose face is marred by dust and sweat and blood . . . who knows the great enthusiasms, the great devotions—and spends himself in a worthy cause—who at best if he wins knows the thrills of high achievement—and if he fails at least fails while daring greatly—so that his place shall never be with those cold and timid souls who know neither victory nor defeat."

The athletes in this room—you gentlemen—and your colleagues across the country have known victory and defeat, and have accepted both. I salute you.

part 4

Post-Game Rumbles: Essays on History and Philosophy

Thinkers from Plato to Paul Weiss have found in sports material for systematic speculation and have used the phenomena of sports as a meaningful index of human nature, civilized behavior, and social concerns. Plato, for example, assigns an important role to athletics in his political system because his view of human nature includes both the mind and body as central features. Marshall McLuhan claims great psychological import for sports because, in his view, they play a central role in the collective life of a society; Arnold Toynbee measures the advance or decay of a civilization by its attitude toward the professionalization of sports. In contrast to these views, Paul Weiss holds that sports are events "cut off from the rest of the world." He believes it is not legitimate to extend the domain of sport, with its specific rules and forms, to either human nature or the broader society.

Weiss argues against athletics as the imitation of life, which is exemplified by war in his essay. His thesis runs counter to the general view of sports that has been held since Plato. Historically, imitation theories present sport as a microcosm of the larger society, either in the psychological terms of Thorstein Veblen or in the sociological ones of Lewis Mumford. Perhaps the most concise expression of this mimetic view of sports is McLuhan's statement that "games become faithful models of a culture." Johan Huizinga amusingly stands this notion on its head by saying, "Business becomes play." In his view, culture becomes a faithful model of games.

Arguing from an existentialist framework, Howard Slusher proposes sport as the "ground of being," and carries the mimetic theory into the metaphysical realm. Basically, Slusher feels that athletics furnish the arena in which human potential can reach its most complete fulfillment.

This view is diametrically opposed to that of Timothy Dwight, the eighteenth-century president of Yale who is mentioned in Henry Adams's essay. Dwight saw sports as immoral, a common view in Puritan America, and argued that they debased the human species. The differences between these two antagonists in time and theory point up one of the most interesting aspects of sports: Athletics provide us with a medium for an exchange with the past, even if that exchange is sometimes contentious. Clearly, over the reach of time we have explored and tried to understand our universe by speculating on sports.

from The Republic

Plato

(The first speaker in the dialogue is Socrates, the second Glaucon.)

MUSIC AND GYMNASTIC

"Did you never observe," I said, the effect on the mind itself of exclusive devotion to gymnastic, or the opposite effect of an exclusive devotion to music?"

"In what way shown?" he said.

"The one producing a temper of hardness and ferocity, the other of softness and effeminacy," I replied.

"Yes," he said, "I am quite aware that the mere athlete becomes too much of a savage, and that the mere musician is melted and softened beyond what is good for him."

"Yet surely," I said, "this ferocity only comes from spirit, which, if rightly educated, would give courage, but, if too much intensified, is liable to become hard and brutal."

"That I quite think."

"On the other hand, the philosopher will have the quality of gentleness. And this also, when too much indulged, will turn to softness, but, if educated rightly, will be gentle and moderate."

"True."

"And in our opinion the guardians ought to have both these qualities?"

"Assuredly."

"And both should be in harmony?"

"Beyond question."

"And the harmonious soul is both temperate and courageous?"

"Yes."

"And the inharmonious is cowardly and boorish?"

"Very true."

"And, when a man allows music to play upon him and to pour into his soul through the funnel of his ears those sweet and soft and melancholy airs of which we were just now speaking, and his whole life is passed in warbling and the delights of song; in the first stage of the process the passion or spirit which is in him is tempered like iron, and made useful, instead of brittle and useless. But, if he carries on the softening and soothing process, in the next stage he begins to melt and waste, until he has wasted away his spirit and cut out the sinews of his soul; and he becomes a feeble warrior."

"Very true."

"If the element of spirit is naturally weak in him the change is speedily accomplished, but if he have a good deal, then the power of music weakening the spirit renders him excitable;—on the least provocation he flames up at once, and is speedily extinguished; instead of having spirit he grows irritable and passionate and is quite impracticable."

"Exactly."

"And so in gymnastics, if a man takes violent exercise and is a great feeder, and the reverse of a great student of music and philosophy, at first the high condition of his body fills him with pride and spirit, and he becomes twice the man that he was."

"Certainly."

"And what happens? if he do nothing else, and holds no converse with the Muses, does not even that intelligence which there may be in him, having no taste of any sort of learning or inquiry or thought or culture, grow feeble and dull and blind, his mind never waking up or receiving nourishment, and his senses not being purged of their mists?"

"True," he said.

"And he ends by becoming a hater of philosophy, uncivilized, never using the weapon of persuasion—he is like a wild beast, all violence and fierceness, and knows no other way of dealing; and he lives in all ignorance and evil conditions, and has no sense of propriety and grace."

"That is quite true," he said.

"And as there are two principles of human nature, one the spirited and the other the philosophical, some God, as I should say, has given mankind two arts answering to them (and only indirectly to the soul and body), in order that these two principles (like the strings of an instrument) may be relaxed or drawn tighter until they are duly harmonized."

"That appears to be the intention."

"And he who mingles music with gymnastic in the fairest proportions, and best attempers them to the soul, may be rightly called the true musician and harmonist in a far higher sense than the tuner of the strings."

"You are quite right, Socrates."

"And such a presiding genius will be always required in our State if the government is to last."

"Yes, he will be absolutely necessary."

WOMEN AND ATHLETIC TRAINING

"And can you mention any pursuit of mankind in which the male sex has not all these gifts and qualities in a higher degree than the female? Need I waste time in speaking of the art of weaving, and the management of pancakes and preserves, in which womankind does really appear to be great, and in which for her to be beaten by a man is of all things the most absurd?"

"You are quite right," he replied, "in maintaining the general inferiority of the female sex: although many women are in many things superior to many men, yet on the whole what you say is true."

"And if so, my friend," I said, "there is no special faculty of administration in a state which a woman has because she is a woman, or which a man has by virtue of his sex, but the gifts of nature are alike diffused in both; all the pursuits of men are the pursuits of women also, but in all of them a woman is inferior to a man."

"Very true."

"Then are we to impose all our enactments on men and none of them on women?"

"That will never do."

"One woman has a gift of healing, another not; one is a musician, and another has no music in her nature?"

"Very true."

"And one woman has a turn for gymnastic and military exercises, and another is unwarlike and hates gymnastics?"

"Certainly."

"And one woman is a philosopher, and another is an enemy of philosophy; one has spirit, and another is without spirit?"

"That is also true."

"Then one woman will have the temper of a guardian, and another not. Was not the selection of the male guardians determined by differences of this sort?"

"Yes."

"Men and women alike possess the qualities which make a guardian; they differ only in their comparative strength or weakness."

"Obviously."

"And those women who have such qualities are to be selected as the companions and colleagues of men who have similar qualities and whom they resemble in capacity and in character?"

"Very true."

"And ought not the same natures to have the same pursuits?"

"They ought."

"Then, as we were saying before, there is nothing unnatural in assigning music and gymnastic to the wives of the guardians—to that point we come round again."

"Certainly not."

"The law which we then enacted was agreeable to nature, and therefore not an impossibility or mere aspiration; and the contrary practice, which prevails at present, is in reality a violation of nature."

"That appears to be true."

"We had to consider, first, whether our proposals were possible, and secondly whether they were the most beneficial?"

"Yes."

"And the possibility has been acknowledged?"

"Yes."

"The very great benefit has next to be established?"

"Quite so."

"You will admit that the same education which makes a man a good guardian will make a woman a good guardian; for their original nature is the same?"

"Yes."

"I should like to ask you a question."

"What is it?"

"Would you say that all men are equal in excellence, or is one man better than another?"

"The latter."

"And in the commonwealth which we were founding do you conceive the guardians who have been brought up on our model system to be more perfect men, or the cobblers whose education has been cobbling?"

"What a ridiculous question!"

"You have answered me," I replied: "Well, and may we not further say that our guardians are the best of our citizens?"

"By far the best."

"And will not their wives be the best women?"

"Yes, by far the best."

"And can there be anything better for the interests of the State than that the men and women of a State should be as good as possible?"

"There can be nothing better."

"And this is what the arts of music and gymnastic, when present in such manner as we have described, will accomplish?"

"Certainly."

"Then we have made an enactment not only possible but in the highest degree beneficial to the State?"

"True."

"Then let the wives of our guardians strip, for their virtue will be their robe, and let them share in the toils of war and the defense of their country; only in the distribution of labors the lighter are to be assigned to the women, who are the weaker natures, but in other respects their duties are to be the same. And as for the man who laughs at naked women exercising their bodies from the best of motives, in his laughter he is plucking 'A fruit of unripe wisdom,' and he himself is ignorant of what he is laughing at, or what he is about;—for that is, and ever will be, the best of sayings, 'That the useful is the noble and the hurtful is the base.' "

Translated by Benjamin Jowett

The Ancient Ways

Edith Hamilton

The Greeks were the first people in the world to play, and they played on a great scale. All over Greece there were games, all sorts of games; athletic contests of every description: races—horse-, boat-, foot-, torch-races; contests in music, where one side outsung the other; in dancing—on greased skins sometimes to display a nice skill of foot and balance of body; games where men leaped in and out of flying chariots; games so many one grows weary with the list of them. They are embodied in the statues familiar to all, the disc thrower, the charioteer, the wrestling boys, the dancing flute players. The great games—there were four that came at stated seasons—were so important, when one was held, a truce of God was proclaimed so that all Greece might come in safety without fear. There "glorious-limbed youth"—the phrase is Pindar's, the athlete's poet—strove for an honor so coveted as hardly anything else in Greece. An Olympic victor—triumphing generals would give place to him. His crown of wild olives was set beside the prize of the tragedian. Splendor attended him, processions, sacrifices, banquets, songs the greatest poets were glad to write. Thucydides, the brief, the severe, the historian of that bitter time, the fall of Athens, pauses, when one of his personages has conquered in the games, to give the fact full place of honor. If we had no other knowledge of what the Greeks were like, if nothing were left of Greek art and literature, the fact that they were in love with play and played magnificently would be proof enough of how they lived and how they looked at life. . . . They had physical vigor and high spirits and time, too, for fun. The witness of the games is conclusive. And when Greece died and her reading of the great enigma was buried with her statues, play, too, died out of the world. The brutal, bloody Roman games had nothing to do with the spirit of play. They were fathered by the Orient, not by Greece. Play died when Greece died and many and many a century passed before it was resurrected.

To rejoice in life, to find the world beautiful and delightful to live in, was a mark of the Greek spirit which distinguished it from all that had gone before. It is a vital distinction. The joy of life is written upon everything the Greeks left behind and they who leave it out of account fail to reckon with something that is of first importance in understanding how the Greek achievement came to pass in the world of antiquity. It is not a fact that jumps to the eye for the reason that their literature is marked as strongly by sorrow. The Greeks knew to the full how bitter life is as well as how sweet. Joy and sorrow, exultation and tragedy, stand

---

Excerpted from *The Greek Way* and *The Roman Way.*

hand in hand in Greek literature, but there is no contradiction involved thereby. Those who do not know the one do not really know the other either. It is the depressed, the gray-minded people, who cannot rejoice just as they cannot agonize. The Greeks were not the victims of depression. Greek literature is not done in gray or with a low palette. It is all black and shining white or black and scarlet and gold. The Greeks were keenly aware, terribly aware, of life's uncertainty and the imminence of death. Over and over again they emphasize the brevity and the failure of all human endeavor, the swift passing of all that is beautiful and joyful. To Pindar, even as he glorifies the victor in the games, life is "a shadow's dream." But never, not in their darkest moments, do they lose their taste for life. It is always a wonder and a delight, the world a place of beauty, and they themselves rejoicing to be alive in it. . . .

What constitutes Rome's greatness, in the last analysis, is that powerful as these were in her people there was something still more powerful; ingrained in them was the idea of discipline, the soldier's fundamental idea. However fierce the urge of their nature was, the feeling for law and order was deeper, the deepest thing in them. Their outbreaks were terrible; civil wars such as our world has not seen again; dealings with conquered enemies which are a fearful page in history. Nevertheless, the outstanding fact about Rome is her unwavering adherence to the idea of a controlled life, subject not to this or that individual, but to a system embodying the principles of justice and fair dealing.

How savage the Roman nature was which the Roman law controlled is seen written large in Rome's favorite amusements, too familiar to need more than a cursory mention: wild beast hunts—so-called, the hunting place was the arena; naval battles for which the circus was flooded by means of hidden canals; and, most usual and best loved by the people, the gladiators, when the great amphitheatre was packed close tier upon tier, all Rome there to see human beings by the tens and hundreds killing each other, to give the victor in a contest the signal for death and eagerly watch the upraised dagger plunge into the helpless body and the blood spurt forth.

That was Rome's dearest delight and her unique contribution to the sport of the world. None of these spectacles were Greek. They entered Greece only under Roman leadership and Athens, it is claimed, never allowed gladiators. Twice, we are told, the citizens stopped a fight as it was about to begin, both times aroused by the protest of a great man. "Athenians," cried one of them, "before you admit the gladiators, come with me and destroy the altar to Pity," and the people with one voice declared that their theatre should never be so defiled. The second time, a revered and beloved philosopher denounced the brutality they were about to witness, and the result was the same. But everywhere else Rome went the bloody games followed, and all the time they grew more bloody and more extravagant. On one occasion we read of a hundred lions perishing and as many lionesses. On another, five thousand animals were killed, bulls, tigers, panthers, elephants. The poet Martial, who wrote endless epigrams to flatter the great Vespasian's son, the Emperor Domitian, some seventy-five years after Augustus, says: "The hunter by the Ganges has not to fear in the countries of the Orient as many tigers as Rome has seen. This city can no longer count her joys. Caesar, your arena surpasses the triumph and splendor of Bacchus whose car only two tigers draw."

Of how many human beings met their death in these ways no estimate at all can be made. The supply of prisoners of war could not begin to meet the demand and men condemned to die were sent to help fill the gladiatorial schools, as they were called; masters, too, often sold their slaves to them: there were even volunteers. Cicero speaks of these more than once. As the games went on, the exaggeration in every direction resulted in what seems to the modern reader incredible, the creations of a monstrous fantasy. We hear of the arena being sprinkled with gold dust; of dwarfs matched against each other and against wild beasts; women, too. Martial tells of having seen a woman kill a lion. Emperors fought, in carefully arranged contests, of course. The son of Rome's best ruler, Marcus Aurelius, boasted that he had killed or conquered two thousand gladiators, using his left hand only. The account ends by growing monotonous. Human ingenuity in devising new and more diverting ways of slaughter was finally exhausted and all that could be done to satisfy the impatient spectators was to increase the number engaged. In one naval battle when the arena was flooded, it is recorded that twenty-four ships took part, large enough to hold in all nineteen thousand men.

It is impossible to escape the suspicion, as one reads description after description, that journalese was not unknown in Rome. Surely, the reader is driven to reason, a people with a tendency to exaggeration would not always successfully repress it on a subject that almost irresistibly invited it, even though they claimed to be writing accurate historical records. When finally one is told of an emperor in the later days of the empire who "would never dine without human blood," without, that is, watching men kill each other, suspicion becomes a certainty. It is too perfectly the tabloid newspaper headline. How could such a fact be known? The gossip of palace slaves? Or even the assertion of the imperial brute himself, wanting, as a Roman would, to appear to out-Nero Nero? Especially monstrous events in the games and especially enormous numbers of those killed in them are hardly to be accepted as plain history, but they do show what Aristotle called the truth which is truer than history. Romans wrote them for Romans, and Romans enjoyed reading and believing them.

To pass from this contemplation, from the way Rome was pleased to amuse herself, to the consideration of what she really did in the world, is to make a startling transition. The Romans did not trample all nations down before them in ruthless brutality and kill and kill in a savage lust for blood. They created a great civilization. Rome's monumental achievement, never effaced from the world, was law. A people violent by nature, of enormous appetites and brutal force, produced the great Law of Nations which sustained with equal justice the rights of free-born men everywhere. The fact with all its familiarity has the power to astonish whenever it comes to mind, but the reasons are easily to be seen. The little town on the seven hills conquered the other little towns around her, because her citizens could obey orders. No one who knows Rome at all will feel this a mere conjecture. The father who condemned his son to death for winning a victory against orders is a legendary figure of deep significance. The orgy of the arena was a relaxation, in the same way as destroying a captured city was or a murderous civil outbreak. They were incidental merely. The conception of a power outside themselves to which they must and would submit was enduring. Over the lawless earth where petty tribes were forever fighting other petty tribes for the right to live, where there was nothing more enlightened than tribal customs untold ages old, marched the Roman, bringing with him as certainly as his sword and his lance his idea of an ordered life in which no man and no tribe was free, but all bound to obey an impersonal, absolute authority which imposed the necessity of self-controlled action. Along with the tremendous Roman roads and aqueducts went the ideal of which they were the symbol, civilization, founded and upheld by law.

The conception was magnificent, grandiose. It was Rome who spread wherever she went the great idea that a man must be assumed to be innocent until he was proved to be guilty; who pronounced it the height of injustice to carry any law out logically without regard to the practical good or ill which resulted; who never in her law-making quite lost sight of the conception that all, men or women, free or slaves, were "by nature" equal.

The Play-Element in Contemporary Civilization

Johan Huizinga

from HOMO LUDENS

The question to which we address ourselves is this: to what extent does the civilization we live in still develop in play-forms? How far does the play-spirit dominate the lives of those who share that civilization? The 19th century, we observed, had lost many of the play-elements so characteristic of former ages. Has this leeway been made up or has it increased?

It might seem at first sight that certain phenomena in modern social life have more than compensated for the loss of play-forms. Sport and athletics, as social functions, have steadily increased in scope and conquered ever fresh fields both nationally and internationally.

Contests in skill, strength and perseverance have, as we have shown, always occupied an important place in every culture either in connection with ritual or simply for fun and festivity. Feudal society was only really interested in the tournament; the rest was just popular recreation and nothing more. Now the tournament, with its highly dramatic staging and aristocratic embellishments, can hardly be called a sport. It fulfilled one of the functions of the theatre. Only a numerically small upper class took active part in it. This one-sidedness of mediaeval sporting life was due in large measure to the influence of the Church. The Christian ideal left but little room for the organized practice of sport and the cultivation of bodily exercise, except insofar as the latter contributed to gentle education. Similarly, the Renaissance affords fairly numerous examples of body-training cultivated for the sake of perfection, but only on the part of individuals, never groups or classes. If anything, the emphasis laid by the Humanists on learning and erudition tended to perpetuate the old under-estimation of the body, likewise the moral zeal and severe intellectuality of the Reformation and Counter-Reformation. The recognition of games and bodily exercises as important cultural values was withheld right up to the end of the 18th century.

The basic forms of sportive competition are, of course, constant through the ages. In some the trial of strength and speed is the whole essence of the contest, as in running and skating matches, chariot and horse races, weight-lifting, swimming, diving, marksmanship, etc. Though human beings have indulged in such activities since the dawn of time, these only take on the character of organized games to a very slight degree. Yet nobody, bearing in mind the agonistic principle which animates them, would hesitate to call them games in the sense of play—which, as we have seen, can be very serious indeed. There are, however, other forms of contest which develop of their own accord into "sports". These are the ball-games.

What we are concerned with here is the transition from occasional amusement to the system of organized clubs and matches. Dutch pictures of the 17th century show us burghers and peasants intent upon their game of *kolf*; but, so far as I know, nothing is heard of games being organized in clubs or played as matches. It is obvious that a fixed organization of this kind will most readily occur when two groups play against one another. The great ball-games in particular require the existence of permanent teams, and herein lies the starting-point of modern sport. The process arises quite spontaneously in the meeting of village against village, school against school, one part of a town against the rest, etc. That the process started in 19th-century England is understandable up to a point, though how far the specifically Anglo-Saxon bent of mind can be deemed an efficient cause is less certain. But it cannot be doubted that the structure of English social life had much to do with it. Local self-government encouraged the spirit of association and solidarity. The absence of obligatory military training favoured the occasion for, and the need of, physical exercise. The peculiar form of education tended to work in the same direction, and finally the geography of the country and the nature of the terrain, on the whole flat and, in the ubiquitous commons, offering the most perfect playing-fields that could be desired, were of the greatest importance. Thus England became the cradle and focus of modern sporting life.

Ever since the last quarter of the 19th century games, in the guise of sport, have been taken more and more seriously. The rules have become increasingly strict and elaborate. Records are established at a higher, or faster, or longer level than was ever conceivable before. Everybody knows the delightful prints from the first half of the 19th century, showing the cricketers in top-hats. This speaks for itself.

Now, with the increasing systematization and regimentation of sport, something of the pure play-quality is inevitably lost. We see this very clearly in the official distinction between amateurs and professionals (or "gentlemen and players" as used pointedly to be said). It means that the play-group marks out those for whom playing is no longer play, ranking them inferior to the true players in standing but superior in capacity. The spirit of the professional is no longer the true play-spirit; it is lacking in spontaneity and carelessness. This affects the amateur too, who begins to suffer from an inferiority complex. Between them they push sport further and further away from the play-sphere proper until it becomes a thing *sui generis:* neither play nor earnest. In modern social life sport occupies a place alongside and apart from the cultural process. The great competitions in archaic cultures had always formed part of the sacred festivals and were indispensable as health and happiness-bringing activities. This ritual tie has now been completely severed; sport has become profane, "unholy" in every way and has no organic connection whatever with the structure of society, least of all when prescribed by the government. The ability of modern social techniques to stage mass demonstrations with the maximum of outward show in the field of athletics does not alter the fact that neither the Olympiads nor the organized sports of American Universities nor the loudly trumpeted international contests have, in the smallest degree, raised sport to the level of a culture-creating activity. However important it may be for the players or spectators, it remains sterile. The old play-factor has undergone almost complete atrophy.

This view will probably run counter to the popular feeling of to-day, according to which sport is the apotheosis of the play-element in our civilization. Nevertheless popular feeling is wrong. By way of emphasizing the fatal shift towards over-seriousness we would point out that it has also infected the non-athletic games where calculation is everything, such as chess and some card-games.

A great many board-games have been known since the earliest times, some even in primitive society, which attached great importance to them largely on account of their chanceful character. Whether they are games of chance or skill they all contain an element of seriousness. The merry play-mood has little scope here, particularly where chance is at a minimum as in chess, draughts, backgammon, halma, etc. Even so all these games remain within the definition of play as given in our first chapter. Only recently has publicity seized on them and annexed them to athletics by means of public championships, world tournaments, registered records and press reportage in a literary style of its own, highly ridiculous to the innocent outsider.

Card-games differ from board-games in that they never succeed in eliminating chance completely. To the extent that chance predominates they fall into the category of gambling and, as such, are little suited to club life and public competition. The more intellectual card-games, on the other hand, leave plenty of room for associative tendencies. It is in this field that the shift towards seriousness and over-seriousness is so striking. From the days of *ombre* and *quadrille* to whist and bridge, card-games have undergone a process of increasing refinement, but only with bridge have the modern social techniques made themselves master of the game. The paraphernalia of handbooks and systems and professional training has made bridge a deadly earnest business. A recent newspaper article estimated the yearly winnings of the Culbertson couple at more than two hundred thousand dollars. An enormous amount of mental energy is expended in this universal craze for bridge with no more tangible result than the exchange of relatively unimportant sums of money. Society as a whole is neither benefited nor damaged by this futile activity. It seems difficult to speak of it as an elevating recreation in the sense of Aristotle's *diagoge*. Proficiency at bridge is a sterile excellence, sharpening the mental faculties very one-sidedly without enriching the soul in any way, fixing and consuming a quantity of intellectual energy that might have been better applied. The most we can say, I think, is that it might have been applied worse. The status of bridge in modern society would indicate, to all appearances, an immense increase in the play-element today. But appearances are deceptive. Really to play, a man must play like a child. Can we assert that this is so in the case of such an ingenious game as bridge? If not, the virtue has gone out of the game.

The attempt to assess the play-content in the confusion of modern life is bound to lead us to contradictory conclusions. In the case of sport we have an activity nominally known as play but raised to such a pitch of

---

diagoge: course of life; *specifically,* way of passing time; recreation or pastime.

technical organization and scientific thoroughness that the real play-spirit is threatened with extinction. Over against this tendency to over-seriousness, however, there are other phenomena pointing in the opposite direction. Certain activities whose whole *raison d'être* lies in the field of material interest, and which had nothing of play about them in their initial stages, develop what we can only call play-forms as a secondary characteristic. Sport and athletics showed us play stiffening into seriousness but still being felt as play; now we come to serious business degenerating into play but still being called serious. The two phenomena are linked by the strong agonistic habit which still holds universal sway, though in other forms than before.

The impetus given to this agonistic principle which seems to be carrying the world back in the direction of play derives, in the main, from external factors independent of culture proper—in a word, communications, which have made intercourse of every sort so extraordinarily easy for mankind as a whole. Technology, publicity and propaganda everywhere promote the competitive spirit and afford means of satisfying it on an unprecedented scale. Commercial competition does not, of course, belong to the immemorial sacred play-forms. It only appears when trade begins to create fields of activity within which each must try to surpass and outwit his neighbour. Commercial rivalry soon makes limiting rules imperative, namely the trading customs. It remained primitive in essence until quite late, only becoming really intensive with the advent of modern communications, propaganda and statistics. Naturally a certain play-element had entered into business competition at an early stage. Statistics stimulated it with an idea that had originally arisen in sporting life, the idea, namely, of trading records. A record, as the word shows, was once simply a memorandum, a note which the innkeeper scrawled on the walls of his inn to say that such and such a rider or traveller had been the first to arrive after covering so and so many miles. The statistics of trade and production could not fail to introduce a sporting element into economic life. In consequence, there is now a sporting side to almost every triumph of commerce or technology: the highest turnover, the biggest tonnage, the fastest crossing, the greatest altitude, etc. Here a purely ludic element has, for once, got the better of utilitarian considerations, since the experts inform us that smaller units—less monstrous steamers and aircraft, etc.—are more efficient in the long run. Business becomes play. This process goes so far that some of the great business concerns deliberately instil the play-spirit into their workers so as to step up production. The trend is now reversed: play becomes business. A captain of industry, on whom the Rotterdam Academy of Commerce had conferred an honorary degree, spoke as follows:

> "Ever since I first entered the business it has been a race between the technicians and the sales department. One tried to produce so much that the sales department would never be able to sell it, while the other

> tried to sell so much that the technicians would never be able to keep pace. This race has always continued: sometimes one is ahead, sometimes the other. Neither my brother nor myself has regarded the business as a task, but always as a game, the spirit of which it has been our constant endeavour to implant into the younger staff."

These words must, of course, be taken with a grain of salt. Nevertheless there are numerous instances of big concerns forming their own Sports Societies and even engaging workers with a view not so much to their professional capacities as to their fitness for the football eleven. Once more the wheel turns.

It is less simple to fix the play-element in contemporary art than in contemporary trade. As we tried to make clear in our tenth chapter, a certain playfulness is by no means lacking in the process of creating and "producing" a work of art. This was obvious enough in the arts of the Muses or "music" arts, where a strong play-element may be called fundamental, indeed, essential to them. In the plastic arts we found that a play-sense was bound up with all forms of decoration; in other words, that the play-function is especially operative where mind and hand move most freely. Over and above this it asserted itself in the master-piece or show-piece expressly commissioned, *the tour de force,* the wager in skill or ability. The question that now arises is whether the play-element in art has grown stronger or weaker since the end of the 18th century.

A gradual process extending over many centuries has succeeded in defunctionalizing art and making it more and more a free and independent occupation for individuals called artists. One of the landmarks of this emancipation was the victory of framed canvases over panels and murals, likewise of prints over miniatures and illuminations. A similar shift from the social to the individual took place when the Renaissance saw the main task of the architect no longer in the building of churches and palaces but of dwelling-houses; not in splendid galleries but in drawing-rooms and bed-rooms. Art became more intimate, but also more isolated; it became an affair of the individual and his taste. In the same way chamber music and songs expressly designed for the satisfaction of personal aestheticisms began to surpass the more public forms of art both in importance and often in intensity of expression.

Along with these changes in form there went another, even more profound, in the function and appreciation of art. More and more it was recognized as an independent and extremely high cultural value. Right into the 18th century art had occupied a subordinate place in the scale of such values. Art was a superior ornament in the lives of the privileged. Aesthetic enjoyment may have been as high as now, but it was interpreted in terms of religious exaltation or as a sort of curiosity whose purpose was to divert and distract. The artist was an artisan and in many cases a menial, whereas the scientist or scholar had the status at least of a member of the leisured classes.

The great shift began in the middle of the 18th century as a result of new aesthetic impulses which took both romantic and classical form, though the romantic current was the more powerful. Together they brought about an unparalleled rise in aesthetic enjoyment all the more fervent for having to act as a substitute for religion. This is one of the most important phases in the history of civilization. We must leap over the full story of this apotheosis of art and can only point out that the line of art-hierophants runs unbroken from Winckelmann to Ruskin and beyond. All the time, art-worship and connoisseurship remained the privilege of the few. Only towards the end of the 19th century did the appreciation of art, thanks largely to photographic reproduction, reach the broad mass of the simply educated. Art becomes public property, love of art *bon ton.* The idea of the artist as a superior species of being gains acceptance, and the public at large is washed by the mighty waves of snobbery. At the same time a convulsive craving for originality distorts the creative impulse. This constant striving after new and unheard-of forms impels art down the steep slope of Impressionism into the turgidities and excrescences of the 20th century. Art is far more susceptible to the deleterious influences of modern techniques of production than is science. Mechanization, advertising, sensation-mongering have a much greater hold upon art because as a rule it works directly for a market and has a free choice of all the techniques available.

None of these conditions entitles us to speak of a play-element in contemporary art. Since the 18th century art, precisely because recognized as a cultural factor, has to all appearances lost rather than gained in playfulness. But is the net result a gain or a loss? One is tempted to feel, as we felt about music, that it was a blessing for art to be largely unconscious of its high purport and the beauty it creates. When art becomes self-conscious, that is, conscious of its own grace, it is apt to lose something of its eternal child-like innocence.

From another angle, of course, we might say that the play-element in art has been fortified by the very fact that the artist is held to be above the common run of mortals. As a superior being he claims a certain amount of veneration for his due. In order to savour his superiority to the full he will require a reverential public or a circle of kindred spirits, who will pour forth the requisite veneration more understandingly than the public at large with its empty phrases. A certain esotericism is as necessary for art to-day as it was of old. Now all esoterics presuppose a convention: we, the initiates, agree to take such and such a thing thus and thus, so we will understand it, so admire it. In other words, esoterics requires a play-community which shall steep itself in its own mystery. Wherever there is a catch-word ending in *-ism* we are hot on the tracks of a play-community. The modern apparatus of publicity with its puffy art-criticism, exhibitions and lectures is calculated to heighten the play-character of art.

It is a very different thing to try to determine the play-content of modern science, for it brings us up against a fundamental difficulty. In the case of art we took play as a primary datum of experience, a generally accepted quantity; but when it comes to science we are constantly being driven back on our definition of that quantity and having to question it afresh. If we apply to science our definition of play as an activity occurring within certain limits of space, time and meaning, according to fixed rules, we might arrive at the amazing and horrifying conclusion that all the branches of science and learning are so many forms of play because each of them is isolated within its own field and bounded by the strict rules of its own methodology. But if we stick to the full terms of our definition we can see at once that, for an activity to be called play, more is needed than limitations and rules. A game is time-bound, we said; it has no contact with any reality outside itself, and its performance is its own end. Further, it is sustained by the consciousness of being a pleasurable, even mirthful, relaxation from the strains of ordinary life. None of this is applicable to science. Science is not only perpetually seeking contact with reality by its usefulness, i.e. in the sense that it is *applied*, it is perpetually trying to establish a universally valid pattern of reality, i.e. as *pure* science. Its rules, unlike those of play, are not unchallengeable for all time. They are constantly being belied by experience and undergoing modification, whereas the rules of a game cannot be altered without spoiling the game itself.

The conclusion, therefore, that all science is merely a game can be discarded as a piece of wisdom too easily come by. But it is legitimate to enquire whether a science is not liable to indulge in play within the closed precincts of its own method. Thus, for instance, the scientist's continued penchant for systems tends in the direction of play. Ancient science, lacking adequate foundation in empiricism, lost itself in a sterile systematization of all conceivable concepts and properties. Though observation and calculation act as a brake in this respect they do not altogether exclude a certain capriciousness in scientific activities. Even the most delicate experimental analysis can be, not indeed manipulated while actually in progress, but played in the interests of subsequent theory. True, the margin of play is always detected in the end, but this detection proves that it exists. Jurists have of old been reproached with similar manoeuvres. Philologists too are not altogether blameless in this respect, seeing that ever since the Old Testament and the Vedas they have delighted in perilous etymologies, a favourite game to this day for those whose curiosity outstrips their knowledge. And is it so certain that the new schools of psychology are not being led astray by the frivolous and facile use of Freudian terminology at the hands of competents and incompetents alike?

Apart from the possibility of the scientific worker or amateur juggling with his own method he may also be seduced into the paths of play by the competitive impulse proper. Though competition in science is less directly conditioned by economic factors than in art, the logical development of civilization which we call science is more inextricably bound up with dialectics than is the aesthetic. In an earlier chapter we discussed the origins of science and philosophy and found that they lay in the agonistic sphere. Science, as some one has not unjustly said, is polemical. But it is a bad sign when the urge to forestall the other fellow in discovery or to annihilate him with a demonstration, looms too large in the work done. The genuine seeker after truth sets little store by triumphing over a rival.

By way of tentative conclusion we might say that modern science, so long as it adheres to the strict demands of accuracy and veracity, is far less liable to fall into play as we have defined it, than was the case in earlier times and right up to the Renaissance, when scientific thought and method showed unmistakable play-characteristics.

These few observations on the play-factor in modern art and science must suffice here, though much has been left unsaid. We are hastening to an end, and it only remains to consider the play-element in contemporary social life at large and especially in politics. But let us be on our guard against two misunderstandings from the start. Firstly, certain play-forms may be used consciously or unconsciously to cover up some social or political design. In this case we are not dealing with the eternal play-element that has been the theme of this book, but with false play. Secondly, and quite independently of this, it is always possible to come upon phenomena which, to a superficial eye, have all the appearance of play and might be taken for permanent play-tendencies, but are, in point of fact, nothing of the sort. Modern social life is being dominated to an ever-increasing extent by a quality that has something in common with play and yields the illusion of a strongly developed play-factor. This quality I have ventured to call by the name of Puerilism, as being the most appropriate appellation for that blend of adolescence and barbarity which has been rampant all over the world for the last two or three decades.

It would seem as if the mentality and conduct of the adolescent now reigned supreme over large areas of civilized life which had formerly been the province of responsible adults. The habits I have in mind are, in themselves, as old as the world; the difference lies in the place they now occupy in our civilization and the brutality with which they manifest themselves. Of these habits that of gregariousness is perhaps the strongest and most alarming. It results in puerilism of the lowest order: yells or other signs of greeting, the wearing of badges and sundry items of political haberdashery, walking in marching order or at a special pace and the whole rigmarole of collective voodoo and mumbo-jumbo. Closely akin to this, if at a slightly deeper psychological level, is the insatiable thirst for trivial recreation and crude sensationalism, the delight in mass-meetings, mass-demonstrations, parades, etc. The club is a very ancient institution, but it is a disaster when whole nations turn into clubs, for these, besides promoting the precious qualities of friendship and loyalty, are also hotbeds of sectarianism, intolerance, suspicion, superciliousness and quick to defend any illusion that flatters self-love or group-consciousness. We have seen great nations losing every shred of honour, all sense of humour, the very idea of decency and fair play. This is not the place to investigate the causes, growth and extent of this world-wide bastardization of culture; the entry of half-educated masses into the international traffic of the mind, the relaxation of morals and the hypertrophy of technics undoubtedly play a large part.

One example of official puerilism must suffice here. It is, as we know from history, a sign of revolutionary enthusiasm when governments play at nine-pins with names, the venerable names of cities, persons, institutions, the calendar, etc. *Pravda* reported that as a result of their arrears in grain deliveries three *kolkhozy* in the district of Kursk, already christened Budenny, Krupskaya and the equivalent of Red Cornfield, have been re-christened Sluggard, Saboteur and Do-Nothing by the local soviet. Though this *trop de zèle* received an official rebuff from the Central Committee and the offensive soubriquets were withdrawn, the puerilistic attitude could not have been more clearly expressed.

Very different is the great innovation of the late Lord Baden-Powell. His aim was to organize the social force of boyhood as such and turn it to good account. This is not puerilism, for it rests on a deep understanding of the mind and aptitudes of the immature; also the Scout Movement expressly styles itself a game. Here, if anywhere, we have an example of a game that comes as close to the culture-creating play of archaic times as our age allows. But when Boy-Scoutism in degraded form seeps through into politics we may well ask whether the puerilism that flourishes in present-day society is a play-function or not. At first sight the answer appears to be a definite yes, and such has been my interpretation of the phenomenon in other studies. I have now come to a different conclusion. According to our definition of play, puerilism is to be distinguished from playfulness. A child playing is not puerile in the pejorative sense we mean here. And if our modern puerilism were genuine play we ought to see civilization returning to the great archaic forms of recreation where ritual, style and dignity are in perfect unison. The spectacle of a society rapidly goose-stepping into helotry is, for some, the dawn of the millennium. We believe them to be in error.

More and more the sad conclusion forces itself upon us that the play-element in culture has been on the wane ever since the 18th century, when it was in full flower. Civilization to-day is no longer played, and even where it still seems to play it is false play—I had almost said, it plays

---

kolkhozy: collective farms of the Soviet Union.
trop de zèle: excess of enthusiasm.

false, so that it becomes increasingly difficult to tell where play ends and non-play begins. This is particularly true of politics. Not very long ago political life in parliamentary democratic form was full of unmistakable play-features. One of my pupils has recently worked up my observations on this subject into a thesis on parliamentary eloquence in France and England, showing how, ever since the end of the 18th century, debates in the House of Commons have been conducted very largely according to the rules of a game and in the true play-spirit. Personal rivalries are always at work, keeping up a continual match between the players whose object is to checkmate one another, but without prejudice to the interests of the country which they serve with all seriousness. The mood and manners of parliamentary democracy were, until recently, those of fair play both in England and in the countries that had adopted the English model with some felicity. The spirit of fellowship would allow the bitterest opponents a friendly chat even after the most virulent debate. It was in this style that the "Gentleman's Agreement" arose. Unhappily certain parties to it were not always aware of the duties implicit in the word gentleman. There can be no doubt that it is just this play-element that keeps parliamentary life healthy, at least in Great Britain, despite the abuse that has lately been heaped upon it. The elasticity of human relationships underlying the political machinery permits it to "play", thus easing tensions which would otherwise be unendurable or dangerous—for it is the decay of humour that kills. We need hardly add that this play-factor is present in the whole apparatus of elections.

In American politics it is even more evident. Long before the two-party system had reduced itself to two gigantic teams whose political differences were hardly discernible to an outsider, electioneering in America had developed into a kind of national sport. The presidential election of 1840 set the pace for all subsequent elections. The party then calling itself Whig had an excellent candidate, General Harrison of 1812 fame, but no platform. Fortune gave them something infinitely better, a symbol on which they rode to triumph: the log cabin which was the old warrior's modest abode during his retirement. Nomination by majority vote, i.e. by the loudest clamour, was inaugurated in the election of 1860 which brought Lincoln to power. The emotionality of American politics lies deep in the origins of the American nation itself: Americans have ever remained true to the rough and tumble of pioneer life. There is a great deal that is endearing in American politics, something naïve and spontaneous for which we look in vain in the dragoonings and drillings, or worse, of the contemporary European scene.

Though there may be abundant traces of play in domestic politics there would seem, at first sight, to be little opportunity for it in the field of international relationships. The fact, however, that these have touched the nadir of violence and precariousness does not in itself exclude the possibility of play. As we have seen from numerous examples, play can be cruel and bloody and, in addition, can often be false play. Any law-abiding community or community of States will have characteristics linking it in one way or another to a play-community. International law between States is maintained by the mutual recognition of certain principles which, in effect, operate like play-rules despite the fact that they may be founded in metaphysics. Were it otherwise there would be no need to lay down the *pacta sunt servanda* principle, which explicitly recognizes that the integrity of the system rests on a general willingness to keep to the rules. The moment that one or the other party withdraws from this tacit agreement the whole system of international law must, if only temporarily, collapse unless the remaining parties are strong enough to outlaw the "spoilsport".

The maintenance of international law has, at all stages, depended very largely on principles lying outside the strict domain of law, such as honour, decency, and good form. It is not altogether in vain that the European rules of warfare developed out of the code of honour proper to chivalry. International law tacitly assumed that a beaten Power would behave like a gentleman and a good loser, which unhappily it seldom did. It was a point of international decorum to declare your war officially before entering upon it, though the aggressor often neglected to comply with this awkward convention and began by seizing some outlying colony or the like. But it is true to say that until quite recently war was conceived as a noble game—the sport of kings—and that the absolutely binding character of its rules rested on, and still retained, some of the formal play-elements we found in full flower in archaic warfare.

A cant phrase in current German political literature speaks of the change from peace to war as "das Eintreten des Ernstfalles"—roughly, "the serious development of an emergency". In strictly military parlance, or course, the term is correct. Compared with the sham fighting of manoeuvres and drilling and training, real war is undoubtedly what seriousness is to play. But German political theorists mean something more. The term "Ernstfall" avows quite openly that foreign policy has not attained its full degree of seriousness, has not achieved its object or proved its efficiency, until the stage of actual hostilities is reached. The true relation between States is one of war. All diplomatic intercourse, insofar as it moves in the paths of negotiation and agreement, is only a prelude to war or an interlude between two wars. This horrible creed is accepted and indeed professed by many. It is only logical that its adherents, who regard war and the preparations for it as the sole form of serious politics, should deny that war has any connection with the contest and hence with play. The agonistic factor, they tell us, may have been

---

pacta sunt servanda: the agreed upon must be observed.

operative in the primitive stages of civilization, it was all very well then, but war nowadays is far above the competitiveness of mere savages. It is based on the "friend-foe principle". All "real" relationships between nations and States, so they say, are dominated by this eneluctable principle. Any "other" group is always either your friend or your enemy. Enemy, or course, is not to be understood as *inimicus* or ἐχθρός, i.e. a person you hate, let alone a wicked person, but purely and simply as *hostis* or πολέμιος, i. e. the stranger or foreigner who is in your group's way. The theory refuses to regard the enemy even as a rival or adversary. He is merely in your way and is thus to be made away with. If ever anything in history has corresponded to this gross over-simplification of the idea of enmity, which reduces it to an almost mechanical relationship, it is precisely that primitive antagonism between phratries, clans or tribes where, as we saw, the play-element was hypertrophied and distorted. Civilization is supposed to have carried us beyond this stage. I know of no sadder or deeper fall from human reason than Schmitt's barbarous and pathetic delusion about the friend-foe principle. His inhuman cerebrations do not even hold water as a piece of formal logic. For it is not war that is serious, but peace. War and everything to do with it remains fast in the daemonic and magical bonds of play. Only by transcending that pitiable friend-foe relationship will mankind enter into the dignity of man's estate. Schmitt's brand of "seriousness" merely takes us back to the savage level.

Here the bewildering antithesis of play and seriousness presents itself once more. We have gradually become convinced that civilization is rooted in noble play and that, if it is to unfold in full dignity and style, it cannot afford to neglect the play-element. The observance of play-rules is nowhere more imperative than in the relations between countries and States. Once they are broken, society falls into barbarism and chaos. On the other hand we cannot deny that modern warfare has lapsed into the old agonistic attitude of playing at war for the sake of prestige and glory.

Now this is our difficulty: modern warfare has, on the face of it, lost all contact with play. States of the highest cultural pretensions withdraw from the comity of nations and shamelessly announce that "pacta non sunt servanda". By so doing they break the play-rules inherent in any system of international law. To that extent their playing at war, as we have called it, for the sake of prestige is not true play; it, so to speak, plays the play-concept of war false. In contemporary politics, based as they are on the utmost preparedness if not actual preparation for war, there would seem to be hardly any trace of the old play-attitude. The code of honour is flouted, the rules of the game are set aside, international law is broken, and all the ancient associations of war with ritual and religion are gone.

---

inimicus ἐχθρός (echthros): a destestable person.

hostis, πολέμιος (polemios): one who may be an enemy on a temporary basis, not of himself a detested person; sometimes used to describe a political opponent.

Nevertheless the methods by which war-policies are conducted and war-preparations carried out still show abundant traces of the agonistic attitude as found in primitive society. Politics are and have always been something of a game of chance; we have only to think of the challenges, the provocations, the threats and denunciations to realize that war and the policies leading up to it are always, in the nature of things, a gamble, as Neville Chamberlain said in the first days of September 1939. Despite appearances to the contrary, therefore, war has not freed itself from the magic circle of play.

Does this mean that war is still a game, even for the aggressed, the persecuted, those who fight for their rights and their liberty? Here our gnawing doubt whether war is really play or earnest finds unequivocal answer. It is the *moral* content of an action that makes it serious. When the combat has an ethical value it ceases to be play. The way out of this vexing dilemma is only closed to those who deny the objective value and validity of ethical standards. Carl Schmitt's acceptance of the formula that war is the "serious development of an emergency" is therefore correct—but in a very different sense from that which he intended. His point of view is that of the aggressor who is not bound by ethical considerations. The fact remains that politics and war are deeply rooted in the primitive soil of culture played in and as contest. Only through an ethos that transcends the friend-foe relationship and recognizes a higher goal than the gratification of the self, the group or the nation will a political society pass beyond the "play" of war to true seriousness.

So that by a devious route we have reached the following conclusion: real civilization cannot exist in the absence of a certain play-element, for civilization presupposes limitation and mastery of the self, the ability not to confuse its own tendencies with the ultimate and highest goal, but to understand that it is enclosed within certain bounds freely accepted. Civilization will, in a sense, always be played according to certain rules, and true civilization will always demand fair play. Fair play is nothing less than good faith expressed in play terms. Hence the cheat or the spoil-sport shatters civilization itself. To be a sound culture-creating force this play-element must be pure. It must not consist in the darkening or debasing of standards set up by reason, faith or humanity. It must not be a false seeming, a masking of political purposes behind the illusion of genuine play-forms. True play knows no propaganda; its aim is in itself, and its familiar spirit is happy inspiration.

In treating of our theme so far we have tried to keep to a play-concept which starts from the positive and generally recognized characteristics of play. We took play in its immediate everyday sense and tried to avoid the philosophical short-circuit that would assert all human action to be play. Now, at the end of our argument, this point of view awaits us and demands to be taken into account.

"Child's play was what he called all human opinions", says late Greek tradition of Heraclitus. As a pendant to this lapidary saying let us quote at greater length the profound words of Plato which we introduced into our first chapter: "Though human affairs are not worthy of great seriousness it is yet necessary to be serious; happiness is another thing. . . . I say that a man must be serious with the serious, and not the other way about. God alone is worthy of supreme seriousness, but man is made God's plaything, and that is the best part of him. Therefore every man and woman should live life accordingly, and play the noblest games, and be of another mind from what they are at present. For they deem war a serious thing, though in war there is neither play nor culture worthy the name, which are the things *we* deem most serious. Hence all must live in peace as well as they possibly can. What, then, is the right way of living? Life must be lived as play, playing certain games, making sacrifices, singing and dancing, and then a man will be able to propitiate the gods, and defend himself against his enemies, and win in the contest". Thus "men will live according to Nature since in most respects they are puppets, yet having a small part in truth". To which Plato's companion rejoins: "You make humanity wholly bad for us, friend, if you say that". And Plato answers: "Forgive me. It was with my eyes on God and moved by Him that I spoke so. If you like, then, humanity is not wholly bad, but worthy of some consideration."

The human mind can only disengage itself from the magic circle of play by turning towards the ultimate. Logical thinking does not go far enough. Surveying all the treasures of the mind and all the splendours of its achievements we shall still find, at the bottom of every serious judgement, something problematical left. In our heart of hearts we know that none of our pronouncements is absolutely conclusive. At that point, where our judgement begins to waver, the feeling that the world is serious after all wavers with it. Instead of the old saw: "All is vanity", the more positive conclusion forces itself upon us that "all is play". A cheap metaphor, no doubt, mere impotence of the mind; yet it is the wisdom Plato arrived at when he called man the plaything of the gods. In singular imagery the thought comes back again in the *Book of Proverbs*, where Wisdom says: "The Lord possessed me in the beginning of his ways, before he made any thing from the beginning. I was set up from eternity, and of old before the earth was made . . . I was with him forming all things: and was delighted every day, playing before him at all times; playing in the world. And my delights were to be with the children of men."

Whenever we are seized with vertigo at the ceaseless shuttlings and spinnings in our mind of the thought: What is play? What is serious? we shall find the fixed, unmoving point that logic denies us, once more in the sphere of ethics. Play, we began by saying, lies outside morals. In itself it is neither good nor bad. But if we have to decide whether an action to which our will impels us is a serious duty or is licit as play, our moral conscience will at once provide the touchstone. As soon as truth and justice, compassion and forgiveness have part in our resolve to act, our anxious question loses all meaning. One drop of pity is enough to lift our doing beyond intellectual distinctions. Springing as it does from a belief in justice and divine grace, conscience, which is moral awareness, will always whelm the question that eludes and deludes us to the end, in a lasting silence.

Translated by R. F. C. HULL

from A Study of History

Arnold Toynbee

The ἰδιώτης, in the fifth-century Greek usage of the word, was a superior personality who committed the social offence of 'living to himself' instead of putting his personal gifts at the service of the common weal; and the light in which such behaviour was regarded in the classical Hellenic World is illustrated by the fact that, in our modern Western vernacular languages, a derivative of this Greek word ἰδιώτης has acquired the meaning of 'mental imbecile'. This far-fetched meaning has been imported into the word 'idiot' on the strength of its moral connotation in Hellenic minds. The connotation has been so strong that the meaning has been changed by it out of all recognition. It is amusing to reflect that, if we had managed to forget the original connotation and to carry the original meaning over into the un-Hellenic moral environment of our own code of social ethics, then the English word 'idiot' would presumably be used to-day as a laudatory term; for it would then still signify a man of parts who has devoted his abilities to the acquisition of a personal fortune through private business enterprise; and this classical Hellenic *bête noire* is our latter-day Western hero.

In the Hellenic Society of the fifth century B.C. the free male citizens, who alone lived to the full the intense social life of the city-state, were

---

ἰδιώτης (idiotes): a private person; for example, one who is not involved in political activity.

virtually behaving as *ἰδιῶται* towards the women and the slaves, who had been left behind in the advance of the Hellenic Civilization from the Homeric to the Attic stage. The women and the slaves found themselves virtually outside the social pale of the master institution in which the results of the free male citizens' advance had been embodied. From this point of view it is significant that one of the promptest constructive reactions to the breakdown of the Hellenic Civilization in 431 B.C. was a movement to bring the women and the slaves back into social partnership with the free male citizens as recognized and active members of the commonwealth. This movement declared itself in Athens, 'the Education of Hellas', while the Atheno-Peloponnesian War, which was the beginning of the Hellenic 'Time of Troubles', was still being fought—as witness the war-plays of Aristophanes; and the emancipation of these two great classes in the Hellenic body social may be judged to have reached its apogee during the first century of the third chapter of Hellenic history: a century that began with Alexander's passage of the Dardanelles in 334 B.C. and closed with the outbreak of the Hannibalic War in 218 B.C.

At the opposite extreme to the *ἰδιώτης* stood the *βάναυσος*, who was the other bugbear of fifth-century Hellas. The *βάναυσος* meant a person whose activity was specialized, through a concentration of his energies upon some particular technique, at the expense of his all-round development as a 'social animal'. The kind of technique which was usually in people's minds when they used this term of abuse was some manual or mechanical trade which was practised for private profit. Making money out of industry was as ill looked upon in fifth-century Hellas as it has been well looked upon in the English-speaking communities of a nineteenth-century Western Society; and in the old-fashioned aristocratic Boeotian community of Thebes the social stigma was so severe that it carried a political disqualification with it. The Hellenic horror of *βαναυσία*, however, went farther than this. It implanted in Hellenic minds a deep distrust of all professionalism, even when the medium was something finer than stone or iron or wood or leather and the motive something nobler than money-making.

For example, under the Lycurgean *agôgê* or 'way of life' at Sparta, the Spartiate 'Peers' were forbidden not only to master and practise any lucrative manual trade, but even to train for and take part in any of the international athletic competitions which were held periodically in the Hellenic World—notwithstanding the two facts that, at the four great Pan-Hellenic festivals, the prizes were not objects of material value but were simple wreaths of green-stuff, and that, in all other Hellenic commu-

---

ἰδιῶται (idiotai): the plural form of idiotes.

βάναυσος (banausos): a professional, specialist, or expert.

βαναυσία (banausia): professional skill or expertise used for private gain; money-making job especially looked down on if in political office, oratory, or the creative arts.

nities, the winning of one of these wreaths was regarded as the highest honour which a man could possibly gain for himself and for his country. The Spartans, of course, defeated their own ends—and discredited their parochial policy of diverging from the main channel of Hellenic Civilization into a peculiar backwater—by specializing professionally in the Art of War, with disastrous social, and in the end even disastrous military, consequences. It was the paradox and the irony of Spartan history that Spartan militarism, at its height, became *βαναυσία* incarnate. On the other hand the subtler Athenians did not allow themselves to fall into this insidious pitfall. They were on their guard against *βαναυσία* even in the cultivation of those abilities and activities and arts which they were most prone to admire; and they did not hesitate to criticize the professionalism of a countryman of their own who was the most brilliant political genius that Attica had produced and who had used his specialized ability, with dazzling success, to save his country from destruction and to make her great.

> In refined and cultivated society Themistocles used to be girded at by people of so-called liberal education [for his lack of accomplishments] and used to be driven into making the rather cheap defence that he certainly could do nothing with a musical instrument, but that, if you were to put into his hands a country that was small and obscure, he knew how to turn it into a great country and a famous one.

This sensitiveness to the dangers of *βαναυσία*, which comes out so strongly in Hellenic social life, can also be observed in the institutions of other societies. For example, the social function of the Jewish Sabbath—and of the sabbatarian Sunday of Scotland, England, and the Transmarine English-speaking countries of our modern Western World—is to insure that, for one whole day out of every seven, a creature who has been specializing for six successive days in the week in sordid business for private gain shall remember his Creator and shall live, for a recurrent twenty-four hours, the life of an integral human soul instead of quite uninterruptedly performing the vain repetitions of a money-making machine. Again, it is no accident that in England mountaineering and 'organized games' and other sports should have come into fashion simultaneously with the rise of Industrialism at the turn of the eighteenth and nineteenth centures; and that this new passion for Sport should since have spread, *pari passu* with Industrialism, from England over the World. For Sport, in this latter-day sense of the term, is a conscious attempt at 'recreation' from the soul-destroying exaggeration of the Division of Labour which the Industrial System of economy entails.

---

pari passu: with equal step; along, beside, or together with.

In our latter-day Western World, however, this attempt to adjust Life to Industrialism through Sport has been partially defeated because the spirit and the rhythm of Industrialism have become so insistent and so pervasive that they have invaded and infected Sport itself—just as the *βαναυσία* which the Spartans sought so earnestly to keep at bay eluded their vigilance after all by capturing their own peculiar profession of arms. In the Western World of to-day professional athletes—more narrowly specialized and more extravagantly paid than the most consummate industrial technicians—now vie with the professional entertainers in providing us with horrifying examples of *βαναυσία* at its acme.

In the mind of the writer of this Study this disconcerting industrialization of Sport is summed up in the pictures of three football-fields that are all printed sharply upon his visual memory. One was an English field at Sheffield which he happened once to see out of the railway-carriage window *en route* from York to Oxford. At the parched latter end of summer, when the football season was about to reopen, the grass on this plot of ground was being kept artificially green by hydrants which tapped the municipal water-supply and so made the local groundsman independent of the rain from heaven. And all around this manufactured greensward rose tiers upon tiers of seats, on which thousands of human beings would presently 'take their recreation' in an even closer congestion—with still more pounds of human flesh to the cubic yard of urban space—than during their working hours in shop or office or factory. The other two football-grounds in the writer's mental picture-gallery are to be found on the campuses of two colleges in the United States. One of them was floodlighted, by an ingenious lighting-system which was said to reproduce the exact effect of sunshine, in order that football-players might be manufactured there by night as well as by day, in continuous shifts, as motor-cars or gramophones are produced in factories which run without a break throughout the twenty-four hours. The other American football-ground was roofed over in order that practice might go on whatever the weather. The roof was supported on four immense girders which sprang from the four corners and met above the centre without any interior support. It was said to be the largest span of roof in existence at that moment in the World, and its erection had cost a fabulous sum. Round the sides were ranged beds for the reception of exhausted or wounded warriors. On both these American grounds I found on inquiry that the actual players in any given year were never more in number than an infinitesimal fraction of the total student body; and I was also told that these boys looked forward to the ordeal of playing a match with much the same grim apprehension as their elder brothers had felt when they went into the trenches in 1918. In truth this Anglo-Saxon football was not a game at all. It was the Industrial System celebrating a triumph over its vanquished antidote, Sport, by masquerading in its guise.

from History of the United States during the Jefferson and Madison Administrations

Henry Adams

"The principal amusements of the inhabitants," said Dwight, "are visiting, dancing, music, conversation, walking, riding, sailing, shooting at a mark, draughts, chess, and unhappily, in some of the larger towns, cards and dramatic exhibitions. A considerable amusement is also furnished in many places by the examination and exhibitions of the superior schools; and a more considerable one by the public exhibitions of colleges. Our countrymen also fish and hunt. Journeys taken for pleasure are very numerous, and are a very favorite object. Boys and young men play at foot-ball, cricket, quoits, and at many other sports of an athletic cast, and in the winter are peculiarly fond of skating. Riding in a sleigh, or sledge, is also a favorite diversion in New England."

President Dwight was sincere in his belief that college commencements and sleigh-riding satisfied the wants of his people; he looked upon whist as an unhappy dissipation, and upon the theatre as immoral. He had no occasion to condemn horse-racing, for no race-course was to be found in New England. The horse and the dog existed only in varieties little suited for sport. In colonial days New England produced one breed of horses worth preserving and developing—the Narragansett pacer; but, to the regret even of the clergy, this animal almost disappeared, and in 1800 New England could show nothing to take its place. The germ of the trotter and the trotting-match, the first general popular amusement, could be seen in almost any country village, where the owners of horses were in the habit of trotting what were called scratch-races, for a quarter or half a mile from the door of the tavern, along the public road. Perhaps this amusement had already a right to be called a New-England habit, showing defined tastes; but the force of the popular instinct was not fully felt in Massachusetts, or even in New York, although there it was given full play. New York possessed a race-course, and made in 1792 a great stride toward popularity by importing the famous stallion "Messenger" to become the source of endless interest for future generations; but Virginia was the region where the American showed his true character as a lover of sport. Long before the Revolution the race-course was commonly established in Virginia and Maryland; English running-horses of pure blood—

descendants of the Darley Arabian and the Godolphin Arabian—were imported, and racing became the chief popular entertainment. The long Revolutionary War, and the general ruin it caused, checked the habit and deteriorated the breed; but with returning prosperity Virginia showed that the instinct was stronger than ever. In 1798 "Diomed," famous as the sire of racers, was imported into the State, and future rivalry between Virginia and New York could be foreseen. In 1800 the Virginia race-course still remained at the head of American popular amusements.

In an age when the Prince of Wales and crowds of English gentlemen attended every prize-fight, and patronized Tom Crib, Dutch Sam, the Jew Mendoza, and the negro Molyneux, an Englishman could hardly have expected that a Virginia race-course should be free from vice; and perhaps travellers showed best the general morality of the people by their practice of dwelling on Virginia vices. They charged the Virginians with fondness for horse-racing, cock-fighting, betting, and drinking; but the popular habit which most shocked them, and with which books of travel filled pages of description, was the so-called rough-and-tumble fight. The practice was not one on which authors seemed likely to dwell; yet foreigners like Weld, and Americans like Judge Longstreet in "Georgia Scenes," united to give it a sort of grotesque dignity like that of a bull-fight, and under their treatment it became interesting as a popular habit. The rough-and-tumble fight differed from the ordinary prize-fight, or boxing-match, by the absence of rules. Neither kicking, tearing, biting, nor gouging was forbidden by the law of the ring. Brutal as the practice was, it was neither new nor exclusively Virginian. The English travellers who described it as American barbarism, might have seen the same sight in Yorkshire at the same date. The rough-and-tumble fight was English in origin, and was brought to Virginia and the Carolinas in early days, whence it spread to the Ohio and Mississippi. The habit attracted general notice because of its brutality in a society that showed few brutal instincts. Friendly foreigners like Liancourt were honestly shocked by it; others showed somewhat too plainly their pleasure at finding a vicious habit which they could consider a natural product of democratic society. Perhaps the description written by Thomas Ashe showed best not only the ferocity of the fight but also the antipathies of the writer, for Ashe had something of the artist in his touch, and he felt no love for Americans. The scene was at Wheeling. A Kentuckian and a Virginian were the combatants.

> Bulk and bone were in favor of the Kentuckian; science and craft in that of the Virginian. The former promised himself victory from his power; the latter from his science. Very few rounds had taken place or fatal blows given, before the Virginian contracted his whole form, drew up his arms to his face, with his hands nearly closed in a concave by the fingers being bent to the full extension of the flexors, and summoning

> up all his energy for one act of desperation, pitched himself into the bosom of his opponent. Before the effects of this could be ascertained, the sky was rent by the shouts of the multitude; and I could learn that the Virginian had expressed as much beauty and skill in his retraction and bound, as if he had been bred in a menagerie and practised action and attitude among panthers and wolves. The shock received by the Kentuckian, and the want of breath, brought him instantly to the ground. The Virginian never lost his hold. Like those bats of the South who never quit the subject on which they fasten till they taste blood, he kept his knees in his enemy's body; fixing his claws in his hair and his thumbs on his eyes, gave them an instantaneous start from their sockets. The sufferer roared aloud, but uttered no complaint. The citizens again shouted with joy.

. . . . .

Against [the] Federalist and conservative view of democratic tendencies, democrats protested in a thousand forms, but never in any mode of expression which satisfied them all, or explained their whole character. Probably Jefferson came nearest to the mark, for he represented the hopes of science as well as the prejudices of Virginia; but Jefferson's writings may be searched from beginning to end without revealing the whole measure of the man, far less of the movement. Here and there in his letters a suggestion was thrown out, as though by chance, revealing larger hopes—as in 1815, at a moment of despondency, he wrote: "I fear from the experience of the last twenty-five years that morals do not of necessity advance hand in hand with the sciences." In 1800, in the flush of triumph, he believed that his task in the world was to establish a democratic republic, with the sciences for an intellectual field, and physical and moral advancement keeping pace with their advance. Without an excessive introduction of more recent ideas, he might be imagined to define democratic progress, in the somewhat affected precision of his French philosophy: "Progress is either physical or intellectual. If we can bring it about that men are on the average an inch taller in the next generation than in this; if they are an inch larger round the chest; if their brain is an ounce or two heavier, and their life a year or two longer,—that is progress. If fifty years hence the average man shall invariably argue from two ascertained premises where he now jumps to a conclusion from a single supposed revelation,—that is progress. I expect it to be made here, under our democratic stimulants, on a great scale, until every man is potentially an athlete in body and an Aristotle in mind." To this doctrine the New Englander replied, "What will you do for moral progress?" Every possible answer to this question opened a chasm. No doubt Jefferson held the faith that men would improve morally with their physical and intellectual growth; but he had no idea of any moral improvement other than that which came by nature. He could not tolerate a priesthood, a state church, or revealed religion. Conservatives, who could tolerate no society without such pillars of order, were, from their point of view, right in answering, "Give us rather the worst despotism of Europe,—there our souls at least may have a chance of salvation!" To their minds vice and virtue were not relative, but fixed terms. The Church was a divine institution. How could a ship hope to reach port when the crew threw overboard sails, spars, and compass, unshipped their rudder, and all the long day thought only of eating and drinking? Nay, even should the new experiment succeed in a worldly sense, what was a man profited if he gained the whole world, and lost his own soul? The Lord God was a jealous God, and visited the sins of the parents upon the children; but what worse sin could be conceived than for a whole nation to join their chief in chanting the strange hymn with which Jefferson, a new false prophet, was deceiving and betraying his people: "It does me no injury for my neighbor to say there are twenty Gods or no God!"

On this ground conservatism took its stand, as it had hitherto done with success in every similar emergency in the world's history, and fixing its eyes on moral standards of its own, refused to deal with the subject as further open to argument. The two parties stood facing opposite ways, and could see no common ground of contact.

Survivals of Prowess

Thorstein Veblen

from THE THEORY OF THE LEISURE CLASS

Sports of all kinds are of the same general character, including prize-fights, bull-fights, athletics, shooting, angling, yachting, and games of skill, even where the element of destructive physical efficiency is not an obtrusive feature. Sports shade off from the basis of hostile combat, through skill, to cunning and chicanery, without its being possible to draw a line at any point. The ground of an addiction to sports is an archaic spiritual constitution—the possession of the predatory emulative propensity in a relatively high potency. A strong proclivity to adventuresome exploit and to the infliction of damage is especially pronounced in those employments which are in colloquial usage specifically called sportsmanship.

It is perhaps truer, or at least more evident, as regards sports than as regards the other expressions of predatory emulation already spoken of, that the temperament which inclines men to them is essentially a boyish temperament. The addiction to sports, therefore, in a peculiar degree marks an arrested development of the man's moral nature. This peculiar boyishness of temperament in sporting men immediately becomes apparent when attention is directed to the large element of make-believe that is present in all sporting activity. Sports share this character of make-believe with the games and exploits to which children, especially boys, are habitually inclined. Make-believe does not enter in the same proportion into all sports, but it is present in a very appreciable degree in all. It is apparently present in a larger measure in sportsmanship proper and in athletic contests than in set games of skill of a more sedentary character; although this rule may not be found to apply with any great uniformity. It is noticeable, for instance, that even very mild-mannered and matter-of-fact men who go out shooting are apt to carry an excess of arms and accoutrements in order to impress upon their own imagination the seriousness of their undertaking. These huntsmen are also prone to a histrionic, prancing gait and to an elaborate exaggeration of the motions, whether of stealth or of onslaught, involved in their deeds of exploit. Similarly in athletic sports there is almost invariably present a good share of rant and swagger and ostensible mystification-features which mark the histrionic nature of these employments. In all this, of course, the reminder of boyish make-believe is plain enough. The slang of athletics, by the way, is in great part made up of extremely sanguinary locutions borrowed from the terminology of warfare. Except where it is adopted as a necessary means of secret communication, the use of a special slang in any employment is probably to be accepted as evidence that the occupation in question is substantially make-believe.

A further feature in which sports differ from the duel and similar disturbances of the peace is the peculiarity that they admit of other motives being assigned for them besides the impulses of exploit and ferocity. There is probably little if any other motive present in any given case, but the fact that other reasons for indulging in sports are frequently assigned goes to say that other grounds are sometimes present in a subsidiary way. Sportsmen—hunters and anglers—are more or less in the habit of assigning a love of nature, the need of recreation, and the like, as the incentives to their favorite pastime. These motives are no doubt frequently present and make up a part of the attractiveness of the sportsman's life; but these can not be the chief incentives. These ostensible needs could be more readily and fully satisfied without the accompaniment of a systematic effort to take the life of those creatures that make up an essential feature of that "nature" that is beloved by the sportsman. It is, indeed, the most noticeable effect of the sportsman's activity to keep nature in a state of chronic desolation by killing off all living things whose destruction he can compass.

Still, there is ground for the sportsman's claim that under the existing conventionalities his need of recreation and of contact with nature can best be satisfied by the course which he takes. Certain canons of good breeding have been imposed by the prescriptive example of a predatory leisure class in the past and have been somewhat painstakingly conserved by the usage of the latter-day representative of that class; and these canons will not permit him, without blame, to seek contact with nature on other terms. From being an honorable employment handed down from the predatory culture as the highest form of everyday leisure, sports have come to be the only form of outdoor activity that has the full sanction of decorum. Among the proximate incentives to shooting and angling, then, may be the need of recreation and outdoor life. The remoter cause which imposes the necessity of seeking these objects under the cover of systematic slaughter is a prescription that can not be violated, except at the risk of disrepute and consequent lesion to one's self-respect.

The case of other kinds of sport is somewhat similar. Of these, athletic games are the best example. Prescriptive usage with respect to what forms of activity, exercise, and recreation are permissible under the code of reputable living is of course present here also. Those who are addicted to athletic sports, or who admire them, set up the claim that these afford the best available means of recreation and of "physical culture." And prescriptive usage gives countenance to the claim. The canons of reputable living exclude from the scheme of life of the leisure class all activity that can not be classed as conspicuous leisure. And consequently they tend by prescription to exclude it also from the scheme of life of the community generally. At the same time purposeless physical exertion is tedious and distasteful beyond tolerance. As has been noticed in another connection, recourse is in such a case had to some form of activity which shall at least afford a colorable pretense of purpose, even if the object assigned be only a make-believe. Sports satisfy these requirements of substantial futility together with a colorable make-believe of purpose. In addition to this they afford scope for emulation, and are attractive also on that account. In order to be decorous, an employment must conform to the leisure-class canon of reputable waste; at the same time all activity, in order to be persisted in as an habitual, even if only partial, expression of life, must conform to the generically human canon of efficiency for some serviceable objective end. The leisure-class canon demands strict and comprehensive futility; the instinct of workmanship demands purposeful action. The leisure-class canon of decorum acts slowly and pervasively, by a selective elimination of all substantially useful or purposeful modes of action from the accredited scheme of life; the instinct of workmanship acts impulsively and may be satisfied, provisionally, with a proximate purpose. It is only as the apprehended ulterior futility of a given line of action enters the reflective complex of consciousness as an element essentially alien to the normally purposeful trend of the life process that its disquieting and deterrent effect on the consciousness of the agent is wrought.

The individual's habits of thought make an organic complex, the trend of which is necessarily in the direction of serviceability to the life process. When it is attempted to assimilate systematic waste or futlity, as an end in life, into this organic complex, there presently supervenes a revulsion. But this revulsion of the organism may be avoided if the attention can be confined to the proximate, unreflected purpose of dexterous or emulative exertion. Sports—hunting, angling, athletic games, and the like—afford an exercise for dexterity and for the emulative ferocity and astuteness characteristic of predatory life. So long as the individual is but slightly gifted with reflection or with a sense of the ulterior trend of his actions—so long as his life is substantially a life of naïve impulsive action—so long the immediate and unreflected purposefulness of sports, in the way of an expression of dominance, will measurably satisfy his instinct of workmanship. This is especially true if his dominant impulses are the unreflecting emulative propensities of the predaceous temperament. At the same time the canons of decorum will commend sports to him as expressions of a pecuniarily blameless life. It is by meeting these two requirements, of ulterior wastefulness and proximate purposefulness, that any given employment holds its place as a traditional and habitual mode of decorous recreation. In the sense that other forms of recreation and exercise are morally impossible to persons of good breeding and delicate sensibilities, then, sports are the best available means of recreation under existing circumstances.

But those members of respectable society who advocate athletic games commonly justify their attitude on this head to themselves and to their neighbors on the ground that these games serve as an invaluable means of development. They not only improve the contestant's physique, but it is commonly added that they also foster a manly spirit, both in the participants and in the spectators. Football is the particular game which will probably first occur to any one in this community when the question of the serviceability of athletic games is raised, as this form of athletic contest is at present uppermost in the mind of those who plead for or against games as a means of physical or moral salvation. This typical athletic sport may, therefore, serve to illustrate the bearing of athletics upon the development of the contestant's character and physique. It has been said, not inaptly, that the relation of football to physical culture is much the same as that of the bull-fight to agriculture. Serviceability for these lusory institutions requires sedulous training or breeding. The material used, whether brute or human, is subjected to careful selection and discipline, in order to secure and accentuate certain aptitudes and propensities which are characteristic of the ferine state, and which tend to obsolescence under domestication. This does not mean that the result in either case is an all-around and consistent rehabilitation of the ferine or barbarian habit of mind and body. The result is rather a one-sided return to barbarism or to the *ferae natura*—a rehabilitation and accentuation of those ferine traits which make for damage and desolation, without a corresponding development of the traits which would serve the individual's self-preservation and fullness of life in a ferine environment. The culture bestowed in football gives a product of exotic ferocity and cunning. It is a rehabilitation of the early barbarian temperament, together with a suppression of those details of temperament, which as seen from the standpoint of the social and economic exigencies, are the redeeming features of the savage character.

The physical vigor acquired in the training for athletic games—so far as the training may be said to have this effect—is of advantage both to the individual and to the collectivity, in that, other things being equal, it conduces to economic serviceability. The spiritual traits which go with athletic sports are likewise economically advantageous to the individual, as contradistinguished from the interests of the collectivity. This holds true in any community where these traits are present in some degree in the population. Modern competition is in large part a process of self-assertion on the basis of these traits of predatory human nature. In the sophisticated form in which they enter into the modern, peaceable emulation, the possession of these traits in some measure is almost a necessary of life to the civilized man. But while they are indispensable to the competitive individual, they are not directly serviceable to the community. So far as regards the serviceability of the individual for the purposes of the collective life, emulative efficiency is of use only indirectly if at all. Ferocity and cunning are of no use to the community except in its hostile dealings with other communities; and they are useful to the individual only because there is so large a proportion of the same traits actively present in the human environment to which he is exposed. Any individual who enters the competitive struggle without the due endowment of these traits is at a disadvantage, somewhat as a hornless steer would find himself at a disadvantage in a drove of horned cattle.

The possession and the cultivation of the predatory traits of character may, of course, be desirable on other than economic grounds. There is a prevalent aesthetic or ethical predilection for the barbarian aptitudes, and the traits in question minister so effectively to this predilection that their serviceability in the aesthetic or ethical respect probably offsets any economic unserviceability which they may give. But for the present purpose that is beside the point. Therefore nothing is said here as to the desirability or advisability of sports on the whole, or as to their value on other than economic grounds.

---

ferae natura: nature untamed or undefiled including savagery and uncontrolled human nature.

In popular apprehension there is much that is admirable in the type of manhood which the life of sport fosters. There is self-reliance and good-fellowship, so termed in the somewhat loose colloquial use of the words. From a different point of view the qualities currently so characterized might be described as truculence and clannishness. The reason for the current approval and admiration of these manly qualities, as well as for their being called manly, is the same as the reason for their usefulness to the individual. The members of the community, and especially that class of the community which sets the pace in canons of taste, are endowed with this range of propensities in sufficient measure to make their absence in others felt as a shortcoming, and to make their possession in an exceptional degree appreciated as an attribute of superior merit. The traits of predatory man are by no means obsolete in the common run of modern populations. They are present and can be called out in bold relief at any time by any appeal to the sentiments in which they express themselves—unless this appeal should clash with the specific activities that make up our habitual occupations and comprise the general range of our everyday interests. The common run of the population of any industrial community is emancipated from these, economically considered, untoward propensities only in the sense that, through partial and temporary disuse, they have lapsed into the background of sub-conscious motives. With varying degrees of potency in different individuals, they remain available for the aggressive shaping of men's actions and sentiments whenever a stimulus of more than everyday intensity comes in to call them forth. And they assert themselves forcibly in any case where no occupation alien to the predatory culture has usurped the individual's everyday range of interest and sentiment. This is the case among the leisure class and among certain portions of the population which are ancillary to that class. Hence the facility with which any new accessions to the leisure class take to sports; and hence the rapid growth of sports and of the sporting sentiment in any industrial community where wealth has accumulated sufficiently to exempt a considerable part of the population from work.

A Mad Fight Song for William S. Carpenter, 1966

James Wright

Varus, varus, gib mir meine Legionen wieder

Quick on my feet in those Novembers of my loneliness,
I tossed a short pass,
Almost the instant I got the ball, right over the head
Of Barrel Terry before he knocked me cold.

When I woke, I found myself crying out
Latin conjugations, and the new snow falling
At the edge of a green field.

Lemoyne Crone had caught the pass, while I lay
Unconscious and raging
Alone with the fire ghost of Catullus, the contemptuous graces
tossing
Garlands and hendecasyllabics over the head
Of Cornelius Nepos the mastodon,
The huge volume.

At the edges of southeast Asia this afternoon
The quarterbacks and the lines are beginning to fall,
A spring snow,

And terrified young men
Quick on their feet
Lob one another's skulls across
Wings of strange birds that are burning
Themselves alive.

Captain Carpenter, a graduate of West Point, called for his own troops to be napalmed rather than have them surrender. General Westmoreland called him a "hero" and made him his aide, and President Johnson awarded him a silver star for courage.

Varus, Varus, give me back my legions.

Belief in Luck

Thorstein Veblen

from THE THEORY OF THE LEISURE CLASS

The gambling propensity is another subsidiary trait of the barbarian temperament. It is a concomitant variation of character of almost universal prevalence among sporting men and among men given to warlike and emulative activities generally. This trait also has a direct economic value. It is recognized to be a hindrance to the highest industrial efficiency of the aggregate in any community where it prevails in an appreciable degree.

The gambling proclivity is doubtfully to be classed as a feature belonging exclusively to the predatory type of human nature. The chief factor in the gambling habit is the belief in luck; and this belief is apparently traceable, at least in its elements, to a stage in human evolution antedating the predatory culture. It may well have been under the predatory culture that the belief in luck was developed into the form in which it is present, as the chief element of the gambling proclivity, in the sporting temperament. It probably owes the specific form under which it occurs in the modern culture to the predatory discipline. But the belief in luck is in substance a habit of more ancient date than the predatory culture. It is one form of the animistic apprehension of things. The belief seems to be a trait carried over in substance from an earlier phase into the barbarian culture, and transmuted and transmitted through that culture to a later stage of human development under a specific form imposed by the predatory discipline. But in any case, it is to be taken as an archaic trait, inherited from a more or less remote past, more or less incompatible with the requirements of the modern industrial process, and more or less of a hindrance to the fullest efficiency of the collective economic life of the present.

While the belief in luck is the basis of the gambling habit, it is not the only element that enters into the habit of betting. Betting on the issue of contests of strength and skill proceeds on a further motive, without which the belief in luck would scarcely come in as a prominent feature of sporting life. This further motive is the desire of the anticipated winner, or the partisan of the anticipated winning side, to heighten his side's ascendency at the cost of the loser. Not only does the stronger side score a more signal victory, and the losing side suffer a more painful and humiliating defeat, in proportion as the pecuniary gain and loss in the wager is large; although this alone is a consideration of material weight. But the wager is commonly laid also with a view, not avowed in words nor even recognized in set terms *in petto*, to enhancing the chances of success for the contestant on which it is laid. It is felt that substance and solicitude expended to this end can not go for naught in the issue. There is here a special manifestation of the instinct of workmanship, backed by an even more manifest sense that the animistic congruity of things must decide for a victorious outcome for the side in whose behalf the propensity inherent in events has been propitiated and fortified by so much of conative and kinetic urging. This incentive to the wager expresses itself freely under the form of backing one's favorite in any contest, and it is unmistakably a predatory feature. It is as ancillary to the predaceous impulse proper that the belief in luck expresses itself in a wager. So that it may be set down that in so far as the belief in luck comes to expression in the form of laying a wager, it is to be accounted an integral element of the predatory type of character. The belief is, in its elements, an archaic habit which belongs substantially to early, undifferentiated human nature; but when this belief is helped out by the predatory emulative impulse, and so is differentiated into the specific form of the gambling habit, it is, in this higher-developed and specific form, to be classed as a trait of the barbarian character.

---

in petto: secretly.

The Old Horse Player

Damon Runyon

For forty years he's followed the track
And played them hosses to Helenback,
And they ain't a thing he shouldn't know, that bloke.
So I sez to him, "I want advice
On beatin' this dodge at a decent price.
And what have you got to tell me, old soak?"
"Well, son," he sez, "I've bet and won,
And I've bet and lost, and when all is done
I'm sure of one thing—and only one—
All hawss players must die broke!"

Sez I, "But I see a-many a chump
With plenty o' sugar around this dump"—
Sez I, "What system do they employ, or what is the brand they
smoke?
You study the form, you study the dope
And you're goin' O.K., or so I hope,
I want you to gimme a line or two on how I can fill my poke!"
"Well, son," sez he, "this racket's tough,
And I try to learn as I do my stuff,
And I haven't learned much but I've learned enough—
All hawss players must die broke!"

Sez he, "Some live to be very old,
Till their hair gits gray and their blood gits cold,
And some of 'em almost fall apart before they up and croak."
Sez he, "I've seen 'em, these noble men
Up in the dough, and out again,
In fact, I bin there a-many a time myself—and that's no joke!"
Sez he, "I've seen 'em in limousines
With rocks on their dukes and dough in their jeans,
But they're all alike when they quit their scenes—
All hawss players must die broke!"

Sport and the 'Bitch-goddess'

Lewis Mumford

The romantic movements were important as a corrective to the machine because they called attention to essential elements in life that were left out of the mechanical world-picture: they themselves prepared some of the materials for a richer synthesis. But there is within modern civilization a whole series of compensatory functions that, so far from making better integration possible, only serve to stabilize the existing state—and finally they themselves become part of the very regimentation they exist to combat. The chief of these institutions is perhaps mass-sports. One may define these sports as those forms of organized play in which the spectator is more important than the player, and in which a good part of the meaning is lost when the game is played for itself. Mass-sport is primarily a spectacle.

Unlike play, mass-sport usually requires an element of mortal chance or hazard as one of its main ingredients: but instead of the chance's occurring spontaneously, as in mountain climbing, it must take place in accordance with the rules of the game and must be increased when the spectacle begins to bore the spectators. Play in one form or another is found in every human society and among a great many animal species: but sport in the sense of a mass-spectacle, with death to add to the underlying excitement, comes into existence when a population has been drilled and regimented and depressed to such an extent that it needs at least a vicarious participation in difficult feats of strength or skill or heroism in order to sustain its waning life-sense. The demand for circuses, and when the milder spectacles are still insufficiently life-arousing, the demand for sadistic exploits and finally for blood is characteristic of civilizations that are losing their grip: Rome under the Caesars, Mexico at the time of Montezuma, Germany under the Nazis. These forms of surrogate manliness and bravado are the surest signs of a collective impotence and a pervasive death wish. The dangerous symptoms of that ultimate decay one finds everywhere today in machine civilization under the guise of mass-sport.

The invention of new forms of sport and the conversion of play into sport were two of the distinctive marks of the last century: baseball is an example of the first, and the transformation of tennis and golf into tournament spectacles, within our own day, is an example of the second. Unlike play, sport has an existence in our mechanical civilization even in its most abstract possible manifestation: the crowd that does not witness the ball game will huddle around the scoreboard in the metropolis to watch the change of counters. If it does not see the aviator finish a record flight around the world, it will listen over the radio to the report of his landing and hear the frantic shouts of the mob on the field: should the hero attempt to avoid a public reception and parade, he would be regarded as cheating. At times, as in horse-racing, the elements may be reduced to names and betting odds: participation need go no further than the newspaper and the betting booth, provided that the element of chance be there. Since the principal aim of our mechanical routine in industry is to reduce the domain of chance, it is in the glorification of chance and the unexpected, which sport provides, that the element extruded by the machine returns, with an accumulated emotional charge, to life in general. In the latest forms of mass-sport, like air races and motor races, the thrill of the spectacle is intensified by the promise of immediate death or fatal injury. The cry of horror that escapes from the crowd when the motor car overturns or the airplane crashes is not one of surprise but of fulfilled expectation: is it not fundamentally for the sake of exciting just such bloodlust that the competition itself is held and widely attended? By means of the talking picture that spectacle and that thrill are repeated in a thousand theatres throughout the world as a mere incident in the presentation of the week's news: so that a steady habituation to blood-letting and exhibitionistic murder and suicide accompanies the spread of the machine and, becoming stale by repetition in its milder forms, encourages the demand for more massive and desperate exhibitions of brutality.

Sport presents three main elements: the spectacle, the competition, and the personalities of the gladiators. The spectacle itself introduces the esthetic element, so often lacking in the paleotechnic industrial environment itself. The race is run or the game is played within a frame of spectators, tightly massed: the movements of this mass, their cries, their songs, their cheers, are a constant accompaniment of the spectacle: they play, in effect, the part of the Greek chorus in the new machine-drama, announcing what is about to occur and underlining the events of the contest. Through his place in the chorus, the spectator finds his special release: usually cut off from close physical associations by his impersonal routine, he is now at one with a primitive undifferentiated group. His muscles contract or relax with the progress of the game, his breath comes quick or slow, his shouts heighten the excitement of the moment and increase his internal sense of the drama: in moments of frenzy he pounds his neighbor's back or embraces him. The spectator feels himself contributing by his presence to the victory of his side, and sometimes, more by hostility to the enemy than encouragement to the friend, he does perhaps exercize a visible effect on the contest. It is a relief from the passive rôle of taking orders and automatically filling them, of conforming by means of a reduced "I" to a magnified "It," for in the sports arena the spectator has the illusion of being completely mobilized and utilized. Moreover, the spectacle itself is one of the richest satisfactions for the esthetic sense that the machine civilization offers to those that have no key to any other form of culture: the spectator knows the style of his favorite contestants in the way that the painter knows the characteristic line or palette of his master, and he reacts to the bowler, the pitcher, the punter, the server, the air ace, with a view, not only to his success in scoring, but to the esthetic spectacle itself. This point has been stressed in bull-fighting; but of course it applies to every form of sport. There remains, nevertheless, a conflict between the desire for a skilled exhibition and the desire for a brutal outcome: the maceration or death of one or more of the contestants.

Now in the competition two elements are in conflict: chance and record-making. Chance is the sauce that stimulates the excitement of the spectator and increases his zest for gambling: whippet-racing and horse-racing are as effective in this relation as games where a greater degree of human skill is involved. But the habits of the mechanical régime are as difficult to combat in sport as in the realm of sexual behavior: hence one of the most significant elements in modern sport is the fact that an abstract interest in record-making has become one of its main preoccupations. To cut the fifth of a second off the time of running a race, to swim the English channel twenty minutes faster than another swimmer, to stay up in the air an hour longer than one's rival did—these interests come into the competition and turn it from a purely human contest to one in which the real opponent is the previous record: time takes the place of a visible rival. Sometimes, as in dance marathons or flag-pole squattings, the record goes to feats of inane endurance: the blankest and dreariest of sub-human spectacles. With the increase in professionalized skill that accompanies this change, the element of chance is further reduced: the sport, which was originally a drama, becomes an exhibition. As soon as specialism reaches this point, the whole performance is arranged as far as possible for the end of making possible the victory of the popular favorite: the other contestants are, so to say, thrown to the lions. Instead of "Fair Play" the rule now becomes "Success at Any Price."

Finally, in addition to the spectacle and the competition, there comes onto the stage, further to differentiate sport from play, the new type of popular hero, the professional player or sportsman. He is as specialized for the vocation as a soldier or an opera singer: he represents virility, courage, gameness, those talents in exercizing and commanding the body which have so small a part in the new mechanical regimen itself: if the hero is a girl, her qualities must be Amazonian in character. The sports hero represents the masculine virtues, the Mars complex, as the popular motion picture actress or the bathing beauty contestant represents Venus. He exhibits that complete skill to which the amateur vainly aspires. Instead of being looked upon as a servile and ignoble being, because of the very perfection of his physical efforts, as the Athenians in Socrates' time looked upon the professional athletes and dancers, this new hero represents the summit of the amateur's effort, not at pleasure but at efficiency. The hero is handsomely paid for his efforts, as well as being rewarded by praise and publicity, and he thus further restores to sport its connection with the very commercialized existence from which it is supposed to provide relief—restores it and thereby sanctifies it. The few heroes who resist this vulgarization—notably Lindbergh—fall into popular or at least into journalistic disfavor, for they are only playing the less important part of the game. The really successful sports hero, to satisfy the mass-demand, must be midway between a pander and a prostitute.

Sport, then, in this mechanized society, is no longer a mere game empty of any reward other than the playing: it is a profitable business: millions are invested in arenas, equipment, and players, and the maintenance of sport becomes as important as the maintenance of any other form of profit-making mechanism. And the technique of mass-sport infects other activities: scientific expeditions and geographic explorations are conducted in the manner of a speed stunt or a prizefight—*and for the same reason.* Business or recreation or mass spectacle, sport is always a means:

even when it is reduced to athletic and military exercizes held with great pomp within the sports arenas, the aim is to gather a record-breaking crowd of performers and spectators, and thus testify to the success or importance of the movement that is represented. Thus sport, which began originally, perhaps, as a spontaneous reaction against the machine, has become one of the mass-duties of the machine age. It is a part of that universal regimentation of life—for the sake of private profits or nationalistic exploit—from which its excitement provides a temporary and only a superficial release. Sport has turned out, in short, to be one of the least effective reactions against the machine. There is only one other reaction less effective in its final result: the most ambitious as well as the most disastrous. I mean war.

Ripper Collins' Legacy

Don Johnson

On the blue corner's top rope
the rumored missing link,
Pampero Firpo, looms gigantic.
Launched, the "pampas bull"
balloons in mid-flight, shutting
the crowd's shouts like a clamped
hatch, blotting the ring lights
out before becoming Whitewolf,
who can fly, and does. Rising
only to descend and rise
again, the grinning Indian's
face distends and shrinks
the long night long. His knee hangs
fixed three feet above the mat,
about to float abruptly
through the Ripper's kidneys.

"This is me in Pittsburgh
as the Crusher, the year
I won the Tri-State tag
team belt with Yukon Ike.

In the beginning
I had hopes,
but by then I only played
at playing roles.
You can't do that."

Winter nights the knife
wound suffered when some fan
forgot himself in Carolina
aches, keeps him awake,
and, fortunately, dreamless.
In the dark he picks
through scattered lies
he'd lied about for ages
hoping to choose the one
best suited for the match
upcoming with the Masked Executioner.

Games: The Extensions of Man

Marshall McLuhan

from UNDERSTANDING MEDIA

Alcohol and gambling have very different meanings in different cultures. In our intensely individualist and fragmented Western world, "booze" is a social bond and a means of festive involvement. By contrast, in closely knit tribal society, "booze" is destructive of all social pattern and is even used as a means to mystical experience.

In tribal societies, gambling, on the other hand, is a welcome avenue of entrepreneurial effort and individual initiative. Carried into an individualist society, the same gambling games and sweepstakes seem to threaten the whole social order. Gambling pushes individual initiative to the point of mocking the individualist social structure. The tribal virtue is the capitalist vice.

When the boys came home from the mud and blood baths of the Western Front in 1918 and 1919, they encountered the Volstead Prohibition Act. It was the social and political recognition that the war had fraternalized and tribalized us to the point where alcohol was a threat to an individualist society. When we too are prepared to legalize gambling, we shall, like the English, announce to the world the end of individualist society and the trek back to tribal ways.

We think of humor as a mark of sanity for a good reason: in fun and play we recover the integral person, who in the workaday world or in professional life can use only a small sector of his being. Philip Deane, in *Captive in Korea*, tells a story about games in the midst of successive brainwashings that is to the point.

> There came a time when I had to stop reading those books, to stop practising Russian because with the study of language the absurd and constant assertion began to leave its mark, began to find an echo, and I felt my thinking processes getting tangled, my critical faculties getting blunted. . . . then they made a mistake. They gave us Robert Louis Stevenson's *Treasure Island* in English. . . . I could read Marx again, and question myself honestly without fear. Robert Louis Stevenson made us lighthearted, so we started dancing lessons.

Games are popular art, collective, social *reactions* to the main drive or action of any culture. Games, like institutions, are extensions of social man and of the body politic, as technologies are extensions of the animal organism. Both games and technologies are counter-irritants or ways of adjusting to the stress of the specialized actions that occur in any social group. As extensions of the popular response to the workaday stress, games become faithful models of a culture. They incorporate both the action and the reaction of whole populations in a single dynamic image.

A Reuters dispatch for December 13, 1962, reported from Tokyo:

> Business Is a Battlefield
>
> Latest fashion among Japanese businessmen is the study of classical military strategy and tactics in order to apply them to business operations. . . . It has been reported that one of the largest advertising companies in Japan has even made these books compulsory reading for all its employees.

Long centuries of tight tribal organization now stand the Japanese in very good stead in the trade and commerce of the electric age. A few decades ago they underwent enough literacy and industrial fragmentation to release aggressive individual energies. The close teamwork and tribal loyalty now demanded by electrical intercom again puts the Japanese in positive relation to their ancient traditions. Our own tribal ways are much too remote to be of any social avail. We have begun retribalizing with the same painful groping with which a preliterate society begins to read and write, and to organize its life visually in three-dimensional space. . . .

Games are dramatic models of our psychological lives providing release of particular tensions. They are collective and popular art forms with strict conventions. Ancient and nonliterate societies naturally regarded games as live dramatic models of the universe or of the outer cosmic drama. The Olympic games were direct enactments of the *agon*, or struggle of the Sun god. The runners moved around a track adorned with the zodiacal signs in imitation of the daily circuit of the sun chariot. With games and plays that were dramatic enactments of a cosmic struggle, the spectator role was plainly religious. The participation in these rituals kept the cosmos on the right track, as well as providing a booster shot for the tribe. The tribe or the city was a dim replica of that cosmos, as much as were the games, the dances, and the icons. How art became a sort of civilized substitute for magical games and rituals is the story of the detribalization which came with literacy. Art, like games, became a mimetic echo of, and relief from, the old magic of total involvement. As the audience for the magic games and plays became more individualistic, the role of art and ritual shifted from the cosmic to the humanly psychological, as in Greek drama. Even the ritual became more verbal and less mimetic or dancelike. Finally, the verbal narrative from Homer and Ovid became a romantic literary substitute for the corporate liturgy and group participation. Much of the scholarly effort of the past century in many fields has been devoted to a minute reconstruction of the conditions of primitive art and ritual, for it has been felt that this course offers the key to understanding the mind of primitive man. The key to this understanding, however, is also available in our new electric technology that is so swiftly and profoundly re-creating the conditions and attitudes of primitive tribal man in ourselves.

The wide appeal of the games of recent times—the popular sports of baseball and football and ice hockey—seen as outer models of inner psychological life, become understandable. As models, they are collective rather than private dramatizations of inner life. Like our vernacular tongues, all games are media of interpersonal communication, and they could have neither existence nor meaning except as extensions of our immediate inner lives. If we take a tennis racket in hand, or thirteen playing cards, we consent to being a part of a dynamic mechanism in an artificially contrived situation. Is this not the reason we enjoy those games most that mimic other situations in our work and social lives? Do not our favorite games provide a release from the monopolistic tyranny of the social machine? In a word, does not Aristotle's idea of drama as a mimetic reenactment and relief from our besetting pressures apply perfectly to all kinds of games and dance and fun? For fun or games to be welcome, they must convey an echo of workaday life. On the other hand, a man or society without games is one sunk in the zombie trance of the automaton. Art and games enable us to stand aside from the material pressures of routine and convention, observing and questioning. Games as popular art forms offer to all an immediate means of participation in the full life of a society, such as no single role or job can offer to any man. Hence the contradiction in "professional" sport. When the games door opening into the free life leads into a merely specialist job, everybody senses an incongruity. . . .

The social practices of one generation tend to get codified into the "game" of the next. Finally, the game is passed on as a joke, like a skeleton stripped of its flesh. This is especially true of periods of suddenly altered attitudes, resulting from some radically new technology. It is the inclusive mesh of the TV image, in particular, that spells for a while, at least, the doom of baseball. For baseball is a game of one-thing-at-a-time, fixed positions and visibly delegated specialist jobs such as belonged to the now passing mechanical age, with its fragmented tasks and its staff and line in management organization. TV, as the very image of the new corporate and participant ways of electric living, fosters habits of unified awareness and social interdependence that alienate us from the peculiar style of baseball, with its specialist and positional stress. When cultures change, so do games. Baseball, that had become the elegant abstract image of an industrial society living by split-second timing, has in the new TV decade lost its psychic and social relevance for our new way of life. The ball game has been dislodged from the social center and been conveyed to the periphery of American life.

In contrast, American football is nonpositional, and any or all of the players can switch to any role during play. It is, therefore, a game that at the present is supplanting baseball in general acceptance. It agrees very well with the new needs of decentralized team play in the electric age. Offhand, it might be supposed that the tight tribal unity of football would make it a game that the Russians would cultivate. Their devotion to ice hockey and soccer, two very individualist forms of game, would seem little suited to the psychic needs of a collectivist society. But Russia is still in the main an oral, tribal world that is undergoing detribalization and just now discovering individualism as a novelty. Soccer and ice hockey have for them, therefore, an exotic and Utopian quality of promise that they do not convey to the West. This is the quality that we tend to call "snob value," and *we* might derive some similar "value" from owning race horses, polo ponies, or twelve-meter yachts.

The Urge to Win

Paul Weiss

from SPORT: A PHILOSOPHIC INQUIRY

A game incorporates an "agon"—hence our "agony,"—a struggle. It entrains fatigue, sometimes exhaustion, and almost always some discomfort. The emotions it involves are subject to control and are not, as they sometimes are in ordinary life, allowed to come out explosively. But they are expressed with comparatively little modulation, and consequently not so sensitively as they are in the creation of art.

Victory is what is normally signalized at the close of a game. This seems to be characteristic of games in every epoch and in every place.

The romantics exaggerated and thereby falsified the Greek outlook on sport; they supposed that the Greeks viewed victory in a spirit quite different from our own. Nothing base or vulgar was supposed to cross the Greek mind. The victors, we were taught to believe, were content to receive a mere wreath; the spectators also behaved admirably, applauding all those who won fairly in a clear exhibition of excellence. But as Erich Segal has observed,

> The single aim in all Greek athletics was—as the etymology (from athlon, "prize") suggests—to win. There were no awards for second place; in fact losing was considered a disgrace. . . . It is generally believed that wars were suspended so that the Greeks could hold their Olympic Games. But no Greek historian ever mentions such an armistice, nor is there any evidence that fighting abated during Olympic years. . . . The ancient Olympic victor may have won merely a simple wreath, but when he returned to his home town, gifts were lavished upon him, and he usually received an income for life.[1]

The cry, "It is not the winning, but the taking part, not the conquering, but the playing fair" (attributed to Baron de Coubertin), is not the ancient view. The Greeks found room for and apparently approved of trickery and cunning. What the Greeks practiced, we practice in a muted form. Like theirs, our athletes also strive to win.

If a player would win, he should try to win, should strive to win, should want to win. To obtain maximum results in a game, he must give himself to it. He can then sometimes come close to getting what he desires. And this he will do if he is a true athlete.

---

[1] Erich Segal, "It Is Not Strength, But Art, Obtains the Prize," *The Yale Review*, LVI, No. 4 (June 1967)

The athlete must have a strong urge to defeat his opponent, and must carry out that urge in the form of actions which will enable him to outdistance all. This requires him to be aggressive. Man's aggression, as has already been remarked, is thought by some to exhibit in a vigorous but harmless form an inescapable but dangerous aggressiveness characteristic of us all. Aggression, on this view, is part of man's very nature, rooted deep in the unconscious, in the history of the race, and in the early experiences of the child. It is always and inevitably expressed; mankind is fortunate in having found ways for releasing it without much injury to anyone.

So much aggression seems to be expressed in games that to many an observer a game appears to be like a war, that outstanding example of aggressiveness. Though some sports seem to have been invented to promote physical fitness, skill, and dexterity, or for the purpose of using up surplus energy enjoyably, others—archery, fencing, shooting, judo, evidently, and conceivably boxing, wrestling, dressage, running, weight lifting, and the relay—have instead a military origin or a military objective. These, and perhaps others, refine and promote activities which are parts of the art of war. The fact has tempted some to think of games as a substitute for war. If they were, hopefully they might some day usurp the place that war has assumed in what we like to call "the civilized world." Unfortunately, it does not appear that there is much ground for that expectation, in part because war and game are quite distinct in nature, and in the role they give to aggressiveness.

Both war and game aim at victory. Both usually end in a clearly evidenced superiority of one side over the other, though draws and stalemates are not unknown. Only games *must* conform to rules, though in modern times we try to make wars conform to them too. But it is paradoxical to expect both sides in a war to submit to common rules. Each side seeks to annihilate the other; it would be foolish for either to allow its efforts to be restrained or blocked by an effort to conform to rules it has agreed, with its enemy, to abide by. A genuine war is a ruthless affair, paying for victory with the lives of men and the destruction of property and works of art. Omnivorous, it sweeps away for the time any meaning to a common acceptance of any rule, and jeopardizes every civilized value. If the antagonists could agree upon anything one would expect them to agree to stop the war; when advantage is thought of in terms of what life is and what gives it value, war is evidently to the advantage of neither. It is because they can find no basis for agreement that they go to war seriously, with the intent to render the enemy impotent and sometimes even to destroy him utterly. Wars begin with a disagreement precluding the acceptance of common rules.

Men poised to destroy one another cannot, except foolishly and futilely, agree on conforming to certain rules. There is no punishment which the violators of rules need fear. If they win no one will punish them, and if they lose their loss is inseparable from whatever punishment they thereby suffer. The loser could be punished, over and above what is normally the case, because of his violations of a supposed agreement made in happier days, but since the punishment is meted out by the victor, as he sees fit, it is arbitrary to claim that a closer adherence to the rules would have resulted in a less severe punishment. Only where it is the object of a war to restrain or warn is there much point in keeping to common rules.

It is possible, and it may even be desirable, to act aggressively toward others in a game, but one must, to play with them, act with good will. An intent to cripple and destroy goes counter to the purpose of a game. The aggressiveness exhibited in it is an aggressiveness which conforms to rules, or one is doing violence to the game.

The soldier seeks victory. He must be aggressive. Of course, without a strong desire to defeat his opponent, no athlete can have much hope of victory either. He, too, insists on himself. But there is too much self-sacrifice, humility, team play, together with an acceptance of official neutral decisions and a conformity to objectively stated and applied prescriptions, to make the expression of aggression represent the primary or essential goal, or the motive for athletic activity.

The Geneva conventions and the Red Cross offer limits beyond which one is asked not to go. He who accepts them does so, more likely than not, because he fears retaliation. He then lives through a rule-dominated, traditionalized, conventionalized interlude in the life of mankind, and so far participates in a game which, like a bullfight, takes crippling and death to be prospects not alien to its intent. Nevertheless, a war cannot be taken to be only a game. War and game are distinct both in fact and in theory. The two have different times, spaces, causalities, objectives, and tests. Their origins, procedures, and intentions rarely coincide. Both may accept common rules and follow agreed-upon conventions. But if they do, they do so for different reasons.

The time of a game is cut off from the rest of time to make it the sequential measure of an island of occurrences, having little commerce with the main. The time of a war is a special time, entraining a host of new issues and occurrences, but it is a time which is nevertheless continuous with the time of normal politics and the interaction of various nations. War, it has rightly been said, is politics continued by other means. But a game is only a game.

The geometry of a space is constituted by the kind of roles, positions, and functions which the men and other items in it carry out. Forwards and goalies constitute one type of space; lieutenants and privates constitute another. And each type of space is traversed by its own distinctive time. The space and time of a war differ in nature from those characteristic of a sport.

The causality characteristic of a game is intended to stop at its borders. Awards, injuries, reports, and records outlast the game, and have resonances outside it, but they do not carry the causality of the game outside the game itself. But the causality of a war has an effect on what takes place after the war is over; the actual fighting that goes on, the deployment of troops, the carrying out of a particular strategy all have effects outside the war. Where the one remains within a distinctive, causal, bounded domain, the other has a bearing on the rest of life. . . .

There are war games, and there are games that are warlike. A past war can be recaptured in a study and used as a model in teaching. Men can engage in sham attacks and repulsions. The models and the sham fighting are not parts of a true game; they are parts of a preliminary session, offering one opportunities to practice and to rehearse for the serious war business ahead. The most warlike of games, on the other hand, with its hard-fought victories, spontaneities, and improvizations, is not yet war. Men contest there not to see how much they can destroy, but to see how well they meet the test of being fulfilled men who have accepted their bodies, identified themselves with their equipment, and acted as representatives of all others.

Even if we are inordinately considerate in a war, we will not make it approximate the shape of a game. Nor will the most belligerent of players make a game approximate a state of war. The one is a serious enterprise casting its shadow over the whole of life; the other is a serious enterprise encapsulated by rules which bind and define an isolated domain.

It is possible to speak, with some benefit, of a game as a battle carried out in another way, provided only that the differences between the two are not then blurred. Yet such blurring will most likely occur if we are not exceptionally alert to the great difference there is between using material advantages according to one's will, and having matched competitors follow out agreed upon rules, and if we do not attend to the even greater difference that exists between those who aim to injure or destroy their opponents and their property, and those who seek to determine who is the better, and therefore the representative of a better man.

Even the defeated gain from a game. They benefit from the mere fact that they have engaged in a contest, that they have encountered a display of great skill, that they have made the exhibition of that skill possible or desirable, that they have exerted themselves to the limit, and that they have made a game come to be. New technologies are sometimes produced under the pressure of war; possible dictators may be given pause; law and order may be reinstituted with considerable effectiveness as a consequence of a resounding victory. The results of war may benefit both sides eventually, but it will take a long while, if ever, for these gains to overbalance the irreparable, irreversible loss which the war produces in men, creativity, inquiry, and sheer joyous existence.

Games are desirable, but war is regrettable. A war hurts even the victors. They too must pay in some loss of life and property, and must turn away from their primary task of promoting civilization through the encouragement of art, science, and commerce, to deal instead with what they take to be obstacles in the way.

A good deal of sport can serve as an attractive means for preparing men to become warriors. Our service academies see this; they take athletics to offer an opportunity for training men to meet that final, crucial test which war provides. Sport does promote physical fitness, and physical fitness is an almost indispensable precondition for success in battle, particularly when it is long drawn out and hotly contested. But no one really knows whether some other kind of preparation would not have been better; nor is it unreasonable to suppose that there are advantages, beyond that of promoting fitness, which sport gives to the prospective officer.

There is just as much plausibility to the argument that the service academies' involvement in sport has no particular pertinence to the activities in which their men will participate as there is in the argument that the sports of other institutions have a special relevance to a possible warrior's career. When the service academies compete with other institutions they in fact show the same fine spirit that the others do. They are then no more aggressive or warlike, and are just as considerate toward their opponents as those who do not take themselves to be preparing for, substituting for, or imitating actual combat. The service academies rightly encourage their men to know mathematics, poetry, and philosophy, not because this will make them better able to fight or even to lead, but because these subjects presumably contribute to the making of better men. The same reasons suffice to justify their encouragement of sport.

What is desirable to learn in order to be an officer is not necessarily that which anticipates a participation in war, but whatever enables a young man to achieve a rich maturity. Sport seems to contribute to that result. But neither its history nor its present use in the service academies warrants the conclusion that sport makes use of similar powers, proceeds along similar lines, feeds on similar motives and drives, or aims at goals which are similar to those involved in war.

These differences do not make altogether invalid an attempt to look at a game as an opportunity to express aggression in a harmless way. But the aggression, it must then be remembered, is only one factor; there are other factors as well, all of which have distinctive meanings when they are exhibited within the confines of a game. Sport is not aggression controlled and harmless. It is a constructive activity in which aggression plays a role together with dedication, cooperation, restraint, self-denial, and a respect for the rights and dignity of others.

A game, it cannot be too often insisted, is an event cut off from the rest of the world, though every occurrence in it may have effects in the world outside. Practical concerns are put aside by one who truly plays a game. That is why he is able to concentrate on the production of the game in accordance with accepted rules. But a game is like every other production, practical or otherwise, in that it cannot be entirely prepared for. It is never what it was imagined or predicted to be.

To Nikê

Rainer Maria Rilke

In merely catching your own casting all's
mere cleverness and indecisive winning:—
only when all at once you're catching balls
an everlasting partner hurtles spinning
into your very centre, with trajecture
exactly calculated, curvingly
recalling God's stupendous pontifecture,—
only then catching's capability,
not yours, a world's. And if, not resting here,
you'd strength and will to throw them back again,—
no,—wonderfullier!—forgot all that, and then
found you'd already thrown . . . (as, twice a year,
the flocking birds are thrown, the birds that wander,
thrown from an older to a younger, yonder,
ultramarine warmth),—in that mood of sheer
abandon you'd be equal to the game.

Both ease and difficulty would disappear:
you'd simply throw. A meteor would flame
out of your hands and tear through its own spaces . . .

Translated by J. B. Leishman

Sport as a Human Absurdity

Howard S. Slusher

Although I would be the first to admit sport reflects the culture and thus is often limited by its "mimic" character, I would like to submit that sport is more than a demonstration of existing movement patterns. Knowledge of the variables assists man in his involvement; but unlike science, sport goes beyond the empirical. Somehow we cannot explain all the forces that are an intricate part of sport. Does anyone really know what is meant by the "spirit" of a team? What is involved with getting a team "up"? How can we explain the "peak performances" that by definition are so very infrequent? How do we explain the irregular performance? What is involved with man's "feel" for a specific activity? How do you explain the sudden rapture of a sport thrill, such as gliding down a ski trail or capturing the board as you ride the wave?

Strongly based in an objective world we tend to say these "elements" are part of our existence and they are brought to our awareness. Perhaps this is so. But is it possible—in our transcendence—that these feelings come from *no where?* Irrational? Yes! But remember we do need to go beyond our objective shells to understand what objectivity does not allow us to comprehend. To go *beyond* our human experiences is perhaps the most *human* experience we can have. This does not mean we *accept* or believe each and every input that is not reasonable. Rather we admit that objectivity is but *one* system and we will employ other systems in a continuing, searching concern to discover the truth of human existence. To do less would be inhuman; to do more would not be human.

The sports performer goes beyond assuming responsibility for personal choices. Learning well from the thin-lipped naturalist Emile, the pole vaulter defies gravity, the sprinter explodes through resistance, and the swimmer dares massive forces and load, all see that the sport *movement* must be in keeping with the *essence* of nature. Thus, *control* over self and environment becomes a higher priority than freedom. It is this element, among others, that makes *discipline* such a very important part of the sport experience. Many would like to think of the man of sport as being *freed* by nature; in truth his restrictions are personal *and* natural. Let us, individuals with an interest in sport, not forget that a wide gap *might* well exist between what is natural and what is nature. The former is no doubt almost a replica of the latter. A most *unnatural* point to remember.

Yet it is the restriction of the *natural man* that is a factor in the dehumanization of man which has become such a popular theme in modern literature. As we witness the increase in mechanical and technical "assistance"—such as electric timers, replay machines, exercise "gadgets"—one can hardly wonder if we are increasing our "efficiency" at the cost of de-humanizing mankind. Personally, I cherish my modern conveniences and greatly enjoy the superior performances of the latter half of the twentieth century. But I must wonder if this is what sport is all about. Does man need *hide* from himself and his fellowman in order to escape his personal commitment? If so, I question the place of sport in the development of a strong culture. Materialistically successful but not strong—this is the plight of man. Like society sport crumbles from a disease of dehumanization.

If we are to view sport as anything more than "play time," then we must understand the irrational as a part of human experience. The immediate reaction to such a proposal might well be a scream of "ridiculous!" Does this not mean that sport may well be absurd? The answer is an unequivocal yes. Sport *may* well be absurd. To see man attempt artificially to control internalized and externalized nature may well be absurd. To see man be encapsulated by determined stimuli, under the most adverse conditions, may well be absurd. And for man to estrange himself deliberately from his brother might, indeed, be absurd. To understand the value and meaning attached to sport is to begin to appreciate, if not comprehend, man.

It is no wonder, with all the opportunities for choice that confront the performer, he often demonstrates overt signs of displeasure. Faced, and in fact condemned to, infinite freedom, man finds it difficult and often frustrating to make a choice. Anguish can be seen as a result of the threat of the present. And sport is focused on the present. Man knows almost immediately with the act if he is achieving or not. Entering the game, committed to all that is involved, he is "forced" within a frame of near anguish. When the situation becomes too absurd, when he is faced with too much tension, the hopelessness of the situation brings reality to him in the form of concrete existence. It is unlikely this awareness diminishes man's performance; on the contrary, sport flourishes when anxiety is increased within acceptable limitations. It is almost as if the performer recognizes "what counts" cannot be achieved and rather than continue in the futile search for a meaningful existence, he "cashes in" on the obvious prize—victory.

At this stage it should be pointed out that sport is not the only area of human life that may be touched by the absurd. Contemporary art has fostered this quality as a direct challenge to mankind. To rid itself of "copy" and to increase man's potential to assimilate and embrace existence is but one part of the intentions and achievements of sport.

How could any area of human involvement be considered as providing meaningful experiences to man and then be confined only to the rational. To do this is to assume man is a unity *of* reason. An extension of this thesis is one, I trust, man could hardly accept. Sport *does* provide an experience of mystical dimension. Man communicates with himself and others (and perhaps *the* other) when he "cracks" man. Speaking as a participant of a "contact" sport, I found when I tackled a man that there was *more* than the hit. To say it was satisfaction is true. To say it was a feeling of security is true. To say it was a cathartic experience might well be true. But it was more. It is more. To say I understood it, or understand now, would be to admit the absurd is accessible through reason.

There is, to be sure, a certain degree of *completion* in sport. The player on skates attempts to perfect movement. The routine of the gymnast is complete. Each participant attempts to cover "the holes." But truly this is a function of self-communication. The performer sees himself in the world; and as such sport provides a connective link for structured expression. To the degree that the self and surroundings are understood is the degree man achieves meaning in sport. To assume this is not a function of self-exploration and awareness is to convey apathy to human existence.

> . . . my invisible self, my personality . . . a world which has true infinity, but which is traceable only by the understanding . . . a countless multitude of worlds annihilates as it were my importance as an animal creature, which after it has been for a short time provided with vital power, one knows not how, must again give back the matter of which it was formed to the planet it inhabits. (Kant, 1889, p. 1)

Sport as much as any area of human involvement points to the impossibility of offering a *reasonable* explanation between the inner and outer world of man. To assume that we know why man takes part in sport is presumptuous—no matter what the behavioral sciences might indicate. Again, human action cannot be accounted for by demonstration of empirical data. Man, in his freedom, is basically non-prophetic. To ask even this much from the man of sport is to demand he be a "sooth-sayer."

It is rather odd that in man's attempt to *be* human he needs to seek the transcendental, which is beyond humanity. But this really is not *too* strange, for great men of all civilizations—Socrates, Christ, to mention a couple—reached beyond their own time to achieve that special touch of humanity. But *it is strange* that, as the very area of human life which stresses the development of the *whole man*, sport must admit to a dualistic quality. This is not the typical split of mind-body and reason-emotion but it touches on an equal dimension, if not one of greater depth, namely, sport "pays a premium" to the man who transcends the real. As a "recognizer" of both *what is* and *more than is* sport establishes a strong conflict. Is this any way *to be* absurd? "You bet it is!"

Sport *is* so very popular because it can and does cater to all of mankind. Its raw brutality greatly appeals to the animal in man; while its rhythm and grace appeal to the aesthetic in man. It is no wonder we get confused by categorically assigning rugby and figure skating the same name, sport. At best the classification is most artificial. Yet both fuse the dualistic segments of man's existence. But there is more, much more. In both activities man conclusively demonstrates his desire for nature, romantic as it might be. It is in the sport experience that man can receive tangible evidence of his efforts. The "feed-back" is direct and immediate. There are few places in life where man can "keep score" with such facility. It is not unlike man to think he can achieve meaning by determining the facts. As he remains prey to his material culture he still believes the more he "collects," the more he will *possess.* Absurd? Who knows? He is still playing the game. And *some* say he is winning.

As the performer attains recognition he becomes what Nietzsche would call a *Superman.* He wins. He achieves. He defeats. But man is not *all* animal. Man needs more. Soon the athlete looks to the social and the spiritual phenomena of life. It is *here* sport becomes absurd. The demands of competition, victory and personal achievement do not readily afford *real* amity and symmetry between man and man and/or man and nature. Romantic literature might well speak of this idealization but in truth it is *not* present. The very structure of sport argues against *this* form of transcendence as a general happening. Man cannot be turned on and off much like a water fountain. If sent out to conquer or defeat, he will do so. But to turn from killer to lover, at the happen-chance demands of the idealists, is just not what *is.*

Sport as an Absurd Dehumanizer. To ask what exists in sport is to inquire into the nature of sport. To be sure, sport develops its heroes. But in truth these noble images are not *of themselves.* Instead their individuality conforms to the mass of society. "His body is the carcass lived in by the masses" (Wolf, 1966, p. 2). To a degree the man of sport becomes anonymous. He loses his freedom as he becomes "a member of the team," or "the unsung hero." Who has not heard a coach say, almost as an afterthought, "Let's not forget our line"? This type of felt "necessity," by the coach or backfield men in football is communicated to me as a projection of guilt. A guilt of *using* fellow man as an *instrument* to achieve an end. The "instrument" might well reach worldly success, but he never does reach personal truth. A feeling that goes beyond the roar of the crowd and the touch of gold coins. He loses his humanity; for he really is little more than a "puppet" doing little more than *acting* as a mimic of the objective world.

Sport is marked by its involvement with the *numerous.* In the world, the participant deals with "many faces" of both known and unknown dimensions. The problem is not *the activity* which demands contact with the *mass,* but the constrictions that are placed on man's efforts. To think of man as an individual *in* his own right, and not an instrument of victory or defeat, is the dilemma of sport. "The individual is in the truth even if he should happen to be thus related to what is not true" (Kierkegaard, 1944, p. 178).

This is the crux of the problem. Man risks his basic existence when he enters sport. Is he to be himself or is he to assume the character of the group? Again, we come to the importance of freedom as a function of the "authentic" in sport. If sport is to react against absurdity, then it must provide a truly human experience. Man cannot be forgotten as a grain of sand on the beach. He needs to be *considered.* Man faces, all around him, overwhelming threats to this personhood. The social emphasis upon technology and mechanization indicates man will be nothing but a by-product of advancement. Instead of limiting the thought of man by demanding he conform to established patterns of movement, sport has the *potential* of providing the environment for actualization. It is on the field man *could* be what he is. But this is *more* than skill development; rather, it is development of the self. It is man saying I am more than the culmination. It is man convinced that truth is to be found in the real experience. To be a winner or champion is not necessarily to be man.

> There is a view of life which says that where the masses are, there too is truth, that there is an urge in truth itself to have the masses on its side. There is another view of life which says that wherever the masses are is untruth, so that although every individual, each for himself silently possessed the truth, if they all came together (in such a way however that the many acquired any decisive importance whatsoever noisy and loud), then untruth would immediately be present. (Kierkegaard, 1938, p. 179)

How man uses his freedom in sport will be the determining factor of the truth which is found in sport. To look for anything less would, indeed, be absurd. Man must keep his own style. He must maintain his own individual character. To settle for less is what Sartre would call the "stealing of freedom."

The man of sports knows this only too well. The athlete meets another man. *In* the self the football player is proud he is what he is. He honestly believes he is worthy. Fellow man conveys a negative reaction to the athlete; although, not knowing why, the player feels guilty for being an athlete. In a word, he has let the societal man *steal his freedom.* He is robbed of what he is. Now he is that much less. Authenticity can never be attained if the individual prevents himself from *being.* Only he knows the truth of his own human existence. To prevent submission is possible because of the unique *action* of sport. But to bring this potentiality to reality is a mission that is apparently slipping away from man.

Sport encourages man to give up his freedom. On the field and off the field the stress is not individuality but adaptability. Truth does not come to man only through the sport action experience. It must be brought to awareness. The importance of *absurdity* is in the recognition. The recognition that man is constantly fighting to maintain *being;* yet he is willing to trade it for the first hint of calm. Ironically, sport is the place for the violent.

The excitement of sport is not only directly related to the *events* themselves but, as has been indicated, can be specifically attributed to unusual defiance of reason. Baseball managers "play the percentages" and football coaches stay "close to the book"; but these admissions in themselves indicate the high proportion of instances where rational deduction is not applicable. In this way, among others, sport avoids a sterile direction toward prediction. The players, coaches, and spectators are all engrossed with the unknown, if not the absurd. For years the trademark of the "Brooklyn Bums" baseball team was the unexpected. "It could only happen in Brooklyn" became a national slogan. But in truth "it" happened with great frequency everywhere sport was played. Wherever men of sport convened, the "unbelievable" became quite believable. The pragmatic control of objects and men is both plausible and impossible when it comes to sport.

The analyst of sport is left with no choice but to reduce the game to its elements and circumstances. To a degree this explains the almost neurotic preoccupation with some coaching staffs for projection rooms, "area-frequency" charts and their narcissist-like manner of observing and recording each trait and ability of a "prospect." With little desire, and perhaps ability, to transcend into the abstract, personnel have "guessed" incorrectly as frequently as they have made the correct evaluation of future athletic talents. In attempting to describe the elusive qualities that go into making the composite of an athlete, which cannot be measured by a tape or stop watch, individuals have attempted to express their thought through such clichés as "He gives that extra something"; or "he just seems to come through in the clutch."

What has not been clearly admitted is that the human potential is unified. It is the whole man through his sensations, intellect, will, and *all* his "content" who affords any form of causation. It is the cognitive experience which must be totally evaluated since it reflects the totality of being. This in no way indicates that the specific elements of the sport cannot be vitally and accurately evaluated. One could not argue that man in sport could be stripped of basic essence, but by the same token I must insist that he be given the efficacy of his emotions.

In sport man is plunged into his own existence with concomitant tensions. Existence, for the participant, is not only important but vital to his technical advances as well as to his true significance of purpose. Sport turns man to himself by making existence a personal matter and causing him to "face up" to each crisis as it unfolds. Existence transcends beyond the individual's subjectivity and speculation. There is no logical way in which man can express his desire to strike at a ball, "rack-up" another human, run the lonely track or follow a little ball for hole after hole. These are experiences which possess the potential for personal feelings—so personal that at times we don't care to reveal them to anyone including ourselves and, therefore, certainly cannot be translated into universalities.

It is clear that not all occurrences can be made available to rational explanation. It is in this domain that sport is both limiting and challenging. As we have seen, we do not make sport more real simply by measuring the concrete. Somehow it needs to be something more than just "absurd." Through study and analysis, insights into personal being must be achieved in order to afford meaning to what could be an *it* world. The authenticity of sport rests ultimately in its recognition of the human reality for each of those who hope to attain oneness. Thus, existence is grounded not in the mode but in the being himself.

Looking at sport this way, as it exists, we could see that which *is occurring,* as a sport entity, is that which is of value. Every phenomenon, as it relates to man's participation in sport, is a human fact and therefore, by definition, it is significant. For the runner leaving the "blocks," the swimmer making her "touch," the golfer gripping his club and coxswain beating the count to his crew, the *objectivity* of the phenomenon is what is important. It is what *is* as it appears. Take it out of its context and the meaning is altered. It is this that makes sport what it is. The value, the importance, the significance of the sport act, are both *all and none.* If one desires to speak as naively as indicating its "novel" contribution, then the act, whatever it be, is *in* sport; and as such is of great import, for the sport is of import. Thus, to criticize the scholar of sport by making reference to the fact that similar phenomena occur in other areas of human endeavor is simply to demonstrate ignorance of the value of *the* phenomenon in *the* context. A phenomenon cannot exist in a vacuum and thus its importance lies in its *existence.* In this case it is in sport.

Suggestions for Discussion and Writing

The following questions are as suggestive and open-ended as possible and are intended to provide topics for short reports or long papers. Some of the questions will require outside reading. The editors hope these will provide students with valuable research experience as well as with some depth in understanding the issues raised by sports in literature and in life. Although most of the questions relate to specific selections, a few do not. In these instances, the editors believe students will broaden their scope in dealing with the sporting spirit.

1. Explain "Dream of a Baseball Star" by analyzing the imagery in the dream. Compare and contrast the theme here with that in the lines from "Olympia 8" by Pindar. What contrasting view of sport is present in the two poems? How does the imagery reflect, in a concentrated fashion, the differing attitudes of the two poets?

2. In *Aspects of the Novel*, E. M. Forster distinguishes between "flat" and "round" characters, the flat character being two dimensional and simple, and the round character three dimensional and complex. With these criteria in mind, examine the characterization in "Jamesie." Is Jamesie changed significantly by events in the story? If so, what does he learn about life?

3. Describe the plot in "The Eighty-Yard Run" in terms of its main character. How does character determine action in the story? What is the implied significance, if any, in the name "Christian Darling"? Does an author's selection of a name in any way reflect his or her point of view?

4. In *The Absurd Hero in American Fiction*, David D. Galloway has said of John Updike's poem "Superman," "In a world of such hyperbolic and self-defeating superlatives scant room exists for the hero except in athletic events which seem increasingly to occupy contemporary America's minds." Have athletes, however, also come to "swim in supercolossality" with the rest of us? In what way are the meanings of superlatives abused by sportswriters, sports announcers, and even athletes? For example, what is meant by the term "Super Bowl"? How is the Super Bowl better or bigger than other bowls? Does "Super Bowl" mean that teams participating in it are bigger or better than those participating in the Rose Bowl or the Cotton Bowl? Is it fair to compare a professional event with

an amateur event or are bowl-type teams also professional? Which athletes publicly boast of being "supermen" or "the best"? Do you think such boasting is a display of arrogance, a form of self-advertising, a kind of fun and play, or an expression of bravery and confidence that we expect the hero to possess? Or do you think it is a combination of all?

5. Examine the use of "Baby" in "The Eighty-Yard Run" and "Ace in the Hole." What effects crucial to the meanings of both stories are achieved by this one word?

6. Discuss the revelation of character in "Crowd Pleaser" through dialogue, cliché, and epithet. How does the dialogue of the spectators both reflect the action in the ring and advance the narrative?

7. In Carson McCullers's "The Jockey," the reader is immediately struck by the feeling that much more is implied than told. What can be inferred from the behavior of the jockey and from the comments he makes—especially "You Libertines"?

8. Discuss the attributes of the race horse in Sherwood Anderson's stories in *Horses and Men.* Why have horses, much like athletes, often been regarded as divine symbols? What hidden role do horses play in Carson McCullers's story? From what is implied, describe the accident that injured the jockey's friend. Taking the horse as a divine symbol, would you say it is a god of destruction or a god of life? Why?

9. A. E. Housman's "To an Athlete Dying Young" implies a theme that is common in American fiction, the dismal life of an ex-hero, the washed-up jock, for example. Discuss the treatment of this theme in Irwin Shaw's "The Eighty-Yard Run" and John Updike's "Ace in the Hole."What is common to the treatment of the washed-up jock in these narratives?

10. Ernest Hemingway once remarked that bullfighting is not sport but drama. Read "The Undefeated," *Death in the Afternoon,* or *The Sun Also Rises,* and support or refute this statement. Also with reference to Hemingway's works, compare and contrast bullfighting and boxing as either sport or drama.

11. Irony has been defined as the difference between expectation and result. Discuss the manner in which irony is revealed in Hemingway's "The Capital of the World." Compare the use of irony in this story with that in "The Short Happy Life of Francis Macomber," also by Hemingway.

12. What humorous effects in Ring Lardner's "A Caddy's Diary" are attributable to point of view? Describe "the voice" in this story. Does it remind you of either Huck Finn or Holden Caulfield, or both? What values are revealed in the story?

13. Lardner's characters speak and write what is called substandard English. With reference to "A Caddy's Diary," describe the features of this form of English by an examination of spelling, punctuation, slang, and abbreviations. Why does the sports world, especially, seem to lend itself to the use of jargon?

14. Read several selections—for example, "The Captured Shadow," "The Freshest Boy," and "Basil and Cleopatra"—in *The Stories of F. Scott Fitzgerald.* Discuss the way sports-consciousness is taken for granted by Fitzgerald, who epitomized a period popularly known as "The Golden Age of Sport."

15. Robert Frost has written that education by poetry is education by metaphor. Examine a number of poems in this text and show how the poets have used metaphors to say one thing in terms of another. Why do poets proceed by indirection? Why do sports provide such a good source for metaphors that make larger statements about life?

16. Many films have dealt with athletics. Analyze any one of the following, or compare several, noting particularly that the visual narrative can effectively communicate the actualities of athletic events: *Roller Ball, Death Race 2000, Loneliness of the Long Distance Runner, This Sporting Life, Bang the Drum Slowly, Golden Boy, Champion, Requiem for a Heavyweight, Winning, Grand Prix, Bite the Bullet, Olympiad.*

17. Connections between literature and art—especially painting and sculpture—have proved to be valuable critical tools in both historical and esthetic research. Examine the artistic treatment of the athlete in any period or medium, for example, in the sculpture of ancient Greece—and discuss what seems to you an appropriate or corresponding literary treatment.

18. "Such field sports as fishing and hunting have provided a fascinating metaphor for life since they ceased being solely a means for a culture's livelihood." Discuss this statement in relation to Ernest Hemingway's "Big Two-Hearted River" or William Faulkner's "The Bear."

19. Henry James, Sr., in *Moralism and Christianity,* describes the defiant hero-artist as a "man of whatsoever function, who in fulfilling it obeys his own inspiration and taste, uncontrolled either by his physical necessities or his social obligations." Richard Poirier, in *A World Elsewhere,* adds that "the artist-hero may be, as he often is in American literature, an athlete, a detective, or a cowboy, his technical skills being as disciplined as the skills of art." Can you support these ideas from your reading in American literature? What is the connection, if any, between Henry James, Sr.'s idea and that of Richard Poirier? What is meant by discipline in art?

20. The world of sport has generated many anecdotes and humorous stories. What is there about sport that makes it such a fitting subject for humor? Read the selections by Mark Twain, James Thurber, and H. L. Mencken, and relate these stories to either the theory that humor is based on a sense of incongruity or the theory that it derives from a sudden recognition of one's own superiority over another. Which seems more incongruous: the great journalist and scholar H. L. Mencken in the gymnasium or the star athlete Bolenciecwcz in the classroon? What myths about athletes and intellectuals are underscored by these two selections? Is the Mark Twain selection based on an incongruous situation or on a sense of superiority? Is Mencken superior to the athlete or to Y.M.C.A. pieties?

21. Discuss the issue of sexism in sports. Is *macho* a necessary element of heroism? Does it have a female equivalent? What is right or wrong in athletic competitions between sexes, such as that described by Diana Nyad in this text and by Billy Jean King in an interview with *Seventeen* (May 1974). Build a case for or against standardization and handicapping so that persons can compete despite differences in age, sex, and experience.

22. In *Instant Replay*, Jerry Kramer speaks of devotional services and post-game prayers; most athletic events are preceded by anthems or prayers. What is the connection between sports and religion or between sports and politics? Is it a parasitic or a symbiotic relationship? What values are exchanged in such relationships? Discuss such institutions as the Fellowship of Christian Athletes or such traditions as the emphasis on athletics at our national service academies.

23. The appreciation of literature requires the ability to read clues; a reader has to infer the meaning of a work from suggestions made by its author. By analogy, the same can be said of competitive sports. Athletes have to be able to read clues given by their opponents in order to counter their moves. Gene Tunney's approach to boxing was, in this sense, the same as a critic's approach to literature. Describe Tunney's analysis of Dempsey's fighting style and his own responses to it. Draw parallels between Tunney's approach and that of literary criticism. For example, what in a work of literature would be analogous to a fighter telegraphing a punch?

24. Eugen Herrigel, in *Zen in the Art of Archery*, says, "The effortlessness of a performance for which great strength is needed is a spectacle of whose aesthetic beauty the East has an exceedingly sensitive and grateful appreciation." Can the same be said for Western appreciation of such apparently effortless performances as Joe DiMaggio running down a fly ball, Fergy Jenkins pitching, Tom Okker serving, Evonne Goolagong

Cawley volleying, Clyde or Chenier jump-shooting, Duane Thomas or O. J. Simpson running with the ball, Paul Warfield running a pass pattern, Julius Boros swinging a golf club, or Turischeva doing school exercises on the parallel bars? Is there a spiritual dimension to sports that appeals to spectators as much as to participants like Mike Spino? Write an appreciation of a sporting event that you witnessed in terms parallel to Mike Spino's description of his running experience.

25. Many former athletes say that what they miss most is the fellowship and comradeship of their teammates and peers. Scientists might refer this feeling to a "male bonding" principle inherited from or related to the behavior of certain herding animals. This suggestion might be pursued profitably by reading the animal behavior studies of Konrad Lorenz, Robert Ardrey, or Desmond Morris and drawing parallels to contemporary athletic phenomena. Describe Muhammad Ali's prefight behavior in terms of Ardrey's, Morris's and, especially Lorenz's theories. Would you say the sporting instinct is innate? Why or why not?

26. The place of big-time athletics on campuses is an issue. What is the justification for commercial athletics under the aegis of higher education? Are academic standards endangered by an emphasis on sports? How do educational and, especially, humanistic values conflict with athletic values? How do they complement each other? Are Theodore Roosevelt's and Byron White's arguments valid? Are Xenophanes's?

27. Are violence in sport, violence in art, and violence in society reflections of one another? Are they mutually exclusive phenomena? In psychological terms, is sadomasochism an inevitable element in sport? Does the agon or conflict accurately symbolize our perception of reality? How would Norman Mailer answer these questions? Budd Schulberg?

28. William Faulkner has offered a definition of sport in "An Innocent at Rinkside." What do you think sport is? Which activities would you include in sports? Is horse racing a sport? How about dog racing? Roller derby? Weightlifting? Armwrestling? Moto-cross? Professional wrestling? Gymnastics?

29. A biography of William Faulkner says that his "pleasure in sports seemed to increase in direct relation to their amateur nature." To what extent is this view supported in "An Innocent at Rinkside"? Do sports lose something of their amateur nature when moved indoors? Is it conceivable that people will someday hunt and fish indoors beneath the "pall of spectator tobacco," or is Faulkner only joking?

30. Thomas Jefferson said that "games played with a ball stamp no character on the mind," an opinion generally supported by the findings of psychologists who study athletics. Do such findings invalidate the views of Theodore Roosevelt, Robert Frost, and Marianne Moore?

31. Using the theme "Winning Isn't Everything," write a paper discussing the different views represented in the selections by Robert Frost and Marianne Moore. Keep in mind Frost's statement that the pitcher Ed Lewis "looked on a poem as a performance one had to win," and Moore's statement that "dexterity—with a logic of memory that makes strategy possible" is the source of her pleasure in baseball. What values are implied by these contrasting attitudes? Which view do you share?

32. William Lyon Phelps and Sherwood Anderson disagree in their assessment of Gene Tunney. Based on your reading of the selection by Tunney, who do you think is right? Give reasons for your choice.

33. Recently charges of racism have been directed at the American sports establishment. Discuss this subject with reference to the appropriate *Suggestions for Further Reading* and, particularly, Harry Edwards's essay "The Myth of the Racially Superior Athlete." How convincing are Edwards's arguments? Compare his view to that of Jesse Owens.

34. Where does society find its heroes? Contrast the heroic types represented by John F. Kennedy and Muhammad Ali. Why might a politician cultivate the companionship of an athlete? Why are writers like Norman Mailer, George Plimpton, and Budd Schulberg drawn to sports? Under what circumstances can athletic prowess be given an ideological content? What were the ways in which Schulberg made Ali into an ideological symbol? What does Ali symbolize?

35. It is often said that sport should be regarded as an art form. How is this argument supported by W. H. Auden's "Runner," Marianne Moore's "Baseball and Writing," and Maxine Kumin's "400-meter Freestyle"? Or by Eleanor Metheny's "Symbolic Forms of Movement: The Feminine Image in Sports"?

36. The modern philosopher Jose Ortega y Gasset has said, "All modern art begins to appear comprehensible and in a way great when it is interpreted as an attempt to instill youthfulness into an ancient world. Other styles must be interpreted in connection with dramatic social or political movements, or with profound religious and philosophical currents. The new style only asks to be linked to the triumph of sports and games. It is of the same kind and origin with them." Does this statement, or the sports-mindedness it implies, illuminate modern art, theater, or fiction? In what way does this statement about the fine arts illuminate sports? What meaning does sports seem to have in this statement? Compare this meaning with the sports meanings you can infer from Virgil, A. E. Housman, W. H. Auden, E. A. Robinson, and Marianne Moore.

37. Much has been written recently on drug use and abuse in big-time athletics. What is said about this in Peter Gent's *North Dallas Forty*? How does the situation described in the novel compare with research findings you have read about in magazines and other periodicals?

38. Compare Hitler's view on sport as described by Jesse Owens with those in the selection from Plato's *Republic*. How has the state in both ancient and modern times used the Olympic games for political ends? Can sport be separated from politics? If not, can sport be used to promote justice?

39. With reference to Updike's "Ace in the Hole," Mencken's "Adventures of a Y.M.C.A. Lad," Schulberg's "The Chinese Boxes of Muhammad Ali," and Plato's "Music and Gymnastic," comment on the relationship between the athlete and the intellectual, or the physical life and the life of the mind. How does this relationship help to create dramatic tension? What does it reveal about Western culture? About the human condition?

40. The moral quality associated with the Greek athletic ideal was known as *aidos*. Examine this term in E. N. Gardiner's *Athletics of the Ancient World*, Edith Hamilton's *Mythology*, and Werner Jaeger's *Paideia*, and discuss those contemporary athletes, real or fictional, who appear to possess this trait. Were the ancient Greeks wrong in believing this quality to be incompatible with the commercial spirit? Relate *aidos* to their concern with the dangers of professionalism, as described by Arnold Toynbee in the selection from *A Study of History*.

41. Apollo was the Greek god of order; Dionysus was the Greek god of abandonment. Vince Lombardi, among others, preached "abandon" in football, yet insisted on order. Do football and other sports embody a synthesis of polar opposites? Is that the source of their powerful attraction for both participant and spectator? Do cultures reach their greatest heights in Apollonian-Dionysian syntheses? What do you imagine Plato's answer to this question would be? Do you think Edith Hamilton would say that the ancient Greeks achieved an Apollonian-Dionysian synthesis? In what way does Arnold Toynbee see sport as the medium for achieving a balanced approach to life in contemporary society? According to Toynbee, how has this possibility been frustrated?

42. Popular culture reflects our society's saturation with sport, sporting events, and sports heroes. Consider this in the light of television or comic strips. Note the presence of athletic figures in the foreground, in the background, and in the embodiment of athletic attributes in such roles as detective, westerner, astronaut, lawyer, and paramedic. In what way does

this saturation influence the "play-element" described by Johan Huizinga in the selection from *Homo Ludens*? Why does he say the medieval tournament was not a sport? In your view, is mass participation or enjoyment a necessary part of the definition of sport? What are the implications of the broad diffusion of athletic values for sports and our culture? Discuss Huizinga's suggestion that trade and politics have been influenced by the agonistic spirit.

43. Reread Henry Adams's imagined exchange between John Adams and Thomas Jefferson, paying special attention to Adams's question, "What will you do for moral progress?" Does the integration of physical and intellectual excellence in an individual or nation guarantee moral progress, as Henry Adams believed Jefferson thought? What is the soul, and what is its relationship to body and mind? Has sport contributed to moral progress in America? Has literature, or the church? What would constitute moral progress?

44. The connection between sport and gambling extends back to the origins of both. Only in the Middle Ages, after thousands of years of practice, did the church come to regard gambling a sin, a subtype of the deadly Sloth. How and where did gambling evolve from sin to crime? With what justification was gambling made a sin? What is the contemporary attitude toward sport and gambling? Are Thorstein Veblen's strictures still viable? Is Lewis Mumford's view generally valid?

45. Thorstein Veblen observes that the language of sports is frequently adapted from the language of warfare. In recent times the language of sports has itself been adapted to the languages of war, politics, and diplomacy. What are the other sources of the language of sports? What other areas are influenced by the sports idiom? Explain what one can learn about the nature, the structure, the dynamics, and the appeal of sport by studying its language.

46. To what degree are Veblen's theories on sport confirmed by *The Sun Also Rises; The Great Gatsby; All the King's Men;* and *Goodbye, Columbus?*

47. Keeping in mind society's apparent need for myth and drama, as suggested by Marshall McLuhan and Lewis Mumford, discuss the role of the media in creating heroes, legends, and dramatic spectacles from athletics. In ancient Greece it was the poet who celebrated the achievement of the athlete in a verse form called *epinicion.* To what extent has the sportswriter or sports announcer assumed this function? When does such reportage become artistic invention, and toward what ends is the artistic invention directed? Discuss the treatment of the sportswriter in Mark Harris's *The Southpaw* and Bernard Malamud's *The Natural.*

48. What is the correlation between sport and war that is implied in James Wright's poem "A Mad Fight Song for William S. Carpenter, 1966"? What is the significance of the epigraph to the poem? Describe the place that, according to Edith Hamilton, sport occupied in the Roman Empire. Does Paul Weiss's view of sport and war seem more valid than Veblen's? As nations' defenses become more technologically sophisticated, what happens to the myth of sport as the proper training for warriors, which is classically immortalized in the Victorian cliché "The battle of Waterloo was won on the playing fields of Eton"?

49. Read the section on *areté* in Werner Jaeger's *Paideia: The Ideals of Greek Culture*, and compare this notion with Paul Weiss's concept of excellence in *Sport: A Philosophic Inquiry*. Also compare Weiss's concept with the discussion of *areté* and quality in Robert M. Pirsig's *Zen and the Art of Motorcycle Maintenance*. How does the striving for excellence differ from competition? Can excellence in sports be achieved without competition? Can it be achieved without competition in nonsporting endeavors? Assuming that capitalism is competitive, is sport, by nature, "capitalistic"?

50. The selection by Howard Slusher raises metaphysical questions. To what extent may sport be regarded as an epistemological endeavor—that is, as a means of knowing? Does all "knowing" involve logic, memory, and intellectual processes, or are there ways of comprehending reality through the body? What does Slusher say "reality" is? What does he say is the "meaning" of sport? Why does Slusher say that "in sport man is plunged into his own existence"? After reading *Existentialism* by Jean-Paul Sartre and *The Myth of Sisyphus* or *The Rebel* by Albert Camus, discuss what Slusher means by "the absurd." For those who are interested in pursuing this question, read some of the plays of Samuel Beckett, Eugene Ionesco, or other writers of the Theatre of the Absurd.

Suggestions for Further Reading

Fiction

Algren, Nelson. *Never Come Morning.* 1942
Anderson, Sherwood. *Horses and Men.* 1923
———. *Sherwood Anderson's Memoirs.* 1942
Asinof, Eliot. *Man on Spikes.* 1955.
Atkinson, Hugh. *The Games.* 1967.
Auchincloss, Louis. *The Rector of Justin.* 1964.
Brosnan, Jim. *The Pennant Race.* 1961.
Cheever, John. *The Housebreaker of Shady Hill and Other Stories.* 1958.
Coover, Robert. *The Universal Baseball Association.* 1968.
DeLillo, Don. *End Zone.* 1973.
Einstein, Charles. *The Only Game in Town.* 1955.
Exley, Frederick. *A Fan's Notes.* 1974.
Farrell, James T. *The Life Adventurous.* 1947.
———. *Side Street and Other Stories.* 1961.
———. *The Young Manhood of Studs Lonigan.* 1973.
Faulkner, William. *The Big Woods.* 1955.
———. *The Hamlet.* 1940.
Fitzgerald, F. Scott. *All the Sad Young Men.* 1926.
———. *The Basil and Josephine Stories.* 1973.
———. *Flappers and Philosophers.* 1920.
———. *The Great Gatsby.* 1925.
———. *This Side of Paradise.* 1920.
Gent, Peter. *North Dallas Forty.* 1973.
Glanville, Brian. *The Olympian.* 1969.
———. *The Rise of Gerry Logan.* 1965.
Harris, Frank. *Undream'd of Shores.* 1924.
Harris, Mark. *Bang the Drum Slowly.* 1956.
———. *The Southpaw.* 1953.
———. *A Ticket for a Seamstitch.* 1957.
Heinz, W. C. *The Professional.* 1958.
Hemingway, Ernest. *The Old Man and the Sea.* 1952.
———. *The Short Stories of Ernest Hemingway.* 1953.
———. *The Sun Also Rises.* 1926.
Hughes, Thomas. *Tom Brown's School Days.* 1968.
Jenkins, Dan. *Semi-Tough.* 1972.

Knowles, John. *A Separate Peace.* 1954.
Lampell, Millard. *The Hero.* 1949.
Lardner, Ring. *How to Write Short Stories.* 1975.
———. *Lose with a Smile.* 1933.
———. *The Ring Lardner Reader,* ed. Maxwell Geismar. 1963.
———. *You Know Me, Al.* 1916.
Larner, Jeremy. *Drive, He Said.* 1964.
Lewis, Sinclair. *Babbit.* 1949.
———. *Elmer Gantry.* 1927.
———. *Gideon Planish.* 1943.
London, Jack. *The Abysmal Brute.* 1913.
———. *The Best Short Stories of Jack London.* 1964.
———. *The Game.* 1905.
McGuane, Thomas. *Ninety-Two in the Shade.* 1956.
Malamud, Bernard. *The Natural.* 1965.
Meredith, George. *The Ordeal of Richard Feverel.* 1974.
Morris, Wright. *The Huge Season.* 1954.
Norris, Frank. *The Third Circle.* 1928.
Percy, Walker. *Love in Ruins.* 1972.
Quigly, Martin. *Today's Game.* 1965.
Roth, Phillip. *Goodbye, Columbus.* 1968.
———. *The Great American Novel.* 1972.
Runyon, Damon. *Guys and Dolls.* 1934.
———. *A Treasury of Damon Runyon.* 1958.
Schwed, Peter, and Herbert Warren Wind, eds. *Great Stories from the World of Sport.* 1958.
Shaw, G. B. *Cashel Byron's Profession.* 1968.
Shaw, Irwin. *Mixed Company.* 1950.
———. *Voices of a Summer Day.* 1966.
Shulberg, Budd. *Some Faces in the Crowd.* 1953.
———. *The Harder They Fall.* 1947.
Sillitoe, Alan. *The Loneliness of the Long-Distance Runner.* 1960.
Steinbeck, John. *Burning Bright.* 1950.
———. *Of Mice and Men.* 1937.
Storey, David. *This Sporting Life.* 1960.
Thurber, James. *The Thurber Carnival.* 1945.
Twain, Mark. *The Complete Short Stories of Mark Twain.* 1964.
———. *A Connecticut Yankee in King Arthur's Court.* 1964.
———. *Life on the Mississippi.* 1950.
Updike, John. *Rabbit Redux.* 1971.
———. *Rabbit Run.* 1960.
———. *The Same Door.* 1968.
Warren, Robert Penn. *All the King's Men.* 1963.
Whitehead, James. *Joiner.* 1973.

Williams, Tennessee. *One Arm.* 1967.
Wolfe, Thomas. *You Can't Go Home Again.* 1947.
———. *The Web and the Rock.* 1939.

Drama and Poetry

Albee, Edward. *Who's Afraid of Virginia Woolf?* 1966.
Hewitt, Geof. *Quickly Aging Here: Some Poets of the 1970's.* 1969.
Homer. *The Iliad,* trans. Richmond Lattimore or Robert Fitzgerald.
———. *The Odyssey,* trans. Richmond Lattimore or Robert Fitzgerald.
Inge, William. *Come Back, Little Sheba.* 1950.
———. *Picnic.* 1955.
Jarrell, Randall. *The Complete Poems.* 1969.
Juvenal, *The Sixteen Satires,* trans. Peter Green. 1967.
Miller, Arthur. *Death of a Salesman.* 1950.
Moore, Marianne. *Complete Poems.* 1967.
Morrison, Lillian, ed. *Sprints and Distances.* 1965.
Odets, Clifford. *Golden Boy.* 1939.
O'Neill, Eugene. *Strange Interlude.* 1955.
Patchen, Kenneth. *Selected Poems.* 1957.
Pindar. *The Odes of Pindar,* trans. Richmond Lattimore. 1966.
Rilke, Rainer Maria. *Poems 1906 to 1926,* trans. J. B. Leishman. 1957.
Sackler, Howard. *The Great White Hope.* 1974.
Sherwood, Robert. *The Petrified Forest.* 1941.
Thurber, James and Eliot Nugent. *The Male Animal.* 1941.
Virgil. *The Aeneid,* trans. C. Day Lewis. 1953.
Whitman, Walt. *Leaves of Grass.* 1965.
Williams, Tennessee. *Cat on a Hot Tin Roof.* 1955.
Williams, William Carlos. *Collected Poems, 1921–1931.* 1934.

Nonfiction

Angell, Roger. *The Summer Game.* 1972.
Ardrey, Robert. *Territorial Imperative.* 1966.
Arlott, John, ed. *The Oxford Companion to World Sports and Games.* 1975.
Arnold, Matthew. *Culture and Anarchy.* 1934.
Axthelm, Pete. *The City Game.* 1970.
Betts, John R. *America's Sporting Heritage 1850–1950.* 1974.
Blotner, Joseph. *Faulkner.* 1974.
Bouton, Jim. *Ball Four.* 1970.
Boyle, Robert H. *Sport-Mirror of American Life.* 1963.

Brash, R. *How Did Sports Begin?* 1970.
Castiglione, Baldassare. *The Book of the Courtier,* trans. Leonard Eckstein Opdycke. 1929.
Clark, Kenneth. *The Nude: A Study in Ideal Form.* 1956.
Cook, Alistair, ed. *The Vintage Mencken.* 1955.
Davies, John. "It's Baker! . . . Going for Another Touchdown!" *Esquire* (September 1966), pp. 132–35, 171.
Denney, Reuel. *The Astonished Muse.* 1957.
Edward, Harry. *The Revolt of the Black Athlete.* 1970.
Finley, M. I., and H. W. Pleket. *The Olympic Games: The First Thousand Years,* 1976.
Gardiner, E. Norman. *Athletics of the Ancient World.* 1930.
Gay, John. *Rural Sports.* 1930.
Halberstam, Michael J. "Stover at the Barricades," *American Scholar* (1969), pp. 470–80.
Haley, Bruce. "Sports and the Victorian World," *Western Humanities Review,* 22 (1968), pp. 115–25.
Harris, Dorothy V. *Involvement in Sport.* 1973.
Harris, H. A. *Greek Athletes and Athletics.* 1966.
Hart, M. Marie, ed. *Sport in the Socio-Cultural Process.* 1972.
Hemingway, Ernest. *The Wild Years.* 1967.
Henderson, Robert. *Ball, Bat, and Bishop.* 1947.
———. *Early American Sport.* 1953.
Herrigel, Eugen. *Zen in the Art of Archery.* 1971.
Hitler, Adolph. *Mein Kampf.* 1939.
Hoch, Paul. *Rip Off the Big Game.* 1972.
Huizinga, Johan. *Homo Ludens: A Study of the Play Element in Culture,* trans. R. F. C. Hull. 1960.
Isaacs, Neil D. *All the Moves: A History of College Basketball.* 1975.
Johnson, Jack. *Jack Johnson Is a Dandy: An Autobiography,* intro. by Dick Schaap. 1969.
Jaeger, Werner. *Paideia: The Ideals of Greek Culture,* trans. Gilbert Highet. 1945.
Kaye, Ivan. *Good Clean Violence: A History of College Football.* 1973.
Kieran, John. "The Sportsman's Lexicon," *Saturday Review of Literature* (July 22, 1933), pp. 1–3.
———. *The Story of the Olympic Games, 776 B.C.–1936 A.D.* 1936.
Koestler, Arthur. *The Lotus and the Robot.* 1961.
Kozar, Andrew J. *R. Tait Mackenzie: The Sculptor of Athletes.* 1975.
Kramer, Jerry. *Instant Replay.* 1968.
Krout, John. *Annals of American Sport.* 1929.
Lardner, John. *White Hopes and Other Tigers.* 1951.
Leonard, George B. "Winning Isn't Everything. It's Nothing," *Intellectual Digest* (October 1973), pp 45–47.
———. *The Ultimate Athlete.* 1975.

Lichtenstein, Grace. "Straight Talk from Billie Jean King," *Seventeen* (May 1974).

Lorenz, Konrad. *On Aggression.* 1971.

McLuhan, Marshall. *Understanding Media.* 1964.

Magoun, Francis P., Jr. *History of Football from the Beginning to 1871.* 1966.

Mailer, Norman. *The Fight.* 1975.

———. *Presidential Papers.* 1963.

Manchester, Herbert. *Four Centuries of Sport in America, 1490–1890.* 1931.

Meggyesy, Dave. *Out of Their League.* 1970.

Metheny, Eleanor. *Connotations of Movement in Sport and Dance.* 1965.

Morris, Desmond. *Naked Ape.* 1968.

Morton, Henry W. *Soviet Sport: Mirror of Soviet Society.* 1963.

Mumford, Lewis. *Technics and Civilization.* 1936.

Murphy, Michael. *Golf in the Kingdom.* 1972.

Nietzsche, Friedrich. *The Portable Nietzsche,* ed. Walter Kaufman. 1964.

Novak, Michael. *The Joy of Sports.* 1976.

Ogilvie, Bruce C. and Thomas A. Tutko. *Sport: If You Want to Build Character, Try Something Else, Psychology Today* (October 1971), pp. 61–63.

Orr, Jack. *The Black Athlete.* 1970

Ortega y Gasset, Jose. *The Dehumanization of Art.* 1972.

Owens, Jesse. *Blackthink.* 1970.

Patten, Gilbert (Burt L. Standish). *Frank Merriwell's Father.* 1964.

Paxson, Frederick L. "The Rise of Sport," *Mississippi Valley Historical Review* (September 1917), pp. 143–168.

Pirsig, Robert. *Zen and the Art of Motorcycle Maintenance.* 1974.

Plato. *Republic: Book III, Five Great Dialogues,* trans. Benjamin Jowett.

Plimpton, George. *Paper Lion.* 1966.

Poirier, Richard. *A World Elsewhere.* 1966.

Raglan, Lord. *The Hero: A Study in Tradition, Myth, and Drama.* 1949.

Rank, Otto. *The Myth of the Birth of the Hero.* 1964.

Rice, Grantland. *The Tumult and the Shouting.* 1939.

Robinson, Rachel S. *Sources for the History of Greek Athletics.* 1955.

Sage, George, ed. *Sport and American Society.* 1970.

Saveth, Edward N., ed. *Henry Adams.* 1963.

Schulman, David, "Baseball's Bright Lexicon," *American Speech* (1951), pp. 29–34.

Scott, Jack. *The Athletic Revolution.* 1971.

Shaw, Gary. *Meat on the Hoof.* 1972.

Sisk, John P. "Hot Sporting Blood," *Intellectual Digest* (November 1973) pp. 46–47.
Slusher, Howard S. *Man, Sport, and Existence.* 1967.
Snyder, Eldon E., ed. *Sport: A Social Scoreboard,* 1975.
Super Sports. Special Edition of *Esquire* (October 1974).
Toynbee, Arnold. *A Study of History.* 1962.
Ummlinger, Walter. *Superman, Heroes, and Gods: The Story of Sport Through the Ages,* trans. James Clark. 1963.
Umphlett, Wiley Lee. *The Sporting Myth and the American Experience.* 1975.
Updike, John. *Assorted Prose.* 1965.
Veblen, Thorstein. *The Theory of the Leisure Class.* 1953.
Walton, Izaak. *Compleat Angler.* 1974.
Weiss, Paul. *Sport: A Philosophic Inquiry.* 1969.
Wind, Herbert Warren, ed. *The Realm of Sport.* 1966.
Yates, Norris W. *William T. Porter and the Spirit of the Times.* 1957.

Index of Authors and Titles

Continued from page iv.

HARCOURT BRACE JOVANOVICH, INC. For "Sport and the 'Bitch-goddess' " from *Technics and Civilization*, copyright © 1934 by Harcourt Brace Jovanovich, Inc.; renewed, 1962, by Lewis Mumford. Reprinted by permission of the publishers.

HARPER & ROW, PUBLISHERS For "Superman" from *The Carpentered Hen and Other Tame Creatures* (1958) by John Updike. By permission of Harper & Row, Publishers.

THE HOGARTH PRESS For "To Nikê" from *Poems 1906–1926* by Rainer Maria Rilke, translated by J. B. Leishman. Reprinted by permission of St. John's College, Oxford, and The Hogarth Press.

HOLT, RINEHART AND WINSTON, INC. For "Perfect Day—A Day of Prowess" from *Selected Prose of Robert Frost* edited by Hyde Cox and Edward Connery Lathem. Copyright 1939, 1954, © 1966, 1967 by Holt, Rinehart and Winston. Copyright 1946, © 1959 by Robert Frost. Copyright © 1956 by The Estate of Robert Frost; for "To an Athlete Dying Young" from "A Shropshire Lad"—Authorised Edition—from *The Collected Poems of A. E. Housman*. Copyright 1939, 1940, © 1965 by Holt, Rinehart and Winston. Copyright © 1967, 1968 by Robert E. Symons; and for "400-meter Freestyle" from *Halfway* by Maxine W. Kumin. Copyright © 1957, 1958, 1959, 1960, 1961 by Maxine W. Kumin. All are reprinted by permission of Holt, Rinehart and Winston, Publishers.

DON JOHNSON For "Ripper Collins' Legacy" by Don Johnson.

KING FEATURES SYNDICATE, INC. For "The Old Horse Player" by Damon Runyon. © King Features Syndicate, Inc. 1958.

ALFRED A. KNOPF, INC. For "Adventures of a Y.M.C.A. Lad" from *The Vintage Mencken* by H. L. Mencken, edited by Alistair Cook. Copyright 1943 by Alfred A. Knopf, Inc.; and for "Ace in the Hole" from *The Same Door* by John Updike. Copyright © 1955 by John Updike. Originally appeared in *The New Yorker*. Both are reprinted by permission of Alfred A. Knopf, Inc.

THE LANTZ OFFICE For "The Jockey" by Carson McCullers. Reprinted by permission of The Lantz Office.

LEA & FEBIGER For "Sport as a Human Absurdity" from *Man, Sport and Existence: A Critical Analysis* by Howard S. Slusher. Published by Lea & Febiger, 1967, and reprinted with their permission.

LOUISIANA STATE UNIVERSITY PRESS For "The Stadium" from *Depth of Field* by William Heyen. Reprinted by permission.

MC GRAW-HILL BOOK COMPANY For "Games: The Extensions of Man" from *Understanding Media* by Marshall McLuhan. Copyright © 1964 by Marshall McLuhan. Used with permission of McGraw-Hill Book Company.

MACMILLAN PUBLISHING CO. For "A Mighty Runner (Variation of a Greek Theme)" from *Collected Poems of Edwin Arlington Robinson*. Copyright 1915 by Edwin Arlington Robinson, renewed 1943 by Ruth Nivison; and for "Running as a Spiritual Experience" by Mike Spino from *The Athletic Revolution* by Jack Scott. Copyright © 1971 by The Free Press, a

Division of The Macmillan Publishing Co., Inc. Both are reprinted with permission of The Macmillan Publishing Co., Inc.

ELEANOR METHENY For "Symbolic Forms of Movement: The Feminine Image in Sports" from *Connotations of Movement in Sport and Dance* by Eleanor Metheny. Reprinted by permission.

JIM WAYNE MILLER For "Cheerleader" by Jim Wayne Miller. Reprinted by permission.

WILLIAM MORROW & COMPANY, INC. For "Open Letter to a Young Negro" from *Blackthink* by Jesse Owens and Paul G. Neimark. Copyright © 1970 by Jesse Owens and Paul G. Neimark. Reprinted by permission of William Morrow & Co., Inc.

HENRY W. MORTON For "Sport and Society: USSR vs. U.S." from *Soviet Sport: Mirror of Soviet Society* by Henry W. Morton. Reprinted by permission.

THE NEW AMERICAN LIBRARY, INC. For the excerpt from *Instant Replay* by Jerry Kramer. Copyright © 1968 by Jerry Kramer and Dick Schaap. By arrangement with The New American Library, Inc., New York, N.Y.

NEW DIRECTIONS PUBLISHING CORPORATION For "Dream of a Baseball Star" from Gregory Corso, *The Happy Birthday of Death.* Copyright © 1960 by New Directions Publishing Corporation; for "Now I Went Down to the Ringside and Little Henry Armstrong Was There" from Kenneth Patchen, *Collected Poems.* Copyright 1943 by Kenneth Patchen; for "To Nikê" from Rainer Maria Rilke, *Poems 1906–1926,* translated by J. B. Leishman. Copyright © 1957 by New Directions Publishing Corporation; and for "At the Ball Game" from William Carlos Williams, *Collected Earlier Poems.* Copyright 1938 by New Directions Publishing Corporation. All are reprinted by permission of New Directions Publishing Corporation.

W. W. NORTON & COMPANY, INC. For the excerpt from *The Greek Way* by Edith Hamilton. Copyright 1930, 1943 by W. W. Norton & Company, Inc. Copyright renewed 1958, 1971; and for the excerpt from *The Roman Way* by Edith Hamilton. Copyright 1932 by W. W. Norton & Company, Inc. Copyright renewed 1960 by Edith Hamilton. Both are reprinted by permission of W. W. Norton & Company, Inc.

HAROLD OBER ASSOCIATES INCORPORATED For "Prize Fighters and Authors" from *No Swank* by Sherwood Anderson. Copyright 1934 by Sherwood Anderson. Copyright renewed by Eleanor Copenhaven Anderson, 1960; and for "An Innocent at Rinkside" by William Faulkner from *Sports Illustrated,* January 14, 1955. Copyright 1955 by Estelle Faulkner and Jill Faulkner Summers. Both are reprinted by permission of Harold Ober Associates Incorporated.

CELESTE PHELPS OSGOOD For "Gene Tunney" from *Autobiography with Letters* by William Lyon Phelps. Reprinted by permission.

OXFORD UNIVERSITY PRESS For the excerpt from *The Breakdown of Civilizations,* Volume 4 of *A Study of History* by Arnold J. Toynbee, Oxford University Press, 1939. Reprinted by permission.

PENGUIN BOOKS LTD. For the excerpt from Satire VI in Juvenal: *The Sixteen Satires*, translated by Peter Green (Penguin Classics 1967) p. 136. Copyright © Peter Green, 1967. Reprinted by permission of Penguin Books Ltd.

J. F. POWERS For "Jamesie" from *Prince of Darkness and Other Stories* by J. F. Powers. Reprinted by permission.

G. P. PUTNAM'S SONS For "The Death of Benny Paret" from *The Presidential Papers* by Norman Mailer. Copyright © 1960, 1961, 1962, 1963 by Norman Mailer. Reprinted by permission of G. P. Putnam's Sons.

RANDOM HOUSE, INC. For "Autolycus" by Euripides, translated by Moses Hadas. From *The Greek Poets*, edited by Moses Hadas. Copyright 1953 by Random House, Inc; and for "The Eighty-Yard Run" from *Selected Short Stories of Irwin Shaw*. Copyright 1940 and renewed 1968 by Irwin Shaw. Both are reprinted by permission of Random House, Inc.

AD SCHULBERG For "Crowd Pleaser" from *Some Faces in the Crowd* by Budd Schulberg; and for "The Chinese Boxes of Muhammad Ali" by Budd Schulberg from *Saturday Review*, February 26, 1972. Reprinted by permission.

CHARLES SCRIBNER'S SONS For "The Capital of the World" (copyright 1936 Ernest Hemingway) from *The Short Stories of Ernest Hemingway*; for "The Boxing Match" from Book V of *The Aeneid of Virgil*, translated by Rolfe Humphries. Copyright 1951 Charles Scribner's Sons; and for "A Caddy's Diary" (copyright 1922 Curtis Publishing Company) from *How to Write Short Stories* by Ring Lardner. All are reprinted by permission of Charles Scribner's Sons.

SIMON & SCHUSTER, INC. For "My Fights with Jack Dempsey" by Gene Tunney from *The Aspirin Age*, edited by Isabel Leighton. Copyright © 1949 by Simon & Schuster, Inc. Reprinted by permission of Simon & Schuster, Inc.

THE SOCIETY OF AUTHORS For "To an Athlete Dying Young" from "A Shropshire Lad" from *Collected Poems* by A. E. Housman. Reprinted by permission of the Society of Authors as the literary representative of the Estate of A. E. Housman, and Jonathan Cape Ltd., publishers of A. E. Housman's *Collected Poems*.

SOUTHERN ILLINOIS UNIVERSITY PRESS For "The Urge to Win" from *Sport: A Philosophic Inquiry* by Paul Weiss. Copyright © 1969 by Southern Illinois University Press. Reprinted by permission of Southern Illinois University Press.

SPORTS ILLUSTRATED For "Testament of a Samurai" by Yukio Mishima, translated by Michael Gallagher. Reprinted by permission from *Sports Illustrated*, January 11, 1971. Copyright 1971 by Time Inc. All rights reserved.

HELEN THURBER For the excerpt from "University Days," in *My Life and Hard Times* by James Thurber. Originally printed in *The New Yorker*.

DENNIS TRUDELL For "The Jump Shooter" by Dennis Trudell. Reprinted by permission.

THE UNIVERSITY OF CHICAGO PRESS For the excerpt from "Olympia 8" by Pindar. Reprinted from *The Odes of Pindar*, translated by Richmond Lattimore, by permission of The University of Chicago Press. © 1947, 1976 by The University of Chicago. All rights reserved.

UNIVERSITY OF PITTSBURGH PRESS For "First Practice" by Gary Gildner. Reprinted from *First Practice* by Gary Gildner by permission of the University of Pittsburgh Press. © 1969 by The University of Pittsburgh Press.

VIKING PENGUIN, INC. For "Baseball and Writing" from *The Complete Poems of Marianne Moore*. Copyright © 1961 by Marianne Moore. Originally appeared in *The New Yorker*. Reprinted by permission of Viking Penguin, Inc.

WESLEYAN UNIVERSITY PRESS For "A Mad Fight Song for William S. Carpenter, 1966" by James Wright. Copyright © 1971 by James Wright. Reprinted from *Collected Poems* by James Wright by permission of Wesleyan University Press.

BYRON R. WHITE For "Athletics: . . . 'Unquenchably the Same'?" by Byron R. White. Reprinted by permission.

A 6
B 7
C 8
D 9
E 0
F 1
G 2
H 3
I 4
J 5